DRAGON AGE ORIGINS AWAKENING

PRIMA Official Game Guide

Written by

Mike Searle

The Prima Games logo is a registered trademark of Random House, Inc., registered in the United States and other countries. Primagames.com is a registered trademark of Random House, Inc., registered in the United States. Prima Games is an imprint of Random House, Inc.

© 2010 Electronic Arts Inc. EA and EA logo are trademarks or registered trademarks of Electronic Arts Inc. in the U.S. and/or other countries. All Rights Reserved. BioWare, BioWare logo, Dragon Age and Dragon Age logo are trademarks or registered trademarks of EA International (Studio and Publishing) Ltd. in the U.S. and/or other countries. All other trademarks are the property of their respective owners.

No part of this book may be reproduced or transmitted in any form or by any means, electronic or mechanical, including photocopying, recording, or by any information storage or retrieval system without written permission from Electronic Arts Inc.

Product Manager: Todd Manning
Associate Product Managers: Sean Scheuble & Shaida Boroumand
Copyeditor: Asha Johnson
Design & Layout: Bryan Neff & Jody Seltzer
Manufacturing: Stephanie Sanchez
eProduction: Suzanne Goodwin

Prima would like to thank Chris Corfe for his invaluable support and assistance on this guide.

Please be advised that the ESRB Ratings icons, "EC," "E," "E10+," "T," "M," "AO," and "RP" are trademarks owned by the Entertainment Software Association, and may only be used with their permission and authority. For information regarding whether a product has been rated by the ESRB, please visit www.esrb.org. For permission to use the Rating icons, please contact marketing at esrb.org.

Important:
Prima Games has made every effort to determine that the information contained in this book is accurate. However, the publisher makes no warranty, either expressed or implied, as to the accuracy, effectiveness, or completeness of the material in this book; nor does the publisher assume liability for damages, either incidental or consequential, that may result from using the information in this book. The publisher cannot provide any additional information or support regarding gameplay, hints and strategies, or problems with hardware or software. Such questions should be directed to the support numbers provided by the game and/or device manufacturers as set forth in their documentation. Some game tricks require precise timing and may require repeated attempts before the desired result is achieved.

ISBN: 978-0-3074-6835-2
Library of Congress Catalog Card Number: 2010901992
Printed in the United States of America

10 11 12 13 LL 10 9 8 7 6 5 4 3 2 1

Prima Games
An Imprint of Random House, Inc.
3000 Lava Ridge Court, Suite 100
Roseville, CA 95661
www.primagames.com

About the Author

Mike Searle remembers playing the simple yet addictive *Missile Command*, and the days of Atari *Adventure*, where your square hero could end up in a hollow dragon stomach. His desire to play computer games into the wee hours of the morning really took hold when his parents made him play outside, instead of on the console, so the first chance he got, he bought a PC to play the *Ultima* series, *Doom*, and countless others. Mike started working with Prima Games in 2002 and has written more than 30 strategy guides, including *Lord of the Rings Online: Shadows of Angmar*, *Jurassic Park: Operation Genesis*, *Dark Messiah: Might and Magic*, *Pirates of the Burning Sea*, and several guides in the Tom Clancy's *Ghost Recon* and *Splinter Cell* series. He can't wait for thought technology, so game controls can catch up with his brain and stop all that needless in-game dying. At least, that's what he keeps telling himself about his FPS kill ratio.

We want to hear from you! E-mail comments and feedback to msearle@primagames.com.

W9-APE-449

Contents

NOTE - *Brown, italicized* entries are table titles.

Contents

Contents

primagames.com

How to Use This Guide

Dragon Age™: Origins is back with a vengeance, and that vengeance taps into the darkspawn's renewed strength as they rise up to threaten the Grey Wardens' new foothold on the land. With an expansion this vast, you need a guide that's fat with advice, stats, maps, and expert tips to master your new Amaranthine adventures. Look no farther—you've found it all here...

Basics

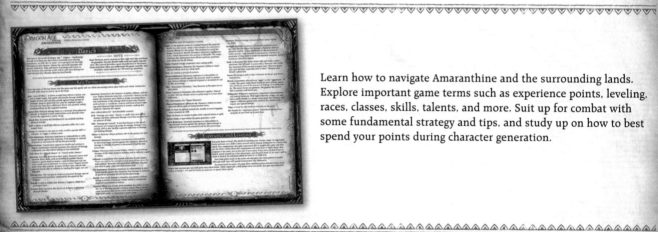

Learn how to navigate Amaranthine and the surrounding lands. Explore important game terms such as experience points, leveling, races, classes, skills, talents, and more. Suit up for combat with some fundamental strategy and tips, and study up on how to best spend your points during character generation.

Classes

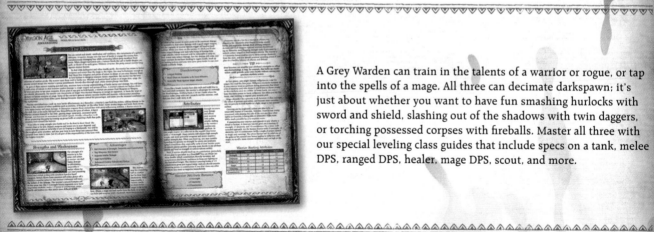

A Grey Warden can train in the talents of a warrior or rogue, or tap into the spells of a mage. All three can decimate darkspawn; it's just about whether you want to have fun smashing hurlocks with sword and shield, slashing out of the shadows with twin daggers, or torching possessed corpses with fireballs. Master all three with our special leveling class guides that include specs on a tank, melee DPS, ranged DPS, healer, mage DPS, scout, and more.

The Party

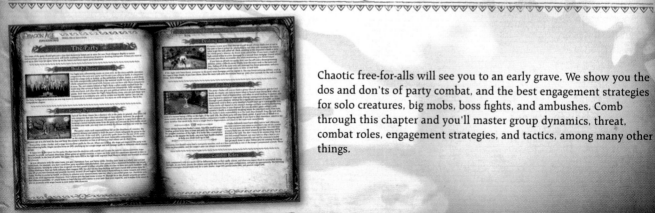

Chaotic free-for-alls will see you to an early grave. We show you the dos and don'ts of party combat, and the best engagement strategies for solo creatures, big mobs, boss fights, and ambushes. Comb through this chapter and you'll master group dynamics, threat, combat roles, engagement strategies, and tactics, among many other things.

How to Use This Guide

Basics ~ Classes ~ The Party ~ Companions ~ Supporting Cast ~ Equipment ~ Bestiary ~ Walkthrough ~ Side Quests ~ Random Encounters ~ Achievements/Trophies

Companions

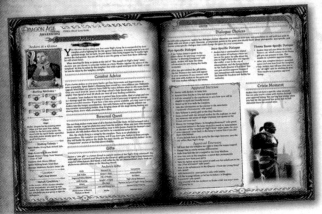

Get into the minds of your trusted companions, learning what secrets they can teach you. Find out how to unlock them all for your party and how to make each the ultimate combatant.

Companions covered include: Anders (mage), Justice (warrior), Mhairi (warrior), Nathaniel Howe (rogue), Sigrun (rogue), Velanna (mage), and one faithful companion from *Dragon Age: Origins*.

Supporting Cast

Who is the Architect? Can the Dark Wolf thwart a plot on your life? How deep is the baroness's cruelty? The lands of Amaranthine aren't just about you and your companions; hundreds of lively non-player characters (NPCs) interact with you and shape this new region. This chapter takes a peek at the most important faces around the land.

Equipment

Gear up with complete specs on all the new *Awakening* weapons, armor, accessories, gifts, runes, crafting and usable items, and more.

primagames.com

The Bestiary

Dragons, genlocks, hurlocks, ogres, and more return from *Dragon Age: Origins*. Uncover all the secrets of returning denizens, plus all the new *Awakening* creatures, in our complete Bestiary chapter.

Walkthroughs

Everything you wanted to know about your Grey Warden quests is here, including super-detailed maps, runthroughs of every major encounter, boss strategies, treasure locations, and even where to find the resources to build Vigil's Keep into a massive fortress.

Side Quests

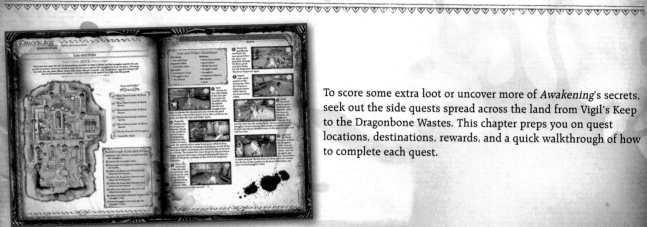

To score some extra loot or uncover more of *Awakening*'s secrets, seek out the side quests spread across the land from Vigil's Keep to the Dragonbone Wastes. This chapter preps you on quest locations, destinations, rewards, and a quick walkthrough of how to complete each quest.

How to Use This Guide

Basics ~ Classes ~ The Party ~ Companions ~ Supporting Cast ~ Equipment ~ Bestiary ~ Walkthrough ~ Side Quests ~ Random Encounters ~ Achievements/Trophies

Random Encounters

Traveling across the countryside isn't always a stroll in the park. You may encounter bandits, blood mages, or even fen witches. Our handy random encounter runthrough lists all the encounters, triggers, important plot points, and strategy tips on how to come out on top.

Achievements & Trophies

Who doesn't have fun collecting titles? Get the scoop on the storyline unlocks, plus what you have to do to master the eight new *Awakening* achievements/trophies.

❖ CAUTION ❖

If you haven't played through *Dragon Age: Origins*, you may want to return to the land of Ferelden and play through the whole original story, or many elements will be spoiled for you should you ever wish to return there. Many plot points and story secrets may be revealed in these chapters while explaining strategy and tips for the game. Please read carefully and look for Spoiler Alerts if you want to avoid learning key turning points in the story.

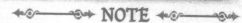

Basics

Welcome to the world of *Dragon Age™: Origins—Awakening*! Our job is to keep you alive and to maximize your playing experience, so with that in mind, we're going to run through the basics in this chapter. Master the essential concepts and ground rules first, then add layers of strategy and tactics to your favorite class and the world will be safe from darkspawn until the last Grey Warden takes his final breath.

→ NOTE →

Stop! We know you're anxious to dive right into tips and hints on gameplay, but you should really read your game manual first. The manual provides a great introduction to the basics. Come back here when you understand the game controls, user interface, menu options, etc. We won't go anywhere.

Key Terms

Here are some of the key terms that the game and this guide will use while discussing various play styles and tactics. Familiarize yourself with these so you're up on the lingo.

AoE: "Area of Effect." A talent or spell that affects a radius, not just a single target. AoE spells and attacks damage multiple targets at once and can help greatly against large groups of enemies. Keep in mind that you may hit multiple targets, but you also may draw additional threat and possibly nullify existing effects on the targeted enemies.

Armor Stat: Reduces damage done to a character from physical attacks. A weapon's armor penetration score directly counteracts the opponent's armor rating.

Attack Stat: Increases the likelihood of successfully landing physical attacks.

Buff: A talent or spell that delivers a positive effect for a prolonged time.

Camp: To remain in one spot in order to kill a specific NPC or monster, or trigger a certain event.

Cold Resistance: Measures resistance or vulnerability to cold-based attacks against the character. Cold damage is reduced (if green) or increased (if red) by this percentage.

Constitution: Constitution represents health and resilience. Higher constitution directly increases the amount of damage a character can take before falling on the battlefield.

Crit: Short for "critical chance" or "critical strike chance."

Cunning: Cunning determines how well a character learns and reasons. Most skills, such as Survival or Combat Tactics, require a quick mind to master—and an observant eye can more easily find weaknesses in enemy armor. Rogues benefit most from this statistic, as many of their class talents and special attacks rely on subtlety or reading the target, not raw strength.

Damage Stat: The equipped weapon's potential damage against an unarmored opponent, adjusted for the speed of the weapon.

Debuff: A skill or ability that delivers a negative effect for a prolonged time.

Defense Stat: Increases the chance of dodging or parrying physical attacks.

Dexterity: Dexterity is the measure of agility, reflexes, and balance. Higher dexterity improves a character's chances to hit, makes the character more likely to dodge incoming blows, and contributes to the damage dealt by piercing weapons such as bows or crossbows. Archery and dual-weapon fighting styles demand high dexterity to master, making this attribute a favorite for rogues.

DLC: Abbreviation for "downloadable content."

DoT: "Damage over time." Talents or spells that deal initial damage and then additional damage every few seconds for a set amount of time.

DPS: "Damage per second." A stat that factors in the speed and power of a weapon to gauge its average damage every second. DPS is also used as a generic reference to damage and dealing damage.

DPSer: A character whose primary role in the group is to deal damage.

Electrical Resistance: Measures resistance or vulnerability to electricity-based attacks against the character. Electrical damage is reduced (if green) or increased (if red) by this percentage.

Fatigue: Wearing armor causes fatigue, which is a percentage increase of the basic mana or stamina cost to activate a spell or talent.

Follower: A companion who travels with you on your quests. There can only be four people in your party at one time: the main (player) character, and up to three followers. The rest stay back at party camp and level as you level.

Fire Resistance: Measures resistance or vulnerability to fire-based attacks against the character. Fire damage is reduced (if green) or increased (if red) by this percentage.

Health: How much damage a character can sustain without falling in battle. A character whose health is completely depleted may sustain an injury.

Injuries: When one of your party members has fallen in combat, he or she may sustain a serious injury. These injuries cause penalties that can be cured with an injury kit, certain high-level spells, or returning to party camp.

Key Terms - Experience and Leveling

Basics ~ Classes ~ The Party ~ Companions ~ Supporting Cast ~ Equipment ~ Bestiary ~ Walkthrough ~ Side Quests ~ Random Encounters ~ Achievements/Trophies

Loot: Another term for treasure or rewards.

Magic: In the general sense, it's energies beyond the material world. In a stat sense, magic is the measure of a character's natural affinity for the arcane. This attribute is crucial for mages, because it directly increases a character's spellpower score, which determines the potency of all spells. The magic attribute also determines how effective potions, poultices, and salves are for all classes.

Mana: Magical energy consumed when casting spells.

Mental Resistance: Measures the character's ability to resist mental effects such as a sleep spell.

Mob: An enemy or group of enemies.

Nature Resistance: Measures resistance or vulnerability to nature-based attacks against the character (such as poisoning). Nature damage is reduced (if green) or increased (if red) by this percentage.

NPC: "Non-player Character." Any character in the game not in your party.

Party: A group of characters who adventure together, limited to four. You can always return to party camp to recruit other followers.

PC: Abbreviation for "Player Character."

Physical Resistance: Measures the character's ability to resist physical effects such as being knocked down.

Pull: To draw an enemy toward you, usually to avoid engaging other enemies as well.

Root: To freeze an enemy in place with a special talent or spell.

Spawn Point: A spot where the game generates a mob.

Spirit Resistance: Measures resistance or vulnerability to spirit-based attacks against the character. Spirit damage is reduced (if green) or increased (if red) by this percentage.

Stamina: Physical energy consumed when using talents or skills.

Strength: Strength measures a character's physical prowess, and directly affects the damage a character deals in physical combat. It also contributes to the accuracy of melee attacks. High strength is essential for warriors, in particular if they wish to wield two-handed weapons, and is nearly as critical for rogues.

Tank: A character who draws threat well and holds a mob's attention. An "off-tank" is a secondary character who holds the attention of the second strongest mob. Warriors generally tank the best, especially with their "Weapon and Shield" talent tree.

Taunt: To enrage a mob so that it focuses its threat and attention on you.

Threat: Sometimes referred to as "aggro" or the "aggression" of a mob. The game ranks threat based on your actions, generally revolving around the amount of damage or healing you do. The more threat you generate, the greater the chance that a monster will attack you.

Willpower: Willpower represents a character's determination and mental fortitude. With high willpower, mages can cast more spells thanks to a deeper mana pool. For warriors and rogues, willpower grants more stamina for combat techniques and special attacks.

Wipe: A term for the death of everyone in the party.

XP: Stands for "experience points." Experience marks your progress as you level up in your class.

Experience and Leveling

Everyone loves to level. The thrill of watching your warrior, mage, or rogue gain levels and earn new skills comes second only to slaying darkspawn in a heroic last stand. Your companions also gain experience (XP) at roughly the same rate that you do. Don't worry about the companions you leave back at Vigil's Keep; they progress at the same rate as the rest of your party. If you leave Anders home at level 8, travel around on a few adventures, and return at level 12, he won't still be stuck at level 8. He will most likely be level 12, or close to it.

Each class gains levels at the same rate and gains the same points to spend, although each class will spend those points very differently.

For every level you gain, you gain three attribute points and one talent point. Mages and warriors get one skill point every three levels, while rogues get a skill point every two levels. You gain specialization points at levels 7, 14, and 22. Points are precious, so spend them wisely.

primagames.com

Your Health

Obviously, staying alive is your first priority whenever you're out adventuring. Those with high constitution scores will have more health, and thus take a lot more hits before perishing. Warriors generally want high health to stay on their feet, despite being the punching bags for enemies. Rogues may have high health, depending on how much they like to mix it up in combat. Mages usually concentrate on less-physical attributes and may be more fragile in the midst of swinging swords and smashing clubs.

Your best ally against loss of health is a healer. A simple Heal spell can do wonders, and Group Heal keeps everyone up in a fight. Health poultices serve the same purpose. Judge how much damage you've taken and use the appropriate level poultice: lesser if your health is still above 50 percent, regular if your health dips below 50 percent, and greater when you're knocking on death's door.

If you do drop in battle, you won't lose the game unless all your party members fall as well. In a fight where you fall, but your allies manage to win the day, you will climb back to your feet after the battle. Check this character for wounds. A persistent injury penalizes you according to the following chart:

Injuries

Injury Name	Penalty To	Injury Name	Penalty To
Bleeding	Health Regeneration	Deafened	Defense
Broken Bone	Dexterity	Gaping Wound	Maximum Health
Concussion	Magic	Head Trauma	Willpower
Coughing Blood	Fatigue	Open Wound	Nature Resistance
Cracked Skull	Cunning	Torn Jugular	Constitution
Crushed Arm	Damage	Wrenched Limb	Attack Speed
Damaged Eye	Attack		

Races and Classes

During character creation, you will choose a race and class, unless you decide to transfer a character over from *Dragon Age: Origins*. Not only do race and class give different bonuses to different stats, but they may affect how certain characters in the game interact with you. Here are brief descriptions of the three races and classes.

Races

Human: The most numerous, yet the most divided of all the races. Only four times have they ever united under a single cause, the last being centuries ago. Religion and the Chantry play a large part in human society. It distinguishes them culturally from elves and dwarves more than anything else. Humans can be warriors, rogues, or mages.

Elf: Once enslaved by humans, most elves have all but lost their culture, scrounging an impoverished living in the slums of human cities. Only the nomadic Dalish tribes still cling to their traditions, living by the bow and the rule of their old gods as they roam the ancient forests, welcome nowhere else. Elves can be warriors, rogues, or mages.

Your Health - Skills, Talents, and Specializations

Basics ~ Classes ~ The Party ~ Companions ~ Supporting Cast ~ Equipment ~ Bestiary ~ Walkthrough ~ Side Quests ~ Random Encounters ~ Achievements/Trophies

Dwarf: Rigidly bound by caste and tradition, the dwarves have been waging a losing war for generations, trying to protect the last stronghold of their once-vast underground empire from the darkspawn. Dwarves are very tough and have a high resistance to all forms of magic, thus preventing them from becoming mages. As such, dwarves can only be warriors or rogues.

Mage: As dangerous as it is potent, magic is a curse for those lacking the will to wield it. Malevolent spirits that wish to enter the world of the living are drawn to mages like beacons, putting the mage and everyone nearby in constant danger. Because of this, mages lead lives of isolation, locked away from the world they threaten.

Classes

Warrior: Warriors are powerful fighters, focusing on melee and ranged weapons to deal with their foes. They can withstand and deliver a great deal of punishment, and have a strong understanding of tactics and strategy.

Rogue: Rogues are skilled adventurers who come from all walks of life. All rogues possess some skill in picking locks and spotting traps, making them valuable assets to any party. Tactically, they are not ideal front-line fighters, but if rogues can circle around behind their target, they can backstab to devastating effect.

Skills, Talents, and Specializations

Besides attributes, your skills, talents or spells, and specializations define who you are and how effective you'll be in combat. Each level you get more powerful as you add points in these areas. For more specifics on skills, talents, and specializations, see the Classes chapter.

Skills

All three classes share the same skill tree, which includes the following: Coercion, Stealing, Trap-Making, Survival, Herbalism, Poison-Making, Combat Training, Combat Tactics, Runecrafting, Vitality, and Clarity. Whether you want to focus on persuading others, detecting enemies, crafting health potions, or learning combat tricks, among other things, you gain skill points every three levels (or one every two levels if you're a rogue) to explore the skill tree. Because you can fill out only two to three skills, put some serious thought into which ones you want to master.

Talents and Spells

Talents are specific to warriors and rogues; mages learn spells. You can't take everything, so choose talents/spells that fit into your play style. For example, a warrior can dual-wield weapons, fight with weapon and shield, rely on a two-handed weapon, or strike at range with bow and arrows. All talents don't complement each other; choose a path and stick with it to unlock the better talents/spells at higher levels.

Talents require stamina, while spells cost mana. Keeping some sustained talents or spells active ties up a certain amount of stamina/mana, which could prevent a character from using other abilities when starting a new encounter. Keep an eye on your stamina/mana levels before and during combat.

Specializations

You unlock your first specialization at level 7, your second at level 14, and your third at level 22. Specializations give an array of attribute bonuses and open up unique talent chains. They are very powerful abilities in the right situation. Specializations for a warrior include Berserker, Templar, Champion, Reaver, Spirit Warrior, and Guardian. Mage specializations include Spirit Healer, Shapeshifter, Arcane Warrior, Blood Mage, Keeper, and Battlemage. Rogue specializations are Ranger, Bard, Duelist, Assassin, Legionnaire Scout, and Shadow.

primagames.com

Items

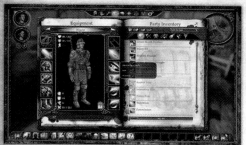

Gear can be just as important as your abilities. The proper items can vault you from normal soldier to tweaked-out death-dealer. Make sure items go to the appropriate party member, depending on his or her role. Equip a warrior focusing in the Weapon and Shield talent train with the best set of armor, while the warrior focused in Archery takes the next best set.

Combat

Parties work the best when you know the strengths, and limitations, of each class and plan your battle strategies accordingly. Each class falls into one of these general categories: tank (warrior), DPS (rogue, mage, warrior), and healer (mage). As the name implies, a tank's job is to draw fire and take as much damage as possible to protect everyone else. This job is executed right at the front lines of a battle and generally never shifts from that location. Tanks have talents that force enemies to attack them for a short time and high damage potential to keep the threat on them instead of their companions. Warriors make the best tanks.

The second category, DPS (or damage), is divided into two subcategories: ranged and melee. Ranged DPS characters do lots of damage, and as a result, generate large amounts of threat and will die very quickly when their ranged advantage is lost and there's no tank protection nearby. Ideally a ranged DPS character should stay in the back of a battle and let the tanks and melee DPS protect them. On the other hand, a melee DPS character is usually more durable and can try to let the tanks take the hits while they kill off enemies directly. Rogues make great DPS characters, as do mages focusing on damage and area-effect spells. Though you generally need one warrior to be a tank, a warrior studying the art of two-handed weapons can deal major DPS.

The third category, the healer, is a key support role in any group. Your job as a healer is to keep everyone alive. For a healer to be successful, they need to stay as far away from the enemies as possible and avoid getting hit. A healer who can do this, while keeping his fellow companions healthy, is one of the most effective members of a group. Just watch your mana and always keep lyrium potions available in case you need to gain extra mana for a crucial healing spell. Mages concentrating on Creation magic prove to be strong healers.

Mobs

Mobs are the monsters and people you fight to complete quests and gain experience. There are two types of mobs: normal and ranked. Normal mobs have a white name above their heads. One of your party members is generally more than a match for a normal monster. Ranked creatures have different colored names. Opponents with yellow names are more challenging and aggressive than average. Orange names represent extremely powerful enemies capable of threatening a full party of adventurers by themselves.

Threat

Threat is a score used to determine who an enemy will attack. Simply put, the more threat you generate toward a target, the greater chance it will attack you, and continue to attack you even after others join in. Threat is commonly generated by damage, so the more DPS you deliver, the greater the chance you'll attract attention. Luckily, there are some threat-reduction talents in the game that allow you to shed the threat temporarily (or possibly completely if you don't jump back into the fight).

Items - The Codex

Basics ~ Classes ~ The Party ~ Companions ~ Supporting Cast ~ Equipment ~ Bestiary ~ Walkthrough ~ Side Quests ~ Random Encounters ~ Achievements/Trophies

Tanks are the ones most concerned with threat. They generate the most threat with special talents (sometimes known as "taunts") that automatically attract an enemy's attention and lock it on the tank. It's generally good form to allow your tank to build up threat by leaving him alone for the first few seconds of the combat as he launches a few damaging attacks. If you have an off-tank, he should be ready to grab threat on any target that breaks free of the main tank or any extra monsters that show up unannounced.

When monsters in *Awakening* perceive a character, they evaluate a base level of threat. That base level is influenced by the class of armor the character is wearing at the moment of perception. Robes generate extremely low levels of threat, while massive armors generate the most. Outfit your party accordingly. You can control the initial flow of threat by distributing gear based on each companion's role. An off-tank, for example, can avoid catching most of the damage by wearing heavy or medium armor, while the main tank wears massive.

TIP

Some specific creatures target casters. Rogues and shrieks are the key monsters with this behavior, and they may beeline for a healer at the start of a fight.

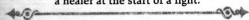

A DPS specialist has a relatively simple task: Don't out-damage the tank so much that you gain threat. It might take some practice in the group, but you'll eventually learn how many talents you can launch, and how frequently, to maximize your damage without surpassing the tank's ability to hold threat. The biggest mistake to avoid as a DPSer is to start attacking too soon in the fight; allow the tank a few seconds to build up threat before you dive in.

Tactics

All characters have tactic slots that can be programmed with automatic behavior based on a certain set of circumstances. You may want to slot an action that says to use a health poultice if your health drops below 50 percent, or an action that dictates you defend the healer whenever they are attacked by an enemy. You can always pause combat and manually choose your characters' action; however, at some point in every fight, your characters will act on their own, and tactics allow them to function effectively based on the skill sets of their fellow party members. For more on tactics, see the "Tactics" section of the Party chapter.

The Map

Of course, you can't really get anywhere unless you understand the map. The map will be used for so many things, but the most useful aspect is to view plot helpers. Unless the option is turned off on the Options menu, plot helper arrows display on the map at various key quest points, especially where you have to go for the next leg of your journey. On the map, a yellow dot represents a party member, and a yellow dot with a circle around it represents the PC. A blue dot signifies an ally, and a red dot equals an enemy. Plot givers show up as white exclamation points, and key locations display as white Xs. A vendor or store looks like a house, and map exit points appear as white-rimmed black circles.

The Codex

The codex is the parchment icon on your Journal screen and is the repository of important knowledge uncovered in the game. It falls into 10 categories: creatures, items, magic and religion, culture and history, characters, books and songs, notes, spell combinations, control, and quest-related. As you unlock a codex entry, a scroll appears in the appropriate category and you can read volumes on the various topics. Check it regularly for information, especially if you need a clue to a puzzling mystery on your current quest.

primagames.com

Character Generation

Unlike *Dragon Age: Origins* where you started from scratch with barely a talent under your belt, *Awakening* presents you with two main options to vault your PC up to level 18: create a new character or import an existing character over from *Dragon Age: Origins*.

Create a New Character

When you choose to create a new character, you get many of the same options that you had if you created a character for *Dragon Age: Origins*. You can choose a race and class (your starting origin story is Grey Wardens only), plus the various face and voice customization options. Remember, though, you're on the fast track to level 18. You get to choose two of your class's original specializations (such as Assassin and Bard for rogue), and you're given 62 points to spend on attributes. See the appropriate class chapter for how you should spend your attribute points. As tempting as it may sound to drop them all in your primary stat, you may regret that decision when you begin to falter in other areas of the game with frail secondary attribute scores.

After attributes, you get to purchase skills and talents/spells up to level 18. Plan how you want to spend all your important talent/spell points before you spend a single one. Does your warrior want to concentrate in the Weapon and Shield tree, or load up on Two-Handed talents? Should your mage spend a full eight points on specializations, thus reducing how many mainline spells he takes? See the appropriate class chapter for suggestions on how to spend your talent/spell points.

Before you begin the game at Vigil's Keep, each new character is given a decent set of starting gear, an inventory of helpful poultices and potions, and 55 sovereigns.

NOTE

Depending on how long and hard you played through *Dragon Age: Origins*, experienced characters may have better gear and more gold than newly created characters. As a general rule of thumb, if your PC is armed to the gills with high-end gear, holds a full inventory of cool loot, or has more than 55 sovereigns socked away, it's probably best to import your old character, even if you aren't the nostalgic sort.

Importing a Character

If you played through *Dragon Age: Origins*, even if you didn't finish the game, you can import a character. Any level character can be imported. Lower level characters will be boosted up to level 18. If you import a character higher than level 18, your imported character maintains its previous level.

You keep your attribute scores, and are awarded extra points to spend to reach level 18. All talents/spells remain the same, as do skills, and you buy new ones if you need to catch up to level 18. As with a new character, see the appropriate class chapter for hints on how best to spend your points for higher level characters.

You also get to keep your equipment. This can be a significant advantage if you stacked your previous character with nifty loot. If you want to ensure that your character has access to the same equipment, you must import your character at the game's start.

TIP

Stock up on crafting ingredients, advanced runes, and anything else you might think useful to carry over into *Awakening*, then save your *Origins* game. Only your main PC's equipment and the general inventory port over to *Awakening*, so load up. Anything on your *Origins* companions will be lost.

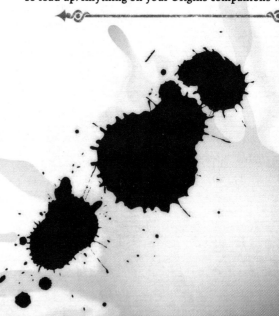

Character Generation ~ Leveling

Basics ~ **Classes** ~ The Party ~ Companions ~ Supporting Cast ~ Equipment ~ Bestiary ~ Walkthrough ~ Side Quests ~ Random Encounters ~ Achievements/Trophies

The Classes

Grey Wardens come from all backgrounds in life, hone many skills, and walk the path of adventure as one of the three classes: warrior, mage, or rogue. As a warrior, you brave the heart of the enemy vanguard with solid steel in hand and sturdy shield to guard your side. You punish foes with great two-handed weapons or a spray of arrow volleys. A mage draws mana from the Fade and bombards enemies with freezing blasts or blistering infernos. Their command of ranged attacks and unparalleled healing powers triumphs on the battlefield. Hiding in the shadows, a rogue slays the unwary from behind and detects dungeon traps with a discerning eye. His thieving hands collect more coin than a covetous merchant. The possibilities are nearly endless no matter which class you choose.

Leveling

Each level you gain three attribute points and one talent point. Attribute points can be spent on raising your core stats, while talent points can purchase new talents (for warriors and rogues) or new spells (for mages). Mages and warriors get one skill point every three levels, while rogues get a skill point every two levels. You gain specialization points at levels 7, 14, and 22. Using this information, spend your points wisely. Don't be caught with a level 18 warrior who has only the first couple of abilities in many chains. His contribution to the party will be limited, and you don't get a second chance at spending these points unless you purchase a special Manual of Focus, which allows you to re-spec your character.

✦ TIP ✦

A useful trick is to re-spec your character after level 24 using the Manual of Focus. This allows you access to a far greater number of high-level abilities than at previous levels. Using this trick also grants you access to both of the new specializations, which can make for a devastating character.

Experience Gain

Character Level	XP required to gain a level	Total current XP at the start of this level	Character Level	XP required to gain a level	Total current XP at the start of this level
1	2,000	0	19	11,000	112,501
2	2,500	2,001	20	11,500	123,501
3	3,000	4,501	21	12,000	135,001
4	3,500	7,501	22	12,500	147,001
5	4,000	11,001	23	13,000	159,501
6	4,500	15,001	24	13,500	172,501
7	5,000	19,501	25	14,500	186,001
8	5,500	24,501	26	15,000	200,501
9	6,000	30,001	27	15,500	215,501
10	6,500	36,001	28	16,000	231,001
11	7,000	42,501	29	16,500	247,001
12	7,500	49,501	30	17,000	263,501
13	8,000	57,001	31	17,500	280,501
14	8,500	65,001	32	18,000	298,001
15	9,000	73,501	33	18,500	316,001
16	9,500	82,501	34	19,000	334,501
17	10,000	92,001	35	Max	353,501
18	10,500	102,001			

✦ NOTE ✦

It is possible to reach level 35 in *Awakening*, but it's a challenging feat to accomplish. You must complete almost everything in both *Origins* and *Awakening* to attain that level.

primagames.com

Skills

All characters have the same set of skills from which to choose (not to be confused with talents/spells, which are unique for each class). Skills range from Coercion, which influences how well you can change NPCs' points of view, to Combat Tactics, which gives you more options in battles, to Runecrafting, which enables you to create runes to power up certain magic weapons and armor. For the most part, your cunning score and level affect how far you can advance in a skill. Raise your cunning to 16 to access all of Coercion, Stealing, Survival, and Combat Tactics. Gaining level 10 opens up all of Trap-Making, Herbalism, and Poison-Making. Combat Training has no restrictions on it. Reach level 20 to begin acquiring the new *Awakening* skills: Runecrafting, Vitality, and Clarity.

When you purchase a skill for the first time, you start at its basic effect, and with each upgrade your ability grows and more options open up. For example, a basic herbalist can create lesser potions, while an improved herbalist can craft normal lyrium and health potions, and so on up the ladder to expert and master Herbalism. Only one skill point is available every three levels (or every two if you're a rogue), so make your skill choices count. At most you will max out two to three skills during the game, or you may master one skill and dabble in others. To aid in choosing the best skills for you, here are some pointers.

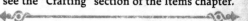

> **NOTE**
>
> For a list of all crafting items, ingredients, and recipes, see the "Crafting" section of the Items chapter.

Coercion

You can access more game areas and information, bargain for better rewards or terms, and talk your way out of many difficult situations with this skill. While all classes can intimidate effectively (given a high Coercion skill and some fearsome party members), warriors can use their strength score (instead of cunning) to gain a bit of an edge in their intimidations. For convincing companions to follow your lead without serious approval drops, you will likely gain the most use out of this skill. When in doubt, put your points into Coercion.

Stealing

You are quick enough to pilfer small items from others, whether friendly or hostile, as long as they aren't too alert. Of course, you may have to pay the price if someone catches you in the act.

Trap-Making

Learning how to make traps and lures seems like a good rogue talent, but this can be very useful for mages as well. If you're not all that strong in melee range, use traps and lures to draw in enemies and deal some preliminary damage while you cast a barrage of spells from afar. Even a warrior can throw a trap around once in a while to root extra enemies.

Survival

The more you advance this skill, the better chance you have to detect creatures on your mini-map before they surprise you. This skill can save you from more than a few ambushes. In addition, you get a bonus to nature resistance, which protects against poison attacks of all sorts as well as spells such as Stonefist, Walking Bomb, and Virulent Walking Bomb.

Herbalism

Gain the ability to make your own potions, poultices, and salves with this skill. These are invaluable items, and you'll always want at least five in any difficult fight. Regardless of class, all parties should have at least one person proficient in Herbalism.

Poison-Making

The ability to create poison works best for rogues, or warriors who want a boost to damage. You need at least one point in Poison-Making to use poisons and bombs. If you already have a character crafting health and mana potions, it never hurts to increase your offensive potential as well, even with just one level in this skill.

Combat Training

The more points you spend here, the better your warrior or rogue performs in combat. It's essential for any melee-based character. Warriors and rogues gain access to new weapon talents, stamina regeneration, attack bonuses, and armor upgrades. Mages can take more damage before it interrupts spellcasting.

Skills

Basics ~ **Classes** ~ The Party ~ Companions ~ Supporting Cast ~ Equipment ~ Bestiary ~ Walkthrough ~ Side Quests ~ Random Encounters ~ Achievements/Trophies

Combat Tactics

Spending points in this skill gives you more tactics slots for your character. If you make all the decisions yourself, it's not that important; if you allow the characters to act on their own in combat, it's a big deal to get more tactics slots to better customize your combat strategies.

Runecrafting

This skill enables you to create your own runes for weapons and armor. It's expensive to craft potent runes, because you must create two runes of a lesser level and then destroy them in the process of creating the higher-level rune. Despite this, the power to customize your weapons and armor with extra abilities is worth having in any party.

Vitality

Bulk up your health with this skill. Each level increases your health gain, which should prove a necessity for warriors or any other characters frequently taking blows in the heart of combat. At higher experience levels, if you don't have any other skills you want to take for a character, think about Vitality to maximize defense.

Clarity

Improve your stamina/mana pool with this skill. Each level increases your stamina or mana gain, which works for just about any character, especially mages and DPSers who constantly rely on heavy stamina talents. At higher experience levels, if you don't have any other skills you want to take for a character, think about Clarity to increase how many spells or talents you can use in a fight.

NPC Crafters

Not every skill has to come from you or your party; some NPCs around the world can craft items for you. You might not have the hands of a blacksmith, for example, but if you bring special items to Herren and Wade in the Vigil's Keep courtyard, they will craft you a superior weapon, piece of armor, bow, or shield, depending on the original materials. Look for help wherever you go.

> **← NOTE →**
>
> See the Side Quests and Random Encounters chapters for details on side quests that lead to special items.

Choosing Skills

You should choose skills that appeal to your play style, and vary it from character to character. A rogue may enjoy Stealing, while Herbalism is a natural fit for a mage because it benefits from a high magic score. That doesn't mean a rogue shouldn't learn Herbalism or a mage learn Stealing. Always have fun with your choices, and remember that between the four characters in your party, you can play with most, if not all, of the game's skills.

However, some skills influence the game directly more than others. Coercion is the most important. It can give you options in dialogue to avoid fights or open up new areas of play that you might not have received without the art of persuasion. Survival points out enemies on the mini-map, which helps you set up your party for fights and avoid deadly ambushes. Herbalism creates super-useful health poultices and lyrium potions. Unless you want to spend tons of coin on these essential accessories, invest in Herbalism to make your own at a fraction of the price. Runecrafting works similar to Herbalism, only with creating runes and with a higher price associated with the crafting materials. Without a doubt, Combat Training is vital to warriors and rogues who want access to top-tier weapon talents.

Warrior Combat Skills

A warrior primarily concerned about combat and dialogue options with eight points to spend on skills might lean toward this configuration to start with:

- Combat Training +4
- Coercion +4
- Survival +1

Mage Healing and Coercion Skills

A mage primarily concerned about dialogue options and healing and with eight points to spend on skills might lean toward this configuration at the outset:

- Coercion +4
- Combat Training +1
- Herbalism +3

Rogue Combat Skills

A rogue primarily concerned about combat and Poison-Making with 11 points to spend on skills might lean toward this configuration when starting out:

- Combat Training +4
- Poison-Making +3
- Stealing +1
- Coercion +3

The biggest choice of your early career comes next: Do you play a warrior, mage, or rogue? All experiences are rewarding, but each is unique in  the origin story you play through, the talents/spells you gain, and your ability to affect combat and influence the storyline. Which type of Grey Warden will you be?

The Warrior

You are sword and shield, retribution and resilience, the cornerstone of a party's defenses. A warrior charges into the heat of battle to engage the enemy first, simultaneously damaging foes while protecting fellow party members from harm. When danger surrounds you, a warrior heeds the call to battle despite cut, gash, or threat of an early grave. Without a warrior, the party cannot survive long against sterner threats.

To deal with darkspawn and other deadly perils, the warrior has access to better weapons and armor than the mage or the rogue. You may be fortunate enough to find these fine weapons and pieces of armor in shops, or you may discover them as loot hidden in dungeon treasure chests; regardless, the warrior has the best selection of combat goods. The warrior uses them well in battle too. Whether in hand-to-hand melee or at longer bow range, the enemy cannot escape the warrior's severe punishment. Swords slice through mail, while arrows plunge into flesh.

As part of their natural training and skill sets, warriors have a strong understanding of battle tactics and strategy. You will have a wide array of talents to deal massive combat damage to single targets and groups of foes. A warrior's talents are broken down by how you plan to use your weapons. If you plan to use gear in both hands, a warrior can pursue Dual Weapons or Weapon and Shield. Alternately, the warrior can concentrate on larger Two-Handed Weapons to savage an opponent, or learn the ways of Archery to harass enemies at range. Some of the warrior's general talents increase health and stamina, reduce armor penalties, draw hostilities away from allies, grant damage bonuses, improve critical hit percentages, and make you the meanest combatant on the battlefield.

Warrior specializations crank up your battle effectiveness. As a Berserker, a warrior's rage fuels his strikes, adding damage to the blows at the expense of other qualities such as stamina. A Templar, on the other hand, hunts enemy mages and beats them down with mana drains and more damage. A Champion inspires those around him with party-influencing abilities. A Reaver revels in the dark side as he sucks life back into himself from the pain of others. A Spirit Warrior attunes himself to the Fade, gaining magic resistance, increased spirit damage, and bonuses to movement and attack speeds. Finally, a Guardian is all about protecting the party by tossing up group buffs or conjuring a field that pulls enemies back toward the warrior.

If you like to jump straight into battle and be the first to draw blood, the warrior class is for you. Superb weapons and armor are at your disposal, and melee damage comes as naturally to you as forging to a blacksmith. You will be the toughest party member, and you may have to save those less armored than yourself from time to time, but it's all part of the responsibility of the hero with the biggest muscles.

Strengths and Weaknesses

The strength of a warrior is in his arms and armor. A warrior can deal major damage to adversaries, especially in melee where he can land pounding blows and critical strikes with excellent hand-to-hand weapons. Return blows from enemies will either glance off a warrior's superior armor or the warrior's defenses will limit the extent of the damage. The warrior's natural bonuses aid in the cause too. His +4 strength bonus augments your most important attribute, and a +3 bonus to constitution raises health and makes you that much more difficult to kill.

Advantages

- Stat Bonuses to Strength, Dexterity, and Constitution
- Top Weapons, Best Armor
- Superior Melee Damage
- High Survivability
- Enhanced Combat Talents and Tactics

The warrior may be a wrecking ball in combat, but he does have limitations. Most importantly, a warrior needs to close on his target to be at his best. Where a mage can hurl spells from the back, or a rogue can hide and surprise with a backstab, most warriors must

The Warrior

get close to his enemy at some point to do maximum damage. It's possible to deal some damage with a good ranged weapon, but the majority of warrior talents trigger off hand-to-hand combat. While you close on the enemy, it's likely you'll take some ranged damage and may take heaps of damage from magic attacks, which warriors will be vulnerable to early on. Your armor may reduce damage, but the damage will come, and most warriors do not have healing to regain health. Stock up on healing potions and stay near your party healer in case your health suddenly drops.

Disadvantages

- Limited Healing
- Must Close on Enemies to Be Most Effective
- Generally Weak Against Magic Attacks

If you like a brash, in-your-face play style and really love to hack and slash monsters, the warrior's advantages far outweigh his disadvantages. Nothing beats a 10-on-1 battle where the warrior walks away with just a scratch and the enemies...well, they just don't walk away at all.

Attributes

Strength increases your damage and affects your accuracy with melee attacks, making it the warrior's number-one attribute. As you might expect, it's reflected in the warrior class bonus with a +4 strength. Many talents will require high strength scores, and more powerful weapons and armor require a higher strength stat. When you level up, you may consider spending two points on strength for every one point you spend somewhere else, especially early in your warrior career to unlock talents quicker (you may even decide to put all three points per level in strength to unlock talents earlier).

Next, a warrior should stock up on constitution, particularly if you plan to specialize as a Guardian. You can always use more health, which constitution directly increases, and constitution also boosts resilience to keep you fighting on the battlefield longer. The warrior's starting bonus of +3 constitution gives you a good jump, and you should consider throwing points to constitution if you don't have any other attribute you want to improve immediately.

Warrior Attribute Bonuses

+4 Strength

+3 Dexterity

+3 Constitution

Dexterity can do a lot for a warrior. It affects your chance to hit, increases your chance to dodge enemy blows, and augments damage from piercing weapons. Archery and dual weapon–specced warriors should load up on dexterity, even forgoing strength early if you need to unlock certain ranged or dual-weapon talents. The warrior's +3 dexterity bonus pushes you to above-average dexterity from the start, and you should continue spending points if you plan on a healthy balance of offense and defense.

TIP

Gear bonuses can amplify your attribute's strengths or offset any shortcomings. A ring, for example, that bulks up constitution could provide some extra health without costing any precious attribute points.

At first glance, you might dismiss willpower as a stat for mages. But read the fine print. Willpower increases stamina, so if your warrior loves to perform daring maneuvers that drain a lot of stamina (and who doesn't) you'll have to throw points to this attribute once in a while. At lower levels, you won't have the extra points to boost willpower, but when you hit the teens, start looking to expand your stamina pool.

Magic shouldn't be a priority at all; however, it does increase the effect of potions and salves, and because most warriors rely on potions to buff health in a fight, magic is not entirely useless.

Cunning can be neglected, unless you plan to be an inexorable master of Coercion. However, if you're not overly concerned with playing the role of the nice guy, your alternative to Coercion is being able to intimidate those same NPCs, made possible by your superior score.

If maximizing your warrior stats appeals to you, choose a dwarf or human. A dwarven warrior gives you a starting 15 strength, 14 dexterity, and 15 constitution. For a more well-rounded approach, try the human warrior with 15 strength, 14 dexterity, and 13 constitution (with a couple of points spread to magic and cunning). The elven warrior isn't as solid out of the gates as his natural race bonus applies to willpower and magic, so an elf's main warrior attributes aren't as high at the start.

Warrior Starting Attributes

Attribute	Human	Elf	Dwarf
Strength	15	14	15
Dexterity	14	13	14
Willpower	10	12	10
Magic	11	12	10
Cunning	11	10	10
Constitution	13	13	15

When entering *Awakening* with a new character, you begin with 62 points to add to your attributes. If you want a powerful and damaging warrior, apply the majority of points to strength. If you want a more defensive juggernaut, spread out your points between strength, dexterity, and constitution. In most cases, though, it's probably best to stick with the standard warrior advice—strength first, then constitution, with dexterity for dual weapons and a little willpower for extra stamina.

Skills

All warriors need to pick up the Combat Training skill as soon as they can. Combat Training opens up the higher tier weapon talents, which you can't live without. Spend your first skill points here to max it out. Other skills can be helpful, such as Trap-Making if you want to add a little AoE damage to your repertoire; however, they aren't essential like Combat Training.

◄► NOTE ◄►

Beyond your starting skills, you're likely to obtain 8 skill points when you start a new character. Pick your two or three favorite skills and stick with them. If you spread your points too thin, you'll end up doing a bunch of things—but not well.

After you finish off your Combat Training, think about Coercion. It's an incredibly useful skill in dialogue; it gives you story options that you won't get access to otherwise. Cunning opens up the Coercion skills, and more cunning will increase your Persuade skill, but in most situations you can use your Intimidate skill in lieu of Persuade. Intimidate works off your strength stat, which fits perfectly with a warrior.

Warrior Skill Recommendations

Assuming you spend 8 skill points at the start, here's a good spread to consider. Note that many other combinations could work better for you, so experiment!

- Combat Training +4
- Coercion +4
- Survival +1

Survival can be a good skill to have because the more you advance it, the better chance you have to detect creatures on your mini-map before they surprise you. You can save yourself from more than a few ambushes with this skill. Don't forget about the bonus to nature resistance too.

If you aren't directly playing your warrior companions (see the Companions chapter for more details) and want one of them to run around on their own, Combat Tactics might be a good investment too. The more tactic slots you open, the more you can shape how your companions behave in battle. Inevitably, even if you plan on controlling your warrior during fights, there will be moments when you don't program your warrior's every move (or something more important is going on) and tactics come into play. One or two points should be good, or max it out if you want the character to go on autopilot.

Talents

Warriors will shine in combat, amid talons scraping at flesh and blood spurting in faces. Like the other classes, the warrior offers more than a single way to play. You can choose the tank role, focusing on defense and holding your team together, or the melee DPS role, concentrating on pounding out as much damage as your two hands can manage. If you want to affect combat from the perimeter, the ranged fighter can be a gem; he may not have the same firepower as a mage, but a warrior archer has many tools and the tough skin to back them up.

◄► NOTE ◄►

It's possible to have three warrior companions in the game: Justice, Mhairi, and the returning Oghren. Develop each differently to have access to a wider arsenal.

All warriors should familiarize themselves with the cooldown component of each talent. The worst situation is to have plenty of stamina and no available talents to use. Branch out into different chains to avoid the cooldown problem. For example, if you develop the Weapon and Shield school primarily for defense, having a talent or two in Two-Handed can help with extra damage and keeping your options open.

Your talents drain stamina from your pool. Watch how much stamina you're using in a fight and act accordingly. If you run short without a healer's Restoration spell to replenish you, it could cost your party a victory. Gauge what you have to do to help the team. There's little sense running off a series of moves that drains three quarters of your stamina on the first opponent when there are three more to go.

The Warrior

Basics ~ **Classes** ~ The Party ~ Companions ~ Supporting Cast ~ Equipment ~ Bestiary ~ Walkthrough ~ Side Quests ~ Random Encounters ~ Achievements/Trophies

Warrior Weapon Sets

Take advantage of your warrior's second set of weapons. Gear your first equipment set for your primary focus, and your secondary set as backup. For example, arm yourself with an excellent two-handed weapon if your focus is in the Two-Handed school, and a crossbow in the second set for a little ranged damage. If you want to broaden your fighting style, pair your main style with one other style. Use a few Archery talents paired with any of the other schools and you have a well-prepared warrior ready for ranged and melee combat. Use Dual Weapons with Weapon and Shield when you want to shift focus from defending and attacking to becoming a whirlwind of attacks. Use Two-Handed with Dual Weapons when you want to go from that whirlwind of attacks to being able to take on giant foes.

Remember, though, as you level up, you'll gain access to specializations, so you'll want to spend points in those talent chains too. Usually by level 18, you'd have enough talent points to max out your Warrior talent school, all but one weapon-type talent chain, and all but one in a specialization talent chain. Also remember that the secondary set of weapons (and accompanying talents for them) are meant to be a backup, so avoid splitting your talent points evenly between both styles or you'll be decent at both but excel at neither.

Warrior School

You have three choices: one for basic defense, one for basic offense, and a new chain with a little bit of everything. The chain that starts with Powerful leans toward defense (though both chains give you offensive and defensive options). Powerful adds extra health and reduces fatigue, which means all of your abilities cost less. Even if you don't want to spec in the Warrior school at all, think about spending an extra point in Powerful because it's a great early ability. The sustained ability Threaten is a must for tanks who get into the thick of things and need to keep threat on themselves. Bravery is all-around good, with its bonuses to damage, resistances, and critical hit chance. Death Blow restores stamina for each foe a warrior fells in battle.

The Precise Striking chain centers around increasing your attacking skills. You sacrifice attack speed with Precise Striking, but you gain a bonus to your attack chance and critical hit chance. Taunt works as another excellent threat-magnet for

tanks who want to suck in everything around them. It can also work with an off-tank to help them control enemies when they need to play the tank role. Disengage reduces threat and allows the warrior to shed enemies when the pressure gets too great; this is another excellent ability for off-tanks who only want to hold a foe for a little while. Perfect Striking gains you a massive attack bonus for a short time.

The new Second Wind chain starts off with a fantastic talent that refills your stamina pool to full upon activation. Peon's Plight hits the enemy hard: lesser foes die outright, elites take a double critical hit, and even bosses take a critical hit. Grievous Insult is like a super Taunt: it draws all enemies immediately toward the warrior. For Massacre, the warriors spins in an arc of death, killing lesser foes, dealing a critical hit to elite enemies and normal damage to bosses.

Dual Weapon School

For those warriors who prefer dexterity, Dual Weapons gives you more offense without relying on strength. You deal damage with two weapons simultaneously; alas, the drawback is that your defense suffers. The focus of your passive abilities is on your second hand: you want to deal as close to normal damage as possible and score close to the same number of critical hits as your main hand.

You gain a bonus to attack and defense with Dual-Weapon Finesse. Dual-Weapon Expert gives a bonus to critical chance and lets you cause bleeding lacerations on your opponent, inflicting damage over time. You may wield full-sized weapons in your off-hand while reducing the stamina cost of all dual weapon talents with Dual-Weapon Mastery.

Increase your attack damage with Dual Striking in the second chain. Score a two-hit combo with a possibility of stunning your opponent and scoring a critical hit with Riposte. Cripple gives you a chance to score a critical hit and inflict your opponent with penalties to movement speed, attack, and defense. Punisher is a three-hit combo that can score a critical hit, knock an opponent down, and cause penalties to movement and attack speed.

Dual-Weapon Sweep deals significant damage with each sweep. Flurry is a three-hit combo, while Momentum increases your attack speed with every hit. Whirlwind is a flurry of constant attacks: the signature of a Dual Weapon expert.

This talent chain can also be a deadly combination with the Warrior talent school. Draw enemies in and knock them down, stun them, cause damage over time, and inflict penalties to movement speed, attack, and defense. Powerful and Bravery give you bonuses to attack, defense, and resistances while Death Blow restores stamina with each kill, making you a whirlwind of death…if you don't get hammered by arrows or spells from opponents.

23

The new Twin Strikes chain scores two automatic critical hits on a target. Find Vitals increases melee critical chance by 10 and critical damage by 20. Low Blow combos with Twin Strikes and leaves opponents unable to move for a short duration. Unending Flurry acts just as you would expect it to: repeated attacks strike the target over and over until you miss or run out of mana.

Archery School

Another school for warriors who build up dexterity, Archery gives ample special effects for a ranged combat enthusiast. Melee Archer lets you fire while being attacked (eliminating some of the pain of being an archer). Master Archer gives you bonuses to activated abilities and eliminates the penalty to attack speed when wearing heavy armor. Aim reduces attack speed but gives bonuses to attack, damage, armor penetration, and critical chance. Defensive Fire gives you a boost to defense but slows your attack speed.

In the second chain, Pinning Shot is a necessity because it impales the victim's leg and either pins it in place or slows its movement speed. Crippling Shot deals normal damage to an enemy and gives it penalties to attack and defense, and Critical Shot delivers maximum damage upon impact. The deadly Arrow of Slaying usually scores a critical hit, often dropping weakened enemies.

Rapid Shot increases attack speed, but you lose the ability to score critical hits. Shattering Shot deals normal damage and opens up an enemy's armor. If a warrior finds open armor, its wearer will be in sore shape. Suppressing Fire is like Rapid Shot, but its foes now take penalties to their attack rating. Scattershot stuns a foe and then shatters, dealing damage to other enemies around it.

When you have room to breathe, Pinning Shot and Crippling Shot turn enemies into sitting ducks for mage attacks, deadly rogues, or more of your carefully aimed arrows. Shattering Shot is excellent against heavily armed foes. Rapid Shot, Suppressing Fire, and Scattershot hack away at the collective hit points of enemy ranks.

TIP

A good combo against a heavily armed foe is Shattering Shot, Crippling Shot, Aim/Rapid Shot, and Arrow of Slaying. Mix in another Shattering Shot if the first armor penalty runs out.

Don't think an archer just scores a hit or two before having to engage an opponent in melee. You can kill a couple enemies in a few hits while pinning others in place and continuing to fire while other attackers swarm you. This turns you into a deadly sniper that enemies need to deal with or suffer the consequences. If the enemy swarms you, switch to Defensive Fire while you have the passive ability Melee Archer. You can fire off arrows while being attacked and still have decent defense.

The new Accuracy chain gives bonuses to your attack and damage scores, as well as ranged critical chance. Arrow Time slows down enemies around the archer, while the phenomenal Burst Shot scores an automatic triple critical hit against a single target and then shatters to deal AoE damage to all other targets around it. Rain of Arrows blankets an area with damage, harming foes and friends alike in the large radius.

Weapon and Shield School

Your standard warrior tank usually dips into the Weapon and Shield school a lot. In the offensive chain, Shield Bash deals normal damage and has a chance to knock an enemy down. Shield Pummel is a two-hit combo that can stun an enemy. Overpower is a three-hit shield combo that might deal a critical hit with the third strike. Assault is a four-hit combo that diminishes in power with each strike. Use any of these with Shield Defense, Shield Wall, or Shield Cover to get in some good, solid hits while bolstering your defenses. Use any of these with Threaten or Taunt in the Warrior talent school to pull enemies in and knock them back on their collective back sides.

Shield Wall or Shield Defense used with Taunt or Threaten from the Warrior talent school makes a great combination because you lure enemies in and beef up your defenses while resisting knockdown effects and shrugging off missiles. The Shield Block passive ability eliminates your enemies' flanking advantage on your shield side, while the Shield Tactics passive ability eliminates your enemies' flanking advantage altogether. This comes in very handy because hordes of enemies swarm your characters in many battles. When they flank you, they score bonuses to attacks and critical hits. Shield Cover and Shield Defense help you shrug off missile attacks. This is very useful, for example, when hurlocks are swarming you while genlock archers are slamming you with arrows.

The many passive abilities in this talent chain give bonuses to the sustained and activated abilities, so they get stronger the more you progress in Weapon and Shield training. Now, if only there were 300 more of these guys in your army at the end of the game...

The new Juggernaut chain allows a tank to run through enemies and knock them aside, which aids in reaching surrounded allies and generally knocking enemies about. Carapace protects the warrior by reducing damage based off the warrior's constitution score; the fourth talent in the chain, Bulwark of the Ages, improves Carapace and makes the tank completely invulnerable for the first half of the Carapace effect. Air of Insolence radiates continuous energy that draws enemies toward the warrior.

The Warrior

Basics ~ **Classes** ~ The Party ~ Companions ~ Supporting Cast ~ Equipment ~ Bestiary ~ Walkthrough ~ Side Quests ~ Random Encounters ~ Achievements/Trophies

Two-Handed School

In this talent school, you get to deal massive damage, but you're slower moving and you don't have as much in the way of defense. The Stunning Blows passive ability adds a chance to stun your target each time you strike. Shattering Blows gives you attack bonuses against golems and other heavily armored foes. Destroyer means that every attack you deal has a chance to sunder an opponent's armor. Two-Handed Strength reduces your attack and defense penalty in Powerful Swings.

Indomitable gives you a bonus to attack while making you immune to stun or knockdown effects. If you're in a swarm of larger enemies, use Indomitable to protect against getting stunned or knocked down, but careful with this because it uses a nice chunk of your stamina. The Powerful Swings sustained ability gives you a nice bonus to damage but reduces your attack and defense.

Pommel Strike knocks an opponent to the ground. Critical Strike is a massive hit that scores a critical hit and sometimes kills a foe outright. Sunder Arms targets an enemy's weapon, giving a penalty to attack, while Sunder Armor targets the armor, giving a penalty to armor and dealing normal damage to the unlucky victim. Mighty Blow can deal a critical hit and reduce the opponent's movement, and Two-Handed Sweep hits enemies in a wide arc, dealing normal damage and knocking them down.

The new Sweeping Strike chain begins with a talent that knocks a group of enemies to the ground (if they fail a physical resistance check), critically hits the primary target and distributes normal damage to the rest. The sustained talent Two-Handed Impact sends out shockwaves that deal damage to other enemies around your primary target. Onslaught advances the warrior several steps, sweeping the weapon in huge arcs that deal damage to multiple foes. Reaving Storm sends the warrior on a furious assault against multiple foes as he or she slashes continuously at all surrounding enemies.

TIP
Try Sunder Arms, Sunder Armor, normal attack, Mighty Blow, and Critical Strike. For some foes, you might not even need Mighty Blow.

Warrior Talents

Chain	Name	Prerequisite	Description	Cost (mana/stamina)	Upkeep (mana/stamina)	Fatigue (% mana/stamina)	Ranged	Cooldown (sec.)	Area of Effect Radius (ft.)
			Warrior School						
Chain 1	Powerful	Strength 10	Through training and hard work, the warrior has gained greater health and reduced the fatigue penalty for wearing armor.	0	0	0	No	0	0
	Threaten	Strength 14, Level 4	The warrior adopts a challenging posture that increases enemy hostility with each melee attack, drawing them away from other allies while this mode is active.	0	35	2	No	15	0
	Bravery	Strength 20, Level 8	The warrior's unwavering courage grants bonuses to damage, physical resistance, and mental resistance, as well as a bonus to critical chance that increases proportionally to the number of enemies above two that the warrior is engaging.	0	0	0	No	0	0
	Death Blow	Strength 25, Level 12	Each time the warrior fells an enemy, the end of the battle seems closer at hand, restoring a portion of the warrior's stamina.	0	0	0	No	0	0
Chain 2	Precise Striking	Dexterity 10	The warrior tries to make each attack count, sacrificing attack speed for a bonus to attack as well as an increased chance to score critical hits for as long as this mode is active.	0	40	5	No	15	0
	Taunt	Strength 14, Level 4	A mocking bellow catches the attention of nearby foes, increasing their hostility toward the warrior. Frightening Appearance increases the effect.	40	0	0	No	20	10
	Disengage	Dexterity 18, Level 8	A relaxed position makes the warrior seem less threatening, reducing the hostility of nearby enemies, who may seek other targets instead.	10	0	0	No	10	10
	Perfect Striking	Strength 22, Level 12	The warrior focuses on precision, gaining a massive attack bonus for a moderate time.	60	0	0	No	30	0
Chain 3	Second Wind	Level 20, Strength 34	Long years of training grant access to deep reserves of vigor, instantly restoring nearly all of the warrior's stamina.	0	0	0	No	120	0
	Peon's Plight	Level 22, Strength 41	The warrior lashes out with a powerful blow intended to eliminate the weakest opposition. A successful attack automatically kills a target of normal or lesser rank, inflicts a double critical hit against an elite target, or inflicts a regular critical hit against a boss.	60	0	0	No	45	0
	Grievous Insult	Level 25, Strength 45	A vile epithet attracts the ire of all enemies nearby, drawing them away from their current targets and toward the warrior.	80	0	0	No	60	10
	Massacre	Level 27, Strength 54	The warrior spins in an arc of death, automatically killing nearby enemies of lower or lesser rank and scoring a critical hit against any elite target, but inflicting normal damage against a boss.	100	0	0	No	60	7.5

primagames.com

Chain	Name	Prerequisite	Description	Cost (mana /stamina)	Upkeep (mana /stamina)	Fatigue (% mana/stamina)	Ranged	Cooldown (sec.)	Area of Effect Radius (ft.)
			Dual Weapon School						
Chain 1	Dual Striking	Dexterity 12	When in this mode, the character strikes with both weapons simultaneously. Attacks cause more damage, but the character cannot inflict regular critical hits or backstabs.	0	50	5	No	10	0
	Riposte	Dexterity 16	The character strikes at a target once, dealing normal damage, as well as stunning the opponent unless it passes a physical resistance check. The character then strikes with the other weapon, generating a critical hit if the target was stunned.	40	0	0	No	20	0
	Cripple	Dexterity 22	The character strikes low at a target, gaining a momentary attack bonus and hitting critically if the attack connects, while crippling the target with penalties to movement speed, attack, and defense unless it passes a physical resistance check.	35	0	0	No	30	0
	Punisher	Dexterity 28	The character makes three blows against a target, dealing normal damage for the first two strikes and generating a critical hit for the final blow, if it connects. The target may also suffer penalties to attack and defense, or be knocked to the ground.	50	0	0	No	40	0
Chain 2	Dual-Weapon Sweep	Dexterity 12	The character sweeps both weapons in a broad forward arc, striking nearby enemies with one or both weapons and inflicting significantly more damage than normal.	20	0	0	No	15	2
	Flurry	Dexterity 18	The character lashes out with a flurry of three blows, dealing normal combat damage with each hit.	40	0	0	No	20	0
	Momentum	Dexterity 24	The character has learned to carry one attack through to the next, increasing attack speed substantially. This mode consumes stamina quickly, however.	0	60	5	No	30	0
	Whirlwind	Dexterity 30	The character flies into a whirling dance of death, striking out at surrounding enemies with both weapons. Each hit deals normal combat damage.	40	0	0	No	40	2
Chain 3	Dual-Weapon Training	Dexterity 12	The character has become more proficient fighting with two weapons, and now deals closer to normal damage bonus with the off-hand weapon.	0	0	0	No	0	0
	Dual-Weapon Finesse	Dexterity 16	The character is extremely skilled at wielding a weapon in each hand, gaining bonuses to attack and defense.	0	0	0	No	0	0
	Dual-Weapon Expert	Dexterity 26	The character has significant experience with two-weapon fighting, gaining a bonus to critical chance, as well as a possibility with each hit to inflict bleeding lacerations that continue to damage a target for a time.	0	0	0	No	0	0
	Dual-Weapon Mastery	Dexterity 36	Only a chosen few truly master the complicated art of fighting with two weapons. The character is now among that elite company, able to wield full-sized weapons in both hands. Stamina costs for all dual-weapon talents are also reduced.	0	0	0	No	0	0
Chain 4	Twin Strikes	Level 20, Dexterity 34	Two devastating strikes in rapid succession each inflict an automatic critical hit. Find Vitals adds additional damage to each hit. If the target is affected by Low Blow, it cannot move for a short time.	50	0	0	No	30	0
	Find Vitals	Dexterity 40	The character is a force of nature when wielding two weapons, gaining permanent bonuses to melee critical chance and critical damage. Twin Strikes now inflicts additional bleeding damage (melee critical chance +10, critical damage +20).	Passive	0	0	No	0	0
	Low Blow	Dexterity 46	The character strikes at the legs of surrounding enemies, imposing penalties to movement speed and attack speed for a short time. If an opponent is already bleeding from Twin Strikes, it slips and falls to the ground as well.	50	0	0	No	30	2.5
	Unending Flurry	Dexterity 50	The character singles out an enemy for death, stabbing it quickly and repeatedly, consuming a small amount of stamina with each hit. The assault continues until the target dies or flees, or until the character misses or runs out of stamina. If the target is bleeding from Twin Strikes, each swing becomes a critical hit. If the target is slowed by Low Blow, the character cannot miss.	40	0	0	No	60	0
			Archery School						
Chain 1	Melee Archer	Dexterity 12	Experience fighting in tight quarters has taught the archer to fire without interruption, even when being attacked.	0	0	0	No	0	0
	Aim	Dexterity 16	The archer carefully places each shot for maximum effect while in this mode. This decreases rate of fire but grants bonuses to attack, damage, armor penetration, and critical chance. Master Archer further increases these bonuses.	0	35	5	No	10	0
	Defensive Fire	Dexterity 22	While active, the archer changes stance, receiving a bonus to defense but slowing the rate of fire. With the Master Archer talent, the defense bonus increases.	0	40	5	No	15	0
	Master Archer	Dexterity 28	Deadly with both bows and crossbows, master archers receive additional benefits when using Aim, Defensive Fire, Crippling Shot, Critical Shot, Arrow of Slaying, Rapid Shot, and Shattering Shot. This talent also eliminates the penalty to attack speed when wearing heavy armor, although massive armor still carries the penalty.	0	0	0	No	0	0

The Warrior

Basics ~ **Classes** ~ The Party ~ Companions ~ Supporting Cast ~ Equipment ~ Bestiary ~ Walkthrough ~ Side Quests ~ Random Encounters ~ Achievements/Trophies

Chain	Name	Prerequisite	Description	Cost (mana /stamina)	Upkeep (mana /stamina)	Fatigue (% mana/stamina)	Ranged	Cooldown (sec.)	Area of Effect Radius (ft.)
			Archery School (continued)						
Chain 2	Pinning Shot	Dexterity 12	A shot to the target's legs disables the foe, pinning the target in place unless it passes a physical resistance check, and slowing movement speed otherwise.	20	0	0	Yes	15	0
	Crippling Shot	Dexterity 16	A carefully aimed shot hampers the target's ability to fight by reducing attack and defense if it hits, although the shot inflicts only normal damage. The Master Archer talent adds an attack bonus while firing the Crippling Shot.	25	0	0	Yes	10	0
	Critical Shot	Dexterity 21	Finding a chink in the target's defenses, the archer fires an arrow that, if aimed correctly, automatically scores a critical hit and gains a bonus to armor penetration. The Master Archer talent increases the armor penetration bonus.	40	0	0	Yes	10	0
	Arrow of Slaying	Dexterity 30	The archer generates an automatic critical hit if this shot finds its target, although high-level targets may be able to ignore the effect. The archer suffers reduced stamina regeneration for a time. Master Archer adds an extra attack bonus.	80	0	0	Yes	60	0
Chain 3	Rapid Shot	Dexterity 12	Speed wins out over power while this mode is active, as the archer fires more rapidly but without any chance of inflicting regular critical hits. Master Archer increases the rate of fire further still.	0	35	5	No	30	0
	Shattering Shot	Dexterity 16	The archer fires a shot designed to open up a weak spot in the target's armor. The shot deals normal damage if it hits and imposes an armor penalty on the target. Master Archer increases the target's armor penalty.	25	0	0	Yes	15	0
	Suppressing Fire	Dexterity 24	When this mode is active, the archer's shots hamper foes. Each arrow deals regular damage and also encumbers the target with a temporary penalty to attack. This penalty can be applied multiple times.	0	60	5	No	10	0
	Scattershot	Dexterity 27	The archer fires a single arrow that automatically hits, stunning the target and dealing normal damage. The arrow then shatters, hitting all nearby enemies with the same effect.	50	0	0	Yes	40	0
Chain 4	Accuracy	Level 20, Dexterity 34	For as long as this mode is active, the archer's mind is clear of everything except the next shot's trajectory, gaining bonuses to attack, damage, ranged critical chance, and ranged critical damage, all dependent on the archer's dexterity attribute.	0	60	0	No	10	0
	Arrow Time	Dexterity 38	Intense focus slows the archer's perception of time, effectively reducing the movement speed of enemies who come near for as long as this mode is active, excepting those of elite rank or higher. This deep concentration drains stamina constantly.	0	40	10	No	10	0
	Burst Shot	Dexterity 44	The archer looses a special shaft that scores an automatic triple critical hit against the targeted enemy, then shatters, inflicting half the effect on those unfortunate enough to be in the vicinity. Friendly fire possible.	60	0	0	Yes	60	3
	Rain of Arrows	Dexterity 52	The archer's bow points to the sky, firing multiple projectiles which then rain down over time in the targeted area. Friendly fire possible.	80	0	0	Yes	60	0
			Weapons and Shield School						
Chain 1	Shield Bash	Strength 11	The character shield-bashes a target, dealing normal damage as well as knocking the target off its feet unless it passes a physical resistance check. Shield Mastery doubles the strength bonus for this attack.	25	0	0	No	20	0
	Shield Pummel	Strength 15	The character follows up an attack with two hits from the shield, dealing normal damage with each attack. If the target fails a physical resistance check, it is stunned. Shield Mastery doubles the character's strength bonus for each strike.	30	0	0	No	20	0
	Overpower	Strength 25	The character lashes out with the shield three times. The first two hits inflict normal damage. The last strike is a critical hit if it connects, knocking the target down unless it passes a physical resistance check. Shield Mastery increases the damage.	30	0	0	No	20	0
	Assault	Strength 32	The character quickly strikes a target four times, but dealing reduced damage with each hit. If the character has Shield Mastery, the damage from each hit increases.	40	0	0	No	20	0
Chain 2	Shield Block	Dexterity 10	Practice fighting with a shield improves the character's guard. Enemies can no longer flank the character on the shield-carrying side.	0	0	0	No	0	0
	Shield Cover	Dexterity 16	While in this mode, the warrior's shield provides a greater chance of deflecting missile attacks. Shield Mastery increases this bonus further.	0	20	5	No	15	0
	Shield Tactics	Dexterity 20	The character is proficient enough with a shield to defend from all angles, so that attackers no longer benefit from flanking strikes.	0	0	0	No	0	0
	Shield Mastery	Dexterity 26	The character has mastered the use of the shield for both offense and defense, and receives additional benefits when using Shield Bash, Shield Pummel, Assault, Overpower, Shield Defense, Shield Wall, and Shield Cover.	0	0	0	No	0	0

primagames.com

Chain	Name	Prerequisite	Description	Cost (mana /stamina)	Upkeep (mana /stamina)	Fatigue (% mana/stamina)	Ranged	Cooldown (sec.)	Area of Effect Radius (ft.)
			Weapons and Shield School (continued)						
Chain 3	Shield Defense	Strength 11	While this mode is active, the character drops into a defensive stance that favors the shield, gaining a bonus to defense and an increased chance to shrug off missile attacks, but taking a penalty to attack. With Shield Balance, the attack penalty is reduced. With Shield Expertise, the defense bonus increases. With Shield Mastery, the defense bonus increases further.	0	35	5	No	5	0
	Shield Balance	Strength 14	The character has learned to compensate for the weight of a shield in combat and no longer suffers an attack penalty while using Shield Defense.	0	0	0	No	0	0
	Shield Wall	Strength 20	In this mode, the character's shield becomes nearly a fortress, adding a significant bonus to armor and a greater likelihood of shrugging off missile attacks, but at the cost of reduced damage. Shield Expertise makes the character immune to direct knockdown attacks while in this mode, and Shield Mastery gives a bonus to defense.	0	55	5	No	15	0
	Shield Expertise	Strength 26	The character's experience using a shield in combat has made certain abilities more efficient, increasing the defense bonus for Shield Defense and making the character immune to direct knockdown attacks while using Shield Wall.	0	0	0	No	0	0
Chain 4	Juggernaut	Level 20, Strength 26	A powerful physique allows the character to knock aside any enemies who are in the way while this mode is active and the character is moving. Each knockback drains a small amount of stamina.	0	60	10	No	10	0
	Carapace	Strength 32	No attack gets past this shield completely. For a moderate duration, all damage is reduced by an amount proportional to the character's constitution modifier. Bulwark of the Ages improves the protection, making the character completely immune to damage for the first half of this effect.	40	0	0	No	60	0
	Air of Insolence	Strength 36	While this mode is active, the character adopts an intimidating posture that continuously draws the attention of nearby enemies, consuming stamina constantly.	0	100	10	No	10	0
	Bulwark of the Ages	Strength 40	The warrior is one with the shield. This talent improves the effect of Carapace, now making the character completely immune to damage for the first half of that effect.	0	0	0	No	0	0
			Two-Handed School						
Chain 1	Mighty Blow	Strength 15	The character puts extra weight and effort behind a single strike, gaining a bonus to attack. If it hits, the blow deals critical damage and imposes a penalty to movement speed unless the target passes a physical resistance check.	40	0	0	No	20	0
	Powerful Swings	Strength 21	While in this mode, the character puts extra muscle behind each swing, gaining a bonus to damage but suffering penalties to attack and defense. Two-Handed Strength reduces the penalties to attack and defense.	0	30	5	No	10	0
	Two-Handed Strength	Strength 28	The character has learned to wield two-handed weapons more effectively, reducing the penalties to attack and defense from Powerful Swings.	0	0	0	No	0	0
	Two-Handed Sweep	Strength 36, Level 10	The character swings a two-handed weapon through enemies in a vicious arc, dealing normal damage to those it hits and knocking them down unless they pass a physical resistance check.	40	0	0	No	20	3
Chain 2	Pommel Strike	Strength 12	Instead of going for the fatal attack an enemy expects, the player strikes out with a weapon's blunt end, knocking the opponent to the ground unless it passes a physical resistance check.	20	0	0	No	10	0
	Indomitable	Strength 20	Through sheer force of will, the character remains in control on the battlefield, gaining a slight increase to attack damage while being immune to stun or knock down effects for the duration of this mode.	0	60	5	No	30	0
	Stunning Blows	Strength 28	The character's fondness for massive two-handed weapons means that each attack offers a chance to stun the opponent due to the sheer weight behind the blow.	0	0	0	No	0	0
	Critical Strike	Strength 34	The character makes a single massive swing at the target, gaining a bonus to attack. If the strike connects, it is an automatic critical hit, possibly killing the opponent outright if its health is low enough.	40	0	0	No	60	0
Chain 3	Sunder Arms	Strength 18	The character attempts to hinder a target's ability to fight back, rather than going directly for a killing blow. Unless the target passes a physical resistance check, it suffers a penalty to attack for a short time.	25	0	0	No	10	0
	Shattering Blows	Strength 23	The character is as adept at destruction as at death and gains a large damage bonus against golems and other constructs.	0	0	0	No	0	0
	Sunder Armor	Strength 28, Level 10	The character aims a destructive blow at the target's armor or natural defenses. The attack deals normal damage, but also damages the armor unless the target passes a physical resistance check.	40	0	0	No	20	0
	Destroyer	Strength 40, Level 14	Few can stand against the savage blows of a destroyer. Every attack sunders the target's armor, reducing its effectiveness for a short time. The effects of multiple blows are not cumulative.	0	0	0	No	0	0

The Warrior

Basics ~ **Classes** ~ The Party ~ Companions ~ Supporting Cast ~ Equipment ~ Bestiary ~ Walkthrough ~ Side Quests ~ Random Encounters ~ Achievements/Trophies

Chain	Name	Prerequisite	Description	Cost (mana/stamina)	Upkeep (mana/stamina)	Fatigue (% mana/stamina)	Ranged	Cooldown (sec.)	Area of Effect Radius (ft.)
Two-Handed School (continued)									
Chain 4	Sweeping Strike	Level 20, Strength 30	A massive swing plows through a cone of enemies, inflicting a critical hit against the primary target and normal damage against others in the cone. Affected enemies are also knocked to the ground unless they pass a physical resistance check.	30	0	0	Yes	10	60
	Two-Handed Impact	Strength 38	While in this mode, each blow from the character's heavy two-hander generates a small shockwave that damages other enemies near the target. This mode drains stamina constantly.	0	40	10	No	10	0
	Onslaught	Strength 44	The character advances several times, sweeping the weapon in huge arcs that hit multiple enemies.	50	0	0	No	30	2.5
	Reaving Storm	Strength 50	While this mode is active, the character turns continuously to attack surrounding enemies, slashing in wild arcs but spending stamina with each hit. This mode can only be activated during combat.	0	0	10	No	30	0
Power of Blood School (downloadable content only)									
Chain 1	Blood Thirst	None	The warrior's own tainted blood spills in sacrifice, increasing movement speed, attack speed, and critical hit chance. For as long as the mode is active, however, the warrior suffers greater damage and continuously diminishing health.	30	30	5	No	5	0
	Blood Fury	None	The warrior sprays tainted blood in order to knock back nearby enemies, which they may resist by passing a physical resistance check. The gush of blood, however, results in a loss of personal health.	30 Stam. & 40 Health	0	0	No	10	5

Specializations

Each class can learn three out of the six possible specializations throughout the course of the game. Your first specialization can be learned at level 7; your second at level 14; and your third at level 22. Specializations are difficult to achieve, but very rewarding if you gain one. In *Awakening*, all specializations are learned via Manuals. As long as the specific abilities fit with your play style and character breakdown, a specialization is generally worth spending points in over regular talents.

Definitely experiment with specializations. A tank could, for example, specialize in Templar to take out spellcasters even if he can't get to them directly. However, here are some suggested play style fits for the six specializations:

Warrior Specialization Manual Locations

In *Awakening*, all your new specializations are learned from manuals. Track them down at the following locations:

- **Guardian Manual:** Herren's Merchandise in Vigil's Keep
- **Reaver Manual:** Dwarven bartender in Amaranthine's Crown and Lion Inn
- **Spirit Warrior Manual:** Octham's Goods in Amaranthine

Berserker

- **Primary:** DPS (max out damage at the expense of stamina)
- **Secondary:** Knockout punch (use Final Blow to finish off a foe but exhausts you in a long fight)

Champion

- **Primary:** Party buffer (increase attack and defense bonuses for everyone)
- **Secondary:** Enemy control (use Superiority to knock enemy groups off their feet)

Reaver

- **Primary:** AoE DPS (radiate spirit damage and fear)
- **Secondary:** Health resilient (absorb health from nearby corpses)

Templar

- **Primary:** Mage killer (pound enemy mages with abilities)
- **Secondary:** Dispel magic (clean area of spell effects)

Spirit Warrior

- **Primary:** Anti-magic (resist spells to augment defense)
- **Secondary:** Fade killer (slay enemies from the Fade easier)

Guardian

- **Primary:** Damage shield (defend the whole party at once)
- **Secondary:** Defense aura (pull enemies back to warrior)

Warrior Specializations

Talent Name	Prerequisite Level	Description	Cost (mana /stamina)	Upkeep (mana /stamina)	Fatigue (% mana/stamina)	Ranged	Cooldown (sec.)	Area of Effect Radius (ft.)
Specialization: Berserker								
Berserk	7	The stench of blood and death drives the Berserker into a willing fury, providing a bonus to damage. Rages incur a penalty to stamina regeneration, however, which Constraint reduces. Resilience adds a bonus to health regeneration in this mode.	0	20	5	No	30	0
Resilience	8	Rages no longer wear so heavily on the Berserker's body. The stamina regeneration penalty applied by Berserk is reduced, and the Berserker gains a bonus to nature resistance.	0	0	0	No	0	0
Constraint	10	The Berserker has learned to retain control during rages, reducing Berserk's penalty to stamina regeneration.	0	0	0	No	0	0
Final Blow	12	All the Berserker's stamina goes into a single swing. If the blow connects, the attack inflicts extra damage proportional to the amount of stamina lost.	5	0	0	No	60	0
Specialization: Champion								
War Cry	7	The Champion lets out a fearsome cry that gives nearby enemies a penalty to attack. With Superiority, nearby enemies are also knocked down unless they pass a physical resistance check.	25	0	0	No	20	10
Rally	12	The Champion's presence inspires nearby allies, giving them bonuses to attack and defense while this mode is active. When coupled with Motivate, the attack bonus increases.	0	50	5	No	30	10
Motivate	14	The Champion inspires allies to attack with renewed vigor. The Rally talent now increases attack, in addition to its defense bonus.	40	30	0	No	0	0
Superiority	16	The Champion is so fearsome that War Cry now knocks nearby opponents off their feet unless they pass a physical resistance check.	60	0	0	No	0	0
Specialization: Reaver								
Devour	7	The Reaver revels in death, absorbing the lingering energy of all nearby corpses, each of which partially restores the Reaver's own health.	25	0	0	No	30	5
Frightening Appearance	12	This talent focuses the Reaver's unsettling countenance into a weapon, making a target cower in fear unless it passes a mental resistance check. Frightening Appearance also increases the effectiveness of Taunt and Threaten.	25	0	0	No	20	0
Aura of Pain	14	Radiating an aura of psychic pain, the Reaver takes constant spirit damage while this mode is active, as do all enemies nearby.	0	60	5	No	45	4
Blood Frenzy	16	Driven by pain, the Reaver gains larger bonuses to damage whenever health decreases. Because this mode also incurs a penalty to health regeneration, the Reaver flirts with death the longer the frenzy persists.	0	60	5	No	60	0

The Warrior

Basics ~ **Classes** ~ The Party ~ Companions ~ Supporting Cast ~ Equipment ~ Bestiary ~ Walkthrough ~ Side Quests ~ Random Encounters ~ Achievements/Trophies

Talent Name	Prerequisite Level	Description	Cost (mana /stamina)	Upkeep (mana /stamina)	Fatigue (% mana/stamina)	Ranged	Cooldown (sec.)	Area of Effect Radius (ft.)
Specialization: Templar								
Righteous Strike	7	Templars are enforcers specifically chosen to control mages and slay abominations. Each of the Templar's melee hits against an enemy spellcaster drains its mana.	0	0	0	No	0	0
Cleanse Area	9	The Templar purges the area of magic, removing all dispellable effects from those nearby. Friendly fire possible.	40	0	0	No	30	10
Mental Fortress	12	The Templar has learned to focus on duty, gaining a large bonus to mental resistance.	0	0	0	No	0	0
Holy Smite	15	The Templar strikes out with righteous fire, inflicting spirit damage on the target and other nearby enemies. If the target is a spellcaster, it must pass a mental resistance check or else loses mana and takes additional spirit damage proportional to the mana lost. All affected enemies are stunned or knocked back unless they pass physical resistance checks.	75	0	0	Yes	40	5
Specialization: Spirit Warrior								
Beyond the Veil	20	The warrior dons a cloak of mystical energies from the Fade in order to evade a substantial proportion of physical attacks, although the mode drains stamina constantly. If the warrior has Soulbrand, this mode also adds a moderate chance of resisting hostile spells, and the warrior's attacks all deal spirit damage, bypassing enemy armor. If the warrior has Blessing of the Fade, the chance of resisting hostile spells increases further and the warrior gains bonuses to movement speed and attack speed.	0	80	10	No	10	0
Soulbrand	22	The warrior has gained a deeper connection to the spirit world. While Beyond the Veil is active, the warrior gains a moderate chance of resisting hostile spells, and attacks now deal spirit damage, bypassing enemy armor (magic resistance +5, spirit damage +5%).	Passive	0	0	No	0	0
Fade Burst	25	The warrior bursts with energies drawn from the other side of the Veil, dealing spirit damage to all enemies nearby, particularly harming creatures from the Fade. The amount of damage depends on the warrior's willpower attribute. Friendly fire possible.	80	0	0	No	30	7.5
Blessing of the Fade	28	The warrior is able to draw strength from the benevolent spirits of the Fade. While Beyond the Veil is active, the warrior's chance of resisting hostile spells increases further and the warrior gains bonuses to movement speed and attack speed (magic resistance +5, spirit damage +5%).	Passive	0	0	No	0	0
Specialization: Guardian								
Guardian's Shield	20	The Guardian, dedicated to protecting allies, builds a shield around a party member that absorbs an amount of damage based on the Guardian's constitution attribute. Master Guardian increases the strength of the shield.	40	0	0	No	30	0
Fortifying Presence	22	The Guardian sheathes the entire party in mystical protection, granting each member a temporary bonus to armor, with strength and duration both dependent on the Guardian's constitution attribute. Master Guardian increases the armor bonus.	50	0	0	No	10	0
Master Guardian	25	The Guardian has committed to life as a true defender. Guardian's Shield now absorbs more damage, and Fortifying Presence now provides a greater armor bonus.	0	0	0	No	0	0
Aura of the Stalwart Defender	28	While this mode is active, the Guardian makes a personal sacrifice in order to preserve allies, creating a field that pulls a foe back toward the Guardian if it tries to leave the field unless the enemy passes a physical resistance check. This mode can only be activated during combat.	0	100	10	No	10	0

primagames.com

Gear

Warriors get the cream of the crop when it comes to weapons and armor. With so many choices, you really need to decide what talents you'll be concentrating on to pick the best equipment. You don't, for instance, want an awesome two-handed sword if you're training in Weapon and Shields. Any weapon that grants you strength (or dexterity for warriors in Archery and Dual Weapon) should be considered. Bonuses to damage, attack, and criticals can be great too. If you want more defense, bulk up your armor rating, but it's always a fine line between great armor rating and too much fatigue. Armor doesn't do a lot of good if you can't use any of your talents. You can always look for armor with a bonus to armor rating (no fatigue penalty), or even armor that grants constitution bonus or healing bonus.

There's more warrior gear than you could ever hope to equip in a single play through. The general rule of thumb is to wait for loot that serves as an upgrade and snatch it up. If you have extra coin to buy a nice gear upgrade, feel free to spend away, though most of the low-level equipment will be easily replaced by future loot, and the high-level equipment is very expensive (generally bought before a run at the Mother).

NOTE

In *Awakening*, it's out with the old and in with the new. As you journey toward level 35, here are some key items to seek out. Keep in mind that ideal gear varies based on your play style and role in the party. If, for example, you want a high-damage warrior, look for strength/dexterity bonuses and melee crit. If your warrior does a lot of tanking, high constitution and defense are your treasured traits. We've suggested excellent possibilities in each item category. For more possibilities and complete stats on each item, see the Equipment chapter.

Ideal Warrior Equipment

Item Type	Item 1	Item 2
Greatsword / Longsword	Vigilance	Dragonbrand
Longbows	Heartwood Bow	Misery
Crossbows	Longshot	—
Kite Shields	Landsmeet Shield	Heartwood Shield
Tower Shields	Partha	—
Light Chest Armor	Vest of the Nimble	Rainswept
Massive Chest Armor	Golem Shell Armor	—
Heavy Helmets	Stormchaser Helm	Helm of Dragon's Peak
Massive Helmets	Helm of Hirol's Defense	Helm of the Sentinel
Heavy Boots	Fleet Feet	—
Massive Boots	Boots of the Sentinel	—
Heavy Gloves	Stormchaser Gauntlets	—
Massive Gloves	Gauntlets of Hirol's Defense	Gauntlets of the Sentinel
Amulets	Seeker's Chain	Scout's Medal
Belts	Sash of Power	Doge's Dodger
Rings	Tingler	Corin's Proposal

Party Responsibilities

Are you the party's tank or a damage-dealer? If you're the tank, your primary responsibility is holding threat and making sure that none of your companions die. That generally means stocking up on defensive talents and gear. If you're melee or ranged DPS, you can concentrate on offense and how much damage you can deal to enemy combatants. All non-tank warriors need to be aware of threat and avoid pulling too much at once. Learn to time your attacks so you don't create too much threat on yourself, yet deal significant damage to the enemy.

If your warrior is the main PC, the other three companions should fill in talents around you for a well-balanced party. If you're building up a companion warrior, look to fill in where the party is lacking. Not dealing enough damage? Crank up the offense. Tank having trouble holding all the enemies? Invest in some off-tank talents, such as Taunt, to grab enemies when needed. In the final party configuration, your PC should play whatever role you have the most fun with while the other three companions add the components necessary to maximize your combat efficiency.

The warrior ranks highest of the three classes in access to weapons and armor. Your talents and gear allow you to defensively tank for the group, deal huge amounts of single-target damage, and chip in with AoE every once and a while. There's no tougher adventurer in the land, so if you want to get right in the face of a raging hurlock or slash through spider ichor, step into the boots of a warrior.

Role Models

With the game's best weapon talent trees, you can create dozens of warriors who each wield something a little different in combat. Don't feel constrained to play according to the following warrior models to the letter; take bits and pieces that appeal to your play style and add your own spin. However, these are basic models for a tank, melee DPS warrior, or ranged DPS warrior. Each shows you how to choose your talents up to level 30, what talent chains are effective, how specializations fit in, and sample combat strategies for that model.

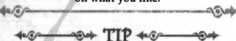
NOTE

If you create a new Grey Warden, you have 21 points to spend, which actually puts you one point ahead of these charts. So if you follow these charts, you'll have one extra point to spend on what you like.

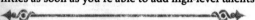
TIP

In Awakening, some amazing new talents become available to you once you reach level 20. Although you can still choose from Origins talents, we recommend focusing on the new Awakening abilities as soon as you're able to add high-level talents.

Tank Warrior Model

Level	Talent
0	Shield Bash
1	Powerful, Shield Defense
2	Shield Balance
3	Shield Wall
4	Threaten
5	Shield Block
6	Shield Cover
7	War Cry (Champion)—*First Specialization Available at This Level*
8	Bravery
9	Shield Tactics
10	Shield Pummel
11	Overpower
12	Shield Mastery
13	Death Blow
14	Rally (Champion)—*Second Specialization Available at This Level*
15	Motivate (Champion)
16	Superiority (Champion)
17	Shield Expertise
18	Assault
19	Pinning Shot
20	Second Wind

Level	Talent
21	Juggernaut
22	Guardian's Shield (Guardian)—*Third Specialization Available at This Level*
23	Fortifying Presence (Guardian)
24	Carapace
25	Master Guardian (Guardian)
26	Air of Insolence
27	Bulwark of the Ages
28	Aura of the Stalwart Defender (Guardian)
29	Beyond the Veil (Spirit Warrior)
30	Soulbrand (Spirit Warrior)

Overview: A tank protects his companions and deals significant damage to boot. He generally concentrates in the Warrior school and the Weapon and Shield school.

Leveling: Sink the majority of your points into strength and dexterity, increasing constitution whenever you have some free points, and spend your skill points on Combat Training, Vitality, and probably Clarity (or spread out points to other skills like Coercion and Survival).

Spending Your Tank's Attribute Points

When you start a new character in *Awakening*, you have 62 attribute points to spend on your level 18 character. Depending on how you want to play your character and what skills/talents you take, you may spend more or less points on individual attribute scores, but this is a good base model for a tank's initial points distribution:

- **Strength:** 26 points
- **Dexterity:** 13 points
- **Willpower:** 8 points
- **Constitution:** 15 points

TIP

If you import an old character and want to tweak attributes, skills, or talents, you can easily buy a Manual of Focus from Herren in Vigil's Keep and re-spec your character.

Pick up Powerful and Shield Defense, then Shield Balance and Shield Wall. Next is an automatic choice: Threaten. You now have the core of your tanking defense ready to go. Shield Defense is a great all-purpose protection stance; Shield Wall defends even better, but at the cost of reduced damage, which may not matter much if you have enough damage-dealers in the party. Shield Balance reduces the penalty to battle with a shield in your off-hand—another crucial talent for a Weapon and Shield warrior. Threaten should stay on in almost any fight to draw most of the threat to you.

primagames.com

◆◆◆ TIP ◆◆◆

If you want a more offensive-minded tank, simply switch some of the earlier defensive talents, such as Shield Block and Shield Cover, and load up on Shield Pummel, Overpower, and Assault.

Add Shield Block and Shield Cover to the mix. You could go with more offense here, but in this model we're concentrating on building the best defensive juggernaut we can to hold the line for your party. Stick with defense first, offense second. You need 16 dexterity to pick up Shield Cover.

You want the Champion specialization if at all possible. You can gain the Champion specialization by completing the "Arl of Redcliffe" and "Urn of Sacred Ashes" quests and freeing Arl Eamon from his illness in *Dragon Age: Origins*; in *Awakening*, it's even easier—you begin with it when making a new character. The first Champion talent, War Cry, hits all nearby enemies with an attack penalty, and it really shines when you add Superiority.

Invest in Bravery. It gives bonuses to damage, physical resistance, mental resistance, and critical chance. In other words, it helps all facets of combat. Continue to add points to dexterity and strength as you level so you're prepared to meet the prerequisites of more advanced talents.

With 20 dexterity, you can add Shield Tactics. This may be the most important talent a good tank needs, because it prevents enemies from scoring flanking bonuses against your warrior. No matter where your tank stands now, which is usually in the middle of an enemy swarm, it's just like he's facing the enemy head on.

Next switch to offense: pick up Shield Pummel, then purchase Overpower. Shield Pummel is a two-hit combo that can stun an opponent; Overpower is a three-hit combo that can knock a target down. Your strength and dexterity scores need to be in the mid-20s to open up your new talents.

Another milestone comes with Shield Mastery. The majority of your offensive and defensive abilities gain bonuses with Shield Mastery. You cap out the Warrior school when you gain Death Blow. Now, whenever your warrior slays an enemy, stamina gets restored. With enough killing, you can continuously operate your talents.

Next, study all the rest of your Champion talents. Rally and Motivate enhance the entire party's offense and defense, but Superiority is the coup de grace. Now when you trigger War Cry, it has a chance to knock down all enemies around you and give you a great advantage in battle.

Fill out the rest of your Weapon and Shield chains. If you lean toward defense, learn Shield Expertise first; if you lean toward offense, get the four-hit combo Assault (requires 32 strength).

Your final point could be spent on almost anything. We'll add a ranged component with Pinning Shot. If you can't reach them on foot, pull out the bow and give them a reason to come to you.

Once you hit level 20, invest in the new Warrior talent Second Wind. It's one of the best in the game, instantly refilling your stamina pool upon activation. It gives you that many more abilities to use during a long fight.

When you reach level 21, pick up the first of the new Weapon and Shield talents: Juggernaut.

At level 22, grab the next available Guardian talent: Guardian's Shield will give you another buff to keep your whole group safe. It works off your constitution score; if you find yourself using it often, crank up your constitution as you level.

At level 23, chose the next Guardian talent, Fortifying Presence, then move on to Master Guardian at level 25, and fill out your Guardian specialization at level 28 with Aura of the Stalwart Defender. You'll be a mountain of defense by this point.

You'll follow at level 24 with Carapace and level 26 with Air of Insolence to bolster personal defense and increase your threat ability, respectively. Level 27 finishes off the new Weapon and Shield talents with Bulwark of the Ages.

Near the end of your leveling, you can branch out into whatever you feel like. For this build, we'll pick up a third specialization: Spirit Warrior. More defense for a tank doesn't hurt, so at level 29 we gain Beyond the Veil and start building up our magic resistance with Soulbrand at level 30.

Talent Choices: A tank concentrates on the defensive gems in the Warrior school, such as Powerful, Threaten, and Bravery. Other than that, a tank maxes out the Weapon and Shield school to take advantage of all its defensive components, with a little offense thrown in for good measure. No matter the enemy configuration, your tank should have an answer for it.

Specialization: The Champion's War Cry hampers enemy attacks. Rally and Motivate increase offense and defense for your party. Superiority knocks enemies off their feet if they fail a physical resistance check. At higher levels, Guardian and Spirit Warrior supplement your defensive prowess.

Battle Tactics: Meet the enemy head on and intercept any attack on your companions. Unless you have Shield Tactics, you don't want to let yourself get surrounded where you fall prey to flanking bonuses. Instead, choose a tactical location that shields you from some enemy attacks while protecting your party's flanks. Use Threaten or Taunt to pull the threat toward you and away from companions.

Study your situation and choose the correct defense accordingly. For strict defense, go with Shield Wall, which boosts armor and prevents you from getting knocked down (a huge headache for your party if you don't have an off-tank ready to jump in). If you want more offense, go with the standard Shield Defense instead. If you're unsure on how the battle will go, always opt for more defense.

Once your defensive position is secure, think about dealing damage back to the monsters nearest you (or any ones who seem like they want to break free of your grasp). You can use Overpower and Assault to inflict serious harm. Save Shield Bash and Shield Pummel when you want to stun or knock down a target, especially if your health is low or an enemy is on another companion.

The Warrior

Basics ~ **Classes** ~ The Party ~ Companions ~ Supporting Cast ~ Equipment ~ Bestiary ~ Walkthrough ~ Side Quests ~ Random Encounters ~ Achievements/Trophies

Melee DPS Warrior Model

Level	Talent
0	Dual-Weapon Sweep
1	Pommel Strike, Powerful
2	Mighty Blow
3	Indomitable
4	Stunning Blows
5	Powerful Swings
6	Critical Strike
7	Berserk (Berserker)—*First Specialization Available at This Level*
8	Resilience (Berserker)
9	Two-Handed Strength
10	Constraint (Berserker)
11	Two-Handed Sweep
12	Final Blow (Berserker)
13	Sunder Arms
14	Shattering Blows—*Second Specialization Available at This Level*
15	Sunder Armor
16	Destroyer
17	Precise Striking
18	Taunt
19	Disengage
20	Second Wind
21	Sweeping Strike
22	Peon's Plight—*Third Specialization Available at This Level*
23	Beyond the Veil (Spirit Warrior)
24	Soulbrand (Spirit Warrior)
25	Two-Handed Impact
26	Onslaught
27	Grievous Insult
28	Fade Burst (Spirit Warrior)
29	Massacre
30	Reaving Storm

Overview: Concentrate on dealing combat damage as quickly as you can without pulling too much threat.

Leveling: Because most of what a melee DPSer loves to do is deal hand-to-hand damage, you only have to worry about strength. Spend the majority of your points on strength, and skill points go to Combat Training, Clarity and prorably Poison-Making.

Spending Your Melee DPSer's Attribute Points

When you start a new character in *Awakening*, you have 62 attribute points to spend on your level 18 character. Depending on how you want to play your character and what skills/talents you take, you may spend more or less points on individual attribute scores, but this is a good base model for a melee DPSer's initial points distribution:

- **Strength:** 35 points
- **Dexterity:** 5 points
- **Willpower:** 12 points
- **Constitution:** 10 points

Select Pommel Strike and Powerful with your first two talent points. Pommel Strike gives you a knockdown attack, and Powerful enhances your health and reduces fatigue; these are useful defensive abilities, but the offense will come in bunches soon.

Mighty Blow begins a run to some major offense. It gives a bonus to attack and, if the blow connects, scores a critical hit on the target. Indomitable serves as a stepping stone talent to reach the better offensive top-tier talents; you may use Indomitable against creatures such as golems who you know will knock you down, but otherwise all your efforts go toward offense and you can leave it off. Make sure you have 28 strength and Expert Combat Training to select Stunning Blows. It's a passive talent that can make a world of difference: all your blows have a chance to stun the enemy. Powerful Swings increases your damage; however, it gives a penalty to attack and defense until you gain Two-Handed Strength.

If you've maxed out your strength and skills properly, you can pick up Critical Strike. Critical Strike promises an automatic critical hit and massive damage to a single target. Use it in any one-on-one fight or when you have lots of stamina in a longer fight.

Dip into the Berserker specialization. Berserk increases damage for each of your strokes, though your stamina will suffer a bit. Resilience helps offset Berserk's stamina penalty, as does Constraint. Speaking of offsetting penalties, Two-Handed Strength minimizes the penalties from Powerful Swings.

Two-Handed Sweep gives you an option against multiple foes. You deal normal damage, but can knock them off their feet. Berserker's Final Blow hits an opponent with a massive blow inflicting damage proportional to all of your stamina (which is expended in the process).

Next, invest in the Sunder chain: Sunder Arms, Shattering Blows, Sunder Armor, and Destroyer (requires 30 strength). If you like, feel free to buy part of this chain earlier for extra damage penetration, but you will lose out on some AoE and suffer penalties while using talents such as Powerful Swings. The chain can dramatically alter a battle against heavily armored foes, or massive foes such as golems.

Pick up the offensive Warrior chain: Precise Striking, Taunt, and Disengage. Taunt lets you off-tank if necessary, while Disengage is a nice option to reduce threat and shed enemies if the onslaught becomes too much.

primagames.com

At level 20, Pick up the essential Second Wind, first of the new Warrior talents, which fills your stamina pool back to full upon activation.

Follow up at level 22 with the second Warrior talent, Peon's Plight, which is an excellent single-target attack that can slay lesser foes instantly.

You might not think it's an ideal fit at level 23, but invest in the Spirit Warrior specialization. You're not as interested in the defensive qualities for your melee DPSer, though it certainly doesn't hurt, but at level 24 you can pick up Soulbrand and convert all your regular damage into spirit damage, which now bypasses foes' armor. Continue with Fade Burst at level 28.

Start the new Two-Handed chain at level 21 with Sweeping Strike. Continue on at level 25 with Two-Handed Impact, followed by Onslaught at level 26, and Reaving Storm at level 30. You won't be at a loss for attacks now when you want to heap on the damage.

Level 27 gives you Grievous Insult, which can be used in an emergency to draw foes to you and off-tank if your main tank is having problems, but it's more important as the stepping stone to reach the major AoE attack Massacre at level 29.

TIP

An alternative option involves re-specing your character at level 21 when you gain Sweeping Strike. Sacrifice Two Handed Sweep or Critical Strike (Sweeping Strike is a good enough replacement), and put the extra point into Peon's Plight. You're then one step ahead, and you'll be able to get the last Spirit Warrior ability: Blessing of the Fade, which increases your hostile spell resistance while giving a bonus to movement and attack speed.

Talent Choices: In this version of a DPS warrior, your combat skills revolve around a two-handed weapon that, though slower, generally deals the most DPS of any weapon. Most of your talents maximize damage potential, with a few that give you AoE or stunning capabilities. It's possible to branch out into Archery and Dual Weapon, but you don't want to spread yourself too thin or you won't max out your two-hander's damage.

Specialization: Berserker is a big plus as soon as you can achieve it. The extra damage from the specialization is exactly what you want in a DPS melee class. The stamina penalty can be rough; however, two of your talents minimize the penalty, and the last talent, Final Blow, will win you some battles. At higher levels, Spirit Warrior converts your normal damage to spirit damage to avoid enemy armor.

Battle Tactics: Be patient. You can deal a huge amount of damage, which means if you attack too swiftly, you may pull the threat off your tank. You won't be much use to the group with four enemies stomping on your shredded corpse. Wait for the tank to set up, then attack from the flank or rear and cut through enemy after enemy. It's fine to go all out on an enemy and even pull it off the tank so long as it dies almost immediately.

Watch the battle and see where you're most needed. If you have off-tank skills, pick up any stragglers that go for the healer or other non-tank companions. The quicker the enemies drop, the less damage the party receives, so bounce from weakest enemy to weakest enemy as you help the tank chop away at the numbers. Save your big special effects (stuns, critical strikes, etc.) for bosses or tough enemies that just won't go down with the normal party tactics. If the tank looks to be in trouble, pull out all the stops and dive into the main enemy line.

Ranged DPS Warrior Model

Level	Talent
0	Powerful
1	Threaten
2	Bravery
3	Righteous Strike
4	Cleanse Area
5	Mental Fortress
6	Holy Smite
7	Melee Archer—First Specialization Available at This Level
8	Aim
9	Defensive Fire
10	Master Archer
11	Pinning Shot
12	Crippling Shot
13	Critical Shot
14	Arrow of Slaying—Second Specialization Available at This Level
15	Rapid Shot
16	Scattering Shot
17	Suppressing Fire
18	Scattershot, Shield Bash
19	Death Blow
20	Second Wind
21	Accuracy
22	Peon's Plight—Third Specialization Available at This Level
23	Arrow Time
24	Burst Shot
25	Rain of Arrows
26	Beyond the Veil
27	Soulbrand
28	Fade Burst
29	Grievous Insult
30	Massacre

Overview: Much like an offensive mage, a ranged DPS warrior concentrates weapons and talents on enemies at a distance. He focuses on the Archery school, and may dip into some talents, such as Dual Weapon and the new *Awakening* Warrior talents, when melee becomes imminent.

TIP

Your draw speed with bows is normally slowed down if you wear heavy or massive armor. However, if you take the Master Archer talent, the penalty on heavy armor is removed, thus you can draw at full speed in everything but massive.

The Warrior

Basics ~ **Classes** ~ The Party ~ Companions ~ Supporting Cast ~ Equipment ~ Bestiary ~ Walkthrough ~ Side Quests ~ Random Encounters ~ Achievements/Trophies

Leveling: As you'll be working with a bow and dual weapons, load up on dexterity. Your goal is to have 27 dexterity and Master Combat Training by level 6.

Spending Your Ranged DPSer's Attribute Points

When you start a new character in *Awakening*, you have 62 attribute points to spend on your level 18 character. Depending on how you want to play your character and what skills/talents you take, you may spend more or less points on individual attribute scores, but this is a good base model for a ranged DPSer's initial points distribution:

- **Strength:** 12 points
- **Dexterity:** 26 points
- **Willpower:** 14 points
- **Constitution:** 10 points

With your first three talent points, invest in the Warrior talents Powerful, Threaten, and Bravery. These are generally useful talents to beef up personal defense and to allow the archer to contribute more in combat situations. These also set up the later Warrior talent Death Blow at level 19.

Tap into the Templar specialization. The first talent, Righteous Strike, lets you drain mana with any successful melee strike against an enemy spellcaster. You may have to get close to use this talent, but it's generally worth it against spellcasters, and it opens the door for Cleanse Area. This removes all magic effects on your party, which is great when you have negative debuffs on the group, but watch that you don't strip the good buffs in the process.

Mental Fortress gives you a huge upgrade to your mental resistance.

Next, select Holy Smite (which decimates enemy spellcasters by dealing damage and draining mana).

Slip in Melee Archer. It's an all-around useful ability: it prevents attacks from interrupting your firing. Next, fill out the rest of the Melee Archer chain: Aim, Defensive Fire, and Master Archer. Use Aim for more offense and Defensive Fire when you fear return fire. Master Archer improves almost every Archery talent.

Now choose Pinning Shot, followed by Crippling Shot, which allows you to hamper someone's attack and defense.

If you have 21 dexterity and Expert Combat Training, select Critical Shot. If you hit, Critical Shot inflicts critical damage and a bonus to armor penetration.

If you can reach 30 dexterity, you gain Arrow of Slaying. This scores an automatic critical hit against all but high-level opponents, and it's another offensive threat you can deliver.

Next, max out your ranged abilities. Reload much faster with Rapid Shot. Shattering Shot imposes an even greater penalty to a foe's defense as it reduces armor value. Follow that up with Suppressing Fire to further encumber targets with attack penalties.

Scattershot is an awesome talent that automatically stuns your target and deals normal damage, then splinters off and does the same to all nearby enemies. Use this effectively against enemy spellcasters or large enemy groups to impede

flanking attempts. If you need additional defense, add to your Weapon and Shield talent chain with Shield Bash.

At level 19, further improve your combat with Death Blow.

You won't be sorry when you buy Second Wind at level 20. Regaining all your stamina at a crucial point in combat can make all the difference.

When you reach level 21, dive into the new Archery talents. Accuracy scores you big bonuses to several combat stats and paves the way for three more talents. At level 23, Arrow Time forces enemies around you to slow down, which gives you that much more time to pick them off. Level 24's Burst Shot devastates a foe with three automatic critical hits, plus half the damage spilled over in AoE around the target. Level 25's Rain of Arrows covers an area with projectiles to strike multiple foes.

Pick up the Spirit Warrior specialization with Beyond the Veil at level 26, Soulbrand at level 27, and Fade Burst at level 28. These improve your defense, and allow you to bypass foes' armor by converting all your regular damage into spirit damage.

At level 22, finish off the new Warrior talents, starting with Peon's Plight. Peon's Plight and Grievous Insult at level 29 give your archer more options in melee combat. It all leads up to Massacre at level 30, which can get you out of a melee jam when surrounded by multiple foes. By this point, you'll destroy them at range, and should they limp into melee range, you're not half-bad nose-to-nose either.

Talent Choices: The Archery school and all its ranged surprises are your bread and butter. Dual Weapons provide some support talents in case an enemy gets close enough to melee.

Specialization: Templar enhances your skill in taking down enemy spellcasters. Righteous Strike can be fantastic once you reach higher levels and can tap into your melee talents. Cleanse Area and Mental Fortress bulk up your defensive abilities. Holy Smite gives you another powerful ranged attack that will destroy an enemy spellcaster in a single energy burst.

Battle Tactics: Once the battle begins, stand your ground. Let the tank and other melee DPSers embrace the enemy. You want to nuke them from afar. Unlike a mage who stays in the rear, however, the ranged DPS warrior can enter melee with his better armor, weapons, and Dual Weapon talents at higher levels.

Survey the battlefield and pick your targets wisely. Concentrate fire on the tank's target to bring it down quicker, or look for injured foes that you can drop with an arrow or two. If you see an enemy spellcaster in the enemy's rear, make it your priority. You don't want it getting off damaging spells. Same goes for enemy archers. If your melee companions can't reach them, it's your job to stop them from pelting the team with damage.

On offense, your rotation goes something like this: Aim, Pinning Shot (against moving targets), Critical Shot (against near-dead targets), Arrow of Slaying. On defense, go Defensive Fire, Crippling Shot, Suppressing Fire, and Scattershot (especially against enemy spellcaster or enemies charging at you).

As a ranged DPS warrior, you have much of the offense of a DPS mage, yet you can still wear most of the better armor and use high quality weapons. Keep on the go to avoid enemy melee encounters and let your arrows serve as warnings to any new darkspawn that stumble across the field of arrow-strewn corpses.

The Mage

You are channeler and healer, death-dealer and life-giver, the spellpower behind the party's muscle. A mage stays in the rear, choosing targets carefully and always thinking ahead to the next damage spell or heal. A mage can conjure fire, encase allies in impenetrable force fields, or drain the very life from a victim. Tapping into any of the four magic schools (Primal, Creation, Spirit, Entropy), the DPS mage supplies firepower, especially against large enemy groups, the healer supports benevolent spells that can turn the tide in a close contest, or the hybrid mage balances both offense and defense in one versatile package.

Though the mage doesn't have the same kind of access to weapons and armor as a warrior or rogue (unless the mage specializes in Arcane Warrior), consider his spell arrays his artillery. The Primal school gives the mage the power of the elements: fire, earth, cold, electricity. By the third spell in any of these chains, the mage can cast devastating AoE attacks that destroy large enemy groups. In the Creation school, healing and buffs take precedent. The power to regenerate health, mana, and stamina fuels your party to greater glory. Your last two schools, Spirit and Entropy, grant mind-bogglingly cool abilities that stretch beyond pure damage or healing. With nearly 80 spells to choose from, no two mages need be the same.

Mage specializations offer the greatest possibilities to transform your class into something outside the normal class boundaries. An Arcane Warrior trades magic score for strength, ditches staff and robe for weapons and armor usually restricted to warriors, and can enter melee as a hand-to-hand brawler. A Blood Mage taps into the life force flowing in most creatures' veins, and uses that dark magic to control minds, damage enemies, convert blood to mana, and heal from the pain of others. A Shapeshifter can change into a combat-oriented spider, bear, and insect swarm, or master them all for potent alternate fighting forms. A Spirit Healer is the ultimate savior, able to heal the entire party at once, cure injuries, and even bring the dead back to life. At level 20 and higher, a Keeper merges with nature itself and forms a powerful union of spellcaster and the surrounding vegetation that traps, hurts, and drains enemies within. Finally, a Battlemage can use all the elements against enemies, freeze them in place, or drain their life. A Battlemage can even regain mana from his own wounds.

If you like to sling spells from tactical positions and play around with the fantastical, the mage class is for you. World-class spells are at your fingertips, and you will rule the battlefield from afar. No other class can touch you when it comes to obliterating hordes of monsters at once. Just remember that if those monsters get up, you'd better have enough mana to knock them back down.

Strengths and Weaknesses

Think of the mage as a cannoneer or a field medic, depending on your play style and spell spec. If you lean toward a DPS mage, your spells can do tremendous damage to single targets (possibly killing them with a single spell) or major damage to a large enemy group. You can even contribute damage over time to opponents with such spells as Fireball and Walking Bomb. If you become a healer, your spells will keep you and your allies alive, even in battles that may seem lost at the start. Either of those skills sets would earn you a place on the team, but you also have crowd control spells (Grease, Earthquake, Cone of Cold, etc.) that keep enemies from swarming the party, and party buffs (the Heroic chain, Spellbloom, etc.) that aid your allies with additional abilities.

Advantages

- Stat Bonuses to Magic, Willpower, and Cunning
- Great Ranged and AoE Damage
- Healing
- Crowd Control Spells
- Party Buffs

With all those great spells a hand gesture away, mages pay the price with armor and weapons: they can use only robes, cowls, staves, and the less powerful armor and weapons. Mages aren't built for hand-to-hand melee, unless they devote several spells to melee offense/defense or seek out the Arcane Warrior and/or Battlemage specializations, and spellcasters can't go toe-to-toe

The Mage

Basics ~ **Classes** ~ The Party ~ Companions ~ Supporting Cast ~ Equipment ~ Bestiary ~ Walkthrough ~ Side Quests ~ Random Encounters ~ Achievements/Trophies

with foes like warriors and rogues can. Even worse, mages' damage spells, especially AoE spells that strike multiple targets, generate significant threat and will pull monsters to you. You need a capable tank to regain the threat or you will find yourself bloodied on the ground.

Disadvantages

- Limited Armor and Weapon Choices
- Generally Weak in Melee
- Damage Spells Can Generate Significant Threat

You may not be the party member who jumps into the thick of melee, but you can be the tactician who stands in the back and surveys the whole battlefield. Whether you like to blow things up or pick your targets off one by one, the mage's spells have you covered. You will have the firepower to bolster your party from competent fighters to veritable forces of nature.

Attributes

Spells are your livelihood as a mage, thus your magic score is essential. Magic directly increases your character's spellpower score, which determines the potency of all spells. The prerequisite for the various schools of magic begins at 18 magic, but goes as high as 61 magic for the most expensive of the newer abilities, so put most of your points here to unlock crucial spells. Magic also determines how effective potions, poultices, and salves are for characters; your mage will gain bigger benefits from lyrium potions and health poultices because of your affinity for magic.

Mage Attribute Bonuses

+5 Magic

+4 Willpower

+1 Cunning

Willpower works in conjunction with magic. The more points you throw into willpower, the larger your mana pool and the more spells you can cast. If you have a party member with good Herbalism, you may be able to stock up on lyrium potions to offset a lower willpower score, but you definitely need to spend as many points here as you can afford. If you have a good tank who holds threat well, and you don't get hit much by monsters in melee, sink all your extra points into growing your mana pool.

TIP

Gear bonuses can amplify your attribute's strengths or offset any shortcomings. A ring, for example, that bulks up constitution could provide some extra health without costing any of your precious attribute points.

After magic and willpower, your attributes will go more according to your play style. In general, you may want to add a little constitution. Every mage, even if they don't plan on beating mobs over the head with a staff, needs health and resilience. The more you have, the longer you'll stay in a fight, and if your tank fails to hold a creature's threat and it comes gunning for you, that extra constitution and health bonus will make a difference.

Cunning contributes to learning skills, and it's huge if you take Coercion and want to persuade NPCs. If you don't invest in Coercion, then feel free to spend these points in constitution and dexterity.

Dexterity has limited use for most mages. It can be helpful to dodge incoming blows, and an Arcane Warrior mage may want some points in dexterity for accuracy while wielding melee weapons. If you do spend points, spend only a few.

Because you shouldn't be engaging foes physically, strength means very little. There's always something better to spend points on, so leave this attribute alone. If you're worried about combat damage, it's probably best to spend the points on constitution instead.

During character creation, feel free to choose a race based on overall story possibilities. However, if maximizing your mage stats appeals to you, choose an elf. An elven mage gives you a starting 17 magic and 16 willpower. A human mage offers one fewer point in magic and two fewer points in willpower. Most of your points are socked away in magic and willpower, so later in your character's evolution you'll need to spread out the points to other attributes. Dwarves cannot be mages; if you want to play a dwarf, you won't be casting spells.

Mage Starting Attributes

Attribute	Human	Elf
Strength	11	10
Dexterity	11	10
Willpower	14	16
Magic	16	17
Cunning	12	11
Constitution	10	10

Once you choose your mage's race, you begin with 62 points to add to your attributes. Most builds require you to spend the majority of your points in magic and willpower. It's important to unlock spells early, and because magic is the main prerequisite for spells, you must reach the 25–30 magic range to unlock most spells, and 40 or higher to unlock the new Mage school spells. In general, think about a 2/1 split between magic and willpower each time you earn attribute points from leveling, or a 1/1/1 split among magic, willpower, and constitution.

primagames.com

Skills

Mages are natural herbalists, so it's fitting that you begin with a skill point in Herbalism (and also one point in Combat Tactics). They stockpile magic attribute points for spell effectiveness, and items produced by Herbalism rely on magic for effectiveness. It's a perfect union. At least one party member must be skilled in Herbalism per party. Otherwise, you lose out on essential healing and mana potions, and won't have the same staying power in fights as a fully stocked party. Unless one of your companions (say, Velanna) supports Herbalism, you should strongly consider it as your top skill.

NOTE

Beyond your starting skills, you're likely to obtain 10–12 skill points throughout the game. Pick your two or three favorite skills and stick with them. If you spread your points too thin, you'll end up doing a bunch of things—but not well.

Because mages gravitate toward magic, Herbalism ranks high, but Coercion is usually the best skill to take. As with any other class, Coercion grants you access to story possibilities that aren't available through brute force. Spend all your skill points here first if you don't plan on becoming a herbalist.

The more points you spend in Combat Training, the more damage you can take before the damage interrupts your spellcasting. If you're a mage who expects to get hit often in combat, or you don't want to blow a key spell because of mob interference, then stock up on Combat Training. Two points is enough to withstand disruption from all but the most damaging attacks.

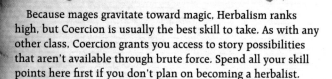

Mage Skill Recommendations

Assuming you spend 8 skill points by level 18, here's a good spread to consider. Note that many other combinations could work better for you, so experiment!

- Herbalism +3
- Combat Training +1
- Coercion +4

Survival can be a good skill to have because the more you advance it, the better chance you have to detect creatures on your mini-map before they surprise you. You can save yourself from more than a few ambushes with this skill. Don't forget about the bonus to nature resistance too.

For companion mages, who you might not always control directly, consider spending skill points in Combat Tactics. The more tactic slots you open, the more you can shape how your companion behaves in battle. Inevitably, even if you

plan on controlling your mage during fights, there will be moments when you don't program your mage's every move (or something more important is going on) and tactics come into play. One or two points should be good, or max it out if you want the character to go on autopilot.

None of the other lower-level skills really fit the mage profile, except perhaps Trap-Making. At first it seems solely a rogue skill, but if your mage isn't strong in ranged damage (a healer, for example), you may want Trap-Making to use traps to lure enemies in. Traps deal decent damage up front while you cast a spell barrage from afar.

Once you reach level 20, spend your skill points on Clarity. The new skill boosts your mana pool by 25 mana per level. If you max out on Clarity that's 100 mana more than you might have had otherwise.

Spells

Mages have access to a vast arsenal of spells, many more than you could attain in the course of the game. Rather than focusing on one school, pick the type of mage you'd like to be (DPS, healer, or blend) then round out your mage with a selection of spells that could deal with an array of situations. For example, you'll want a few spells for AoE, direct attacks on single targets, buffs, etc. Notice how the stronger spells are at the end of individual chains. With that in mind, develop individual chains rather than focusing on an entire school.

You start with one point in the Mage spell school and 62 more points to spend wherever you like. In addition, you receive one point for every level you gain during your journey through *Awakening*. It might seem like a lot, but you really have to plan what spell chains you want, because you'll cap only four or five regular chains if you decide to specialize.

NOTE

It's possible to have three mages in the game: Anders, Velanna, and you. Develop each differently to have access to a wider arsenal of magic.

All mages need to familiarize themselves with the cooldown component of each spell. The worst situation is to have plenty of mana and no available spells to cast. Branch out into different spells to avoid the cooldown problem. Yes, you may love to cast Lightning on a target, but you need a follow-up damage spell or two to use while Lightning reloads. You also want to branch out into different chains so that your spell rotation cycles through separate damage types. For example, if you develop the Fire chain as your sole damage source and run into rage demons, who are resistant to fire, you won't do too well. But if you have Winter's Grasp or Cone of Cold in your arsenal, you can contribute massive damage.

The Mage

Basics ~ **Classes** ~ The Party ~ Companions ~ Supporting Cast ~ Equipment ~ Bestiary ~ Walkthrough ~ Side Quests ~ Random Encounters ~ Achievements/Trophies

Even DPS mages should carry a Heal spell. It's always a luxury to have a mage who can serve the same function as a health poultice, only on a continuous basis with sometimes greater effect. In the same regard, don't under-value your defensive spells. Your main priority may be to deal damage as a DPS mage, but at some point you will need to protect yourself. Spells such as Arcane Shield and Force Field minimize damage that would otherwise kill you in an encounter.

Your spells draw mana from your pool. Watch how much mana you're using in a fight and cast accordingly. If you run short without ample lyrium potions to replenish, you could cost your party a victory. Gauge what you have to do to help the team. There's no sense casting a huge Chain Lightning spell on a group of enemies that go down with one or two swings, just as you may want to hold back on that Petrify spell if the tank has the situation under control. Save your mana. You never know when the next fight will start, and you'll be grateful you didn't waste mana.

Spell Combos

- Earthquake + Grease + Fireball + Walking Bomb should stymie most groups before they can do too much harm to your party.

- A fire spell on Grease works great at lower levels or when you don't have all kinds of time.

- Glyph of Paralysis + Glyph of Repulsion causes an explosive effect that paralyzes those nearby.

- Blizzard + Tempest becomes Storm of the Century (spectacular electrical storm).

- Cast Blizzard on a burning Grease slick to extinguish it.

- Send a tank to draw all kinds of threat from a mob away from the party. Cast Force Field on the tank for immunity from all damage and then follow with Inferno to engulf the entire area. The enemies burn while fighting a tank that can't die.

- Drain Life and Mana Drain are twice as effective on a target with a Vulnerability Hex.

- Cast Spell Might on yourself and then cast Animate Dead on a skeleton. This skeleton is much more powerful than the ordinary skeletons you can animate.

- Cast Sleep on a target and then cast Horror on it. This inflicts massive spirit damage on the target, often killing many lesser foes outright. Those who survive emerge in a state of fear.

- Immobilize a target with Cone of Cold or Petrify. When the target is in that vulnerable state, a critical hit from any weapon, a hit from the Stonefist spell, or the effects of the Crushing Prison spell will shatter it. (Bosses and lieutenants are highly resistant to this.)

- Cast a Death Hex on a target and then cast a Death Cloud in its area. If the target is touched by the Death Cloud, it sustains massive spirit damage.

CAUTION

Many spells have an area of effect much larger than just one target, making friendly fire possible. The higher the spell in the chain, the more damage your party members can take if they're caught in the affected area, so be careful.

Mage School

Arcane Bolt is a basic all-around damage spell with a long range, decent damage, and minor cost. Arcane Shield is a sustained ability that helps divert attacks and bolsters your mage's defense. Staff Focus increases the power of your basic staff attack, and Arcane Mastery grants a permanent bonus to spellpower, augmenting all your spells. Almost any mage build wants Arcane Mastery as soon as it becomes available at level 10. On the attack, cast your powerful spells, then follow them up with Arcane Bolt. When you're being swarmed, use your Arcane Shield, then let your other characters take the threat while you move back and come at your enemies with another wave of spells.

At level 20, the two new Mage school chains open up. The Fade Shield chain increases your mastery of the elements. Fade Shield soups up your Arcane Shield to further defend against magic attacks and reduce physical damage. Elemental Mastery increases elemental damage from other spells while it's in effect. Attunement gives a +10 bonus to willpower, magic, and combat mana regeneration. Time Spiral can win you the day when it resets all your cooldowns and suddenly makes all spells possible for active duty.

If you don't go for that chain, you may want to start with Repulsion Field at level 20. The field knocks back nearby enemies if they fail a physical resistance check, which is fantastic against lesser foes that try to swarm you. Invigorate radiates out to lessen the activation cost of your allies' talents and spells, though it drains your mana continuously. Arcane Field generates waves of spirit damage that smash through nearby foes. Mystic Negation creates a field that continuously negates hostile magic in the area.

Primal School

Your main offensive spells find their home in the Primal school. Mostly focused on activated abilities, both in direct attacks and AoE attacks, Primal taps fire, earth, cold, and electricity for your staple damage attacks. The first spell in each chain gives you a decent damage spell (except for the Earth chain, which gives you Stonefist second), and the third spell grants you a powerful AoE blast.

primagames.com

Monsters will be affected differently based on their resistances and vulnerabilities, and each chain has its own special effects: fire causes damage over time; earth gives you defense and one-shot kill with Petrify; cold hampers enemy movement; electricity forks to adjacent targets.

Creation School

Your primary school as a healer, Creation focuses on restoring health, replenishing mana, enhancing the party, and warding an area with glyphs. The Heal chain is the most important; you'll want Heal right out of the gate and Regeneration as soon as you can reach the 23 magic prerequisite. The Spell Wisp chain can work for any mage as well: Spell Wisp increases spellpower, Grease traps enemies in a flammable AoE, Spellbloom regenerates mana, and Stinging Swarm is like an AoE damage spell as it bounces from target to target, except it doesn't create tons of threat focused on a single creature each time. The Heroic chain is for mages who want to buff the party, sacrificing offense for utility. The Glyph chain gives the mage some crowd control with paralysis, warding, repulsion, and neutralization effects.

Spirit School

Two of the chains can be unexpected powerhouses if used well. The Walking Bomb chain poisons a single target, or explodes a host of similar monsters with Virulent Walking Bomb, plus the chain provides mana regeneration and additional melee support through Animate

Dead. The Mind Blast chain splits between great defensive and great offensive abilities. Mind Blast stuns all nearby enemies (great for when the mage gets swarmed), Force Field nullifies all damage to a target for a short time (the ultimate threat negation), Telekinetic Weapons beefs up armor penetration for your whole squad, and Crushing Prison completely shuts down a target, rooting the enemy in place and causing enough damage to kill weaker targets. The Spell Shield chain is a must for defensive mages, especially Dispel Magic to remove devastating hexes and Anti-Magic Ward to cancel enemy spellcasting on one of your allies. Finally, the Mana chain centers around disrupting enemy spellcasters' mana, and replenishing your own in the process. If your party doesn't have a Templar, think about spending a few points in this chain's abilities.

Entropy School

The Entropy chains slide into the dark side of magic. The Drain/Death chain may be the most useful; the first two abilities net you health, while Curse of Mortality is lethal against healing mobs and Death Cloud is lethal to everything. The Weakness chain strips offense, defense, and movement from enemies, or it outright paralyzes them. The upgrades (Miasma and Mass Paralysis) do it even better, affecting whole groups. The Fear chain begins with Disorient, which inflicts combat penalties, works toward Horror, which causes the targets to cower in fear, and then knocks out enemies with Sleep. Combo Sleep with Waking Nightmare and hostile targets become randomly stunned, attack other enemies, or become the caster's ally for the duration of the spell. The last chain of hexes grants four different effects: vulnerability to resistances, AoE resistance penalties, inaccuracy, and bad luck (all normal hits become critical strikes).

Mage Spells/Talents

Chain	Name	Prerequisite	Description	Cost (mana /stamina)	Upkeep (mana /stamina)	Fatigue (% mana/stamina)	Ranged	Cooldown (sec.)	Area of Effect Radius (ft.)
			Mage School						
Chain 1	Arcane Bolt	None	The caster fires a sphere of magical energy at an enemy, dealing moderate spirit damage.	15	0	0	Yes	6	0
	Arcane Shield	Level 3	The caster generates protective sheath that helps divert incoming attacks, gaining a bonus to defense while this mode is active.	0	30	5	No	10	0
	Staff Focus	Level 7	The character has specialized in direct attacks using a mage staff, gaining a permanent bonus to damage from basic attacks.	0	0	0	No	0	0
	Arcane Mastery	Level 10	The mage has gained a keen familiarity with the arcane arts, granting a permanent bonus to spellpower.	0	0	0	No	0	0

The Mage

Basics ~ **Classes** ~ The Party ~ Companions ~ Supporting Cast ~ Equipment ~ Bestiary ~ Walkthrough ~ Side Quests ~ Random Encounters ~ Achievements/Trophies

Chain	Name	Prerequisite	Description	Cost (mana /stamina)	Upkeep (mana /stamina)	Fatigue (% mana/stamina)	Ranged	Cooldown (sec.)	Area of Effect Radius (ft.)
			Mage School (continued)						
Chain 2	Fade Shield	Level 20, Magic 40	The mage alters Arcane Shield to step partway into the Fade, adding a significant chance of resisting hostile spells or evading physical attacks while that spell is active, and a lesser chance of both when the spell is inactive (displacement +5, magic resistance +5).	Passive	0	0	No	0	0
Chain 2	Elemental Mastery	Level 22, Magic 44	The mage has learned to amplify the effects of each of the elements, increasing any elemental damage inflicted by other attacks while this spell is active.	0	100	10	No	30	0
Chain 2	Attunement	Level 25, Magic 52	The mage has become more attuned to surrounding magical energies, gaining bonuses to willpower, magic, and mana regeneration (willpower +10, magic +10, combat mana regen +10).	Passive	0	0	No	0	0
Chain 2	Time Spiral	Level 28, Magic 61	The mage, through great concentration, is able to alter perception of time, resetting the cooldowns on all spells.	120	0	0	No	180	0
Chain 3	Repulsion Field	Level 20, Magic 43	For as long as this spell is active, waves of repulsive energy emanate from the mage. With every wave, nearby enemies are knocked back unless they pass a physical resistance check. Mana is consumed each time a creature is knocked back.	0	80	10	No	10	0
Chain 3	Invigorate	Level 22, Magic 49	Waves of invigorating energy bolster nearby allies, substantially reducing their fatigue, meaning that their spells or talents will cost less to activate while this spell is active. However, the caster's mana drains continuously.	0	100	20	No	30	0
Chain 3	Arcane Field	Level 24, Magic 55	While this spell is active, the mage radiates arcane energy every few seconds, emitting waves of projectiles that deal spirit damage to enemies within the field. Each projectile consumes a small amount of mana.	0	80	10	No	10	0
Chain 3	Mystic Negation	Level 26, Magic 58	An aura of beneficial magic surrounds the mage while this spell is active. Every few seconds, the spell banishes any magical effects within the field that were created by a hostile creature. Each dispelled effect consumes a small amount of mana.	0	100	10	No	10	0
			Primal School						
Chain 1	Flame Blast	None	The caster's hands erupt with a cone of flame, inflicting fire damage on all targets in the area for a short time. Friendly fire possible.	20	0	0	Yes	10	35
Chain 1	Flaming Weapons	Magic 18	While this spell is active, the caster enchants the party's melee weapons with flame so that they deal additional fire damage with each successful attack.	0	50	5	Yes	10	0
Chain 1	Fireball	Magic 27	The caster's hands erupt with an explosive ball of flame, inflicting lingering fire damage on all targets in the area as well as knocking them off their feet unless they pass a physical resistance check. Friendly fire possible.	40	0	0	Yes	10	7
Chain 1	Inferno	Magic 34	The caster summons a huge column of swirling flame. All targets in the area take constant fire damage as they burn. Friendly fire possible.	70	0	0	Yes	60	10
Chain 2	Lightning	Magic 18	The caster fires a bolt of lightning at a target, dealing electricity damage. Friendly fire possible.	20	0	0	Yes	10	0
Chain 2	Shock	None	The caster's hands erupt with a cone of lightning, damaging all targets in the area. Friendly fire possible.	40	0	0	Yes	15	35
Chain 2	Tempest	Magic 28	The caster unleashes a fierce lightning storm that deals constant electricity damage to anyone in the targeted area. Friendly fire possible.	50	0	0	Yes	40	10
Chain 2	Chain Lightning	Magic 33	The caster's hands erupt with a bolt of lightning that inflicts electricity damage on a target, then forks, sending smaller bolts jumping to those nearby, which fork again. Each fork does less damage than the previous. Friendly fire possible.	60	0	0	Yes	60	0
Chain 3	Rock Armor	None	The caster's skin becomes as hard as stone, granting a bonus to armor for as long as this mode is active.	0	40	5	No	10	0
Chain 3	Stonefist	Magic 18	The caster hurls a stone projectile that knocks down the target and inflicts nature damage, possibly shattering those that have been petrified or frozen solid. Friendly fire possible.	30	0	0	Yes	15	0
Chain 3	Earthquake	Magic 25	The caster disrupts the earth, causing a violent quake that knocks everyone in the targeted area to the ground unless they pass a physical resistance check every few seconds. Friendly fire possible.	40	0	0	Yes	40	10
Chain 3	Petrify	Magic 30	The caster draws from knowledge of the elements to turn the target into stone unless it passes a physical resistance check. While petrified, the target is immobile and vulnerable to shattering from a critical hit. Creatures already made of stone are immune.	40	0	0	Yes	40	0
Chain 4	Winter's Grasp	None	The caster envelops the target in frost, freezing lower-level targets solid. Those that resist suffer a penalty to movement speed.	20	0	0	Yes	8	0
Chain 4	Frost Weapons	Magic 18	While this mode is active, the caster enchants the party's weapons with frost so that they deal additional cold damage with each melee attack.	0	50	5	Yes	10	0
Chain 4	Cone of Cold	Magic 25	The caster's hands erupt with a cone of frost, freezing targets solid unless they pass a physical resistance check, and slowing their movement otherwise. Targets frozen solid by Cone of Cold can be shattered with a critical hit. Friendly fire possible.	40	0	0	Yes	10	35
Chain 4	Blizzard	Magic 34	An ice storm deals continuous cold damage to everyone in the targeted area and slows their movement speed while granting bonuses to defense and fire resistance. Targets can fall or be frozen solid unless they pass a physical resistance check. Friendly fire possible.	70	0	0	Yes	60	10

primagames.com

Chain	Name	Prerequisite	Description	Cost (mana /stamina)	Upkeep (mana /stamina)	Fatigue (% mana/stamina)	Ranged	Cooldown (sec.)	Area of Effect Radius (ft.)
			Creation School						
Chain 1	Glyph of Paralysis	None	The caster inscribes a glyph on the ground that paralyzes the first enemy who crosses its bounds, unless the opponent passes a physical resistance check. A single caster can maintain a limited number of Glyphs of Paralysis at once.	25	0	0	Yes	40	2.5
	Glyph of Warding	Magic 18	The caster inscribes a glyph on the ground that bestows nearby allies with bonuses to defense and mental resistance as well as a bonus against missile attacks.	40	0	0	Yes	30	2.5
	Glyph of Repulsion	Magic 25	The caster inscribes a glyph on the ground that knocks back enemies unless they pass a physical resistance check.	35	0	0	Yes	30	2.5
	Glyph of Neutralization	Magic 33	The caster inscribes a glyph on the ground that neutralizes all magic, dispels all effects, drains all mana, and prevents spellcasting or mana regeneration within its bounds.	60	0	0	Yes	60	2.5
Chain 2	Heal	None	The caster causes flesh to knit miraculously, instantly healing an ally by a moderate amount.	20	0	0	Yes	5	0
	Rejuvenate	Magic 18	The caster channels regenerative energy to the selected ally, granting them a short term boost to mana or stamina regeneration.	25	0	0	Yes	45	0
	Regeneration	Magic 23	The caster infuses an ally with beneficial energy, greatly accelerating health regeneration for a short time.	25	0	0	Yes	5	0
	Mass Rejuvenation	Magic 28	The caster channels a stream of rejuvenating energy to all members of the party, significantly increasing mana and stamina regeneration for a short duration.	45	0	0	No	90	0
Chain 3	Heroic Offense	None	The caster enhances an ally's aptitude in battle, granting a bonus to attack.	20	0	0	Yes	5	0
	Heroic Aura	Magic 15	The caster sheathes an ally in an aura that completely shrugs off most missile attacks for a moderate duration.	30	0	0	Yes	5	0
	Heroic Defense	Magic 20	The caster shields an ally with magic, granting bonuses to defense, cold resistance, electricity resistance, fire resistance, nature resistance, and spirit resistance, although at a penalty to fatigue, meaning that the ally's talents or spells will cost more to activate.	40	0	0	Yes	10	0
	Haste	Magic 30	While this mode is active, the caster imbues the party with speed, allowing them to move and attack significantly faster, although the spell also imposes a small penalty to attack and drains mana rapidly while in combat.	0	60	10	Yes	30	0
Chain 4	Spell Wisp	None	The caster summons a wisp that grants a small bonus to spellpower for as long as this mode is active.	0	30	5	No	5	0
	Grease	Magic 20	The caster summons a grease slick that slows anyone who walks on it, as well as causing them to slip unless they pass a physical resistance check. If the grease is set on fire, it burns intensely for a time. Friendly fire possible.	25	0	0	Yes	20	7.5
	Spellbloom	Magic 23	The caster creates an energizing bloom of magic that grants anyone nearby, friend or foe, a bonus to mana regeneration.	25	0	0	Yes	30	10
	Stinging Swarm	Magic 33	A swarm of biting insects descend on the target, dealing a large amount of damage over a short time. If the targeted creature dies before the swarm dissipates, the insects will jump to another nearby enemy.	50	0	0	Yes	30	0
			Spirit School						
Chain 1	Mana Drain	None	The caster creates a parasitic bond with a spellcasting target, absorbing a small amount of mana from it.	0	0	0	Yes	10	0
	Mana Cleanse	Magic 18	The caster sacrifices personal mana to nullify the mana of enemies in the area.	40	0	0	Yes	20	10
	Spell Might	Magic 25	While in this mode, the caster overflows with magical energy, making spells more powerful, but expending mana rapidly and suffering a penalty to mana regeneration.	0	60	5	No	10	0
	Mana Clash	Magic 33	The caster expels a large amount of mana in direct opposition to enemy spellcasters, who are completely drained of mana and suffer spirit damage proportional to the amount of mana they lost.	50	0	0	Yes	40	10
Chain 2	Mind Blast	None	The caster projects a wave of telekinetic force that stuns enemies caught in the sphere.	20	0	0	No	30	5
	Force Field	Magic 18	The caster erects a telekinetic barrier around a target, who becomes completely immune to damage for the duration of the spell but cannot move. Friendly fire possible.	40	0	0	Yes	30	0
	Telekinetic Weapons	Magic 23	While this mode is active, the caster enchants the party's melee weapons with telekinetic energy that increases armor penetration. The bonus to armor penetration is based on the caster's spellpower and provides greater damage against heavily armored foes.	0	50	5	Yes	5	0
	Crushing Prison	Magic 30	The caster encloses a target in a collapsing cage of telekinetic force, inflicting spirit damage for the duration and possibly shattering those that have been petrified or frozen solid.	60	0	0	Yes	60	0

The Mage

Basics ~ **Classes** ~ The Party ~ Companions ~ Supporting Cast ~ Equipment ~ Bestiary ~ Walkthrough ~ Side Quests ~ Random Encounters ~ Achievements/Trophies

Chain	Name	Prerequisite	Description	Cost (mana /stamina)	Upkeep (mana /stamina)	Fatigue (% mana/stamina)	Ranged	Cooldown (sec.)	Area of Effect Radius (ft.)
			Spirit School (continued)						
Chain 3	Spell Shield	None	While this ability is active, any hostile spell targeted at the caster has a 75% chance of being absorbed into the Fade, draining mana instead. Once all mana has been depleted, the shield collapses.	0	45	5	No	10	0
	Dispel Magic	Magic 18	The caster removes all dispellable effects from the target. Friendly fire possible.	25	0	0	Yes	2	0
	Anti-Magic Ward	Magic 25	The caster wards an ally against all spells and spell effects, beneficial or hostile, for a short time.	40	0	0	Yes	30	0
	Anti-Magic Burst	Magic 33	This burst of energy eliminates all dispellable magical effects in the area. Friendly fire possible.	40	0	0	Yes	30	7
Chain 4	Walking Bomb	None	The caster magically injects a target with corrosive poison that inflicts continual nature damage. If the target dies while the effect is still active, it explodes, damaging all targets nearby. Although this spell is related to Virulent Walking Bomb, the magic behind the two does not interact; a target cannot be infected with both. Friendly fire possible.	30	0	0	Yes	20	0
	Death Syphon	Magic 20	While this mode is active, the caster draws in nearby entropic energy, draining residual power from any dead enemy nearby to restore the caster's mana.	0	45	5	No	10	5
	Virulent Walking Bomb	Magic 25	The caster magically injects a target with corrosive poison that inflicts continual nature damage. If the target dies while the effect is still active, it explodes, damaging nearby targets and possibly infecting them in turn. Although this spell is related to Walking Bomb, the magic behind the two does not interact; a target cannot be infected with both. Friendly fire possible.	40	0	0	Yes	40	0
	Animate Dead	Magic 33	The caster summons a skeleton minion from the corpse of a fallen enemy to fight alongside the party for a short time, although, as a puppet of the caster, it will not use any talents or spells without specific instruction.	0	80	10	No	60	0
			Entropy School						
Chain 1	Disorient	None	The caster engages in subtle mental manipulation that disorients the target for a short time, making the target a less effective combatant by inflicting penalties to attack and defense.	20	0	0	Yes	10	0
	Horror	Magic 18	The caster forces a target to cower in fear, unable to move, unless it passes a mental resistance check. Targets already asleep when the spell is cast cannot resist its effect and take massive spirit damage.	40	0	0	Yes	20	0
	Sleep	Magic 30	All hostile targets in the targeted area fall asleep unless they pass a mental resistance check, although they wake when hit. Sleeping enemies cannot resist the Horror spell, which will inflict additional damage.	35	0	0	Yes	50	10
	Waking Nightmare	Magic 32	Hostile targets are trapped in a waking nightmare unless they pass a mental resistance check. They are randomly stunned, attack other enemies, or become the caster's ally for the duration of the effect. Enemies that are already asleep cannot resist.	40	0	0	Yes	40	5
Chain 2	Drain Life	None	The caster creates a sinister bond with the target, draining its life energy in order to heal the caster.	20	0	0	Yes	10	0
	Death Magic	Magic 20	While active, the caster draws in nearby entropic energy, draining residual life-force from any dead enemy nearby to heal the caster.	0	45	5	No	10	5
	Curse of Mortality	Magic 25	The caster curses a target with the inevitability of true death. While cursed, the target cannot heal or regenerate health and takes continuous spirit damage.	40	0	0	Yes	60	0
	Death Cloud	Magic 34	The caster summons a cloud of leeching entropic energy that deals continuous spirit damage to all who enter. Friendly fire possible.	50	0	0	Yes	60	10
Chain 3	Vulnerability Hex	None	The target suffers a hex that inflicts penalties to cold resistance, electricity resistance, fire resistance, nature resistance, and spirit resistance.	20	0	0	Yes	20	0
	Affliction Hex	Magic 20	A contagious hex inflicts penalties to cold resistance, electricity resistance, fire resistance, nature resistance, and spirit resistance on the target and all other enemies nearby.	40	0	0	Yes	20	10
	Misdirection Hex	Magic 28	The target suffers a frustrating hex of inaccuracy. All hits become misses, while critical hits become normal hits.	45	0	0	Yes	40	0
	Death Hex	Magic 36	The target suffers a hex of lethal bad luck. Every normal hit it suffers becomes a critical hit.	60	0	0	Yes	60	0
Chain 4	Weakness	None	The caster drains a target of energy, inflicting penalties to attack and defense, as well as reducing its movement speed unless it passes a physical resistance check.	20	0	0	Yes	10	0
	Paralyze	Magic 18	The caster saps a target's energy, paralyzing it for a time unless it passes a physical resistance check, in which case its movement speed is reduced instead.	35	0	0	Yes	30	0
	Miasma	Magic 25	While this mode is active, the caster radiates an aura of weakness, hindering nearby enemies with penalties to attack and defense. Unless the opponents pass a physical resistance check, they also suffer a penalty to movement speed.	0	60	5	No	30	0
	Mass Paralysis	Magic 35	All hostile targets in the area are paralyzed for a short time unless they pass a physical resistance check, in which case their movement speed is reduced instead.	70	0	0	Yes	50	8

Chain	Name	Prerequisite	Description	Cost (mana /stamina)	Upkeep (mana /stamina)	Fatigue (% mana/stamina)	Ranged	Cooldown (sec.)	Area of Effect Radius (ft.)
			Power of Blood School (downloadable content only)						
Chain 1	Dark Sustenance	None	A self-inflicted wound lets the mage draw from the power of tainted blood, rapidly regenerating a significant amount of mana but taking a small hit to health.	40 Health (gains 100 mana)	0	0	No	60	0
	Bloody Grasp	None	The mage's own tainted blood becomes a weapon, sapping the caster's health slightly but inflicting spirit damage on the target. Darkspawn targets suffer additional damage for a short period.	15	0	0	Yes	10	0

Specializations

Each class has three specializations (out of six) that they can learn during the game. Your first specialization can be learned at level 7; your second at level 14; and your third at level 22. Some specializations are difficult to achieve, but very rewarding if you gain one. As long as the specific abilities fit with your play style and character breakdown, a specialization is generally worth spending points in over regular spells.

Mage Specialization Manual Locations

In *Awakening*, all your new specializations are learned from manuals. Track them down at the following locations:

- **Battlemage Manual:** Ambassador Cera in the throne room of Vigil's Keep
- **Blood Mage Manual:** Dwarven bartender in Amaranthine's Crown and Lion Inn
- **Keeper Manual:** Henley's Apothecary in Amaranthine

You should definitely experiment with specializations. A pure healer could, for example, specialize in Shapeshifter to add some offense to the mix and some defense if they generate too much threat. Here are some suggested play style fits for the six specializations:

Arcane Warrior
- **Primary:** Melee/ranged mage (standard ranged spells with Arcane Warrior abilities for melee component)
- **Secondary:** Mana powerhouse (use Fade Shroud to regenerate mana faster) or tanking capability

Blood Mage
- **Primary:** Enemy control (use Blood Control to possess enemies to fight for you)
- **Secondary:** Health resilient (use Blood Sacrifice to heal self along with standard healing spells)

Shapeshifter
- **Primary:** DPS mage (Shapeshifter melee attacks complement ranged spells)
- **Secondary:** Health resilient (use Flying Swarm to avoid health damage)

Spirit Healer
- **Primary:** Main party healer (Group Heal essential for party survival)
- **Secondary:** Savior (return dead comrades to life with Revival)

Keeper
- **Primary:** Natural powerhouse (create a small area that taps into the powers of nature)
- **Secondary:** Rooter (paralyze foes with vines and roots)

Battlemage
- **Primary:** Combat veteran (wade into melee with greater healing and damage capabilities)
- **Secondary:** Freezer burn (damage and freeze enemies stone cold)

The Mage

Mage Specializations

Talent Name	Prerequisite Level	Description	Cost (mana /stamina)	Upkeep (mana /stamina)	Fatigue (% mana/stamina)	Ranged	Cooldown (sec.)	Area of Effect Radius (ft.)
Specialization: Arcane Warrior								
Combat Magic	7	While this mode is active, the Arcane Warrior channels magic inward, trading increased fatigue for an attack bonus and the ability to use spell-power to determine combat damage. Aura of Might and Fade Shroud improve the effects. Additionally, regardless of whether the mode is active, an Arcane Warrior who has learned this spell may use the magic attribute to satisfy the strength requirement to equip higher-level weapons or armor.	0	50	50	No	10	0
Aura of Might	12	The Arcane Warrior's prowess with Combat Magic grows, granting additional bonuses to attack, defense, and damage while in that mode.	0	0	0	No	0	0
Shimmering Shield	14	The Arcane Warrior is surrounded by a shimmering shield of energy that blocks most damage and grants large bonuses to armor and all resistances. When active, however, the Shimmering Shield consumes mana rapidly.	0	40	5	No	30	0
Fade Shroud	16	The Arcane Warrior now only partly exists in the physical realm while Combat Magic is active. Spanning the gap between the real world and the Fade grants a bonus to mana regeneration and a chance to avoid attacks.	0	0	0	No	0	0
Specialization: Blood Mage								
Blood Magic	7	For as long as this mode is active, the Blood Mage sacrifices health to power spells instead of expending mana, but effects that heal the Blood Mage are much less effective than normal.	0	0	5	No	10	0
Blood Sacrifice	12	The Blood Mage sucks the life-force from an ally, healing the caster but potentially killing the ally. This healing is not affected by the healing penalty of Blood Magic.	0	0	0	Yes	15	0
Blood Wound	14	The blood of all hostile targets in the area boils within their veins, inflicting severe damage. Targets stand twitching, unable to move unless they pass a physical resistance check. Creatures without blood are immune.	40	0	0	Yes	20	10
Blood Control	16	The Blood Mage forcibly controls the target's blood, making the target an ally of the caster unless it passes a mental resistance check. If the target resists, it instead takes great damage from the manipulation of its blood. Creatures without blood are immune.	40	0	0	Yes	40	0
Specialization: Shapeshifter								
Spider Shape	7	The Shapeshifter can transform into a giant spider, gaining a large bonus to nature resistance as well as the spider's Web and Poison Spit abilities. The caster's spellpower determines how powerful the form is. With Master Shapeshifter, the mage becomes a corrupted spider, growing still stronger and gaining the Overwhelm ability.	0	50	5	No	90	0
Bear Shape	8	The Shapeshifter can transform into a bear, gaining large bonuses to nature resistance and armor as well as the bear's Slam and Rage abilities. The caster's spellpower further enhances this bear's statistics and abilities. With Master Shapeshifter, this form transforms the caster into a powerful bereskarn and gains the Overwhelm ability.	0	60	5	No	90	0
Flying Swarm	10	The Shapeshifter's body explodes into a swarm of stinging insects that inflict nature damage on nearby foes, with the damage increasing based on the caster's spellpower and proximity. While in this form, the caster gains Divide the Storm, and any damage the Shapeshifter suffers is drawn from mana instead of health, but the caster regenerates no mana. The swirling cloud of insects is immune to normal missiles and has a very good chance of evading physical attacks but is extremely vulnerable to fire. With Master Shapeshifter, the character gains health whenever the swarm inflicts damage.	0	30	5	No	60	0
Master Shapeshifter	12	Mastery of the shifter's ways alters the forms of Bear Shape and Spider Shape, allowing the caster to become a bereskarn and a corrupted spider, both considerably more powerful than their base forms. In those forms, the Shapeshifter also gains Overwhelm. Additionally, the Flying Swarm shape drains health from foes whenever the main swarm inflicts damage.	0	0	0	No	0	0
Specialization: Spirit Healer								
Group Heal	7	The caster bathes allies in benevolent energy, instantly healing them by a moderate amount.	40	0	0	Yes	20	0
Revival	8	The caster revives fallen party members in an area, raising them from unconsciousness and restoring some health.	60	0	0	Yes	120	2
Lifeward	12	The caster places a protective ward on an ally that automatically restores health when the ally falls close to death.	55	0	0	Yes	30	0

primagames.com

Specialization	Talent Name	Prerequisite Level	Description	Cost (mana /stamina)	Upkeep (mana /stamina)	Fatigue (% mana/stamina)	Ranged	Cooldown (sec.)	Area of Effect Radius (ft.)
Specialization: Keeper									
Keeper	One with Nature	20	The Keeper's bond with the earth creates a defensive field that immobilizes the Keeper for as long as this spell is active, but inflicts nature damage and a penalty to movement speed on any enemy that enters the field.	0	80	10	No	10	0
	Thornblades	22	The Keeper calls roots from beneath the earth to inflict physical damage on all enemies within the field created by One with Nature. The roots also knock enemies back unless they pass a physical resistance check.	60	0	0	No	30	10
	Replenishment	25	No living thing can escape the cycle of life; all who fall return to the earth. The mage now regains some health whenever a Keeper spell inflicts damage. When an enemy dies within the field of One with Nature, the body is consumed, giving the mage a large bonus to health regeneration for a short time.	80	0	0	No	0	0
	Nature's Vengeance	28	The Keeper summons gigantic roots from within the ground to attack all enemies in the area, impaling the opponents for a short time unless they pass a physical resistance check.	100	0	0	No	60	10
Specialization: Battlemage									
Battlemage	Draining Aura	20	The Battlemage thrives in the heat of combat, creating a field that drains life from nearby enemies to heal the mage for as long as the spell is active. Each time an enemy is drained, the spell consumes a small amount of the Battlemage's mana.	0	100	10	No	10	0
	Hand of Winter	22	The Battlemage releases a burst of intense cold, damaging nearby enemies as well as freezing them unless they pass a physical resistance check, and inflicting a penalty to movement speed otherwise.	80	0	0	No	45	7.5
	Stoic	25	The Battlemage has learned to harness pain and transform it into power, restoring mana whenever the mage suffers damage.	0	0	0	No	0	0
	Elemental Chaos	28	The Battlemage creates a field of chaotic, swirling energy that continuously harms nearby enemies with damage from each of the elements in turn for as long as this spell is active. The spell consumes mana rapidly.	0	140	10	No	10	0

Gear

Mages might not get the pick of the litter for equipment, but the gear they do receive should pump up their main abilities if you shop correctly. Don't worry about defense too much; concentrate on bumping up your magic and willpower scores, or gaining spellpower points to enhance all spells, or adding mana boosts. The goal of all mages is to avoid drawing too much threat, and if you're achieving that goal, armor won't be too much of a factor. If you're worried about taking damage, invest in constitution to increase health and ward you against melee and ranged attacks. The same goes with weapons: don't pick a staff based on DPS; pick one that increases your main attributes. Also, think about your spell preferences. If you invest in fire spells, for example, a ring that generates extra fire damage is a huge boon.

There's more mage gear than you could ever hope to equip in a single play. The general rule of thumb is to wait for loot that serves as an upgrade and snatch it up. If you have extra coin to buy a nice gear upgrade, feel free to spend away, though most of the low-level equipment will be easily replaced by future loot, and the high-level equipment is very expensive (generally bought before a run at the Mother).

NOTE

In *Awakening*, it's out with the old and in with the new. As you journey toward level 35, here are some key items to seek out. Keep in mind that ideal gear varies based on your play style and role in the party. If, for example, you want a high-damage mage, look for the magic attribute or specific damage bonuses based on your school (generally fire, cold, or spirit). If your mage does a lot of healing, willpower for extra mana is your treasured trait. We've suggested excellent possibilities in each item category. For more possibilities and complete stats on each item, see the Equipment chapter.

Ideal Mage Equipment

Item Type	Item 1	Item 2
Staves	Staff of the Lost	Spellfury
Daggers	Voice of Velvet	—
Mage Robes	Spellminder	Robes of the Architect

The Mage

Item Type	Item 1	Item 2
Light Chest Armor	Vest of the Nimble	Rainswept
Light Helmets	Cap of the Nimble	—
Mage Helmets	Toque of the Oblivious	—
Light Boots	Mage's Running Boots	Fadewalker
Light Gloves	Oven Mitts	—
Amulets	Illumination	Seeker's Chain
Belts	Belt of the Architect	Sash of Power
Rings	Ring of Mastery	Ring of Discipline

Party Responsibilities

Ask yourself two questions when playing a mage: "Are you primarily a damage-dealer or a healer?" and "Are you the only mage in the party?" If you want to perform the damage role, you will naturally concentrate on ways to harm your opponent. If you want to play the role of healer, regeneration and rejuvenation spells are in order. If you're the only mage in the party, you must take some healing spells as part of your repertoire.

Another important question: "What need do you fulfill best?" Perhaps, you may look at your other three companions and fill in the void that they lack. For example, if you have a warrior concentrating on two-handed weapons, a backstabbing rogue, and your sword-and-shield tank, DPS would seem to be covered while healing/party buffs are lacking. On the flip side, if you have a Spirit Healer such as Anders in the group, you can stretch out to damage spells and maybe supplement his talents with a heal or two.

In the end, though, choose the role that you want your mage to be and work the team around that. If you want to play DPS, go for it and make sure you have one of your other mages involved in the healing role. If you want to play the healer, make sure you have another DPS-driven companion. If you want to play a little DPS and a little healing, you might be able to swing it as a single mage, or you may need help from one of the companion mages; it all depends on your combat style and tactics.

One thing all mages should strive for is to remain in the background and avoid threat whenever possible. You aren't built for melee combat (unless you spec an Arcane Warrior properly), and if you draw threat, you will die quickly. Don't pull targets away from your tank, except, possibly, if they are near death and easy kills.

The mage ranks highest of the three classes in versatility. You can deal damage, heal, control large enemy groups, buff your party, and more. Save your mana for the right reactions at the correct times and you'll excel in this class. So long as you remember not to lead the battle charge, your magic will work wonders in fights.

Role Models

What role will you play in your party? With tons of spells to choose from and six specializations, you can make myriad mages. Don't feel constrained to play according to the following mage models to the letter; strive for these ideals, but leave room for your own innovation. These are basic models for a DPS mage, healer, or blend mage who balances offense and defense. Each shows you how to choose your spells up to level 30, what spell chains are effective, how specializations fit in, and sample combat strategies for that model. Strive for these ideals, but leave room for your own innovation.

NOTE
If you create a new Grey Warden, you have 21 points to spend, which actually puts you one point ahead of these charts. So if you follow these charts, you'll have one extra point to spend on what you like.

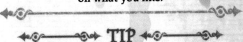
TIP
In *Awakening*, some amazing new talents become available to you once you reach level 20. Although you can still choose from Origins talents, we recommend focusing on the new *Awakening* abilities as soon as you're able to add high-level talents.

DPS Mage Model

Level	Spell/Talent
0	Arcane Bolt
1	Flame Blast, Heal
2	Flaming Weapons
3	Fireball
4	Spell Wisp
5	Grease
6	Walking Bomb
7	Death Syphon—*First Specialization Available at This Level*
8	Arcane Shield
9	Staff Focus
10	Arcane Mastery
11	Virulent Walking Bomb
12	Inferno
13	Lightning
14	Spider Shape —*Second Specialization Available at This Level* (Shapeshifter)
15	Bear Shape (Shapeshifter)

primagames.com

Level	Spell/Talent
16	Flying Swarm (Shapeshifter)
17	Master Shapeshifter
18	Animate Dead
19	Rejuvenate
20	Fade Shield
21	Elemental Mastery
22	Repulsion Field—*Third Specialization Available at This Level*
23	One with Nature
24	Attunement
25	Thornblades
26	Replenishment
27	Time Spiral
28	Nature's Vengeance
29	Invigorate
30	Mystical Negation

Overview: A DPS mage deals heavy damage from medium to long range. He generally concentrates in the Primal and Spirit schools.

Leveling: What does a DPS mage do best? Damage. Naturally, then, you should start off with a Primal chain. In this case, we'll choose the Fire chain, mostly because Fireball is such a great AoE damage spell. You could, of course, start with any of the Primal chains. (The Earth chain, however, may prove a little troublesome at its first rank; it's the only Primal chain that doesn't start out with a damage spell.)

Spending Your DPS Mage's Attribute Points

When you start a new character in *Awakening*, you have 62 attribute points to spend on your level 18 character. Depending on how you want to play your character and what skills/spells you take, you may spend more or less points on individual attribute scores, but this is a good base model for a DPS mage's initial points distribution:

- **Willpower:** 16 points
- **Magic:** 36 points
- **Constitution:** 10 points

Invest in Flame Blast to start the Fire chain and give you an additional attack to Arcane Bolt (all mages start with this basic attack). Pick up Heal as well. Yes, it's a defensive spell, but every mage should carry it to save allies or themselves in a pinch. Take Flaming Weapons for some melee support. Once you learn Fireball, you can roast enemy groups from a great distance. You have fine weapons already, so long as you don't run into fire-resistant mobs.

Choose Spell Wisp and the second spell in that chain, Grease. Spell Wisp increases spellpower, which augments all your damage spells, and Grease causes enemies to slip if they miss a physical resistance check (crowd control) and the slick surface can be set on fire for extra damage, making it a perfect combo for your fire-based spells.

Start your second damage chain with Walking Bomb. This gives you a separate source of poison damage (and sets you up for another lethal AoE attack). The follow-up to Walking Bomb, Death Syphon, restores mana; it's always handy in longer battles.

Now fill out the standard Mage school. Arcane Shield helps divert incoming attacks, giving you some more defense. The overlooked Staff Focus powers up your basic staff attack, which you always use as back-up damage when your mana runs low. The real reason for running these spells in a row here is to ensure that you pick up Arcane Mastery at its earliest availability. Because Arcane Mastery grants a permanent bonus to spellpower, it makes all your DPS stronger no matter what spell you choose.

Next, maximize your two damage chains. Virulent Walking Bomb functions similar to Walking Bomb with one big difference: when targets explode, they have a chance to infect other enemies and start a chain reaction of explosions. Inferno, the top of the Fire chain, engulfs an entire area in continuous flame and will decimate enemies if they can't escape to the cooler perimeter. Note that you need 34 magic to access Inferno.

Branch out into a third damage chain, Lightning. Two separate damage sources are usually enough, but if you rotate three, you should always have a damage spell available as long as your mana lasts.

Try out the Shapeshifter specialization with Spider Shape. With a DPS mage who really wants to hammer out lots of damage, it's best to go with your core damage spells early and slip into a specialization. The Shapeshifter specialization lets you deal melee DPS, which is fantastic for when your mana runs low or if you find yourself under direct melee attack. To gain all the creature abilities from Shapeshifter, we'll invest four points in a row to the specialization, though you could spread them out through level 20 if you like.

At levels 18 through 20, you should fill in with whatever tickles your fancy. At level 18, we pick up Animate Dead to finish off the Walking Bomb chain and gain some combat allies in the process. For level 19, select Rejuvenate; its effect on a party member's stamina/mana is invaluable backup for a healer. By level 20, you have three separate damage chain nearly maxed out, some good support spells, and an entire specialization at your disposal, with one extra point to spend as you wish.

At level 20, invest in the new Mage spell Fade Shield and work your way up to Elemental Mastery at level 21, Attunement at level 24, and Time Spiral at level 27. These are the best spells for a high-level mage looking to maximize damage.

Fill in level 22 with Repulsion Field from the other new Mage school chain. It's a highly effective defensive spell against swarming creatures and may give you the breathing room you need to deal with a threatening group one by one.

The Mage

Basics ~ **Classes** ~ The Party ~ Companions ~ Supporting Cast ~ Equipment ~ Bestiary ~ Walkthrough ~ Side Quests ~ Random Encounters ~ Achievements/Trophies

At level 23, go with your second specialization: Keeper. One with Nature sets up an area around you that damages enemies and slows them. It also roots you in place, but that's not usually a big deal because you don't plan on moving much with a handful of ranged spells at your disposal. Level 25's Thornblades, level 26's Replenishment, and level 28's Nature's Vengeance fill out the specialization and load you up with rooting, healing, and more damage against enemies closer to you.

At level 29, spend a spell point on Invigorate. You may not want to drain through your mana in most situations, but it's good to have in an emergency where your allies are desperate for stamina/mana. Finally, at level 30, select Mystical Negation.

Spell Choices: Fire spells serve as your primary AoE if you have the space to deal damage to your foe without catching the party in friendly fire. The Spell Wisp chain gives you extra spellpower and a crowd control spell in Grease. The Walking Bomb chain focuses on another cycle that can serve as either single-target damage or AoE damage. The Lightning chain gives you a third damage alternative, the effect of bouncing from one target to the next, and another option to avoid cooldown problems.

Specialization: Shapeshifter provides melee DPS so you can conserve on mana and defend yourself if under direct attack. Spider Shape has an effective Web snare, Bear Shape offers a good Overwhelm ability, and Flying Swarm turns into an AoE attack that also protects you from physical damage (all damage comes off your mana instead). Master Shapeshifter improves all forms, and you can hold your own against less powerful mobs. Your higher-level specialization give you more versatility. The Keeper abilities lock down nearby enemies, while harming them and healing you.

Battle Tactics: Your standard tactic is to deal steady damage to enemies without pulling so much threat that the enemies escape your tank's hold and charge toward you. With that in mind, you may have to delay a few seconds at the start of the fight, or during the fight, depending on the enemy position and your tank's ability to lock down the threat.

Your general spell cycle will be Fireball (if you won't hit your party with friendly fire), Walking Bomb, Arcane Bolt, and Lightning (if you've reached level 13 or higher). A neat trick inside dungeons is to open a door and hurl a Fireball at enemies on the far side of the room. The explosion consumes the room and the walls prevent the burst from burning your party; just cast it well away from the door.

Similarly, you can use your higher damage spells, such as Tempest, to hurt enemies you can't even see. Target the spell around a corner or inside another room (if the door is open) and let it rip. Enemies inside will take tons of damage or come running out into your well-positioned party's ambush.

An important part of your job may be to contain rather than destroy. Think of Grease whenever you see a large group ready to flank your party, or if something unexpected happens, such as your tank getting stunned and losing threat. Grease will delay most of the enemies, and you can always follow up with a Flame Blast to ignite the oil and cause great pain to the enemy.

If you're playing pure DPS, you should have another mage, a healer, in your party too. They can do the heavy lifting when it comes to healing and keep the party alive. However, don't ignore the supplemental healer role. In tough fights, throw a Heal into your rotation. If your primary healer is having trouble, you may even heal after every other damage spell. As soon as that Heal spell becomes active, glance at everyone's health bars and kick it off if wounds are piling up. Yes, you are a master DPSer, but if you are the only one standing, it won't do you much good.

Healer Mage Model

Level	Spell/Talent
0	Arcane Bolt
1	Heal, Rejuvenate
2	Regeneration
3	Winter's Grasp
4	Spell Shield
5	Dispel Magic
6	Arcane Shield
7	Group Heal (Spirit Healer)—*First Specialization Available at This Level*
8	Revival (Spirit Healer)
9	Staff Focus
10	Arcane Mastery
11	Mass Rejuvenation
12	Lifeward (Spirit Healer)
13	Frost Weapons
14	Cleansing Aura (Spirit Healer)—*Second Specialization Available at This Level*
15	Cone of Cold
16	Blizzard
17	Vulnerability Hex
18	Affliction Hex
19	Force Field
20	Fade Shield
21	Elemental Mastery
22	Attunement—*Third Specialization Available at This Level*
23	Draining Aura
24	Hand of Winter
25	Time Spiral
26	Repulsion Field
27	Invigorate
28	Arcane Field
29	Stoic
30	Elemental Chaos

Overview: A healer focuses on health regeneration and rejuvenation. These mages generally concentrate in the Creation school.

Leveling: A healer should concentrate in the Creation school, at least until they reach Regeneration and have two solid heals.

Spending Your Healer's Attribute Points

When you start a new character in *Awakening*, you have 62 attribute points to spend on your level 18 character. Depending on how you want to play your character and what skills/spells you take, you may spend more or less points on individual attribute scores, but this is a good base model for a healer's initial points distribution:

- **Willpower:** 28 points
- **Magic:** 34 points

Pick up Heal and Rejuvenate. Heal will be your staple health spell; Rejuvenate helps to restore stamina for warriors and mana for mages. If you increase your magic attribute correctly, you can net Regeneration. It's crucial to have at least two healing spells; otherwise, while Heal is on cooldown, a party member could become gravely wounded and you'll have no healing to help him.

Every healer should have a form of damage as well. In addition to your standard Arcane Bolt, we'll pick up Winter's Grasp. The Cold chain has the built-in effect of freezing a target in place, which serves to slow down foes and help out on defense; this defensive component complements your healing role.

Next, branch out into the Spirit school. Spell Shield comes first as a potential defense against hostile spells, but it's really a prerequisite for Dispel Magic. This is always handy to remove enemy effects on party members, Dispel Magic proves critical to remove Curse of Mortality, which prevents healing and will kill party members if you don't eliminate it fast.

Pick up Arcane Shield. Much like Spell Shield, it's extra defense that may come into play in certain fights, but it's mostly a prerequisite to ramp up to Arcane Mastery later.

No matter what you have to do, you want to gain the Spirit Healer specialization as soon as you can. The first spell in the chain, Group Heal, is *the* most important spell as a healer. The ability to heal all your party members at once will turn the tide in many battles. The Spirit Healer ability Revival may tip the battle scales in your favor when one of your companions drops and you can bring them back from the brink of death.

Fill out your basic Mage school. Choose Staff Focus and Arcane Mastery. Arcane Mastery will augment all your healing spells, which is a very good thing for your party's health.

Mass Rejuvenation comes in big in long battles where everyone needs a boost to stamina and mana. This fills out your main Heal chain.

Grab Lifeward from Spirit Healer. It's another healing spell that works when a companion's near death: a nice luxury to throw on a tank, or someone else that you can't heal immediately.

Frost Weapons inches you up in the Cold chain and lets you boost your party's offense if it looks to be a light fight that won't require much healing.

Cleansing Aura finishes off the Spirit Healer specialization. It's an AoE healing effect, which also cures injuries (and saves on buying injury kits!).

Fill out your Cold chain with Cone of Cold and Blizzard. You won't blast an area too much with Blizzard unless your party is desperate for damage, but you will fire off a Cone of Cold once in a while. Cone of Cold also freezes targets in place, and if your enemies aren't attacking, you don't have to spend mana healing.

Your final four slots leading up to level 20 can go to any spell chain you like. We'll start the Hex chain: Vulnerability and Affliction. The hexes can reduce attack percentages against your party (as well as enemy defenses), which plays to your strength as the group's main defender. At level 18, there's one extra point to spend as you wish.

Choose Force Field at level 19 for the ultimate damage-preventer. It may nullify an ally's offensive production for 30 seconds, but it also makes them invulnerable for that time frame. When someone's nearly down and out, cast Force Field, followed by Regeneration and your ally's health will slowly tick back up near full without further fuss from you.

At level 20, cash in on the first of the new Mage spells: Fade Shield, which boosts your Arcane Shield if you run into trouble. Level 21's Elemental Mastery will serve up extra damage when you use your cold spells, but it's really a stepping stone to reach level 22's Attunement. With gains to magic, willpower, and mana regeneration, what self-respecting healer wouldn't die for this upgrade? At level 25, the cooldown-resetting Time Spiral is a wonder for a healing mage. Imagine being able to cast back-to-back Group Heals.

When you reach levels 23 and 24, begin the Battlemage specialization with Draining Aura and Hand of Winter. Complete the Battlemage specialization with Stoic at level 29 and Elemental Chaos at level 30.

At level 26, pick up Repulsion Field, a highly effective defensive spell against swarming creatures that may give you the breathing room you need to deal with a threatening group. Invigorate at level 27 can boost your allies' stamina/mana in desperate situations (at the expense of your own mana). Choose Arcane Field at level 28; while active the mage radiates arcane projectiles that deal spirit damage.

Spell Choices: Your Heal chain will be the most active as you cycle back and forth between Heal and Regeneration throughout all future battles. The Cold chain gives you offense and defense, because foes may be frozen in place after you hit them with Winter's Grasp or Cone of Cold. Dispel Magic comes out automatically as soon as one of your companions falters to a lingering negative spell effect. At higher levels, your Hex chain supplements your main strategy with spells that reduce the effectiveness of the enemy against your party, and the new Mage school spells boost your overall effectiveness.

Specialization: Spirit healer is paramount. Seek it out as soon as you unlock the specialization potential. Group Heal proves super effective, healing everyone at once. Revival brings a companion back into the fight who would have been useless otherwise. Lifeward prevents an overwhelming amount of damage from finishing off an ally, while Cleansing Aura generates continuous health to all around you.

The Mage

Basics ~ **Classes** ~ The Party ~ Companions ~ Supporting Cast ~ Equipment ~ Bestiary ~ Walkthrough ~ Side Quests ~ Random Encounters ~ Achievements/Trophies

Battle Tactics: All good healers know to stay out of the heat of battle and focus not on spilling enemy blood, but on staunching the blood on your companions' tunics. Stay out of the main confrontation so as not to draw the attention of your foes. Don't waste mana on offense except in dire circumstances where you need to kill something before it kills you, or possibly minor fights where the outcome is never in doubt. Before you leave one encounter for the next, make sure your mana has topped back off.

Learn your allies' armor and health reserves. If you misjudge someone's threshold for damage, they may end up dead before you can heal them. With some practice, you will know when to fire off a Heal to bring a companion back to full health without wasting healing that goes above their max health rating.

Cycle through Heal and Regeneration, throwing in any other healing you have for longer fights. Preventive healing is a good idea; it keeps your companions' health high and avoids the problem of direly needing a heal that's unavailable on cooldown.

Once you gain Group Heal, master it. It's great to use when multiple party members are taking damage: you cast an economical heal that saves several people at once. You can counteract big bursts of damage that wound your team, such as traps or an unexpected Chain Lightning from an enemy spellcaster. Should multiple party members start taking damage over time—such as from a dragon's firebreathing—Group Heal helps boost everyone's health at once and keep the party out of immediate danger.

Heal as often as seems feasible. Unlike a DPS mage, you can't afford to heal conservatively to avoid threat if companions are at risk. Be sure to stock up on lyrium potions to replenish mana. If a DPS mage comes up dry, you might rely on the warrior to belt out the extra damage; if your healer gets stuck on empty, you had better win the fight in a matter of seconds or someone might not make it.

Blend Mage Model

Level	Spell/Talent
0	Arcane Bolt
1	Heal, Rock Armor
2	Stonefist
3	Earthquake
4	Mind Blast
5	Force Field
6	Arcane Shield
7	Combat Magic (Arcane Warrior)—*First Specialization Available at This Level*
8	Petrify
9	Staff Focus
10	Arcane Mastery
11	Telekinetic Weapons
12	Aura of Might (Arcane Warrior)
13	Crushing Prison
14	Shimmering Shield (Arcane Warrior)—*Second Specialization Available at This Level*
15	Lightning
16	Fade Shroud (Arcane Warrior)

Level	Spell/Talent
17	Rejuvenate
18	Regeneration
19	Chain Lightning
20	Draining Aura (Battlemage)
21	Repulsion Field
22	Hand of Winter (Battlemage)—*Third Specialization Available at This Level*
23	Fade Shield
24	Elemental Mastery
25	Stoic (Battlemage)
26	Attunement
27	Invigorate
28	Elemental Chaos (Battlemage)
29	Time Spiral
30	Arcane Field

Overview: A blend mage has the most versatility, splits talents between offense and defense, and may pull spells from all schools.

Leveling: Choose two defensive spells: Heal and Rock Armor. As with all mages, Heal serves as health rejuvenation whenever someone needs a boost. Rock Armor gives you an armor bonus, which you'll need because a blend mage draws more threat and enters melee more than the average mage.

Spending Your Blend Mage's Attribute Points

When you start a new character in *Awakening*, you have 62 attribute points to spend on your level 18 character. Depending on how you want to play your character and what skills/spells you take, you may spend more or less points on individual attribute scores, but this is a good base model for a blend mage's initial points distribution:

- **Willpower:** 14 points
- **Magic:** 36 points
- **Constitution:** 12 points

You'll take two offensive spells: Stonefist and Earthquake. Stonefist is a great offensive spell that pummels a single enemy with damage and can knock it off its feet. Earthquake will be your staple AoE attack. Note that you could take any main damage chain here (fire, cold, or electricity).

Next, enter the Mind Blast chain. Mind Blast can play out hugely when surrounded by large groups. Stun them to prevent a swarm on you, or to give your companions more time to get into position and wield their best attacks. Perhaps the best defensive spell in the game, Force Field nullifies all damage against you or a targeted ally for a short duration. You can almost stack Force Fields one after the other and keep a target alive against ridiculous damage—the

primagames.com

only drawback is the target of the Force Field can't react in any way while defended.

Pick up Arcane Shield as added defense and the second step toward Arcane Mastery.

With this blend build, we want the Arcane Warrior specialization. Learn Combat Magic and suddenly you can equip high-level armor and weapons. You might not be a tank, but you're no slouch in combat any longer.

Next, boost your offense again. Petrify can be a single-target kill spell if they fail a physical resistance check. (Follow up Petrify with Stonefist for shattering results!) Staff Focus increases the damage done with your basic staff attack.

Arcane Mastery improves spellpower and thus increases the effectiveness of all spells.

Telekinetic Weapons enhances your companions' weapons, and even your melee weapon if you wade into melee as an Arcane Warrior. Aura of Might bolsters your attack, defense, and damage. Note that you need to reach 34 magic to access Aura of Might.

Your best offensive spell comes with Crushing Prison. Break this out against single foes and encase them in a prison that roots them to the spot and deals continuous spirit damage.

Shimmering Shield continues your Arcane Warrior abilities. The shield sucks up damage and cranks up resistances; it's great for melee fighting, but it drains mana quickly, so don't count on casting many spells in conjunction with your defense.

Pick up Lightning. It's another damage spell that gives you a new source of damage and single-foe targeting.

Finish off the Arcane Warrior specialization with Fade Shroud. While Combat Magic is active, Fade Shroud increases mana regeneration and gives a chance to avoid attacks.

Next, choose Rejuvenate, followed by Regeneration. You'll have one extra point to spend as you like at this point. Follow these with Chain Lightning at level 19.

At level 20, enter your second specialization: Battlemage. Pop Draining Aura in melee and nearby enemies take damage while healing you. Pick up the other Battlemage spells as soon as you can. Level 22's Hand of Winter serves as a mini-Cone of Cold in a complete circle around you. Level 25's Stoic increases your mana availability; each time you take a hit in combat, you gain mana. At level 28, Elemental Chaos damages nearby foes with each of the elements one after the other, which should hit at least one of the enemy's vulnerabilities.

Grab Repulsion Field at level 21. It's a great weapon in melee as you scatter throngs of enemies and knock some of their feet for easy pickings.

At level 23, pick up the other new Mage school spells. Fade Shield launches the chain, followed by Elemental Mastery at level 24 for extra damage, Attunement at level 26 for upgrades to your stats, and Time Spiral at level 29 to reset your cooldowns and reuse all your most powerful spells quickly.

Finish off your build with a tad more healing. At level 27 invest in Invigorate to help out an ally's dwindling stamina or mana pool (at the expense of your own mana).

At level 30, choose Arcane Field; when active, the mage radiates arcane projectiles that deal spirit damage.

Spell Choices: The Earth chain gives you lots of offensive options: single-target stun with Stonefist, AoE with Earthquake, and single-target kill with Petrify. Mind Blast and Force Field offer excellent defense, all on the way to your best offensive spell in Crushing Prison. The Lightning chain adds an extra damage dimension to your spell rotation, and the higher-level Mage spells improve your melee capabilities dramatically.

Specialization: Arcane Warrior drives this blend build. Rather than drop spells constantly, the Arcane Warrior mixes ranged DPS with defensive spells and hand-to-hand combat. Combat Magic gives the mage access to armor and weapons only the warrior class would normally have. Aura of Might bolsters stats across the board. Shimmering Shield can keep you alive in a melee fight, but will cut you off from spells as your mana drains away. On the opposite extreme, Fade Shroud will replenish your mana and help you avoid damage once you level high enough to unlock it. Your second specialization, Battlemage, dovetails nicely with Arcane Warrior. Because you're already heavy into the middle of melee, the close-contact Battlemage abilities come in handy in almost all situations.

Battle Tactics: Unlike your standard mage who stays in the rear, this blend mage isn't afraid to enter melee after he specializes in Arcane Warrior at level 7. Suddenly, the lowly mage can wear excellent armor and wield weapons normally above his pay grade. The specialization is worth it just for that benefit alone, and it gets better for a brawler mage when you add the next three talents.

On the spell end, your offensive rotation will usually go Earthquake or Chain Lighting (if you can avoid friendly fire), Arcane Bolt or Lightning, Stonefist (targeting any enemy heading directly for you), and Petrify or Crushing Prison for the kill (or against the strongest opponent). You can pick and choose the correct spell for the situation if you forgo pure spellcasting and slip into Arcane Warrior/Battlemage mode.

Your defensive spell rotation generally goes Rock Armor, Mind Blast or Repulsion Field (when enemies close), Heal or Regeneration (whenever necessary), and Force Field for all-out defense. You can do lots of tricks with Force Field. You can, of course, save someone from certain death with a handy Force Field. You can send a tank in against a difficult foe, let him pile on threat, then throw up a Force Field; the enemy will most likely stay on the tank while you deal with the surrounding enemies. Even better still, you can take on bosses yourself. Cast a major spell, such as Earthquake or Fireball, on the enemy and follow up with a few damage spells to get him mad and fixated on you. As soon as the return damage heads your way, throw up a Force Field. While you're trapped in the Force Field, have a second mage cast Rejuvenate on you to replenish your lost mana (or quaff a lyrium potion as soon as you emerge from the Force Field). You can deal a ton of damage over a long time, while barely taking a nick.

As a blend mage, you can tap into anything, dabbling here and there. The idea is to learn a balance of offense and defense to jump into any situation with an answer in hand. To some degree, all good mages are blends.

The Mage ~ The Rogue

Basics ~ **Classes** ~ The Party ~ Companions ~ Supporting Cast ~ Equipment ~ Bestiary ~ Walkthrough ~ Side Quests ~ Random Encounters ~ Achievements/Trophies

The Rogue

You are flashing daggers and a snarl out of the shadows, savagery and subtlety, the jack-of-all trades for the party. A rogue slips into battle unseen and lethal, able to deal deadly damage from behind and escape harm when enemies take notice. When combat is over, the rogue is the only one who can penetrate locked doors and claim extra treasure from almost every dungeon.

The rogue sits between the warrior and the mage in terms of gear access. They can gain almost any suit of armor or weapon that a warrior gets; however, to do that would cost a ton of attribute points in strength and forgo points in dexterity and cunning that enhance most rogue talents. They certainly have higher DPS weapons and sturdier armor than mages.

Talents for a rogue fall into three main categories: Rogue, Dual Weapon, and Archery. The Rogue talents increase damage from backstabs and critical hits, teach you how to evade the enemy's mightiest blows, enable you to lockpick doors and chests, deactivate traps, and hide invisibly in the shadows through stealth. Dual Weapons gives the rogue a weapon in each hand for double the fun, and once they erase the penalties for wielding two weapons, rogues deal tremendous melee damage. If you don't want to go with melee, the rogue can lean toward Archery, where a single shot can stun multiple targets or split a hurlock skull in two.

Rogue specializations delve into a wide array of abilities. Assassin and Duelist give the melee DPSer more combat talents, with Assassin concentrating on pure damage-dealing and Duelist aiding defense as well. Bard is all about crowd control and party buffs. You can stun a single target or hold an entire group fixated on your song, or you can boost all your companions' stats. Ranger allows you to summon animal allies into a fight, adding a pet wolf, bear, or spider to your side. Legionnaire Scout turns your rogue into a tank, beefing up his or her defensive abilities. Shadow allows the rogue to further blend in with the darkness for defensive and offensive purposes.

If you like to play it a bit sinister and secret, yet go ruthlessly offensive once you dive into combat, the rogue class is for you. Outside of combat, your lockpicking and stealth abilities prove useful in innumerable situations. You will be the party's favorite companion just for the extra loot you find.

Strengths and Weaknesses

When an enemy has locked onto a tank and the rogue is free to backstab, you can deal out massive single target damage and kill things very quickly. A rogue should get into backstab position whenever possible. Out of combat, you can gain extra experience and loot from opening locked doors and chests. Enemies sometimes defend their lair with traps; the rogue not only detects them but also disarms them to avoid the brutal consequences from one misstep. Stealth aids a rogue in almost any situation; in combat, you can slip into the perfect position unseen by enemies, and out of combat, you can recon areas or bypass enemies with high enough skill. And rogues get a skill point every two levels, rather than every three.

Advantages

- Single-target DPS
- Lockpicking
- Trap Detection and Disarmament
- Stealth
- Access to More Skill Points

Rogue defense is rather weak, because it's difficult, if not impossible, to wear heavier armor. Being hit by several mobs or a large boss will take you out pretty fast. This makes using AoE attacks difficult because they usually pull threat and get you killed fast unless your party includes an excellent tank. To be most effective, a rogue needs to be behind his target, which isn't always easy to do and may get you into a combat hotspot. You also don't have much defense against magic, other than going into stealth mode and trying to sneak up on enemy casters.

primagames.com

Disadvantages

- Limited Defense
- Must Get Behind Targets to be Most Effective
- Generally Weak Against Magic Attacks

Attributes

Rogue-specific talents focus mostly on the dexterity and cunning attributes, and the weapon talents focus on dexterity and the Combat Training skill, so spend most of your points on dexterity. Early on, devote as many points as you need to dexterity to unlock the talents you wish to obtain; you can always fill in the other attributes later after you have your core talents well underway.

As for the other attributes, spend the required points in dexterity and spread the remainder of the points among cunning (requirement for many other rogue abilities), constitution (for resilience), willpower (for higher stamina), and strength (for power and armor requirements). Don't leave magic too far behind because spending points here will make potions more effective. Make sure to build strength to at least 20 so the character can use Tier 7 armor, and be in easy range of the higher tiers if need be, and dexterity to at least 36 if you plan on getting Dual-Weapon Mastery.

Rogue Attribute Bonuses

+4 Dexterity
+2 Willpower
+4 Cunning

TIP

Gear bonuses can amplify your attribute's strengths or offset any shortcomings. A ring, for example, that bulks up constitution could provide some extra health without costing any of your precious attribute points.

During character creation, feel free to choose a race based on the corresponding background you would like to play as a rogue. However, if maximizing your rogue stats appeals to you, choose a dwarf or human. A human rogue gives you a starting 15 dexterity and 15 cunning. Dwarves are only one point behind in cunning. The elven rogue is the third choice, because elves start with only 14 dexterity and 14 cunning.

Rogue Starting Attributes

Attribute	Human	Elf	Dwarf
Strength	11	10	11
Dexterity	15	14	15
Willpower	12	14	12
Magic	11	12	10
Cunning	15	14	14
Constitution	10	10	12

Once you choose your rogue's race, you begin with 62 points to add to your attributes. If you want a combat-oriented rogue, focus on dexterity and a little strength. If you want a rogue who concentrates on lockpicking and stealth, spend points on cunning and dexterity. See the model rogue templates at the end of the chapter for specific attribute/talent suggestions.

Skills

All rogues need to pick up Combat Training as soon as they can. Combat Training opens up the higher tier weapon talents, which you can't live without. Spend your first skill point here to vault up to at least Improved Combat Training. You need to reach Expert Combat Training by level 6 and Expert Combat Training by level 9 if you want to focus on combat talents.

Poison-Making can help improve your damage totals, so it's probably the second best rogue skill. Buy beyond the first rank to access stronger poisons and different special effects. You could also go the Trap-Making route and branch out a little more into AoE damage.

If you want more options during dialogue, especially to sway people's opinions or avoid certain fights, invest in Coercion. It's an incredibly useful skill in dialogue; it gives you story options that you won't get otherwise. Cunning opens up the Coercion skills, which fits in with many rogue talents.

Don't forget about Stealing. It focuses on a high cunning score, something rogues should have. Use the Stealing skill to grab gear not normally dropped by foes.

NOTE

Beyond your starting skills, you're likely to obtain 11–16 skill points throughout the game. Pick your three or four favorite skills and stick with them. If you spread your points too thin, you'll end up doing a bunch of things—but not well.

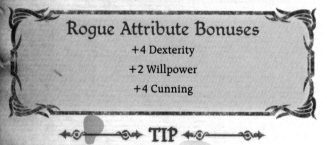

The Rogue

Basics ~ **Classes** ~ The Party ~ Companions ~ Supporting Cast ~ Equipment ~ Bestiary ~ Walkthrough ~ Side Quests ~ Random Encounters ~ Achievements/Trophies

Rogue Skill Recommendations

Assuming you spend at least 11 skill points at the start of your career, here's a good spread to consider. Note that many other combinations could work better for you, so experiment!

- Combat Training +4
- Poison-Making +3
- Coercion +3
- Stealing +1

If you aren't directly playing your rogue companions and want one of them to run around independently, invest in Combat Tactics for extra tactics slots. The more tactic slots you open, the more you can shape how your companion behaves in battle. Inevitably, even if you plan on controlling your rogue during fights, there will be moments when you don't program your rogue's every move (or something more important is going on) and tactics come into play. One or two points should be good, or max it out if you want the character to go on autopilot.

Once you reach level 20, look for the three new *Awakening* skills: Runecrafting, Vitality, and Clarity. Runecrafting creates—you guessed it—runes, which can be added to certain magic weapons and armor to boost abilities. Vitality increases your health by 25 points for every skill point you spend on it. Clarity does the same for you on stamina. Depending on whether you take lots of damage in combat or use up your stamina quickly, you should invest at least a few skill points in Vitality, Clarity, or both.

Talents

Rogues have many areas to spend their points, but not enough points to develop them all (never mind the specializations). So what do you choose? Rogue-specific active and passive talents? Lockpicking and disarming traps? Stealth? The Dual Weapon talent school? The Archer talent school? A specialization or two? If you decide to let your focus slide on the weapon talent chains, you can still use dual weapons and bows, but you won't be nearly as efficient at it. You will be a master at stealth, lockpicking and disarming traps, and your other rogue-specific talents. In addition, you can spend fewer of your skill points on Combat Training and more on Poison-Making, Herbalism, Survival, Coercion, and Stealing. If you choose to focus on one of the weapon talent chains, some of your rogue-specific talents will suffer.

So what kind of rogue do you want to be? Does passing up locked treasure and rooms drive you nuts? Do you love being able to stealth through places and situations? Would you prefer to have a deadly combat rogue? Whatever you choose, make sure it complements the rest of your party. For example, a rogue who is adept in lockpicking, stealth, and rogue-specific talents should be paired with a solid melee rogue or warrior (someone who can take the threat and deal the damage). It also wouldn't hurt to have a good ranged attacker in this party too. You won't be the best one-on-one melee opponent, but you'll be able to:

- Drop your threat
- Evade many incoming attacks
- Stun opponents
- Move deftly in combat
- Gain bonuses to critical chance on all attacks
- Backstab stunned and paralyzed foes
- Deliver penalties to your foes' armor, movement speed, and defense

It's not the most sportsmanlike character, but you'll have a solid advantage in many situations. In addition to your below-the-belt style of dealing with things, you can steal, sneak, and pick your way into many interesting places and treasure chests.

◆ NOTE ◆

It's possible to have three rogues in the game: Nathaniel, Sigrun, and you. Develop each differently to have access to a wider talent arsenal.

All rogues should familiarize themselves with the cooldown component of each talent. The worst situation is to have plenty of stamina and no available talents to use. Branch out into different chains to avoid the cooldown problem.

Your talents drain stamina from your pool. Watch how much stamina you're using in a fight and act accordingly. If you run short without a mage's Restoration spell to replenish you, it could cost your party a victory. Gauge what you have to do to help the team. There's little sense running off a series of moves that drains three quarters of your stamina on the first opponent when there are three more to go. Save your stamina. You never know when the next fight will start, or how long the current fight will go if you have unexpected ambushers, and you'll be grateful you didn't waste stamina.

Full-Sized Weapons vs. Daggers

When you play a dual-wielding rogue, one of the first questions to come to mind is what weapon combination deals the most damage in combat. Obviously, the weapons themselves make the biggest impact on the decision: a high DPS weapon with great bonuses will beat out anything.

Full-Sized Weapons vs. Daggers
(continued)

The only way you can wield two full-sized weapons is by having the Dual Weapon Mastery ability, which also reduces stamina costs for all other dual-weapon abilities. Because two full-sized weapons do more damage than two daggers, your damage-dealing capabilities are enhanced, but you have to spend lots of points in strength to access those weapons, which means fewer points to spend on your core talent needs. Even with the higher damage output, let's not forget about armor penetration and critical chance. Daggers are higher in both. It comes down to the type of enemy or situation you're facing. If you're facing heavily armored foes, the armor penetration and critical chance you get with the Coup de Grace auto backstab, Lethality, Combat Movement, and Evasion rogue abilities are a better choice than a rogue wielding two full-sized weapons coming at the target head on. This is why so many of the rogue abilities require and complement dexterity—not strength and brute force. Because you're building up dexterity for most rogue talents, that's probably the approach you want to take; otherwise, play a warrior. Keep in mind: There is no one dominant strategy for any class versus all enemies and challenges.

Rogue School

In your first chain, Dirty Fighting stuns a target for a short duration. Combat Movement is a passive ability that allows rogues move more swiftly in combat, allowing them a greater chance to flank or get behind their foes (for backstabs and such). Considering that it's sometimes difficult to get directly behind foes in the flow of combat, this one really comes in handy. Coup de Grace is a passive ability that allows your rogue to automatically backstab stunned or paralyzed foes (combos with Dirty Fighting or Dual Strike, warrior's Shield Pummel and Stunning Blows, mage's Mind Blast, to name a few). Feign Death is like the warrior's Disengage: it greatly reduces your threat, making enemies seek other targets.

The second chain holds Below the Belt, an attack that deals normal damage and gives the target penalties to defense and movement speed. Deadly Strike gives you a bonus to armor penetration. Use this on heavily armored foes. Lethality is a passive ability that gains the rogue a bonus on critical chance for all attacks. In addition, if the rogue's cunning score is higher than his strength score, the cunning score affects the attack damage in place of the strength score. If your rogue is high on cunning and low on strength, this is an excellent ability to have. So with this passive ability in the background,

use Dirty Fighting to stun a heavily armored foe, sneak around behind it for an automatic backstab and critical hit (courtesy of Coup de Grace), and then use Deadly Strike to get in another attack with a bonus to armor penetration. Pair this with Mark of Death, Exploit Weakness, Lacerate, and Feast of the Fallen in the Assassin specialty talents, and you'll mark this guy's weak spots for other party members, gain a bonus to your backstab with Coup de Grace, deal damage over time with your Lacerate passive ability, and restore some stamina when your target falls to the ground.

If you've had enough offense, Evasion is a passive ability that gives the rogue a 20 percent chance to dodge physical attacks, including attacks used to stun or knock down the rogue. The Deft Hands chain improves your ability to pick locks and disarm traps; it's a must for rogues who aren't just into combat. One chain down, the more you develop your Stealth talents, the more you can do while stealthed (use potions and other items such as traps and lures, and use stealth while in combat). These are a perfect complement to the new Shadow specialization once you reach level 20.

The new *Awakening* rogue talents begin with Heartseeker. The rogue launches a deadly blow that kills a weakened foe of elite rank or lower on a successful hit, or deals a critical hit if it fails to kill. Ghost is a great escape maneuver, allowing you to disappear from physical attacks for a short time. Weak Points puts a debuff on your opponent that increases the damage he takes. Finally, Flicker is a formidable attack against multiple enemies; all enemies in the targeted area automatically suffer a backstab attack from the rogue.

Dual Weapon School

The Dual Weapon talent school focuses more on activated abilities and attacks. In addition, you get to deal damage with two weapons simultaneously. You don't need the Dual Weapon talent school to be able to wield two weapons, but it's a good school to develop to be more proficient at melee. The focus of your passive abilities is on your second hand—you strive to deal similar damage and a similar rate of critical hits as your main hand. You gain a bonus to attack and defense with Dual-Weapon Finesse. You gain a bonus to critical chance and can cause bleeding lacerations on your opponent, inflicting damage over time with Dual-Weapon Expert. You can wield full-sized weapons in your off hand while reducing the stamina cost of all Dual Weapon talents with Dual-Weapon Mastery.

Increase your attack damage with Dual Striking, but be careful because it eliminates your ability to critical hit or backstab. Next, you can score a two-hit combo with a possibility of stunning your opponent and scoring a critical hit with Riposte. Cripple gives you a chance to score a critical hit and inflict your opponent with penalties to movement speed, attack, and defense. Punisher is a three-hit combo that has a chance to score a critical hit, knock an opponent down, and cause penalties to movement and attack speed.

The Rogue

Basics ~ **Classes** ~ The Party ~ Companions ~ Supporting Cast ~ Equipment ~ Bestiary ~ Walkthrough ~ Side Quests ~ Random Encounters ~ Achievements/Trophies

Dual-Weapon Sweep deals significant damage with each sweep, Flurry is a three-hit combo, Momentum increases your attack speed with every hit, and Whirlwind is a flurry of constant attacks: the signature of a Dual Weapon expert.

The new Twin Strikes chain scores two automatic critical hits on a target. Find Vitals increases melee critical chance by 10 and critical damage by 20. Low Blow combos with Twin Strikes and leaves opponents unable to move for a short duration. Unending Flurry acts just as you would expect it to: repeated attacks strike the target over and over until you miss or run out of stamina.

Archery School

Another school for rogues who build up dexterity, Archery gives ample special effects for a ranged combat enthusiast. Melee Archer lets you fire while being attacked (eliminating some of the pain of being an archer). Master Archer gives you bonuses to activated abilities and eliminates the penalty to attack speed when wearing heavy armor. Aim reduces attack speed but gives bonuses to attack, damage, armor penetration, and critical chance. Defensive Fire gives you a boost to defense but slows your attack speed.

In the second chain, Pinning Shot is a necessity because it impales the victim's leg and either pins it in place or slows its movement speed. Crippling Shot deals normal damage to an enemy and gives it penalties to attack and defense, and Critical Shot delivers maximum damage upon impact. The deadly Arrow of Slaying usually scores a critical hit, often dropping weakened enemies.

Rapid Shot increases attack speed, but you lose the ability to score critical hits. Shattering Shot deals normal damage and opens up an enemy's armor. If a warrior finds that one, it'll be in sore shape. Suppressing Fire is like Rapid Shot, but its foes now take penalties to their attack rating. Scattershot stuns a foe and then shatters, dealing damage to other enemies around it.

When you have room to breathe, Pinning Shot and Crippling Shot turn enemies into sitting ducks for mage attacks, deadly warriors, or more of your carefully aimed arrows. Shattering Shot is excellent against heavily armed foes. Rapid Shot, Suppressing Fire, and Scattershot hack away at the collective hit points of enemy ranks.

TIP

A good combo against a heavily armed foe is Shattering Shot, Crippling Shot, Aim/Rapid Shot, and Arrow of Slaying. Mix in another Shattering Shot if the first armor penalty runs out.

Don't think an archer just scores a hit or two before having to engage an opponent in melee. You can kill off a couple enemies in a few hits while pinning others in place and continuing to fire while other attackers swarm you. This you turns you into a deadly sniper that enemies need to deal with or suffer the consequences. Should the enemy swarm you, switch to Defensive Fire while you have the passive ability Melee Archer. You can fire off arrows while being attacked and still have decent defense.

The new Accuracy chain gives bonuses to your attack and damage scores, as well as ranged critical chance. Arrow Time slows down enemies around the archer, while the phenomenal Burst Shot scores an automatic triple critical hit against a single target and then shatters to deal AoE damage to all other targets around it. Rain of Arrows blankets an area with damage, harming foes and friends alike in the large radius.

Rogue Talents

Chain	Name	Prerequisite	Description	Cost (mana /stamina)	Upkeep (mana /stamina)	Fatigue (% mana/stamina)	Ranged	Cooldown (sec.)	Area of Effect Radius (ft.)
			Rogue School						
Chain 1	Dirty Fighting	Dexterity 10	The rogue incapacitates a target, who takes no damage from the attack but is stunned for a short time.	25	0	0	No	25	0
	Combat Movement	Dexterity 14, Level 4	The quick-stepping rogue can more easily outmaneuver opponents, granting a wider flanking angle that makes backstabs easier to achieve.	0	0	0	No	0	0
	Coup de Grace	Dexterity 18, Level 8	When a target is incapacitated, the opportunistic rogue strikes where it hurts the most, inflicting automatic backstabs against stunned or paralyzed targets.	0	0	0	No	0	0
	Feign Death	Dexterity 22, Level 12	The rogue collapses at enemies' feet, making them lose interest and seek other targets until the rogue gives up the ruse.	0	40	5	No	300	0
Chain 2	Below the Belt	Dexterity 10	The rogue delivers a swift and unsportsmanlike kick to the target, dealing normal combat damage as well as imposing penalties to defense and movement speed unless the target passes a physical resistance check.	25	0	0	No	15	0
	Deadly Strike	Dexterity 14, Level 4	The rogue makes a swift strike at a vulnerable area on the target, dealing normal damage but gaining a bonus to armor penetration.	25	0	0	No	15	0
	Lethality	Dexterity 23, Level 8	The rogue has a keen eye for weak spots and thus gains a bonus to critical chance for all attacks. Additionally, if the rogue's cunning score is greater than strength, sharpness of mind lets the character use the cunning modifier to affect attack damage in place of the strength modifier.	0	0	0	No	0	0
	Evasion	Dexterity 35, Level 12	The rogue gains an almost preternatural ability to sense and avoid danger. This talent grants a one-in-five chance of evading physical attacks, including being stunned or knocked down.	0	0	0	No	0	0

primagames.com

Chain	Name	Prerequisite	Description	Cost (mana /stamina)	Upkeep (mana /stamina)	Fatigue (% mana/stamina)	Ranged	Cooldown (sec.)	Area of Effect Radius (ft.)
			Rogue School (continued)						
Chain 3	Deft Hands	Cunning 10	All rogues have some understanding of opening locks and spotting traps, but particularly dexterous hands and a steady grip give the character a bonus when picking locks or disarming traps. The character's cunning score also contributes to these skills.	0	0	0	No	0	0
	Improved Tools	Cunning 14, Level 4	The rogue has taken to carrying a full set of implements designed to defeat trickier locks and spring traps without harm. These tools add a further bonus when lockpicking or disarming traps, which the character's cunning score also affects.	0	0	0	No	0	0
	Mechanical Expertise	Cunning 18, Level 8	Through practice and research, the rogue has come to possess an encyclopedic knowledge of devices designed to prevent entry. Knowing the right technique for the job lends the rogue yet another bonus when dealing with locks or traps. The character's cunning score also contributes to these skills.	0	0	0	No	0	0
	Device Mastery	Cunning 22, Level 12	Practice makes perfect, and only the most intricate locks or elaborate traps give the rogue pause at this level of mastery. A further bonus applies when lockpicking or disarming traps. The character's cunning score also contributes to these skills.	0	0	0	No	0	0
Chain 4	Stealth	Cunning 10	The rogue has learned to fade from view, although perceptive enemies may not be fooled. Taking any action beyond movement, including engaging in combat or using items, will still attract attention. If the rogue initiates combat while still stealthed, the first strike is an automatic critical hit or backstab.	0	0	5	No	10	0
	Stealthy Item Use	Cunning 14, Level 4	The rogue has learned how to use items while sneaking.	0	0	0	No	0	0
	Combat Stealth	Cunning 18, Level 8	The rogue is stealthy enough to try sneaking during combat, although at a significant penalty.	0	0	0	No	0	0
	Master Stealth	Cunning 22, Level 12	The rogue has mastered the art of stealth, gaining significant bonuses on all stealth checks.	0	0	0	No	0	0
Chain 5	Heartseeker	Level 20, Dexterity 36	The rogue strikes with great precision, attempting to fell weakened enemies in one last blow. If the attack is successful, a target of elite rank or lower is killed instantly if its health is already low enough. If the attack does not kill, it inflicts a critical hit instead.	80	0	0	No	30	0
	Ghost	Level 22, Dexterity 40	The rogue melts into the shadows, completely evading enemies' physical attacks for a short time.	60	0	0	No	60	0
	Weak Points	Level 24, Dexterity 46	While this mode is active, the rogue seeks out enemies' weak points, striking each target in a manner that increases all damage the foe suffers for a short time, no matter the source of the damage.	0	60	10	No	10	0
	Flicker	Level 26, Dexterity 52	The rogue's deadly speed is unmatched. Within a targeted area, the rogue disappears in a blur, sprinting from target to target to backstab each of them.	80	0	0	Yes	60	7.5
			Dual Weapon School						
Chain 1	Dual Striking	Dexterity 12	When in this mode, the character strikes with both weapons simultaneously. Attacks cause more damage, but the character cannot inflict regular critical hits or backstabs.	0	50	5	No	10	0
	Riposte	Dexterity 16	The character strikes at a target once, dealing normal damage, as well as stunning the opponent unless it passes a physical resistance check. The character then strikes with the other weapon, generating a critical hit if the target was stunned.	40	0	0	No	20	0
	Cripple	Dexterity 22	The character strikes low at a target, gaining a momentary attack bonus and hitting critically if the attack connects, while crippling the target with penalties to movement speed, attack, and defense unless it passes a physical resistance check.	35	0	0	No	30	0
	Punisher	Dexterity 28	The character makes three blows against a target, dealing normal damage for the first two strikes and generating a critical hit for the final blow, if it connects. The target may also suffer penalties to attack and defense, or be knocked to the ground.	50	0	0	No	40	0
Chain 2	Dual-Weapon Sweep	Dexterity 12	The character sweeps both weapons in a broad forward arc, striking nearby enemies with one or both weapons and inflicting significantly more damage than normal.	20	0	0	No	15	2
	Flurry	Dexterity 18	The character lashes out with a flurry of three blows, dealing normal combat damage with each hit.	40	0	0	No	20	0
	Momentum	Dexterity 24	The character has learned to carry one attack through to the next, increasing attack speed substantially. This mode consumes stamina quickly, however.	0	60	5	No	30	0
	Whirlwind	Dexterity 30	The character flies into a whirling dance of death, striking out at surrounding enemies with both weapons. Each hit deals normal combat damage.	40	0	0	No	40	2

The Rogue

Basics ~ **Classes** ~ The Party ~ Companions ~ Supporting Cast ~ Equipment ~ Bestiary ~ Walkthrough ~ Side Quests ~ Random Encounters ~ Achievements/Trophies

Chain	Name	Prerequisite	Description	Cost (mana /stamina)	Upkeep (mana /stamina)	Fatigue (% mana/stamina)	Ranged	Cooldown (sec.)	Area of Effect Radius (ft.)
			Dual Weapon School (continued)						
Chain 3	Dual-Weapon Training	Dexterity 12	The character has become more proficient fighting with two weapons, and now deals closer to normal damage bonus with the off-hand weapon.	0	0	0	No	0	0
Chain 3	Dual-Weapon Finesse	Dexterity 16	The character is extremely skilled at wielding a weapon in each hand, gaining bonuses to attack and defense.	0	0	0	No	0	0
Chain 3	Dual-Weapon Expert	Dexterity 26, Level 9	The character has significant experience with two-weapon fighting, gaining a bonus to critical chance, as well as a possibility with each hit to inflict bleeding lacerations that continue to damage a target for a time.	0	0	0	No	0	0
Chain 3	Dual-Weapon Mastery	Dexterity 36, Level 12	Only a chosen few truly master the complicated art of fighting with two weapons. The character is now among that elite company, able to wield full-sized weapons in both hands. Stamina costs for all dual-weapon talents are also reduced.	0	0	0	No	0	0
Chain 4	Twin Strikes	Level 20, Dexterity 34	Two devastating strikes in rapid succession each inflict an automatic critical hit. Find Vitals adds additional damage to each hit. If the target is affected by Low Blow, it cannot move for a short time.	50	0	0	No	30	0
Chain 4	Find Vitals	Dexterity 40	The character is a force of nature when wielding two weapons, gaining permanent bonuses to melee critical chance and critical damage. Twin Strikes now inflicts additional bleeding damage (melee critical chance +10, critical damage +20).	0	0	0	No	0	0
Chain 4	Low Blow	Dexterity 46	The character strikes at the legs of surrounding enemies, imposing penalties to movement speed and attack speed for a short time. If an opponent is already bleeding from Twin Strikes, it slips and falls to the ground as well.	50	0	0	No	30	2.5
Chain 4	Unending Flurry	Dexterity 50	The character singles out an enemy for death, stabbing it quickly and repeatedly, consuming a small amount of stamina with each hit. The assault continues until the target dies or flees, or until the character misses or runs out of stamina. If the target is bleeding from Twin Strikes, each swing becomes a critical hit. If the target is slowed by Low Blow, the character cannot miss.	40	0	0	No	60	0
			Archery School						
Chain 1	Melee Archer	Dexterity 12	Experience fighting in tight quarters has taught the archer to fire without interruption, even when being attacked.	0	0	0	No	0	0
Chain 1	Aim	Dexterity 16	The archer carefully places each shot for maximum effect while in this mode. This decreases rate of fire but grants bonuses to attack, damage, armor penetration, and critical chance. Master Archer further increases these bonuses.	0	35	5	No	10	0
Chain 1	Defensive Fire	Dexterity 22	While active, the archer changes stance, receiving a bonus to defense but slowing the rate of fire. With the Master Archer talent, the defense bonus increases.	0	40	5	No	15	0
Chain 1	Master Archer	Dexterity 28	Deadly with both bows and crossbows, master archers receive additional benefits when using Aim, Defensive Fire, Crippling Shot, Critical Shot, Arrow of Slaying, Rapid Shot, and Shattering Shot. This talent also eliminates the penalty to attack speed when wearing heavy armor, although massive armor still carries the penalty.	0	0	0	No	0	0
Chain 2	Pinning Shot	Dexterity 12	A shot to the target's legs disables the foe, pinning the target in place unless it passes a physical resistance check, and slowing movement speed otherwise.	20	0	0	Yes	15	0
Chain 2	Crippling Shot	Dexterity 16	A carefully aimed shot hampers the target's ability to fight by reducing attack and defense if it hits, although the shot inflicts only normal damage. The Master Archer talent adds an attack bonus while firing the Crippling Shot.	25	0	0	Yes	10	0
Chain 2	Critical Shot	Dexterity 21	Finding a chink in the target's defenses, the archer fires an arrow that, if aimed correctly, automatically scores a critical hit and gains a bonus to armor penetration. The Master Archer talent increases the armor penetration bonus.	40	0	0	Yes	10	0
Chain 2	Arrow of Slaying	Dexterity 30	The archer generates an automatic critical hit if this shot finds its target, although high-level targets may be able to ignore the effect. The archer suffers reduced stamina regeneration for a time. Master Archer adds an extra attack bonus.	80	0	0	Yes	60	0
Chain 3	Rapid Shot	Dexterity 12	Speed wins out over power while this mode is active, as the archer fires more rapidly but without any chance of inflicting regular critical hits. Master Archer increases the rate of fire further still.	0	35	5	No	30	0
Chain 3	Shattering Shot	Dexterity 16	The archer fires a shot designed to open up a weak spot in the target's armor. The shot deals normal damage if it hits and imposes an armor penalty on the target. Master Archer increases the target's armor penalty.	25	0	0	Yes	15	0
Chain 3	Suppressing Fire	Dexterity 24	When this mode is active, the archer's shots hamper foes. Each arrow deals regular damage and also encumbers the target with a temporary penalty to attack. This penalty can be applied multiple times.	0	60	5	No	10	0
Chain 3	Scattershot	Dexterity 27	The archer fires a single arrow that automatically hits, stunning the target and dealing normal damage. The arrow then shatters, hitting all nearby enemies with the same effect.	50	0	0	Yes	40	0

primagames.com

Chain	Name	Prerequisite	Description	Cost (mana /stamina)	Upkeep (mana /stamina)	Fatigue (% mana/stamina)	Ranged	Cooldown (sec.)	Area of Effect Radius (ft.)
	Archery School (continued)								
Chain 4	Accuracy	Level 20, Dexterity 34	For as long as this mode is active, the archer's mind is clear of everything except the next shot's trajectory, gaining bonuses to attack, damage, ranged critical chance, and ranged critical damage, all dependent on the archer's dexterity attribute.	0	60	0	No	10	0
	Arrow Time	Dexterity 38	Intense focus slows the archer's perception of time, effectively reducing the movement speed of enemies who come near for as long as this mode is active, excepting those of elite rank or higher. This deep concentration drains stamina constantly.	0	40	10	No	10	0
	Burst Shot	Dexterity 44	The archer looses a special shaft that scores an automatic triple critical hit against the targeted enemy, then shatters, inflicting half the effect on those unfortunate enough to be in the vicinity. Friendly fire possible.	60	0	0	Yes	60	3
	Rain of Arrows	Dexterity 52	The archer's bow points to the sky, firing multiple projectiles which then rain down over time in the targeted area. Friendly fire possible.	80	0	0	Yes	60	0
	Power of Blood School (downloadable content only)								
Chain 1	Dark Passage	None	Tapping the power of tainted blood makes the rogue more nimble, able to move more quickly while using Stealth and more likely to dodge a physical attack.	0	0	0	No	0	0
	The Tainted Blade	None	The rogue's blood gushes forth, coating the edges of weapons with a deadly taint. The character gains a bonus to damage determined by the cunning attribute, but suffers continuously depleting health in return.	40	40	5	No	5	0

Specializations

Each class has three specializations (out of six) that they can learn during the game. Your first specialization can be learned at level 7; your second

at level 14; and your third at level 22. Specializations are difficult to achieve, but very rewarding if you gain one. As long as the specific abilities fit with your play style and character breakdown, a specialization is generally worth spending points on over regular talents.

Rogue Specialization Manual Locations

In *Awakening*, all your new specializations are learned from manuals. Track them down at the following locations:

- **Legionnaire Scout Manual:** Glassric's Wares in Amaranthine
- **Shadow Manual:** Yuriah's Wares in the Vigil's Keep throne room

Definitely experiment with specializations. A DPS rogue could, for example, specialize in Ranger to add an extra "companion" to a fight for more support. Here are some suggested play style fits for the six specializations:

Assassin

- **Primary:** DPS (all-out offense to max out damage)
- **Secondary:** Stamina replenishment (use Feast of the Fallen to recoup lost stamina)

Bard

- **Primary:** Enemy control (Captivating Song can corral whole crowds)
- **Secondary:** Party buffer (replenish party mana/stamina or augment offense/defense)

Duelist

- **Primary:** Balanced DPS (excellent offense with a touch of defense)
- **Secondary:** Crit-happy (reach Pinpoint Strike for multiple critical successes in a row)

Ranger

- **Primary:** Pet lover (summon beasties for party support)
- **Secondary:** Off-tank (summoned creatures tank for you)

Legionnaire Scout

- **Primary:** Mini-tank (transform into a defensive juggernaut)
- **Secondary:** Anti-magic (avoid all spells, hostile and friendly)

Shadow

- **Primary:** Stealth happy (blend into the shadow for major attacks and defense)
- **Secondary:** Pandemonium player (confuse enemies with an airborne toxin)

The Rogue

Basics ~ **Classes** ~ The Party ~ Companions ~ Supporting Cast ~ Equipment ~ Bestiary ~ Walkthrough ~ Side Quests ~ Random Encounters ~ Achievements/Trophies

Rogue Specializations

Talent Name	Prerequisite Level	Description	Cost (mana/stamina)	Upkeep (mana/stamina)	Fatigue (% mana/stamina)	Ranged	Cooldown (sec.)	Area of Effect Radius (ft.)
Specialization: Assassin								
Mark of Death	7	The Assassin marks a target, revealing weaknesses that others can exploit. All attacks against a marked target deal additional damage.	40	0	0	Yes	60	0
Exploit Weakness	12	A keen eye and a killer instinct help the Assassin exploit a target's weak points. During a successful backstab attack, the Assassin gains additional damage based on cunning.	0	0	0	No	0	0
Lacerate	14	Whenever a backstab deals enough damage, the Assassin's foe is riddled with bleeding wounds that inflict additional damage for a short time.	0	0	0	No	60	0
Feast of the Fallen	16	The Assassin thrives on the moment of death. Stamina is partially restored whenever the Assassin fells an opponent with a backstab.	0	0	0	No	0	0
Specialization: Bard								
Song of Valor	7	The Bard sings an ancient tale of valorous heroes, granting the party bonuses to mana or stamina regeneration at a rate affected by the Bard's cunning. The Bard can only sing one song at a time.	0	50	5	No	30	10
Distraction	8	The Bard's performance, replete with dizzying flourishes, is designed to distract and confuse. The target forgets who it was fighting and becomes disoriented unless it passes a mental resistance check.	40	0	0	Yes	30	0
Song of Courage	10	The Bard launches into an epic song of the party's exploits, granting them bonuses to attack, damage, and critical chance. The size of the bonuses are affected by the Bard's cunning. The Bard can only sing one song at a time.	0	50	5	No	30	10
Captivating Song	12	The Bard begins an entrancing song that stuns hostile targets nearby unless they pass a mental resistance check every few seconds. Continuing the song does not drain stamina, but the Bard cannot move or take any other action while singing.	0	60	5	No	30	4
Specialization: Duelist								
Dueling	7	The Duelist focuses on proper form, gaining a bonus to attack while the mode is active. Keen Defense adds a bonus to defense while in this mode.	0	30	5	No	5	0
Upset Balance	12	The Duelist executes a quick move that throws the opponent off balance, imposing penalties to movement speed and defense unless the target passes a physical resistance check.	25	0	0	No	15	0
Keen Defense	14	The Duelist has an uncanny knack for simply not being there when the enemy attacks, receiving a bonus to defense.	0	0	0	No	0	0
Pinpoint Strike	16	The Duelist has learned to strike the vitals of an enemy with pinpoint accuracy and from any angle. For a moderate duration, all successful attacks generate automatic critical hits.	60	0	0	No	180	0
Specialization: Ranger								
Summon Wolf	7	The Ranger calls a great forest wolf to fight alongside the party.	0	50	5	No	60	0
Summon Bear	8	The Ranger calls a powerful bear to fight alongside the party.	0	50	5	No	90	0
Summon Spider	10	The Ranger calls a large spider to fight alongside the party.	0	50	5	No	120	0
Master Ranger	12	The Ranger has learned to summon stronger companion animals. Animals summoned by a Master Ranger are significantly more powerful in combat than their normal counterparts.	0	0	0	No	0	0
Specialization: Legionnaire Scout								
Mark of the Legion	20	Life in the Legion of the Dead is difficult, but those who manage to survive develop great fortitude, gaining large bonuses to strength and constitution (strength +10, constitution +10).	Passive	0	0	No	0	0
Strength of Stone	22	Through will alone, a legionnaire can become as implacable as the stone of the Deep Roads. When activated, the legionnaire becomes immune to damage or knockdown effects for a moderate time.	60	0	0	No	60	0
Endure Hardship	25	What is pain to one who is already dead? For as long as this mode is active, the legionnaire's health is unaffected by damage, which depletes stamina instead.	0	60	10	No	60	0
Blessing of the Ancestors	28	Long days among the veins of unrefined lyrium in the Deep Roads have given the legionnaire the ability to resist magic. While Strength of Stone is active, the character is also immune to spells, whether hostile or friendly.	0	0	0	No	0	0

Talent Name	Prerequisite Level	Description	Cost (mana /stamina)	Upkeep (mana /stamina)	Fatigue (% mana/stamina)	Ranged	Cooldown (sec.)	Area of Effect Radius (ft.)
		Specialization: Shadow						
Shadow Form	20	While this mode is active, the shadow flits in and out of concealment. Because enemies cannot concentrate on the character, each hit reduces their interest in the attacker. This mode consumes stamina continuously.	0	50	10	No	10	0
Decoy	22	The shadow is a master of misdirection, creating a personal decoy that keeps enemies occupied for a short time while the actual character escapes in stealth.	60	0	0	No	45	0
Deep Striking	25	The shadow has become more experienced in ambush and deception, gaining a large bonus to backstab damage while using Shadow Form as well as a permanent bonus to melee critical chance (critical chance +5).	Passive	0	0	No	0	0
Pandemonium	28	The shadow releases an airborne toxin that confuses all enemies within range, causing them to either flee or attack a random target, whether friend or foe.	80	0	0	No	90	5

Gear

Daggers are a natural weapon for a rogue to use, given their high speed, armor penetration, and critical chance. Other one-handed weapons work well too, but you won't be able to dual wield them until you reach Dual-Weapon Mastery at 36 dexterity. And definitely dual wield, even if it's not something you planned to spec in, because another weapon never hurts.

Carry a bow in the backup weapon slot and make good use of it. You need to build dexterity anyway for the Dual Weapon school, so you might as well use it to complement a bow, right?

There's more rogue gear than you could ever hope to equip in a single play. The general rule of thumb is to wait for loot that serves as an upgrade and snatch it up. If you have extra coin to buy a nice gear upgrade, feel free to spend away, though most of the low-level equipment will be easily replaced by future loot, and the high-level equipment is very expensive (generally bought before a run at the Mother).

 NOTE

In *Awakening*, it's out with the old and in with the new. As you journey toward level 35, here are some key items to seek out. Keep in mind that ideal gear varies based on your play style and role in the party. If, for example, you want a high-damage rogue, look for strength/dexterity bonuses and melee crit. If your rogue does a lot of tanking, high constitution and defense are your treasured traits. We've suggested excellent possibilities in each item category. For more possibilities and complete stats on each item, see the Equipment chapter.

Ideal Rogue Equipment

Item Type	Item 1	Item 2
Greatsword / Longsword	Vigilance	Dragonbrand
Daggers	Voice of Velvet	—
Longbows	Heartwood Bow	Misery
Crossbows	Longshot	—
Kite Shields	Landsmeet Shield	Heartwood Shield
Tower Shields	Partha	—
Light Chest Armor	Vest of the Nimble	Rainswept
Light Helmets	Cap of the Nimble	—
Light Boots	Blackblade Boots	Wolf Treads
Light Gloves	The Slippery Ferret's Gloves	—
Amulets	Nature's Blessing	Scout's Medal
Belts	Doge's Dodger	Wasp's Sting
Rings	Ring of Subtlety	Ring of Severity

The Rogue

Basics ~ **Classes** ~ The Party ~ Companions ~ Supporting Cast ~ Equipment ~ Bestiary ~ Walkthrough ~ Side Quests ~ Random Encounters ~ Achievements/Trophies

Party Responsibilities

Are you the party's damage-dealer or scout? If you're DPS-focused, your primary responsibility is dealing melee or ranged damage. That generally means stocking up on offensive talents and gear. If you're picking a lot of locks and stealthing around, spread more points to the non-combat talents; think balance over cutthroat combat expertise. All rogues need to be aware of threat and avoid pulling too much at once. Learn to time your attacks so you don't draw too much threat but still deal significant damage to the enemy.

If your rogue is the main PC, the other three companions should fill in talents around you for a well-balanced party. If you're building up a companion rogue, look to fill in where the party is lacking. Not dealing enough damage? Crank up the offense. Want to avoid more traps and earn more treasure? Make sure you build up those nimble-fingered talents. In the final party configuration, your PC should play whatever role you have the most fun with while the other three companions add the components necessary to maximize your combat efficiency.

The rogue ranks very well in terms of armor, weapons, and all-purpose talents. Those talents and gear enable you to surprise your foes with killer damage, slip in and out of combat for great defense, and deal with non-combat dungeon obstacles (traps, locks) that other companions cannot. From whirlwind flair in a sea of armor to steady precision with lockpick tools, the rogue covers everything that warriors and mages can't—all with a wink and smile.

Role Models

With the game's best weapon talent trees, you can create dozens of rogues who each wield something a little different in combat. Don't feel constrained to play according to the following rogue models to the letter; take bits and pieces that appeal to your play style and add your own spin. However, these are basic models for a melee DPS rogue, ranged DPS rogue, and scout rogue. Each shows you how to choose your talents up to level 30, what talent chains are effective, how specializations fit in, and sample combat strategies for that model.

NOTE

If you create a new Grey Warden, you have 21 points to spend, which actually puts you one point ahead of these charts. So if you follow these charts, you'll have one extra point to spend on what you like.

TIP

In *Awakening*, some amazing new talents become available to you once you reach level 20. Although you can still choose from Origins talents, we recommend focusing on the new *Awakening* abilities as soon as you're able to add high-level talents.

Melee DPS Rogue Model

Level	Talent
0	Dirty Fighting
1	Below the Belt, Dual-Weapon Training
2	Dual Striking
3	Dual-Weapon Finesse
4	Combat Movement
5	Deadly Strike
6	Riposte
7	Mark of Death (Assassin)—*First Specialization Available at This Level*
8	Lethality
9	Dual-Weapon Expert
10	Coup de Grace
11	Cripple
12	Dual-Weapon Mastery
13	Punisher
14	Exploit Weakness (Assassin)—*Second Specialization Available at This Level*
15	Lacerate (Assassin)
16	Feast of the Fallen (Assassin)
17	Evasion
18	Feign Death
19	Dual-Weapon Sweep
20	Twin Strikes
21	Find Vitals
22	Shadow Form—*Third Specialization Available at This Level*
23	Decoy
24	Heartseeker
25	Ghost
26	Weak Points
27	Flicker
28	Low Blow
29	Deep Striking
30	Pandemonium

Overview: The name of the game is to deal damage quickly. Generally, Dual Weapon talents combined with the backstabbing Rogue talents work best.

Leveling: You begin with Dirty Fighting talent, an excellent starting skill and always useful. You can stun, then move behind the enemy to get in a couple of backstabs. This skill helps tremendously when you are forced to fight face-to-face, or for helping out a healer or teammate about to die.

primagames.com

Spending Your Melee DPSer's Attribute Points

When you start a new character in *Awakening*, you have 62 attribute points to spend on your level 18 character. Depending on how you want to play your character and what skills/spells you take, you may spend more or less points on individual attribute scores, but this is a good base model for a melee DPSer's initial points distribution:

- **Strength:** 14 points
- **Dexterity:** 26 points
- **Willpower:** 12 points
- **Constitution:** 10 points

Below the Belt gives you a decent attack that can slow down enemies so they can't escape or can't pursue. Dual-Weapon Training starts the first Dual Weapon chain, which will be your primary focus. Continue your Dual Weapon basics with Dual Striking and Dual-Weapon Finesse. Make sure you take Improved Combat Training by this point.

Next, Combat Movement presents a wider flanking area to produce backstabs easier. In the bigger fights with bodies all bunched together, it's difficult to get directly behind a target in time, so this helps a lot. Next, pick up Deadly Strike as a precursor to Lethality and extra armor penetration. Then, pick up Riposte to add another stun to your arsenal. With Coup de Grace, you prevent damage to your party while hacking away for criticals.

Once you gain your specialization, you could go with Duelist, but Assassin concentrates on damage, and that's your priority. Mark of Death increases all damage against a single target. It's perfect against bosses and tougher foes that require that special touch.

The passive talent Lethality increases your critical chance and converts cunning to strength for damage purposes. Dual-Weapon Expert adds even more critical chance. You need 26 dexterity and Expert Combat Training by this point.

Coup de Grace and Cripple pile on the damage with more chances for backstabs and critical hits. Top off your two Dual Weapon chains with Dual-Weapon Mastery and Punisher. You can deal with huge threats now, wield full-sized weapons in both hands, use more talents because your stamina costs are reduced, and punish an opponent with three crushing blows. You must have 36 dexterity and Master Combat Training by now.

Complete your Assassin specialization: Exploit Weaknesses increases your damage potential by finding holes in your enemy's defenses, Lacerate gives you a damage-over-time effect, and Feast of the Fallen replenishes your stamina with every kill.

Now that you've nearly maxed out your offense, add a little defense with Evasion and Feign Death. You can always gain these defensive talents earlier if you find yourself hit a lot in combat. With a good party, though, you probably want to favor the offense. At this point, you may have an extra point to spend as you like.

You can finish up your talents through level 20 with virtually anything you want. Here we'll add Dual-Weapon Sweep and Twin Strikes. Twin Strikes lands two critical hits in a row, and when you combine it with level 21's Find Vitals, which improves melee critical chance by 10 and melee critical damage by 20, you deal massive hits.

Start the Shadow specialization at level 22 with Shadow Form, followed by Decoy at level 23. Shadow Form allows the shadow to flit in and out of concealment, making you harder to hit. Decoy keeps enemies occupied while the shadow escapes.

At level 24, switch to the new Rogue chain and buy them all in succession: Heartseeker (level 24), Ghost (level 25), Weak Points (level 26), and Flicker (level 27). Heartseeker adds more offense, Ghost may be your best defense, Weak Points improves all melee talents, and Flicker deals backstabs to all foes in a targeted area.

Pick another Dual Weapon talent at level 28, Low Blow.

Finish with two more Shadow specialization talents: Deep Striking at level 29 grants a large bonus to backstab damage and melee critical chance. Finally, Pandemonium at level 30 confuses all enemies within range.

Talent Choices: Melee DPS tends toward Dual Weapon talents as a natural fit. You can dabble in the cunning Rogue talents, but to maximize your offensive potential, stick with most, if not all, of the dexterity Rogue talents.

Specialization: Assassin is all about enough damage to kill targets before they kill you. It's possible to go with the Duelist specialization as well, if you want a little defense mixed in with your offense, but for all-out DPS, Assassin slays the competition.

Battle Tactics: Wait a few seconds for the tank and other companions to engage the enemy. Angle into the fight from the side or rear, and always position yourself for a backstab attempt. In general, you want to help the tank eliminate his prime adversary, but if you see targets of opportunity with half health or less, make quick work of them.

Based on the position and number of foes, select your attacks appropriately. Tank's target putting up a fight? Hit from behind with Coup de Grace and Punisher. Enemy turning its attention on you? Stun it with Dirty Fighting or Riposte, or slow it down with Cripple so you can escape. Boss lumbering into view? Hit it with Mark of Death so everyone piles on extra damage.

The Rogue

Basics ~ **Classes** ~ The Party ~ Companions ~ Supporting Cast ~ Equipment ~ Bestiary ~ Walkthrough ~ Side Quests ~ Random Encounters ~ Achievements/Trophies

Ranged DPS Rogue Model

Level	Talent
0	Dirty Fighting
1	Pinning Shot, Rapid Shot
2	Below the Belt
3	Crippling Shot
4	Shattering Shot
5	Deadly Strike
6	Critical Shot
7	Suppressing Fire—*First Specialization Available at This Level*
8	Lethality
9	Scattershot
10	Arrow of Slaying
11	Melee Archer
12	Aim
13	Defensive Fire
14	Master Archer—*Second Specialization Available at This Level*
15	Dueling (Duelist)
16	Upset Balance (Duelist)
17	Keen Defense (Duelist)
18	Pinpoint Strike (Duelist)
19	Deft Hands
20	Accuracy
21	Arrow Time
22	Burst Shot—*Third Specialization Available at This Level*
23	Rain of Arrows
24	Heartseeker
25	Ghost
26	Weak Points
27	Flicker
28	Improved Tools
29	Mechanical Expertise
30	Device Mastery

Overview: Much like an offensive mage, a ranged DPS rogue concentrates weapons and talents on enemies at a distance. He focuses on the  Archery school, and may dip into some talents, such as the Duelist specialization, when melee becomes imminent.

Leveling: You begin with Dirty Fighting. It's not ideal for range, but very helpful when an enemy closes on you and you need a quick stun to get your distance again. As you'll be working with a bow, load up on dexterity.

Spending Your Ranged DPSer's Attribute Points

When you start a new character in *Awakening*, you have 62 attribute points to spend on your level 18 character. Depending on how you want to play your character and what skills/spells you take, you may spend more or less points on individual attribute scores, but this is a good base model for a ranged DPSer's initial points distribution:

- **Strength:** 10 points
- **Dexterity:** 30 points
- **Willpower:** 12 points
- **Constitution:** 10 points

With your first two talent points, choose Pinning Shot and Rapid Shot. You now can hamper someone's movement with Pinning Shot or reload much faster with Rapid Shot. Below the Belt gives you another melee talent, which also helps you avoid prolonged face-to-face encounters.

Gain the Improved Combat Training skill and start working on the next tier of talents. Crippling Shot hampers a foe's offense and defense, while Shattering Shot and Deadly Strike put holes in enemy's armor.

If you have 21 dexterity and Expert Combat Training, select Critical Shot. If you hit, Critical Shot inflicts critical damage and a bonus to armor penetration. Follow that up with Suppressing Fire at the next level to further encumber targets with attack penalties.

Purchase Lethality. It's an all-around excellent ability: it increases the critical chance for all attacks and possibly replaces cunning for strength when considering damage bonuses.

You reach your first pinnacle with Scattershot. This awesome talent automatically stuns your target and deals normal damage, then splinters off and does the same to all nearby enemies. Use this effectively against enemy spellcasters or large enemy groups to impede flanking attempts.

If you can reach 30 dexterity, you gain Arrow of Slaying. This scores an automatic critical hit against all but high-level opponents.

At this point, concentrate on the Melee Archer chain. Melee Archer prevents attacks from interrupting your firing, while Aim and Defensive Fire provide offensive and defensive oriented bonuses, respectively. Finish the chain with Master Archer. You can fire arrows while taking damage, gain bonuses to offense and damage, slow the rate of fire to gain bonuses to defense, and bulk up almost all your Archery talents with Master Archer. This skill also allows the rogue to wear heavy armor without attack speed penalties.

Now it's time for some melee talents in case enemies get close. Dueling and Pinpoint Strike ratchet up your offense while Upset Balance and Keen Defense ensure you won't go down so easily with swords and claws flying.

At level 19, dip into the cunning Rogue talent, with one point for lockpicking's Deft Hands. If you aren't pure ranged DPS, you'll want these talents earlier, and you'll pick up the rest of lockpicking at the end with Improved Tools at level 28, Mechanical Expertise at level 29, and Device Mastery at level 30.

When you reach level 20, go right for the new Archery talents. Level 20's Accuracy improves all your bow stats, level 21's Arrow Time slows down enemies around you, level 22's Burst Shot scores three successive critical hits, and level 23's Rain of Arrows delivers much needed AoE damage.

At level 24, it's time for the new Rogue talents. Pick these up in a row, starting with Heartseeker at level 24 for a potent melee attack, Ghost at level 25 for a great escape talent, Weak Points at level 26 for added damage, and Flicker at level 27 for a backstab explosion against multiple foes.

Talent Choices: The Archery school and all its ranged surprises are your go-to talents. Duelist provides some melee talents in case an enemy gets close enough to grab you.

Specialization: The Dueling sustained ability gives a bonus to attack while active. Upset Balance can slow an enemy's movement speed and hinder its defense. The passive Keen Defense does just that: add a permanent bonus to defense. Your top melee talent, Pinpoint Strike, converts all hits into critical strikes for a moderate duration.

Battle Tactics: Once the battle begins, stand your ground. Let the tank and other melee DPSers embrace the enemy. You want to nuke them from afar. Unlike a mage who stays in the rear, however, the ranged DPS rogue can enter melee with his better armor, weapons, and Duelist talents at higher levels.

Survey the battlefield and pick your targets wisely. Concentrate fire on the tank's target to bring it down quicker, or look for injured foes that you can drop with an arrow or two. If you see an enemy spellcaster in the enemy's rear, make it your priority. You don't want it getting off damaging spells. Same goes for enemy archers. If your melee companions can't reach them, it's your job to stop them from pelting the team with damage.

On offense, your rotation goes something like this: Aim, Pinning Shot (against moving targets), Critical Shot (against near-dead targets), and Arrow of Slaying. On defense, go Defensive Fire, Crippling Shot, Suppressing Fire, and Scattershot (especially against enemy spellcasters or enemies charging at you).

As a ranged DPS rogue, you have much of the offense of a DPS mage, yet you still can wear most of the better armor and use high-quality weapons. Keep on the go to avoid enemy melee encounters and let your companions wade through the blood and limbs.

Scout Rogue Model

Level	Talent
0	Dirty Fighting
1	Deft Hands, Stealth
2	Dual-Weapon Training
3	Combat Movement
4	Improved Tools
5	Dual-Weapon Finesse
6	Dual Striking
7	Song of Valor (Bard)—*First Specialization Available at This Level*
8	Mechanical Expertise
9	Dual-Weapon Expert
10	Distraction (Bard)
11	Song of Courage (Bard)
12	Device Mastery
13	Captivating Song (Bard)
14	Dual-Weapon Mastery—*Second Specialization Available at This Level*
15	Riposte
16	Coup de Grace
17	Feign Death
18	Cripple
19	Punisher
20	Stealthy Item Use
21	Combat Stealth
22	Master Stealth—*Third Specialization Available at This Level*
23	Shadow Form (Shadow)
24	Decoy (Shadow)
25	Deep Striking (Shadow)
26	Twin Strikes
27	Find Vitals
28	Pandemonium (Shadow)
29	Low Blow
30	Unending Flurry

Overview: A master thief slinks through the shadows and opens locked doors with a flick of the wrist. A scout rogue can DPS well, but knows more than a thing or two about the business of treasure and traps.

Leveling: From the start, lean toward your key noncombat talents, Deft Hands (for lockpicking and trap detection) and Stealth (for hiding invisibly). The Deft Hands chain is your priority: you want to be able to open locked doors and chests, and it will take up to Device Mastery to open anything that comes your way.

The Rogue

Basics ~ **Classes** ~ The Party ~ Companions ~ Supporting Cast ~ Equipment ~ Bestiary ~ Walkthrough ~ Side Quests ~ Random Encounters ~ Achievements/Trophies

Spending Your Scout's Attribute Points

When you start a new character in *Awakening*, you have 62 attribute points to spend on your level 18 character. Depending on how you want to play your character and what skills/spells you take, you may spend more or less points on individual attribute scores, but this is a good base model for a scout's initial points distribution:

- **Strength:** 12 points
- **Dexterity:** 20 points
- **Willpower:** 12 points
- **Cunning:** 8 points
- **Constitution:** 10 points

Begin on your offense with Dual-Weapon Training and Combat Movement. The following level, pick up Improved Tools to further enhance your lockpicking and trap detection. With this build, you should increase cunning and dexterity to unlock all the necessary talents.

Continue your offense with Dual-Weapon Finesse and Dual Striking. The big penalties to your off-hand weapon will be gone, and you now can attack with a two-hit combo.

Grab the Bard specialization. Song of Valor provides regeneration to mana and stamina, which always proves useful after a long battle. Next, you gain the third lockpicking rank with Mechanical Expertise. You will need 18 cunning.

To become a Dual-Weapon Expert, make sure you have 26 dexterity and Expert Combat Training. Your critical chance increases, and you may inflict lacerations that cause enemies to bleed more damage over time.

Continue down the Bard path. Distraction is a single-target stun, while Song of Courage improves the party's attack, damage, and critical chance scores.

If you have 22 cunning, welcome to the ultimate lockpicking and trap detection talent: Device Mastery. You will never fail to open a locked door or chest (unless it requires a special key), or to detect a trap and disarm it.

You can cap out two more key talent chains. First, the Bard's Captivating Song is the rogue's finest crowd control talent if you have the stamina to use it properly. Dual-Weapon Mastery finishes off your expertise with two weapons, including wielding full-sized weapons if you like.

Now you can fill out talents as desired. Here we went with Riposte and Coup de Grace next for more stunning and backstabbing. Feign Death and Cripple give you options to remove yourself from combat if you have too much threat on you. Punisher gives you a powerful finishing move.

At level 20, Stealthy Item Use improves your stealth to the second rank. Follow with Combat Stealth at level 21 and Master Stealth at level 22.

The new shadow specialization fits in well at level 23. Shadow Form defends the rogue by decreasing threat with each hit against you. Level 24's Decoy also increases defense

with an illusionary doppelganger that seizes the enemy's attention while you slip away in shadow. Level 25's Deep Striking sees you slip out of shadow for attacks and increases backstab damage and critical chance. Finish off the Shadow chain at level 28 with Pandemonium. The talent confuses nearby enemies and forces them to either flee or attack a random target.

At level 26, start in on the new Dual Weapon talents. Level 26's Twin Strikes lands two critical hits, while level 27's Find Vitals increases your melee critical stats. At level 29, Low Blow cuts movement and attack speeds of a foe and will drop them to the ground if previously struck by Twin Strikes. Your final talent at level 30, Unending Flurry, repeatedly stabs a target until you miss or run out of stamina.

Talent Choices: The Rogue cunning abilities come in the most handy, supported by its dexterity talents and some Dual Weapon conditioning.

Specialization: The Bard specialization may not produce extra damage, but it gives the rogue phenomenal control over enemies with the stuns Distraction and Captivating Song. The group buffs Song of Valor and Song of Courage raise the stats of the entire party. If you aren't worried about pure combat, the Bard specialization is the best option for helping out the entire party. The new shadow specialization aids primarily for personal defense, though you can attack out of the shadows for extra damage.

Battle Tactics: You don't have as much DPS as your other companions, so let the tank and other melee specialists roam out into the enemy crowds. You can slip into stealth and pick your best spot to enter combat. At higher levels, once you've stacked up a few Dual Weapon talents, you should hold your own against lesser enemy groups or a stronger one-on-one fight.

Your chief role will be crowd control. Once you have the Bard's Captivating Song at level 13, charge out just behind the tank or other DPSers. Activate Captivating Song once the enemy throng presses in. You won't be able to move, but all enemies within a moderate radius will be stunned unless they pass a mental resistance check every few seconds. Most mobs are susceptible to mental attacks, so the song is very effective. With the song active, you lose stamina over time, and when you hit zero, all enemies break loose. Build up your willpower if you plan on using Captivating Song a lot. By pinning enemies in place, you prevent incoming damage and allow your fellow companions ample free shots on the dazed enemies.

The Party

The name of the game should give you a clue that monstrous beasts are in store for you. From dungeon depths to snowy mountaintops, your four-person party will battle anything from devastating dragons to drooling darkspawn. Unless you want to end up as chew toys for ogres, hone up on the basics and learn expert party dynamics.

Buddy Basics

You begin your adventuring career on your own. As the story unfolds, you meet companions who join your party and become your allies in battle. A companion could be a mage such as Anders, or the unlikeliest of allies, Justice, a spirit from the Fade unexpectedly pulled back to the material world. It's up to you to decide which companions you travel with, because you can have only three companions at once. The rest remain behind at Vigil's Keep, a place easily reached from the world map that serves as haven for you and your companions, fully equipped with merchants and allies who may give you political advice or join you on future quests. Each time you leave the Vigil's Keep throne room, you can pick three new companions to accompany you, and in certain non-hostile regions, you can use the Party Configuration button on your top menu to immediately switch companions. For more on each companion, flip to the Companions chapter.

Group Dynamics

Each of the three classes has a distinct role in the party. In general, class roles fall into categories that take best advantage of class talents. However, be prepared to improvise at any given moment. For example, if you're a rogue bard intent on keeping a second monster away from the party and you see the first enemy about to defeat your tank, you may want to switch to offense and help out with the first enemy.

The party's main tank responsibilities fall on the shoulders of a warrior. His superior defense and ability to hold the mob's threat safeguard the group in the heat of battle. If the tank falls, it generally spells doom for the rest of the party as the enemies split and attack the more vulnerable companions. The warrior's primary job is to the hold the line and keep the enemy's attention on him at all times so that others can do their thing.

Every party needs a healer, and a mage has excellent spells for the job. When not healing, the mage can augment the party with stat-enhancing buffs. Mages can also focus on DPS, stacking up on a single target and AoE damage spells to obliterate whole enemy groups.

A rogue acts as the scout for the party. He slips into the shadows with stealth and recons the area for enemy positions, traps, treasure locations, and quest objectives. When going up against enemies, a rogue can hide until the opportune moment to dart in for a backstab. In the heat of battle, the rogue adds extra DPS to the fight with superior Dual Weapon talents and bonuses to critical hit chances.

As you adventure with the same team, you gain experience, loot, and better skills. Develop your team as a whole and not just individuals. For example, you don't need four party members with Herbalism. One person who's mastered Herbalism can supply all the potions, leaving the others free to spread out their points to other valuable skills. It's fine to have two party members with Poison-Making so they can both enhance their weapon DPS, but also try out Trap-Making, and leave crucial skill points open for your PC to put into Coercion and possibly Survival. At level 20 and higher, look toward Runecrafting to create weapon and armor runes, Vitality to pump up health, or Clarity to enhance your mana/stamina reserves. After a successful quest run, distribute your gear to the most appropriate characters. Don't always give the best items to your PC (though he or she should certainly get great loot whenever possible). It's much better to hand the top-notch armor to your tank than your rogue PC, and it makes little sense to give an accessory with magic bonus to your melee DPS character.

Buddy Basics ~ Combat Roles.

Basics ~ Classes ~ The Party ~ Companions ~ Supporting Cast ~ Equipment ~ Bestiary ~ Walkthrough ~ Side Quests ~ Random Encounters ~ Achievements/Trophies

Dealing with Threat

If anyone in your party does manage to pull threat, always make sure to run to the tank to have it picked up. Attempting to run away only increases the time it takes to get the mob pulled off, likely resulting in the character's death or even the whole party's. Monitor the threat from critical hits. If you land a couple of high critical strikes in a row, disengage for a second then reengage. Critical strikes increase your threat, so consider this when monitoring your threat output.

If you have an off-tank in a party, don't use the off-tank's threat-generating abilities unless a difficult enemy breaks from the main tank or the main tank dies. Pulling off of the main tank will interrupt his threat generation, and your healer may not have enough mana, or time, to heal both.

If the main tank loses threat, everyone in the party must disengage until he regains it. Use any threat-reducing abilities, such as the rogue's Feign Death, if you have them. Once the main tank picks the enemies back up, wait a few seconds for the tank to build threat, then reengage.

Healing

The party's healer will save or damn a group when an encounter gets hot and heavy. As a healer, you have to know when to launch your Group Heal, when to throw around a Heal or Regeneration, and when to avoid healing. In general, save your big heal to counteract large spike damage (unexpected damage that crits through a party members' defense for a significant amount of health), or if you desperately need to float a party member's health back up to a manageable level. Those levels will depend on the enemy's damage and how much backup healing and mana you have at your disposal, but you shouldn't panic unless a party member's health is consistently dropping below the one-third mark. Even then, the healer's main responsibility is to the tank, then himself. Keep the tank alive, even if it means losing a DPSer in the fight. If the tank falls, the whole party will most likely perish. A good rule of thumb is to never switch off the main tank unless another companion's health is dropping rapidly. If you have to heal elsewhere, switch to the party member that needs help, throw a single Heal or Regeneration, and return to the main tank immediately.

TIP

Don't always burn your healer's mana. You may need to pop a healing potion from time to time and save the healer's magic for tougher stretches of the fight. If it looks like a companion is going to die despite the heals, use your best health poultice to help you climb back up to full.

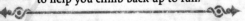

A healer definitely must learn when *not* to heal. Obviously, you must conserve your mana so you don't run out at a crucial time, but you must also look at the big picture. You only have so many heals you can throw around, and the majority will be directed at the tank. You don't want to let anyone drop, but if you find yourself limited, you may have to skip a heal or two that you would have normally cast and let everyone's health bars get much closer to zero. Unless you are cruising through an encounter, you should never heal a non-party member, such as a blue-circled ally or one of the ranger's summoned animals. These allies are expendable, and the ranger's pets can always be re-summoned.

Combat Roles

Each companion's role in a party will be different based on their spells, talents, and what you expect them to accomplish during the fight. As you level, choose the talents and spells that best fit your party configuration, and gear up appropriately. The following general strategies should work well for a tank, healer, mage DPS, general melee DPS, and general ranged DPS.

primagames.com

Tank

A tank doesn't muck around with fancy spells or dainty arrows; he charges at a foe and hacks at it with his weapon of choice. It's the tank's job to engage all enemies and direct their attention on him. Taunt abilities, such as Threaten and Taunt (of course!), increase threat against a target and force that target to become more hostile toward the tank; you can never get a foe mad enough as a tank, so load up the threat and keep those enemies foaming at the mouth! Also, keep aware of the ever-changing battlefield, because it only takes one stray mob to veer toward one of your fellow DPSers (even worse, a healer) to turn an otherwise controlled fight into a free-for-all. Make sure you rope in all the enemies so others are free to aid the party as they should. Because all the damage is focused on you, carry a lot of health poultices and the best gear you can scrounge up. Good gear will mitigate damage, making the healer's job easier and allowing you to go longer in fights, especially boss fights and ones where you handle several foes at once.

Healer

Harnessing great magical powers, a mage healer's primary role is that of savior in a group. They can deal some damage to enemies, but their focus is keeping the party members, and primarily the tank, alive. The tank is the first priority because he is the keystone of your assault—without him, the group quickly falls apart. The healer may also apply buffs (bonuses) to their party that help them do more damage or defend better. One skill a healer needs to master is where to stand and when to move. Most of their magic requires them to remain motionless, yet on some fights, the party can be spread out so the healer needs to move to get within range. The healer has to balance running around and leaving enough time to heal everyone who needs it, while keeping the tank alive. Anyone can stand in one spot and heal. A truly skilled healer can move, heal, and buff with ease. Remember to watch your mana, and if you have to make tough choices, keep the tank alive first and yourself second. A dead healer is no use to the party.

Mage DPS

Some mages incinerate their enemies from afar, others freeze them solid or crumble the earth down around them. The end result is always the same: mass destruction. Their damage makes them extremely valuable in a party, but they also need to control their power, allowing the tank enough time to build up threat before they unleash their destruction. DPS mages do so much damage in such a spectacular way that they often attract unwanted attention. If an opponent gets too close, the mage, wearing only basic robes, could be done for. Mage spells also have decent range. If a mage stands far from the tank and draws the monster's threat, it becomes harder for fellow companions to save the mage. So the mage needs to stand in the right spot and learn the right spell timing. It often is not about how fast one can cast, but knowing when to cast.

Melee DPS

The rogue DPS character, or the non-tank warrior DPSer, relies on cunning and savagery to take down his target as quickly as possible. Melee DPSers are not built for long one-on-one fights like a tank, nor can they usually handle large groups of foes; however, they are excellent damage-dealers who offer support DPS in a party. After the tank engages and holds threat, a rogue DPSer can prowl unseen behind the enemy, then unleash crippling backstab blows to stagger the opponent. A warrior DPSer can dish out damage on the tank's target, then grab threat on a stray creature if it breaks from the pack. Because melee DPS characters have the talents to deal huge damage very quickly (especially critical strikes), they must be extremely careful not to pull threat away from the party's tank. This usually means holding back and not running through the best regimen of combos, except on boss fights or with one creature left standing. You may also choose to slow down your combos so you don't trigger them as quickly. Depending on your skill choices, a melee DPSer can add even more support damage through Runecrafting, Poison-Making, Trap-Making, or certain usable items. A competent and poised melee DPSer can be the difference in your party between a long, drawn-out fight that teeters on the edge of failure and a quick, efficient boss execution.

Ranged DPS

Lightly armored but fast, the ranged DPS character adds similar firepower to the party as a mage DPS character. They can close and deal melee damage, but they are at their best when firing a barrage of arrows from afar. In addition to dealing out damage, the ranged DPSer can snare (slow down movement), stun opponents, and set up defensive fire. Because ranged DPSers have few ways to eliminate the threat they generate, they need to remain focused on when to attack and how hard to attack any given opponent. It is critical to their survival and group success that the monster stays focused on the tank. Make sure to bring health poultices to heal yourself and avoid getting the attention of the mobs.

NOTE

See the Classes chapter for how to spec each of the classes to exactly what you need to satisfy your party's demands.

Configurations and Engagement

The ideal party depends on a number of factors: nature of the encounter, size of the enemy group, play style, and more. Here are four configurations that serve in many all-purpose situations.

Balanced

- Warrior (Tank)
- Mage (Healing)
- Rogue (Scouting, DPS)
- Mage or Warrior (DPS)

Blitzkrieg

- Warrior (Tank)
- Warrior (Off-Tank)
- Mage (Healing)
- Rogue (DPS)

Control

- Warrior (Tank)
- Mage (Healing)
- Rogue (DPS)
- Mage (Crowd Control)

Unbalanced

- Warrior (Tank)
- Warrior (DPS, Off-Tank)
- Warrior (Ranged)
- Mage (Healer)

A balanced party contains a warrior as the tank, mage as the healer, rogue as the scout, and mage or warrior as support. This configuration spreads the talents around and prepares the group for any challenge. Some abilities overlap, which helps in cases where a companion may be overwhelmed at a critical time, or has already fallen in battle.

The "blitzkrieg" configuration emphasizes speed and damage over healing or defense. You carry at least two tanks on the team, a combat-oriented rogue for more damage and some light healing with a mage who also has offensive spells at his fingertips. This type of party plans to rip through one enemy group before a second can engage them; they don't have the defenses for prolonged fighting, so it's got to be swift or not at all.

Engagement 1: Enemy Group

The tank waits for the enemy front line and engages the toughest creature, or the center of an enemy swarm. His job is to hold threat from as many creatures as possible and deal damage as he can. The two DPS characters swing out and attack from the flank (or rear in the case of a rogue). Their jobs are to deal as much damage as possible, without drawing too much threat. The healer holds position in the rear and casts heals as needed to keep the party intact. In general, each companion should target the enemies the tank has and pick off the weakest ones first to reduce the enemy numbers against you.

A party that concentrates on control stands behind healing and crowd control abilities. You still need a warrior tank, and you need a dedicated healer, which falls to a spirit healer mage. The rogue lays down a lot of DPS, but must be flexible enough to off-tank once in a while or throw out some crowd control (such as a bard's Captivating Song). A second mage brings offense to the table, of course, but also spells like Grease and Crushing Prison that can slow or stop extra enemies from engaging. This particular party may enter long fights, battling for continued periods of time with solid healing and abilities that dictate when enemies confront them.

primagames.com

An unbalanced party may not share abilities optimally, but can be a lot of fun nevertheless. The idea is to overbalance with a single class or strategy and pursue it to the max. You can generally get away with any combination, so long as you have a mage healer in the mix (parties without a healer won't do well unless you have unlimited health poultices at your disposal, and that gets very expensive). In this example, we have three warriors, fully armed and armored, who can charge into melee if there aren't any ranged threats, or engage and leave one warrior back to shoot down targets at range and act as bodyguard for the healer in the rear. A three-warrior group dishes out tremendous damage and has serious defensive resilience, even if it lacks the finesse of a rogue's touch or the all-out AoE firepower of a DPS mage.

We all know that the perfect combination of party members doesn't automatically means success. You have to apply your skills and react quickly to the challenges that will inevitably assault you during quests. Smart parties will identify which jobs they can handle and which they can't, and as long as you dodge or control the additional enemies that wander in your direction, your team will thrive in style.

Engagement 2: Boss Fight

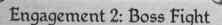

The tank waits for the boss to approach, or charges in if the boss has ranged attacks. His job is to keep the boss's attention focused on him and deal damage when he can. The two DPS characters swing out and attack from the flank (or rear in the case of a rogue). Their jobs are to deal as much damage as possible, without drawing too much threat. The healer holds position in the rear and casts heals as needed to keep the party intact, mainly healing the tank who will likely take big damage spikes from the boss. In general, each companion should go all-out with their best talents/spells as long as they don't pull the boss off the tank. Note that this strategy works the same for a single enemy of any kind; it will just fall that much faster if it's not a boss.

Let's take a look at a sample fight with a tank (warrior), healer (mage) and two DPSers (rogue, mage DPS). You've cleared a path to the boss, and now it's time to take the ugly mug down. Before you launch the first attack, make sure all characters have the proper gear, usable items, and talents ready to go.

As the tank readies his weapon, the healer throws a precautionary Regeneration on him, which serves as a little extra health at the start of the battle and absorbs a few shots. Only

then does the tank charge in and hit the boss with Taunt, or whack him a few times to activate Threaten, to draw the monster's attention for the first few seconds.

The mage DPSer holds his ground. He will out-damage the tank if he rains down destruction alongside the tank. The rogue circles behind the boss to get into backstab position (but not close enough for the boss to strike him with AoE attacks). The tank rolls into his offensive routine, smacking the boss with his best chain of attacks.

After three or four attacks from the tank, it's the DPSers' turn. The mage begins his offensive rotation of spells, while the rogue darts in and backstabs the boss. The rogue continues the assault until the boss turns its attacks on him.

TIP

Let the tank attack twice for every one of the DPSer's attacks unless you're in a position to finish off the boss very quickly.

If this were a full group instead of a single enemy, the roles would stay the same, except the party would generally concentrate damage on the weakest foe to reduce the numbers quicker. If there was a dangerous foe on the battlefield—for example, a genlock emissary casting spells—charge it with your tank and DPSer, unless the ranged DPSers can take it out.

Engagement 3: Strategic Retreat

Given time, all companions retreat to defensive positions in a doorway, corridor, or even a corner. If there isn't time, the tank holds the line with as many creatures as possible, while the group positions itself away from the swarm. If the tank can slowly retreat near the party, he should do so; otherwise, all other companions use single-target ranged attacks. The tank's job is still to hold threat from as many creatures as possible and deal damage. The two DPS characters use ranged attacks, or may be forced to do the best they can head-to-head in melee with creatures. The healer holds position in the rear and casts heals as needed to keep the party intact. In general, each companion should focus on the tank's targets and pick off the weakest ones first to reduce the enemy numbers against you.

Configurations and Engagement - Tactics

Basics ~ Classes ~ **The Party** ~ Companions ~ Supporting Cast ~ Equipment ~ Bestiary ~ Walkthrough ~ Side Quests ~ Random Encounters ~ Achievements/Trophies

With the tank dealing steady damage, the mage and rogue supporting as DPSers, and the healer concentrating heals and regenerations on the tank to keep him healthy, the party will take down the boss after a short fight. If the boss pulls out AoE attacks, or brings in enemy allies, the healer should cast Group Heal when possible to keep everyone's health up.

It's important for every member of the group to keep the self buffs, group buffs, and debuffs up at all times! If it's about to drop, refresh it and continue your DPS on the boss. Group buffs/debuffs can have a dramatic effect over the course of a battle. Remember: Damage-reducing and damage-mitigating buffs can translate directly into heals and mana saved for your healer over the course of a fight.

In the end, a team playing the right roles will conquer dozens of enemies.

Tactics

Tactics are not just about figuring out the correct movement and attack procedure in a battle. In *Dragon Age: Origins—Awakening* the Tactics screen is a tool used to customize your party's actions and reactions based on the current combat situation. Spend skill points in Combat Tactics to unlock more tactic slots, which can be used to customize behavior patterns in various predicaments. If you aren't controlling certain party members directly or you want to play in real time, tactics are an excellent tool.

◆ TIP ◆

Even if you plan to always control your characters, there will be times in long battles where you can't manage them all at once, and tactics will kick into action. Set them anyway!

In the Tactics menu, each character has base preset options and behavior patterns from which to choose. First, set these to the appropriate play style for each character. For example, you should probably set your tank with a "defender" preset and a "defensive" or "default" behavior mode. A ranged DPSer might have an "archer" preset and "ranged" behavior mode.

After the base preset and behavior mode is selected, each character has a number of customizable slots, which really open up your combat options. The first tactic slot will be the first priority and so on down the slots in descending priority order. You can choose options that affect your self, ally, enemy, individual party member, or controlled party member. Tactics can trigger actions based on status (rooted, slowed, grabbing, movement impaired), health percentages, mana or stamina levels, armor type, type of attack, surrounded by enemies, and more. Once conditions are met, you can deactivate and activate whatever combination of talent/spells you desire. For example, you can set one slot to check if you are surrounded by at least

two enemies and then activate Captivating Song, or set your final slot to switch to your melee weapon if all spell options are exhausted. Remember to save your new preset as a Custom save for future use.

Basic Tactics

Choose the following options for the basic tactic combos. Experiment with various conditions to get exactly what you want on the battlefield.

- **Attack:** Enemy, condition (such as nearest or magic-using), Attack (or activate a specific talent/spell)

- **Defense:** Self, condition (such as low health or being attacked), Use Ability or Use Mode (any defensive talent or spell)

- **Aid Ally:** Ally, condition (such as low health or being attacked), Use Ability or Use Mode (any defensive talent or spell)

- **Use Potion (or any item):** Self, condition (such as Health < 50%), Use health poultice (most powerful or least powerful)

Let's take a look at how you could program a balanced party of warrior (tank), mage (healer), rogue (DPS and crowd control), and mage (ranged DPS):

primagames.com

Warrior (Tank)

Preset: Defender

Behavior: Defensive

1. **Enemy:** Rank = Normal (Peon's Plight)
2. **Enemy:** Nearest Visible Mage (Holy Smite)
3. **Self:** Any (Activate: Threaten)
4. **Self:** Being attacked by a ranged attack (Activate: Shield Cover)
5. **Self:** Surrounded by at least two enemies (War Cry)
6. **Enemy:** Health >= 50% (Overpower)

1. Start every fight determining which normal creature needs to die if you have the Peon's Plight talent. A successful attack automatically kills a target of normal or lesser rank, and inflicts critical hits against lieutenants and bosses. Normal spellcasters are prime targets for your opening move.

2. This warrior is also a templar. Whenever he spots an enemy mage, he casts Holy Smite to smack the spellcaster with spirit damage and drain the caster's mana.

3. The warrior activates Threaten at the start of each battle to direct all future threat at himself.

4. If enemies are attacking at range, the warrior activates Shield Cover (instead of standard Shield Defense).

5. This warrior is a champion. When surrounded by more than a single enemy, he triggers War Cry. If he also has Superiority, this combination may knock enemies off their feet in addition to buffing companions.

6. Against a moderately healthy opponent, the warrior tries Overpower second to chip away at health.

NOTE

At higher levels, replace Threaten with Grievous Insult and Overpower with Massacre for a truly deadly warrior.

Mage (Healer)

Preset: Healer

Behavior: Defensive

1. **Self:** Being attacked by a melee or ranged attack (Activate: Fade Shield)
2. **Self:** Mana or Stamina < 50% (Group Heal)
3. **Self:** Mana or Stamina < 25% (Use Lyrium Potion)
4. **Self:** Health < 75% (Heal)
5. **Self:** Health < 75% (Regenerate)
6. **Ally:** Health < 75% (Heal)
7. **Ally:** Health < 75% (Regenerate)
8. **Ally:** Mana or Stamina < 25% (Rejuvenate)
9. **Enemy:** Target using ranged or magic attack (Earthquake)
10. **Enemy:** Target of Justice (Switch to ranged weapon)

1. If an enemy targets the healer, she will activate Fade Shield for a significant chance to resist hostile spells or evade physical attacks.

2. This is a timer effect. You don't want to cast Group Heal early in the fight or it will be mostly useless. Once the healer's mana drops below 50 percent, the tactics will check to cast Group Heal. As soon as its available for the rest of the battle (unless the healer gains mana above 50 percent), Group Heal goes off.

3. Once the healer's mana drops below 25 percent, the healer quaffs a lyrium potion to replenish mana.

4. The healer checks for damage on herself. If health is below 75 percent, she casts Heal on herself.

5. If Heal isn't available due to cooldown, or the healer's health is still below 75 percent, she casts Regenerate on herself.

6. The healer checks for damage on an ally. If health is below 75 percent, she casts Heal on the ally.

7. If Heal isn't available due to cooldown, or the ally's health is still below 75 percent, she casts Regenerate on the ally.

8. If an ally's mana or stamina drops below 25%, the healer casts Rejuvenate to replenish mana or stamina.

9. If all healing options are clear, the healer switches into offensive mode and casts Earthquake (or your favorite AoE spell) at a ranged or magic-wielding enemy. Avoid casting on melee targets or else you may catch your party members in the AoE. To counteract this problem, you can switch to a single-target spell such as Stonefist.

10. If mana is exhausted, or there are no ranged enemy targets, the healer uses her staff to fire at the tank's enemy.

Tactics

Basics ~ Classes ~ **The Party** ~ Companions ~ Supporting Cast ~ Equipment ~ Bestiary ~ Walkthrough ~ Side Quests ~ Random Encounters ~ Achievements/Trophies

Rogue (DPS)

Preset: Scrapper
Behavior: Default
1. **Self:** Any (Venom)
2. **Self:** Any (Dueling)
3. **Enemy:** Target of Justice (Pinpoint Strike)
4. **Enemy:** Target rank is elite or higher (Upset Balance)
5. **Self:** Being attacked by a melee attack (Dirty Fighting)
6. **Enemy:** Target of Justice (Attack)

1. The rogue coats his weapon with poison at the start of the fight for extra DPS.

2. The rogue is a duelist. He activates Dueling for added bonuses.

3. Once he is in position, the rogue will attack the tank's target with a series of critical blows.

4. If the enemy is ranked above the normal foe, the rogue will try to stun the foe with Upset Balance.

5. If an enemy attacks the rogue in melee, he'll stun it with Dirty Fighting.

6. When he's out of special options, the rogue will always attack the tank's target.

Mage (DPS)

Preset: Damager
Behavior: Ranged
1. **Self:** Surrounded by at least two enemies (Repulsion Field)
2. **Enemy:** Target using magic attack (Crushing Prison)
3. **Enemy:** Target between medium and long range (Fireball)
4. **Enemy:** Target rank is elite or higher (Paralyze)
5. **Enemy:** Target using magic attack (Mana Drain)
6. **Enemy:** Nearest visible (Lightning)
7. **Enemy:** Nearest visible (Arcane Bolt)

1. If surrounded by more than a single enemy, the mage defends himself with this spell. Waves of repulsive energy emanate from the mage, which knock back nearby enemies unless they pass a physical resistance check.

2. If a foe is using a magic attack, the mage attempts to root it with Crushing Prison.

3. The mage casts a medium- or long-range Fireball at the enemy.

4. If a foe is ranked higher than normal level, and Crushing Prison failed, is on cooldown, or there is a second opponent who fulfills the conditions, the mage attempts to root it with Paralyze.

5. If the mage spots an enemy spellcaster, he will sap its mana with Mana Drain.

6. Otherwise, the mage will chose the nearest target and blast away with Lightning (or your favorite single-target spell).

7. If Lightning is on cooldown, the mage will hit the nearest target with Arcane Bolt (or another single-target spell).

Companions

If you thought the companions who rallied with you against the archdemon were a fascinating lot, wait till you meet this new group. Companions are your allies in battle, the NPCs who team with your PC and who you control on your quests. Choose companions based on your PC's needs. If you play a mage, you will definitely need a warrior like Justice, possibly a rogue like Nathaniel Howe, and maybe another rogue like Sigrun or another mage like Anders for healing if you concentrate on DPS.

You run into only a handful of companions on your travels, as they are scattered from Knotwood Hills to the Blackmarsh. Know them well, for they are as vital as your own flesh and blood.

Grey Warden Companions

Companion	Class	Location
Anders	Mage	Vigil's Keep
Justice	Warrior	Blackmarsh
Mhairi	Warrior	Vigil's Keep
Nathaniel Howe	Rogue	Vigil's Keep
Oghren	Warrior	Vigil's Keep
Sigrun	Rogue	Knotwood Hills
Velanna	Mage	Wending Wood

Understanding Companions

Companions aren't simple NPCs who point you toward the next quest; they think, have opinions, fall in and out of favor with your decisions, and level along with you. Without companions, you would be a one-person party.

To grasp the intricacies of companion interaction, read through the following pages and familiarize yourself with what works and what doesn't work for your current party make-up. After companion basics, each companion receives a dedicated section with everything you need to know about your favorite ally. The Supporting Cast chapter details other famous characters of the land; consider it a list of the important NPCs and relevant game info to aid you on your quests.

Approval Ratings

Your approval ranges from -100 to 100, with all companions beginning at zero when you first meet them. The higher the approval rating, the more the companion enjoys your company and will be willing to follow your lead. A low approval rating equals a disgruntled companion, and one who might walk out on the group at any moment. In most cases, the approval rating caps at 74 unless you are "friendly" with a companion. You can warm up to companions by talking with them every chance you get and exploring all their dialogue options; you get a friendly rating with a companion by doing each NPC's personal quest.

Approval Chart

Your approval rating with companions ranges from -100 to 100. However, you can only get to max positive approval if you are "friendly" with the companion. You can get "friendly" if you do each companion's personal quest.

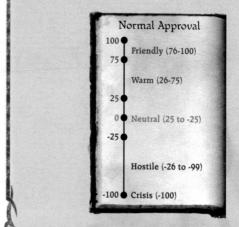

Normal Approval

- 100 — Friendly (76-100)
- 75
- Warm (26-75)
- 25
- 0 — Neutral (25 to -25)
- -25
- Hostile (-26 to -99)
- -100 — Crisis (-100)

Understanding Companions

Basics ~ Classes ~ The Party ~ **Companions** ~ Supporting Cast ~ Equipment ~ Bestiary ~ Walkthrough ~ Side Quests ~ Random Encounters ~ Achievements/Trophies

Gifts

You can give some specific items from your inventory to companions to increase approval. All gifts can be given to all companions, but each companion prefers a specific type of gift that gives a higher approval rating if you match companion and gift appropriately. Dialogue can also be initiated based on gifts being given.

Companion Gifts

To give a gift, switch to the follower in the character record screen, then select an item in your inventory and choose "Gift." A gift given provides a bonus from +1 to +10 to that character's approval rating, depending on how much that follower likes the gift and what their current approval rating is.

Only certain items labeled as "gift" can be given for approval rating boosts. Giving the wrong gift to the wrong companion will raise the companion's approval by only half of what it would if given to the correct companion. "Plot" gifts are given back to the player if they are given to the wrong character. When you donate gifts to companions, listen for the audio clue and watch for the rising heart that displays the approval bump number. Because there are limited gifts in the game, don't just give them away randomly; it's always better to hear a "Wow!" than a "Thanks, I guess."

Companion Quests

Most companions have a personal quest that you can help them undertake. Some are more involved than others. For example, you have to try to steal a phylactery for Anders's personal quest, but only hang out with Oghren at the Vigil Keep's throne room for his. Complete all your companions' quests if you can, because this will solidify your friendship with them. See the individual companion sections for how to unlock each one.

Plot Abilities

Companions can be inspired by your leadership. If you increase a companion's approval rating high enough, they will gain one of several bonuses to their primary attribute. For example, a warm Velanna will gain "Inspired: Minor Magic" and a warm Justice will gain "Inspired: Minor Constitution." There are four levels for the plot abilities—minor, moderate, major, and massive—and each level increases the bonus the companion gets to an attribute, so keep pumping up the approval rating of the companions you prefer to travel with, and they'll become better party members. Plot abilities can degrade, though, if you lose sufficient approval with a companion.

Crisis Moments

When talking to the companions, or if you make decisions in the game that are contrary to a companion's goals, the companion will definitely not approve. If they disapprove, you lose approval rating and they will certainly have words with you.

If you continue on this negative approval path, they will reach a "crisis" point where they say they have to leave. You still have a chance to talk them out of it, and if you're successful, they will stay. But if they reach crisis for a second time, it's over. The companion will leave for good. See the individual companion sections for possible crisis moments and how to avoid them.

primagames.com

Anders

Anders at a Glance

~ Starting Attributes ~

Strength **11**	Dexterity **11**
Willpower **33**	Magic **41**
Cunning **17**	Constitution **17**

~ Class ~
Mage

Healer: Despite his fire-roasting stunt when you first meet him, Anders makes for the best party healer. He starts with the Spirit Healer specialization with points already spent on a good healing base.

~ Starting Talents ~

Spirit Healer: Group Heal, Revival, Lifeward

Mage: Arcane Bolt, Arcane Shield

Primal: Winter's Grasp, Frost Weapons, Cone of Cold

Creation: Heal, Heroic Offense

Spirit: Walking Bomb, Mind Blast

Entropy: Weakness, Paralyze, Drain Life

~ Location ~
Vigil's Keep Interior

~ Unlock Condition ~
In the corridor off the entrance chamber in the keep interior, you meet up with Anders. He's slain some templars after him, but will gladly join your group to fight the darkspawn.

Spoiler Alert

You discover Anders when you first enter Vigil's Keep; he is surrounded by dead templars and is fighting for his life against darkspawn. It would seem he's an evil apostate mage, but in truth, he just doesn't like being trapped (he'll readily fight against the darkspawn). You can ask him to join the party, or leave him there (although he will return later).

When meeting the king or queen at the end of "The Assault on Vigil's Keep" introduction, you can choose to conscript Anders as a Grey Warden (against the advice of the templars), let him be taken by the templars (but with a good word put in for him), or just let him be taken by the templars outright.

Combat Advice

If you choose Anders as your party healer, get him Rejuvenate and Regeneration as soon as possible. Spirit Healer's Cleansing Aura would be a nice addition too. Definitely upgrade Mind Blast one point to Force Field for extra defense when an ally nears death. Once you reach level 20, invest in the Mage school's Fade Shield chain, especially for the mighty Time Spiral at level 28 which can reset all your healing cooldowns.

In combat, leave Anders in the rear to protect him from melee. Heal at range and toss in a damage spell like Winter's Grasp or Cone of Cold if you want to speed up damage against wounded enemies. If you have a few extra points available, you may want to spec Anders into the Keeper specialization. One with Nature and its upgrade abilities can trap enemies surrounding Anders, thus keeping them off the mage during healing and slowing them down while attacking other allies.

Personal Quest

The one thing Anders wants most of all is freedom from the Circle. He had arranged with a cohort, Namaya, to get his phylactery away from the templars. When you meet with Namaya in the city of Amaranthine (see Amaranthine map in Side Quests chapter for Namaya's exact location), she tells Anders where he can find it: in a warehouse across the city.

Alas, the whole thing is a setup by the templars. There is no phylactery in Amaranthine. The templars are waiting, and if you don't give Anders to them outright, they will battle the party to the death. For more details, see "Freedom for Anders" in the "Companions" section of the Side Quest chapter.

Gifts

Anders's "plot gift" is a kitten (found in eastern section of the Vigil's Keep courtyard). His other gifts are a knitted scarf (found in the Chantry), gold earring (Vigil's Keep basement), engraved silver bracers (Kal'Hirol), a bell collar for the cat (Amaranthine), and a book on phylacteries (Silverite Mine in the Wending Wood).

Anders's Gifts

Gift	Found In	Location
Bell Collar	Homer's Toys	Amaranthine
Engraved Silver Bracers	Pile of Bones	Kal'Hirol
Gold Earring	Knight's Corpse	Vigil's Keep Basement
Kitten	Plot Item	Eastern Section of Vigil's Keep Courtyard
Knitted Scarf	Lost and Found Box	Amaranthine Chantry
Phylacteries: A History Written in Blood	Books	Silverite Mine

Anders

Basics ~ Classes ~ The Party ~ **Companions** ~ Supporting Cast ~ Equipment ~ Bestiary ~ Walkthrough ~ Side Quests ~ Random Encounters ~ Achievements/Trophies

Dialogue Choices

As with any companion, Anders has dialogue choices whenever you interact with him, and sometimes he will pull you aside to speak with you about a topic. However, at important points in the game, you should know about plot-specific, area-specific, and throne room-specific dialogue that could change the game for your companion.

Plot-Specific Dialogue

- If Ser Tamra doesn't speak to the player about the growing conspiracy for the "A Brewing Conspiracy" side quest, Anders will have the same information for you during the fealty ceremony.
- After you give Anders the gift kitten, the Ser Pounce-a-Lot item will appear in your inventory. If you interact with this item with Anders in the party, you will hear Anders talking to the kitten.

Area-Specific Dialogue

- Anders has a conversation related to the statue of Andraste (there are two in the game: he talks about the one in Vigil's Keep after you upgrade the walls), a tree in the city of Amaranthine, and the lyrium basket in the Trade Quarter of Kal'Hirol. You can gain serious approval bumps if you sympathize with Anders about his hopes for freedom and dislike for authority.

Throne Room-Specific Dialogue

- Anders may tell you about the Circle Tower's cat, which relates to the kitten gift you can present to him. This results in a positive approval bump.
- After you complete Anders's personal quest and save him from the templars' trap, Anders may tell you that you're an "all right" sort for sticking by him. This results in a positive approval bump.

Approval Increase

- Banter with Anders, or tease him.
- Remind him that he is free and appreciated.
- Kill the templars in the warehouse to save him (you will be eligible to reach his friendly status).
- Stand up for him with the templars.
- Take the information on the statues to the merchants ("Maferath's Monuments" side quest).
- Hire Velanna (a pretty girl) to the Grey Wardens.
- Mess around with the revered mother for the orphans, or steal her sermons (the series of Blight Orphans side quests in the Crown and Lion Inn).
- Rescue the hostage Eileen ("A Daughter Ransomed" side quest).
- Leave him behind at the keep when you march to Amaranthine at the start of the "Assault on Vigil's Keep" main quest. For even more approval, come back to the keep to rescue him if you did leave him behind.
- If you include him in the party for the siege, however, save the city rather than Vigil's Keep.

Approval Decrease

- Tell him that the templars are right to keep the mages trapped.
- Engage him in overly serious conversation.
- Make him feel like he's trapped in the Grey Wardens.
- Give him over to the templars—a move that permanently removes him from your party.
- Take Ser Rylien up on her quest to seek out the maleficars in the city ("Out of Control" side quest).
- Turn in the sylvanwood to the Chantry ("From the Living Wood" side quest).
- Add Nathaniel to your party.
- Side with Justice instead of the baroness.
- Kill the hostage Eileen, or let her be killed ("A Daughter Ransomed" side quest).
- Ally yourself with the Architect in Drake's Fall. He disapproves, but won't leave the party for it.

Crisis Moment

Anders does not have a specific crisis moment. You can only reach a crisis with Anders through poor approval rating. You can beg him to stay when you first hit the approval low point, but he will definitely leave the second time.

Justice

Justice at a Glance

Spoiler Alert

Justice is a good spirit from the Fade, a spirit of justice (it's not his name so much as what he is) that was accidentally sucked into the real world with you and is now stuck in the body of a dead Grey Warden. He embodies the concept of justice completely: he is righteous and noble, always focused on the black and white dichotomy of right and wrong, nothing in between. Interesting enough, Justice is the only companion who doesn't need to take the Joining ritual, because the decomposing body of Kristoff has already joined.

Combat Advice

If you choose Justice as your tank warrior, fill out his Weapon and Shield talents as soon as you can, especially Shield Mastery and Assault. Rather than continue with the Precise Striking chain in the Warrior school, concentrate on the Powerful chain instead (better for defense). With your extra talent points, start on the new Second Wind chain, continue with the Spirit Warrior specialization, and fill out the new Weapon and Shield talents, beginning with Juggernaut at level 20. You may want to specialize in Guardian or Champion, or both, to increase Justice's ability to protect the party.

In combat, send Justice into the fray. He excels in the midst of constant melee where his Weapon and Shield talents shine. Once you reach higher levels, invest in the new Weapon and Shield's Carapace (for super defense) and Air of Insolence (the ultimate taunting ability). Justice will take a pounding, and his dead body will live to tell about it.

Personal Quest

After the events in the Blackmarsh, when you return to Vigil's Keep with Justice, you run into Kristoff's wife, Aura. She's very upset to see her dead husband's body walking around with another spirit inside. Justice tries to explain, but Aura runs off. Justice asks you to help find her so he can make amends. Find Aura in the Amaranthine Chantry, and she and Justice come to an understanding when they finally talk. You can reach friendly status with Justice after this quest completes. For more details see "Justice for Kristoff" in the "Companions" section of the Side Quest chapter.

Gifts

Justice's "plot gift" is a lyrium ring (found in Kal'Hirol's Main Hall); he tells the PC at one point that lyrium calls to him, and that he wishes to have an object made of it. His other gifts are a book on lyrium (warehouse in Amaranthine), Kristoff's locket (Blackmarsh), a book of poetry about the Fade (Vigil's Keep throne room), a box of Kristoff's mementos (Crown and Lion Inn), and the elven prayer for the dead (Wending Wood).

~ Starting Attributes ~

Strength	49
Dexterity	31
Willpower	20
Magic	11
Cunning	11
Constitution	20

~ Class ~

Warrior

Tank: Unless your main character wants to tank, Justice is the best warrior at holding a party together in the heat of combat.

~ Starting Talents ~

Spirit Warrior: Beyond the Veil

Warrior: Powerful, Precise Striking, Taunt

Weapon and Shield: Shield Bash, Shield Pummel, Overpower, Shield Block, Shield Cover, Shield Tactics, Shield Defense, Shield Balance, Shield Wall, Shield Expertise

~ Location ~

Blackmarsh Undying (the Fade)

~ Unlock Condition ~

In the Blackmarsh Undying, Justice tries to help the villagers who have been trapped in the Fade by the evil baroness. When you slay the baroness, Justice may join the party or leave his body to travel the world unhindered.

Justice's Gifts

Gift	Found In	Location
Elven Prayer for the Dead	Crate	Wending Wood
Kristoff's Locket	Pile of Rocks	Blackmarsh
Kristoff's Mementos	Chest	Crown and Lion Inn
Lyrium Ring	Chest	Kal'Hirol's Main Hall
Lyrium: The Voice of the Maker	Bookshelf	Abandoned Warehouse in Amaranthine
Verses of Dreams	Pile of Books	Vigil's Keep Throne Room

Justice

Basics ~ Classes ~ The Party ~ **Companions** ~ Supporting Cast ~ Equipment ~ Bestiary ~ Walkthrough ~ Side Quests ~ Random Encounters ~ Achievements/Trophies

Dialogue Choices

As with any companion, Justice has dialogue choices whenever you interact with him, and sometimes he will pull you aside to speak with you about a topic. However, at important points in the game, you should know about plot-specific, area-specific, and throne room-specific dialogue that could change the game for your companion.

Plot-Specific Dialogue

- When you find the lyrium ring in the depths of Kal'Hirol (see the Main Hall map in the "Last of the Legion" chapter), Justice appreciates your efforts to bring him happiness and jumps up a significant amount on the approval meter.

Area-Specific Dialogue

- The statue of Andraste in Amaranthine invokes a conversation with Justice. As with all the area-specific dialogue possibilities, if you seek to console and befriend Justice, you gain positive approval.

- The elven body in the Dalish camp in the Wending Wood, where you finally confront Velanna during "The Righteous Path" quest, presents another opportunity to gain positive approval if you listen sympathetically to Justice.

- Taking Justice back to the Crown and Lion, where Kristoff was staying, gets some interesting reactions from the patrons.

Throne Room-Specific Dialogue

- Kristoff's chest behind Justice in the throne room gives you more insight into the spirit inhabiting the Grey Warden body.

- Justice may tell you about his attachment to lyrium in the throne room, which puts you on the path for lyrium ring in Kal'Hirol.

- After his talk with Aura in the Chantry, Justice may tell you about his feelings on humanity.

Approval Increase

- Encourage him to follow his human side.
- Explain how his situation is different from demons.
- Appreciate him and thank him.
- Seek justice, even vengeance, on any occasion.
- Aid Constable Aidan against the smugglers ("Law and Order" side quest).
- Rescue the hostage during the "A Daughter Ransomed" side quest, even if you kill the hostage-takers after promising them money.
- Kill the Statue of War's foe, the animated magister corpse ("Brothers of Stone" side quest in the Wending Wood).
- Tell Velanna she doesn't deserve the honor of being a Grey Warden.
- Give Melisse flowers in the final "Making Amends" ("Blight Orphans") side quest.
- Take him to Amaranthine for the siege, or leave him and then come back to rescue him.
- Choose saving the city over saving Vigil's Keep.

Approval Decrease

- Be sarcastic with him.
- Hold his ignorance against him.
- Dismiss his opinions.
- Make him feel bad for being in Kristoff's body.
- Aid the smugglers against Constable Aidan ("Law and Order" side quest).
- Kill Steafan in the cage in Kal'Hirol ("Wrong Place, Wrong Time" side quest).
- Kill the hostage or let her be killed ("A Daughter Ransomed" side quest).
- Take Velanna into the Grey Wardens, or into the party at all.
- Take Nathaniel into the party.
- Cause the revered mother difficulties on the orphans' behalf; give the orphans the sermons, or scare Melisse, the orphan's ex-girlfriend, with the scarecrow ("Blight Orphans" side quests).
- Release the Architect's messenger during the siege on Amaranthine.

Crisis Moment

Justice will not abide by a decision to help the Architect in Drake's Fall as you approach the Mother's nest. He considers aiding the Architect an evil act. Justice may actually leave and battle the party if you still choose to side with the Architect, although Justice can be persuaded to stay if you're friendly with him.

primagames.com

Nathaniel Howe

Nathaniel at a Glance

~ Starting Attributes ~

Strength	Dexterity
24	38

Willpower	Magic
23	11

Cunning	Constitution
36	10

~ Class ~

Rogue

Ranged DPS: The party's resident archer can deal formidable damage if he stays out of melee combat. Nathaniel can break out a backstab in combat if the situation calls for it, but he's more comfortable putting an arrow between the eyes.

~ Starting Talents ~

Assassin: Mark of Death

Rogue: Dirty Fighting, Combat Movement, Below the Belt, Deft Hands, Improved Tools

Archery: Melee Archer, Aim, Defensive Fire, Pinning Shot, Crippling Shot, Critical Shot, Arrow of Slaying, Rapid Shot, Shattering Shot

~ Location ~

Vigil's Keep Dungeon

~ Unlock Condition ~

The private outside the Vigil's Keep throne room informs you that a prisoner has been taken in the dungeon. When you investigate during "The Prisoner" quest, you learn that Nathaniel Howe returned home to try to kill you, then changed his mind and was simply looking for a family keepsake when the guards caught him. You can conscript Nathaniel into the Grey Wardens on the spot, or set him free, in which case he'll return later in a random encounter and ask to join the Wardens.

Spoiler Alert

Before the war, the Howe family name was respected. However, Nathaniel's father sided with Loghain during the events of the last Blight and was executed for the treachery. Now the Grey Wardens have assumed his land, and Nathaniel, not believing the accusations against his father, blames the Grey Wardens for his family's ruin. He just wants to restore his family name, and resents that he's been forced to become a pariah, when he believes the Howes deserve better.

Combat Advice

If you choose Nathaniel as your party rogue and ranged DPS contributor, spend points to fill out his Archery school as quickly as possible, especially to gain Master Archer and Scattershot. Buy the four new Archery talents as soon as you can (Nathaniel's starting dexterity score will enable you to purchase Accuracy and Arrow Time immediately). His starting Assassin specialization isn't a must, unless you plan on using him in melee frequently. Once you reach level 20, invest in the new Rogue talents, particularly Ghost and Weak Points.

In combat, let Nathaniel hang back out of the usual melee brawl. Pick off targets at range, keying on the tank's target or any enemy low on health. Nathaniel can build up his critical chance to deal the most single-target damage in the group, which is a huge bonus to a party already strong in melee DPS.

Personal Quest

Nathaniel learns from the keep's groundskeeper, Samuel, that his sister Delilah is alive and married to a shopkeeper in the city of Amaranthine ("The Howe Family" side quest). When you find Delilah in Amaranthine (see the Amaranthine map in the Side Quests chapter), Nathaniel and Delilah catch up. Delilah tells him that she's happy to be where she is; that she loves her husband; and that their father, Rendon Howe, was not the hero that Nathaniel has been led to believe. After this conversation, Nathaniel can become friendly with the player.

Gifts

Nathaniel's "plot gift" is a his grandfather's bow (found in Vigil's Keep's basement). He tells the PC at one point about his grandfather the Grey Warden (although he probably failed the Joining) and how he would like to have something of his as a memento.

His other gifts are his sister's letters (Vigil's Keep's basement), locksmith's tools (Smuggler's Cave), a bronze sextant (Wending Wood), a golden vase (a store in Amaranthine) and a whetstone (Kal'Hirol).

Nathaniel's Gifts

Gift	Found In	Location
Bronze Sextant	Corpse	Wending Wood
Delilah Howe's Letters	Howe Correspondence	Vigil's Keep Basement
Golden Vase	Octham's Goods	Amaranthine
The Howe Bow	Bag	Vigil's Keep Basement
Locksmith's Tools	Crate	Smuggler's Cove
Whetstone	Stone Container	Kal'Hirol

Nathaniel Howe

Basics ~ Classes ~ The Party ~ **Companions** ~ Supporting Cast ~ Equipment ~ Bestiary ~ Walkthrough ~ Side Quests ~ Random Encounters ~ Achievements/Trophies

Dialogue Choices

As with any companion, Nathaniel has dialogue choices whenever you interact with him, and sometimes he will pull you aside to speak with you about a topic. However, at important points in the game, you should know about plot-specific, area-specific, and throne room-specific dialogue that could change the game for your companion.

Plot-Specific Dialogue

- When you find the Howe Bow at the end of the "Dark Theurge" side quest chain, Nathaniel will be most grateful. Expect a large approval increase.

Area-Specific Dialogue

- The statue of Andraste in Amaranthine triggers a discussion with Nathaniel.
- A tree just inside the Blackmarsh triggers a discussion with Nathaniel about the swamp's creepy landscape and haunted reputation.

- If you are a male human noble from *Dragon Age: Origins*, Nathaniel's sister Delilah will make disparaging remarks about the suitor her father had found for her—and then realize it was you.

Throne Room-Specific Dialogue

- Behind where Nathaniel stands in the throne room hangs a portrait of his mother. He's not too happy with her, but if you sympathize with his tough times, you can gain some positive approval.
- Nathaniel may tell you about his grandfather who was a Grey Warden.
- After his talk with Delilah, Nathaniel may apologize for misjudging you.

Approval Increase

- Speak well, or at least soothingly, of his family.
- Encouraged him to redeem his family name as a Grey Warden.
- Allow him to see himself as a hero.
- Allow Velanna to join the party.
- Aid Constable Aidan against the smugglers during the "Law and Order" side quest.
- Give money to the merchant Mervis for the families of the slain in Amaranthine.
- Give flowers to Melisse, an ex-girlfriend of one of the orphans ("Blight Orphans" side quests).
- Offer to help Keenan in the Silverite Mine ("Last Wishes" side quest).
- Help the Statue of Peace (the Wending Wood's "Brothers of Stone" side quest).
- Rescue Eileen, even if it means killing her kidnappers ("A Daughter Ransomed" side quest).
- Gently look after the dog in the keep basement.
- Side with Justice rather than the baroness.
- Choose him to go to Amaranthine for the siege (if he is warm or higher).
- Rescue him if you leave him behind for the siege.
- Save Vigil's Keep instead of the city of Amaranthine.

Approval Decrease

- Insult his family.
- Dismiss his quest.
- Aid the smugglers against Constable Aidan ("Law and Order" side quest).
- Give up Anders to the templars in the warehouse during Anders's "Freedom for Anders" personal quest.
- Cause the revered mother trouble on behalf of the orphans, or give the orphans the sermon ("Blight Orphans" side quests).
- Kill Steafan in the cage in Kal'Hirol during the "Wrong Time, Wrong Place" side quest.
- Kill Eileen or let her die ("A Daughter Ransomed" side quest).
- Don't choose him to go to Amaranthine for the siege.
- Release the Architect's messenger during the Amaranthine siege.
- Deny the Architect and miss the opportunity to end the Blights.

Crisis Moment

Nathaniel Howe does not have a specific crisis moment. You can only reach a crisis with Nathaniel through poor approval rating. You can beg him to stay when you first hit the approval low point, but he will definitely leave the second time.

primagames.com

Oghren

Oghren at a Glance

~ Starting Attributes ~

Strength **48**	Dexterity **18**
Willpower **23**	Magic **10**
Cunning **10**	Constitution **24**

~ Class ~

Warrior

DPSer or Off-Tank: In a pinch, Oghren can tank in place of Justice. If you do that, however, you negate his specialization: Berserker. The Berserker talents increase damage, which fits into a DPS role, and the only way a stamina-deprived Berserker can hold threat well is to out-damage everyone else.

~ Starting Talents ~

Berserker: Berserk

Warrior: Powerful, Threaten, Bravery, Death Blow

Two-Handed: Pommel Strike, Indomitable, Stunning Blows, Sunder Arms, Shattering Blows, Sunder Armor, Destroyer, Mighty Blow, Powerful Swings, Two-Handed Strength

~ Location ~

Vigil's Keep (Inner Keep)

~ Unlock Condition ~

During the "Assault on Vigil's Keep" introduction, you meet Oghren near the end of your run through the Inner Keep before you encounter the Withered. He joins you automatically and wants to become a Grey Warden.

Spoiler Alert

One of your fellow companions from *Dragon Age: Origins* has returned! Oghren, the gruff but amusing dwarf warrior, beats you to the keep to take on the darkspawn. This time around he's ready to become a Grey Warden and really hew some heads.

Combat Advice

Fill out Oghren's Berserker specialization and Two-Handed school as soon as you get the chance, especially Critical Strike. By adding all the Two-Handed talents, including all the way up to the new Reaving Storm, you can seriously increase his damage potential and make him an excellent DPS addition to the party. As with rogues, Oghren should allow the tank to control enemy groups and then attack from the rear or flank. Because Oghren is so durable, he doesn't have to watch his spacing as much as a rogue, and he can off-tank easily if you need him to grab a creature that the tank can't hold threat on. His skills are best used with heavy or massive armor, either sword and shield or two-handed weapons, with a crossbow for ranged attacks.

Berserk ramps up Oghren's damage and a well-placed Mighty Blow or Critical Strike can hammer an adversary. Sunder Armor rips through a heavily defensive melee attacker, while Pommel Strike and Stunning Blows can knock an enemy out of combat for several seconds. Two-Handed Sweep is great at the end of the fight, or at striking multiple foes—as long as you don't steal threat away from the tank. Final Blow deals massive damage but drains the rest of Oghren's stamina. The new Reaving Storm can wreck multiple foes in a tight melee free-for-all.

Personal Quest

Shortly after your adventures begin, Oghren's wife, Felsi, tracks him down at Vigil's Keep. She angrily accuses him of abandoning their family, which he doesn't disagree with, but he tells her that marriage really isn't for him. Regardless of whether you say anything or simply sit back and listen to the whole thing, Oghren will be eligible for friendly status after the conversation.

Gifts

Oghren's "plot gift" is a toy horse (found in the Blackmarsh), and he tells you that he wants his own horse one day. His other gifts are all alcohol-related, and may be found at the Crown and Lion, Hubert's Den, the warehouse in Amaranthine, Knotwood Hills, and the Vigil's Keep basement.

Oghren's Gifts

Gift	Found In	Location
Aqua Magus	Crate	Abandoned Warehouse in Amaranthine
"Dragon-Piss"	Crate	Hubert's Den in Amaranthine
Hirol's Lava Burst	Chest	Knotwood Hills
Mackay's Epic Single Malt	Crate	Crown and Lion Inn
Toy Horse	On the Ground	Blackmarsh
West Hill Brandy	Crate Vigil's	Keep Basement

Oghren

Basics ~ Classes ~ The Party ~ **Companions** ~ Supporting Cast ~ Equipment ~ Bestiary ~ Walkthrough ~ Side Quests ~ Random Encounters ~ Achievements/Trophies

Dialogue Choices

As with any companion, Oghren has dialogue choices whenever you interact with him, and sometimes he will pull you aside to speak with you about a topic. However, at important points in the game, you should know about plot-specific, area-specific, and throne room-specific dialogue that could change the game for your companion.

Plot-Specific Dialogue

- Bizarre as it might sound, Oghren's special gift is a toy horse, which brings back fond memories for the dwarf. You'll get a big approval bump by handing him this prize and not making fun of him.

Area-Specific Dialogue

- If you interact with the boat when you first enter the Fade, Oghren spouts angrily about how dwarves don't dream and aren't supposed to be in the Fade.
- There is an anvil in Kal'Hirol that Oghren talks to you about.
- At the inn in Amaranthine, interact with the message board outside; Oghren pulls you aside and talks to you too.

Throne Room-Specific Dialogue

- If you interact with the cask behind Oghren, you catch the dwarf in a drunken stupor. Be careful not to offend him too much or you'll lose approval. You can interact with the cask multiple times for different drunken reactions from Oghren.
- While in the throne room, Oghren will ask about Grey Warden dreams.
- Oghren will also ask about Grey Warden salaries in the throne room, which is when you find out about his desire for a pony.
- After Felsi's visit, if your relationship is warm, Oghren will eventually discuss his feelings of guilt about leaving his family.

Approval Increase

- Appreciate him.
- Occasionally "straight talk" with him.
- Encourage him to try harder in the future.
- Tease him.
- Ask how he's feeling.
- Tell him he's a great warrior.
- Recruit him.
- Recruit Sigrun to the Grey Wardens.
- Help the Statue of War ("Brothers of Stone" side quest).
- Kill the hostage-takers ("A Daughter Ransomed" side quest).
- Side with either Justice or the baroness, as long as there's a fight to be had!
- Help the orphans' with their pranks against the revered mother and Melisse ("Blight Orphans" side quests).
- Take him with you to the siege on Amaranthine, especially if you're a woman.
- Leave him behind from the siege, but come back to rescue him.
- Save Vigil's Keep instead of Amaranthine during the siege.
- Side with the Architect to get rid of the Blights.

Approval Decrease

- Tell him he did a bad thing with his family.
- Make fun of him (especially about Branka, his ex-wife who left him for a woman).
- Mock him for drinking too much.
- Leave Sigrun behind.
- Kill Eileen ("A Daughter Ransomed" side quest).
- Deny the Architect and miss the chance to get rid of the Blights.

Crisis Moment

Oghren does not have a specific crisis moment. You can only reach a crisis with Oghren through poor approval rating. You can beg him to stay when you first hit the approval low point, but he will definitely leave the second time.

primagames.com

Sigrun

Sigrun at a Glance

~ Starting Attributes ~

Strength **47**	Dexterity **46**
Willpower **20**	Magic **10**
Cunning **15**	Constitution **16**

~ Class ~

Rogue

...lee DPSer: With all the Dual Weapon ...alents in her repertoire, Sigrun is made ...or dealing heavy damage in melee com-...at. You can tweak her to tank too if you ...ake the rest of the Legionnaire Scout ...specialization.

~ Starting Talents ~

...ionnaire Scout: Mark of the Legion

...gue: Dirty Fighting, Below the Belt, ...Deadly Strike, Lethality, Stealth

...al Weapon: Dual-Weapon Training, ...Dual-Weapon Finesse, Dual-Weapon ...xpert, Dual-Weapon Mastery, Dual ...triking, Riposte, Dual-Weapon Sweep, ...lurry, Momentum

~ Location ~

Knotwood Hills

~ Unlock Condition ~

...ring the "Last of the Legion" main ...st, you come upon Sigrun at the ...rance to Kal'Hirol, being attacked by ...kspawn. The PC can rescue her and ask ...to join them, or let her go on her own.

Spoiler Alert

Sigrun was a former casteless cutpurse, who was convicted of a crime and sentenced to fight for the Legion of the Dead. She went with the Legion to Kal'Hirol, where the darkspawn slaughtered her entire regiment. Sigrun survived when she ran away in fear. She wishes to return to see if she can avenge the Legion.

Combat Advice

When spending Sigrun's points, you can fill in the Rogue and Dual Weapon schools, and the Legionnaire Scout specialization. Start with the Dual Weapon and Rogue schools. You can fill those in early, because the older talents don't have level restrictions. Start with Cripple, Punisher, and Whirlwind in Dual Weapon, then pick up Evasion, Combat Movement, Coup de Grace, and Feign Death in Rogue. Once you hit the level thresholds for the new Rogue talents, grab them immediately.

The Rogue and Dual Weapon talents will increase your effectiveness in melee combat. Let the tank grab the threat and then strike away from the rear. If you want to gain more toughness and tank a little, dip into the remaining three Legionnaire Scout talents: Strength of Stone, Endure Hardship, and Blessing of the Ancestors.

Personal Quest

If you have Sigrun in your party, you will eventually bump into the merchant Mischa in Amaranthine, who recognizes Sigrun and accuses her of being a thief and of betraying their friendship. Later, Sigrun will ask if you can go back to find Mischa again. Mischa is at the Crown and Lion Inn. Sigrun offers a ring as an apology for her previous wrong-doings. The player can let Sigrun give her the ring, or offer money instead to pay the debt. Mischa is satisfied with either of these, and Sigrun feels better about having let down her friend (and will be "friendly" eligible at this point).

Gifts

Sigrun's "plot gift" is a spyglass (found in the Silverite Mine). Her other gifts are a snow globe (can be bought in a store), a toy chariot (Smuggler's Cave), a potted plant (outside the Amaranthine Chantry), a book on warriors (throne room) and soap on a rope (Vigil's Keep dungeon).

Sigrun's Gifts

Gift	Found In	Location
Potted Plant	Pot	Outside Amaranthine Chantry
Snow Globe	Glassric's Wares	Amaranthine
Soap on a Rope	Supplies	Vigil's Keep Dungeon
Spyglass	Soldier's Corpse	Silverite Mine
Toy Chariot	Toy Box	Smuggler's Cove
The Warrior's Heart	Pile of Books	Vigil's Keep Throne Room

Sigrun

Basics ~ Classes ~ The Party ~ **Companions** ~ Supporting Cast ~ Equipment ~ Bestiary ~ Walkthrough ~ Side Quests ~ Random Encounters ~ Achievements/Trophies

Dialogue Choices

As with any companion, Sigrun has dialogue choices whenever you interact with her, and sometimes she will pull you aside to speak with you about a topic. However, at important points in the game, you should know about plot-specific, area-specific, and throne room-specific dialogue that could change the game for your companion.

Plot-Specific Dialogue

- Sigrun has conversations all through Kal'Hirol as she guides the party through the area.

Area-Specific Dialogue

- Sigrun has a conversation about a tree in the Wending Wood.
- At a market stall in Amaranthine, Sigrun worries about being able to afford to buy things.

Throne Room-Specific Dialogue

- If you examine the books behind Sigrun in the throne room, she engages in conversation with you about literature and reading. Keep a friendly tone with her and you'll gain positive approval.
- Sigrun discusses her desire for a spyglass.
- She talks about her guilt over betraying Mischa after meeting the merchant in Amaranthine.
- After making amends with Mischa, Sigrun thanks you for recruiting her to the Grey Wardens, but swears she will return to the Legion after she has finished her tasks with the Grey Wardens and Amaranthine.

Approval Increase

- Stick up for her.
- Give her your trust.
- Understand that the Legion is important to her, and she still belongs to it.
- Talk about how the Grey Wardens differ from the Legion.
- Help Constable Aidan against the smugglers ("Law and Order" side quest).
- Give money to the merchant Mervis to help the families of those who were killed in Amaranthine.
- Give Melisse flowers ("Blight Orphans" side quests).
- Kill the kidnappers ("A Daughter Ransomed" side quest).
- Help the Statue of Peace ("Brothers of Stone" side quest in the Wending Woods).
- Help Keenan send his last words to his wife ("Last Wishes" side quest).
- Ask Velanna to join the Grey Wardens.
- Side with Justice.
- Choose her to go to the siege of Amaranthine.
- Rescue her if she's left behind at the keep.
- Kill the Architect's messenger who comes to Amaranthine after the siege.
- Save Amaranthine during the siege.

Approval Decrease

- Denigrate her choices as stupid.
- Kill Steafan while he is caged in Kal'Hirol ("Wrong Place, Wrong Time" side quest).
- Help the orphans' with their scarecrow or itching powder pranks ("Blight Orphans" side quests).
- Give Anders over to the templars.
- Kill or allow Eileen to be killed ("A Daughter Ransomed" side quest).
- Side with the baroness.
- Let the Architect's messenger who comes to Amaranthine after the seige go.

Crisis Moment

Sigrun will not abide by a decision to help the Architect in Drake's Fall as you approach the Mother's nest. She considers aiding the Architect an evil act. Sigrun may actually leave and battle the party if you still choose to side with the Architect, although Sigrun can be persuaded to stay if you're friendly with her.

primagames.com

Velanna

Velanna at a Glance

Spoiler Alert

An angry elf who intensely dislikes humans because of what they have done to her people in the past, Velanna runs into the party as the primary figure in "The Righteous Path" main quest. Velanna is strong-willed and often defensive, and she has a tendency to lash out at people. She is, however, devoted to her people and very protective of her sister, Seranni, her only family.

Combat Advice

You can take Velanna in many different ways with her extra talent points. Assuming you don't need an extra healer, fill out her Entropy school with Death Hex and Death Cloud. Pick up the last two Primal earth spells: Earthquake and Petrify. In keeping with her nature theme, buy the three remaining Keeper abilities: Thornblades, Replenishment, and Nature's Vengeance. The rest of her points can go toward new Mage school spells and another Primal attack chain.

In combat, avoid melee and drop powerful AoEs on enemy groups, such as Earthquake, or blast them dead with single-target spells such as Drain Life. If the enemy comes to Velanna, use One with Nature to set up a natural barricade around her. With the various upgrades to Keeper, she can root and crush opponents.

Personal Quest

With Velanna in your party, you may come across a random encounter of Dalish elves. You learn that Velanna was cast out of her clan because of her fanatical hatred of humans. Later on, she may confide in you how this came about. For more details see "Velanna's Exile" in the "Companions" section of the Side Quest chapter.

~ Starting Attributes ~

Strength	Dexterity
10	10
Willpower	Magic
40	50
Cunning	Constitution
18	20

~ Class ~

Mage

Ranged DPS: With death magic, nature magic, and a little fire thrown in for good measure, Velanna can slay or stifle even the most ruthless of enemy mobs.

~ Starting Talents ~

Keeper: One with Nature

Mage: Arcane Bolt

Primal: Flame Blast, Flaming Weapons, Fireball, Inferno, Rock Armor, Stonefist

Creation: Heal

Entropy: Vulnerability Hex, Affliction Hex, Misdirection Hex, Drain Life, Death Magic, Curse of Mortality

~ Location ~

Wending Wood

~ Unlock Condition ~

Velanna will interact with the party a number of times in the Wending Wood. Eventually she will battle you as you confront her on the truth about what's happened to her clanmates. When she finally surrenders, she may join your party.

Gifts

Velanna's "plot gift" is a blank journal (found in the Chantry). She tells you at one point that she wishes the Dalish had more records of their history and stories, and you give her the blank book to write them in. Her other gifts are a discarded journal (Amaranthine), shiny malachite (Silverite Mine), an ornate silver bowl (Blackmarsh), an elven runestone (Deep Roads), and a carved greenstone (Kal'Hirol).

Velanna's Gifts

Gift	Found In	Location
Blank Journal	Pile of Books	Amaranthine Chantry
Carved Greenstone	Stone Container	Trade Quarter in Kal'Hirol
Discarded Journal	Crate	Amaranthine
Elven Runestone	Pile of Rocks	Vigil's Keep Deep Roads
Ornate Silver Bowl	Pile of Filth	Blackmarsh
Shiny Malachite	Pile of Rocks	Silverite Mine

Velanna

Basics ~ Classes ~ The Party ~ **Companions** ~ Supporting Cast ~ Equipment ~ Bestiary ~ Walkthrough ~ Side Quests ~ Random Encounters ~ Achievements/Trophies

Dialogue Choices

As with any companion, Velanna has dialogue choices whenever you interact with her, and sometimes she will pull you aside to speak with you about a topic. However, at important points in the game, you should know about plot-specific, area-specific, and throne room-specific dialogue that could change the game for your companion.

Plot-Specific Dialogue

- Inside the Silverite Mine, Velanna has several conversations relating to the quest as she guides you from chamber to chamber.
- Velanna wants desperately to save her sister; she is willing to spare the Architect's life in Drake's Fall just to get her sister back.
- If you give her the blank journal, at first she scoffs at the gift. However, keep your tone friendly and eventually she comes around and you gain positive approval.

Area-Specific Dialogue

- At the statue of Andraste in the Vigil's Keep courtyard after you've upgraded the walls, Velanna will start up a conversation with you.
- Velanna has a conversation with some city elves outside Amaranthine about a Vhenadahl tree in the city.

Throne Room-Specific Dialogue

- Velanna may tell you about her sorrow that the Dalish have lost their history.
- After completing her personal quest, if you are warm with her, Velanna may confide in you what happened with her clan. After this conversation, you are eligible to be friendly.

Approval Increase

- Stand up for her.
- Tell her she's interesting.
- Show her new ideas or perspectives on the world.
- Give her hope for finding her sister.
- Offer to aid her sister Seranni when you meet her in the Silverite Mine.
- Don't tease her in front of the merchant Mervis. ("The Righteous Path" side quest).
- Stand up for yourself with the Dark Wolf ("A Brewing Conspiracy" side quest).
- Speak harshly to the bartender or the innkeeper Inside the Crown and Lion Inn.
- Steal the sermons for the orphans ("Blight Orphans" side quests).
- Stick up for Anders with the templars in the warehouse during the "Freedom for Anders" side quest.
- Kill the kidnappers during the "A Daughter Ransomed" side quest.
- Side with the baroness to get out of the Fade.
- Choose her to fight at the siege of Amaranthine
- Rescue her if she's left behind at the keep.
- Save Vigil's Keep instead saving the city during the siege.

Approval Decrease

- Lump her in with city elves.
- Call her on her harshness.
- Apologize on her behalf.
- Reminded her of what she couldn't have.
- Defend the Chantry, humans, or city elves.
- Tell her she made a bad decision, or that sister can't be rescued.
- Ignore her, tease her, or be sarcastic with her.
- Speak harshly to her sister Seranni when you meet her in the Silverite Mine.
- Take Keenan's side quest ("Last Wishes").
- Insult her for being cynical about Keenan's request ("Last Wishes" side quest).
- Tease her in front of the merchant Mervis ("The Righteous Path" side quest).
- Give the sylvanwood to the Chantry ("From the Living Wood" side quest).
- Kill Eileen, or allow her to be killed during the "A Daughter Ransomed" side quest.
- Side with Justice to get out of the Fade.
- Kill the Architect before the final battle against the Mother.
- Help the Architect before the final battle against the Mother.

Crisis Moment

Velanna does not have a specific crisis moment. You can only reach a crisis with Velanna through poor approval rating. You can beg her to stay when you first hit the approval low point, but she will definitely leave the second time.

primagames.com

Mhairi

Spoiler Alert

Mhairi at a Glance

Mhairi is a new recruit to the Wardens. She joins you just outside the keep and is as surprised as you to find it under attack. She is determined and eager to prove herself, and her warrior talents will prove helpful in the battle to retake Vigil's Keep from the darkspawn. Unfortunately, becoming a Grey Warden is not as easy as wielding a sword and repeating an oath. After the "Assault on Vigil's Keep" quest completes, Mhairi perishes in the Joining ritual and another shining spirit is sacrificed to the cause.

Combat Advice

It's just you and Mhairi at the beginning of your story as you approach Vigil's Keep. If you're a warrior yourself and specced to Sword and Shield, plunge into the fray and let Mhairi serve as extra damage. If you aren't a tank, allow Mhairi to take the lead and grab threat from approaching darkspawn. Give her a few seconds to hammer at a foe, then break out your offense. A mage can sit back and pick off targets with damage spells (being careful not to catch Mhairi in any AoE attacks), while melee warriors and rogues can sneak in from the side or rear to devastate the enemy.

For the most part Mhairi is the party's early damage shield, sucking up as many hits as possible, and should think defense first. Trigger Shield Bash and Shield Pummel when you want to keep foes off balance, especially if they break free to harass other party members. When the fight is under control, Mhairi can add a little extra offense herself with Overpower on the main enemy combatant.

Even when your second warrior, Oghren, joins up with you later in the keep, Mhairi should remain the tank. Oghren's talent lies in DPS, and though he can tank in a pinch by dealing large amounts of damage to keep the enemy's attention, Mhairi's talents more naturally fit into defensive tactics. She's a reliable rock, even when the darkspawn tide swells and threatens to sweep you all away.

~ Starting Attributes ~

Strength	Dexterity
42	28
Willpower	Magic
21	14
Cunning	Constitution
15	13

~ Class ~

Warrior

Tank: Unless you are a tank yourself, Mhairi and her Weapon and Shield talents will help keep the darkspawn off of you. Let her soak up damage while you hit the enemy back hard.

~ Starting Talents ~

Champion: War Cry, Rally, Motivate, Superiority

Warrior: Powerful, Threaten, Bravery

Weapon and Shield: Shield Bash, Shield Pummel, Overpower, Shield Block, Shield Cover, Shield Tactics, Shield Mastery, Shield Defense, Shield Balance, Shield Wall, Shield Expertise.

~ Location ~

Vigil's Keep

~ Unlock Condition ~

You begin with Mhairi when you first arrive at Vigil's Keep at the beginning of the game.

Equipment

Mhairi is a warrior and a champion; she can wear any kind of armor and fights with a sword and shield. Save good drops for later companions, unless you need to load her up temporarily to clear out Vigil's Keep.

Gifts

Because Mhairi doesn't survive long, she has no specific gifts associated with her. Don't waste any gifts on her, even though she's a loyal companion during your run through Vigil's Keep. It's much better to save any gifts you may find for future companions.

Dialogue Choices

Mhairi introduces the player to the keep, and later voices the shock the player must feel at finding the keep under siege by the darkspawn, even after the Blight is finished.

Crisis Moment

It's a rather big one, as Mhairi involuntarily leaves the party when she fails the Joining. All other potential companions you meet are safe from the perils of the Joining. Alas, poor Mhairi didn't have the right genes for the job.

Approval Increase

- Make her feel necessary to the cause.
- Try to help her Warden Friend, Rowland

Approval Decrease

- Patronize her as a new recruit.
- Ask her to hold back
- Kill her Warden friend Rowland.

Alec - The Architect

Basics ~ Classes ~ The Party ~ Companions ~ **Supporting Cast** ~ Equipment ~ Bestiary ~ Walkthrough ~ Side Quests ~ Random Encounters ~ Achievements/Trophies

Supporting Cast

Spoiler Alert

Alec

- First Appearance: Vigil's Keep

Alec is a simple shepherd on trial for theft. He is very grateful when he is set free.

Alistair

- First Appearance: Vigil's Keep

Alistair is the son of the late King Maric, and one of the heroes from the original *Dragon Age: Origins*. Alistair may appear in *Awakening* as the king of Ferelden (depending on how your story played out at the end of *Origins*). He charges the new Warden-Commander with the task of rebuilding the Grey Wardens, and also asks that the Grey Wardens look into why the darkspawn have not fully retreated.

Ambassador Cera

- First Appearance: Vigil's Keep

She is a diplomatic Formari emissary who resides in Vigil's Keep's throne room. You can ask Ambassador Cera to enchant items for your party, as well as sell you Runecrafting materials and lyrium potions.

Anora

- First Appearance: Vigil's Keep

Anora is the daughter of Teyrn Loghain and the widow of King Cailan, who died at the beginning of *Origins*. Anora may appear in *Awakening* as the ruling queen of Ferelden (depending on how your story played out at the end of *Origins*). She charges the new Warden-Commander with the task of rebuilding the Grey Wardens, and also asks that the Grey Wardens look into why the darkspawn have not fully retreated (if Alistair is not the king).

The Architect

- First Appearance: Silverite Mine

The Architect was the first darkspawn to be born different from the rest; he was not subject to their compulsions, and thus was an outcast. But he is brilliant and became determined to find a method so other darkspawn could think and speak for themselves. The ends always justify the means, to the Architect. He has no notion of morality and little concept of humanity. He is a brilliant scholar who has learned everything he knows from books, and is nowhere near as civilized as he projects.

The Architect's War Leader

- First Appearance: Kal'Hirol

The disciple commander is the leader of the Architect's forces who are invading Kal'Hirol to destroy the Lost and his brood-mothers.

primagames.com

Spoiler Alert

Armaas

- First Appearance: Silverite Mine

A qunari merchant who no longer follows the Qun (hence he was once of the Tal-Vashoth). He is driven by a desire for coin, and has consented to trade with the darkspawn. He will also trade with the Grey Wardens at Vigil's Keep if convinced that there are profits to be had.

Aura

- First Appearance: Vigil's Keep

Aura is Kristoff's wife. When she heard Vigil's Keep had been attacked, she pays a visit only to discover that her husband is dead and his body is occupied by a spirit from the Fade. Naturally, she doesn't react well to this.

Bann Esmerelle

- First Appearance: Vigil's Keep

She is the richest and most powerful noble in the arling of Amaranthine, and the steward of the namesake city. She's used to getting her way. Esmerelle bears a grudge against Arl Rendon Howe's murderer, and attempts to assassinate the Grey Warden commander.

The Baroness

- First Appearance: Blackmarsh

The baroness is a cruel and sadistic woman who preyed on the children of the village she ruled over, using their blood to power rituals that kept her young. Eventually the villagers rose up against her and burned down her manor with her in it. Before she died, she cast a spell that dragged all of them into the Fade—where they remain, trapped in a dreamworld with the baroness still ruling over them with an iron fist. She is imperious, proud, and so self-entitled she believes that the lives of her subjects are her due.

Captain Garevel

- First Appearance: Vigil's Keep

Captain Garevel is a high-ranking officer in the Grey Wardens. He is a practical man devoted to duty, and he oversees the security of Vigil's Keep.

Clifton

- First Appearance: Amaranthine

Clifton is the owner/operator of the bar at Amaranthine's Crown and Lion Inn. He is a gruff man, not given to putting up with shenanigans from his customers, but not unfriendly either.

Colbert

- First Appearance: Amaranthine

Colbert is a simple man who enjoys hunting and ale. On one such expedition he runs into trouble and has a valuable lead to offer you when you visit Amaranthine.

Armaas ~ Dworkin

Basics ~ Classes ~ The Party ~ Companions ~ **Supporting Cast** ~ Equipment ~ Bestiary ~ Walkthrough ~ Side Quests ~ Random Encounters ~ Achievements/Trophies

Spoiler Alert

Constable Aidan

- First Appearance: Amaranthine

Constable Aidan is in charge of Amaranthine's defense. He loves his city and would do anything to protect it. Speak with him while visiting Amaranthine and he'll offer you a few quests.

Delilah Howe

- First Appearance: Amaranthine

Delilah was once a noblewoman of means, the daughter of Arl Rendon Howe. But when he was executed for treason and her family ruined, she married a commoner—and discovered she was actually much happier away from her father's intrigues and all the bitterness of the family.

Dailan

- First Appearance: Kal'Hirol

The apparition of a courageous dwarven warrior who was willing to look beyond caste and tradition to protect the things he loved, Dailan resided in the long-dead city of Kal'Hirol.

Derren

- First Appearance: Vigil's Keep

This lesser noble is feuding with another noble over land that both believe is theirs. He's one of the few nobles who is a genuine ally of the Warden-Commander, whom he expects to watch his back.

Danella

- First Appearance: Vigil's Keep

Danella is a young soldier from Vigil's Keep who left her post to save her family from the darkspawn. She is on trial for desertion, and if she is treated badly the other soldiers may not be happy.

Dworkin

- First Appearance: Vigil's Keep

Dworkin is known as "Dworkin the Mad." He experiments with different substances to create explosives, and he enjoys blowing things up. If you bring him lyrium sand, he'll make those explosives for you.

Dark Wolf

- First Appearance: Amaranthine

The Dark Wolf is an elusive vigilante figure. He does what he can to strike back at corrupt nobles and has become a bit of a folk hero. Seek him out in Amaranthine if you want help with the conspiracies circulating around your rule at Vigil's Keep. Just bring a ton of coin with you.

primagames.com

Spoiler Alert

Eileen

• First Appearance: Forlorn Cove

Eileen is Ser Edgar Bensley's daughter who is being held ransom by Mosley the Snake and his vile lot. It's up to you to rescue her near the abandoned chantry in Forlorn Cove.

The Herald

• First Appearance: Vigil's Keep

The Herald is general of the Mother's army. When the Architect freed him, he reacted badly to his newfound sentience, and turned to the Mother's side. The Herald revels in violence.

Felsi

• First Appearance: Vigil's Keep

A returning character from *Dragon Age: Origins*, Felsi is Oghren's on-again, off-again companion. They got married after the archdemon was killed and had a child together. However, domestic bliss did not last, and Felsi ended up throwing Oghren out of the house. When she discovers that Oghren has signed up with the Grey Wardens, she goes to Vigil's Keep to confront him.

Herren

• First Appearance: Vigil's Keep

The lesser partner of Master Wade, Herren and Wade have traveled out to Vigil's Keep from their destroyed shop, once in the Denerim Market District. Herren is a good businessman and shopkeeper saddled with a smith who is prone to flights of fancies. Wade makes the final calls, and Herren has to deal with the fallout.

The First

• First Appearance: Blackmarsh

He was the first darkspawn freed from their dominant hive mind by the Architect—hence the name. Once free, however, he found himself confused and bewildered, unable to cope and resentful against his creator. He joined the Mother in her rebellion against the Architect, but soon she betrays him and he finds himself trapped in the Fade. The First is desperate to survive and will do anything to get back to the real world.

Ines

• First Appearance: Wending Wood

Ines is an experienced, older mage. She spends a lot of time in remote areas hunting down rare plants and has very little patience for other people and basic etiquette. She asks you to look for a rare plant, sending you on a quest in the Wending Wood.

Jacen

• First Appearance: Vigil's Keep

A cocky young elf who has been recruited by the Grey Wardens, Jacen is something of a prodigy with a bow and arrow, and knows it.

Eileen - Lord Eddelbrek

Basics ~ Classes ~ The Party ~ Companions ~ **Supporting Cast** ~ Equipment ~ Bestiary ~ Walkthrough ~ Side Quests ~ Random Encounters ~ Achievements/Trophies

Spoiler Alert

Keenan

- First Appearance: Wending Wood

Keenan is a young Grey Warden who is utterly devoted to his duty. He is self-sacrificing and has great respect for the Warden-Commander.

Lilith the Merchant

- First Appearance: Random Encounter

During a random encounter, you find this merchant attacked by darkspawn. She's very grateful if rescued.

Kendrick

- First Appearance: Amaranthine

Kendrick is a merchant who maintains the bulletin board for the Merchants Guild in Amaranthine. He rewards the player for performing the different tasks listed on the board.

Loghain

- First Appearance: Vigil's Keep

A returning character from *Dragon Age: Origins*, Loghain was born a farmer during a time when his country was under foreign occupation. When he was still a boy, he joined the resistance, where his considerable tactical genius quickly became apparent. He became close friends with Prince Maric, the last true heir to the throne, and together they led the rebels to drive out the invading forces of the Orlesian Empire. Maric raised his friend to the nobility, and Loghain is almost more of a symbol to his people than a man: He represents the Fereldan ideals of hard work and independence.

Loghain may appear in *Awakening*, if he was allowed to live in *Origins* and was made into a Grey Warden. He pays his respects to the new commander, and reports that he has been sent away from Ferelden and stationed in Orlais.

Lady Liza Packton

- First Appearance: Vigil's Keep

This lesser noble has been promised some land; however, another noble is disputing her claim.

Lord Eddelbrek

- First Appearance: Vigil's Keep

The second most important noble in Amaranthine, he is the largest land owner in the arling and provides a great deal of the food. He's much more popular than Esmerelle.

Lady Morag

- First Appearance: Vigil's Keep

Lady Morag is Lord Guy's associate, who also does not like Orlesians. She wants to calm Lord Guy down before his rash words get them both killed.

primagames.com

Spoiler Alert

Lord Guy

- First Appearance: Vigil's Keep

A noble who gets drunk at a party. Like many people, he has a deep hostility toward Orlais and if the Warden-Commander is the Orlesian Grey Warden, he will cause a scene. How you deal with it has political implications.

The Messenger

- First Appearance: Siege of Amaranthine

The Messenger works for the Architect. He comes bearing news that the attack on the city of Amaranthine is a feint; he poses a difficult decision for the Warden-Commander. The commander decides if the Messenger is ultimately spared or killed.

The Lost

- First Appearance: Kal'Hirol

The Lost is one of the Mother's lieutenants. He is slightly mad from being able to think for himself, which the darkspawn should not do. He guards the broodmothers in the depths of Kal'Hirol.

Micah

- First Appearance: Amaranthine

Micah is a man of few words. He tends not to speak unless he has something important to say, and then usually only after his partner Colbert has said something first. He prefers to stay out of other's way, and hopes that others will also stay out of his way.

Maverlies

- First Appearance: Vigil's Keep

Maverlies is a soldier dedicated to the defense of Vigil's Keep. She knows the keep extremely well, and warns you of mysterious goings-on in the keep's basement levels.

Mischa

- First Appearance: Amaranthine

Mischa was a merchant in Orzammar who took pity on the young casteless thief, Sigrun, and allowed Sigrun to run errands for her for a bit of money. Sigrun ended up helping the local crime lord frame Mischa for a crime she did not commit. Mischa was exiled and now lives on the surface, having lost everything. She blames Sigrun for her misfortune.

Mervis

- First Appearance: Amaranthine

Mervis is a member of the Merchants Guild in Amaranthine. The guild is having problems with their caravans being attacked and Mervis is desperately looking for a solution to the problem. He doesn't know who or what is attacking the caravans and hopes the Grey Wardens can investigate.

Mistress Woolsey

- First Appearance: Vigil's Keep

Mistress Woolsey is the treasurer for the Grey Wardens. She is experienced and has a great understanding of what's going on in the world.

Lord Guy - Rowland

Basics ~ Classes ~ The Party ~ Companions ~ **Supporting Cast** ~ Equipment ~ Bestiary ~ Walkthrough ~ Side Quests ~ Random Encounters ~ Achievements/Trophies

Spoiler Alert

The Mother

- First Appearance: Lair of the Mother

Once, the Mother was a young human woman. Sadly, she was infected with the Blight and transformed into a monstrous creature built only for birthing darkspawn. Her mind was subsumed by her dark impulses, but when the Architect freed her from those impulses, she regained a bit of her identity. Discovering that she had become a twisted, hideous creature drove her insane. Now she exists as a creature of chaos, a gibbering mad monster determined to be queen of the darkspawn so that she can destroy them, herself, and the world along with her.

Namaya

- First Appearance: Amaranthine

A past companion of Anders, Namaya is supposed to meet Anders in Amaranthine to get him his phylactery back. When she passes the information along, it's up to you to decide whether you aid Anders or not on his personal quest.

Nida

- First Appearance: Amaranthine

Nida is the Grey Warden Keenan's wife. Nida hardly sees her husband. She has endured long years of sadness knowing he'd rather fight darkspawn instead of starting a family with her. Now, he has been assigned to help rebuild the Fereldan Wardens, and has brought her with him. She lives in Amaranthine, a stranger in a city she doesn't know.

Queen of the Blackmarsh

- First Appearance: Blackmarsh

When the baroness first came to Blackmarsh, she helped the villagers get rid of a dragon that had built its nest close to the village. She used powerful, untried magic that had unforeseen effects. The dragon's body remained in the real world, while its essence was banished to the Fade. Fearful that the dragon would somehow return to the real world, the baroness tore its physical body apart, and scattered its bones about the marsh. If you find and gather the bones, you can summon it back to the real world for a confrontation.

Revered Mother

- First Appearance: Amaranthine

A snooty, control freak of a religious figure who is condescending and arrogant in her righteousness, she runs the Chantry in Amaranthine.

Rowland

- First Appearance: Vigil's Keep

This young and idealistic warrior was recruited into the Grey Wardens and served alongside Mhairi. When you encounter him, he is injured and dying.

primagames.com

Spoiler Alert

Rylock

- First Appearance: Amaranthine

She is a commander of the templars, an order of holy knights that watch the mages of society. Rylock is in pursuit of Anders, the escaped mage, and will stop at nothing to bring him to templar justice.

Samuel

- First Appearance: Vigil's Keep

Samuel was a groundskeeper who once worked in the service of Arl Howe. When the Grey Wardens took over the estate, Samuel decided to remain. Nathaniel Howe has fond memories of Samuel, and you should visit with the groundskeeper in the eastern section of Vigil's Keep.

Ser Tamra

- First Appearance: Vigil's Keep

This noblewoman can potentially be swayed to your side and offer you information on a conspiracy against the Warden-Commander. Her main asset is her penchant for spying. She will risk a great deal to help you.

Ser Temmerly the Ox

- First Appearance: Vigil's Keep

A knight accused of murder, he is a strong, burly man, and even though he is accused of a crime, he is proud and defiant.

Ser Timothy

- First Appearance: Vigil's Keep

Lady Esmerelle's associate has arguments with other nobles.

Seranni

- First Appearance: Silverite Mine

Seranni is Velanna's younger sister. She has led a somewhat sheltered life, even as a nomadic Dalish, because Velanna has always protected her. As a result, Seranni is trusting and idealistic. When she springs the group from the Architect's first hideout, she has been infected with the darkspawn disease, and has started to believe that the Architect is not just an evil darkspawn, but something more.

Statue of Peace

- First Appearance: Wending Wood

This ancient Avvar barbarian was turned to stone by a Tevinter magister over a thousand years ago. Unlike his brother (the Statue of War), he has come to terms with his condition. He sleeps for years at a time.

Statue of War

- First Appearance: Wending Wood

This ancient Avvar barbarian was turned to stone by a Tevinter magister over a thousand years ago. He has forgotten a great deal and is consumed by anger and revenge.

Rylock ~ Wynne

Basics ~ Classes ~ The Party ~ Companions ~ **Supporting Cast** ~ Equipment ~ Bestiary ~ Walkthrough ~ Side Quests ~ Random Encounters ~ Achievements/Trophies

Spoiler Alert

Steafan

- First Appearance: Kal'Hirol

Steafan is a young thief who has been captured by the darkspawn. If you choose to free him in Kal'Hirol, he will return safely to Amaranthine.

Wade

- First Appearance: Vigil's Keep

Partner with Herren, travelers from the distant city of Denerim, Wade is a master smith who always longs for a project that will test his abilities. He is an eccentric genius and seeks perfection.

Utha

- First Appearance: Silverite Mine

Utha is one of the Architect's closest allies, and was once a Silent Sister and a Grey Warden. The Architect used her blood to awaken some other darkspawn. Utha is very loyal to the Architect.

The Withered

- First Appearance: Vigil's Keep

This follower of the Architect is in many ways like the Architect—calm and civilized, though he isn't as familiar with speaking the languages of humans. The Withered is the PC's first major encounter with a talking darkspawn.

Varel

- First Appearance: Vigil's Keep

Varel is an educated man, a fifth son from a noble family who has devoted his life to running Vigil's Keep. He has a strong interest in tradition, and he's hoping to have the keep restored now that it has new owners. He manages the affairs of the keep while you are away.

Voldrik

- First Appearance: Vigil's Keep

Voldrik is a master stonemason and Dworkin's brother. He is very serious about his work and proud of what he does. He will aid you in strengthening Vigil Keep's defenses if you have the sovereigns to match his superior tastes.

Wynne

- First Appearance: Amaranthine

A returning character from *Dragon Age: Origins*, Wynne is a spirit healer from the Circle of the Magi. She has served the Circle for most of her life and is a well-respected mentor and mage. Wynne has very strong morals and sense of duty. She believes wholeheartedly in what the Circle does and believes that through discipline, learning, and wisdom, mages can learn to control and use their gifts to serve Ferelden.

Wynne believes that fear of magic stems from a lack of understanding. She is careful in her speech and carries herself with dignity because she knows that she will be judged as a mage, and wants to present herself as someone who is to be respected, but not feared or reviled. Wynne was saved from death by a Spirit of Faith, which has now bonded to her and sustains her. The spirit is weakening and when it can no longer sustain her, Wynne will die. She has made peace with this.

When you meet her, she is preparing to journey to Cumberland, where the College of Enchanters is convening. She may ask a favor of you if you're inclined to help out.

primagames.com

Equipment

NOTE

This chapter includes only the equipment found in *Awakening*. Although you can import other equipment from *Origins* with your character, you will quickly want to upgrade to the better Tier 8 and Tier 9 equipment found only in *Awakening*.

Suit up in the Sentinel armor, intimidating foes with a look as black and scary as the deepest abyss, and you'll love to see your warrior strut into every fight. Gather the exotic components and ask Master Wade to craft you Vigilance, the mightiest sword in the game, and your PC will cut through all but the strongest monsters with a stroke or two. Each upgrade to your gear is another step on the path toward adventuring godhood.

All party members need good weapons, helmets, gloves, chest pieces, boots, and various accessories. Magical or otherwise, these items bulk up your defense, improve attribute scores, and give you special powers. Whatever you don't fit in your character equipment slots goes into your party inventory, which you can draw from with any character.

TIP

Companions back at Vigil's Keep can hold onto items as well. If you don't have enough space in your inventory to store everything, load up your extra companions or drop items in the Personal Storage chest in the throne room.

Weapon and Armor Materials

When purchasing weapons and armor from vendors or upgrading from monster drops or treasure finds, pay close attention to the items' material types. The game breaks items down into nine different tiers in several different materials. For example, Tier 1 iron won't provide as much damage or damage reduction as the Tier 4 veridium. In general, a higher tier means a better item, if you have the requirements to use it. However, some items may hold special bonuses that override the tier system. If, for example, you're a warrior and find a Tier 9 weapon with bonuses to cunning, you may want to hold on to your old Tier 8 weapon with its strength bonus. Unless you rely on a lot of your old equipment, in *Awakening*, you will generally deal only with Tier 8 and Tier 9 gear.

Most of your equipment comes from vendors, monsters, or treasure; however, you can also find very special items as you complete side quests. You can collect the full set of the super-cool Sentinel armor, for example, in the Blackmarsh during your brush with the First and on the "Tears in the Veil" side quest.

	Material Type
Metals	Iron (Tier 1)
	Grey Iron (Tier 2)
	Steel (Tier 3)
	Veridium (Tier 4)
	Red Steel (Tier 5)
	Silverite (Tier 6)
	Dragonbone (Tier 7)
	White Steel (Tier 8)
	Volcanic Aurum (Tier 9)
Woods	Elm (Tier 1)
	Ash (Tier 2)
	Yew (Tier 3)
	Whitewood (Tier 4)
	Ironbark (Tier 5)
	Sylvanwood (Tier 6)
	Dragonthorn (Tier 7)
	Vhenadahl (Tier 8)
	Ancestral Heartwood (Tier 9)
Leathers	Rough Hide (Tier 1)
	Cured Hide (Tier 2)
	Leather (Tier 3)
	Hardened Leather (Tier 4)
	Reinforced Leather (Tier 5)
	Inscribed Leather (Tier 6)
	Drakeskin (Tier 7)
	Dragonwing (Tier 8)
	High Dragon Hide (Tier 9)

Vendor Shopping

Basics ~ Classes ~ The Party ~ Companions ~ Supporting Cast ~ **Equipment** ~ Bestiary ~ Walkthrough ~ Side Quests ~ Random Encounters ~ Achievements/Trophies

Vendor Shopping

In every major city and village, merchant vendors sell their goods to anyone who flashes a coin at them. Some specialize in armor, while others dabble in the elements of crafting. Some places like the Amaranthine Market District are home to many vendors, and you can find just about anything, legal or otherwise.

Backpacks

As soon as you can afford a backpack, go out and buy one. Each backpack increases your inventory capacity by 10 slots. It's well worth the investment to gain extra holding space on those long dungeon treks. You can find backpacks in Amaranthine, Vigil's Keep courtyard, and four backpacks on Yuriah in the throne room. You can access a new backpack from Yuriah each time you upgrade his store through various merchant-related side quests.

- Glassric's Wares (Amaranthine)
- Herren's Merchandise (Vigil's Keep)
- Yuriah's Wares (Throne Room)
- Yuriah's Wares Upgrade 1 (Throne Room)
- Yuriah's Wares Upgrade 2 (Throne Room)
- Yuriah's Wares Upgrade 3 (Throne Room)

Manuals

Most manuals train you in a class specialization, a rare and valuable thing. The Manual of Focus allows you to re-spec your character. You can find manuals at the following vendors:

- Cera's Rune Stock, Throne Room (Manual: Battlemage)
- Dwarven Bartender, The Crown and the Lion Inn (Manual: Blood Mage)
- Dwarven Bartender, The Crown and the Lion Inn (Manual: Reaver)
- Glassric's Wares, Amaranthine (Manual: Legionnaire Scout)
- Henley's Apothecary, Amaranthine (Manual: Keeper)
- Herren's Merchandise, Vigil's Keep (Manual: Guardian)
- Herren's Merchandise, Vigil's Keep (Manual of Focus)
- Octham's Goods, Amaranthine (Manual: Spirit Warrior)
- Yuriah's Wares, Throne Room (Manual: Shadow)

Rune Tracings

Once you level up a bit and have some sovereigns weighing down your pockets, you'll want to invest in top-notch runes to empower your better weapons. Look for the new masterpiece and paragon runes, plus some specialty runes, at the following vendors:

- Cera's Rune Stock, Throne Room (Evasion Rune Tracing)
- Dwarven Bartender, Crown and Lion Inn (Intensifying Rune Tracing)
- Glassric's Wares, Amaranthine (Menacing Rune Tracing)
- Octham's Goods, Amaranthine (Amplification Rune Tracing)

- Yuriah's Wares Upgrade 1, Throne Room (Endurance Rune Tracing)
- Yuriah's Wares Upgrade 1, Throne Room (Masterpiece Lightning Rune Tracing)
- Yuriah's Wares Upgrade 2, Throne Room (Masterpiece Dweomer Rune Tracing)
- Yuriah's Wares Upgrade 2, Throne Room (Masterpiece Silverite Rune Tracing)
- Yuriah's Wares Upgrade 2, Throne Room (Masterpiece Reservoir Rune Tracing)
- Yuriah's Wares Upgrade 2, Throne Room (Paragon Lightning Rune Tracing)
- Yuriah's Wares Upgrade 2, Throne Room (Paragon Reservoir Rune Tracing)
- Yuriah's Wares Upgrade 3, Throne Room (Paragon Dweomer Rune Tracing)
- Yuriah's Wares Upgrade 3, Throne Room (Paragon Silverite Rune Tracing)

Merchant Vendor Lists

Until you can craft items for yourself with Runecrafting, Herbalism, Poison-Making, and Trap-Making, vendors will be your primary source for runes, health poultices, lyrium potions, and any poisons or traps you may want to use in your adventuring. Even after you start crafting, you will visit vendors often to fill up on the components necessary for your crafts. Note which vendors service your needs the best, because you'll return to them often. While shopping, you will spot unique magic items in almost every shop (marked with an "*" in the following vendor lists). Build up your sovereigns to purchase these choice items for your end-game campaign. Also keep in mind that vendors' stores can upgrade later in the game. Stock that was once dull may hold a new surprise or two. Any time that you want to unload items and sell for profit, take a quick glance at the merchandise in case something new, or suddenly relevant, catches your eye.

❧ ── TIP ── ❧

Sell most of your extra inventory at Yuriah's Wares in the Vigil's Keep throne room. Vendors keep the items you sell to them, and you never know when you'll want to buy back that main-hand mace or special rune later in the game. If it's at Yuriah's, you definitely know where to find it.

The following merchant vendor lists show you all saleable items organized by location. If you happen to be passing through Amaranthine or Vigil's Keep, just look up the shops and note anything that you need to stock up on. So gather up some coin and get shopping already!

Merchant Name	Item Name	Item Quantity
Amaranthine		
Glassric's Wares	Aodh*	1
Glassric's Wares	Arrow of Filth	80
Glassric's Wares	Axe	1
Glassric's Wares	Backpack	1
Glassric's Wares	Battleaxe	1
Glassric's Wares	Biteback Axe*	1
Glassric's Wares	Concentrator Agent	1
Glassric's Wares	Corrupter Agent	1
Glassric's Wares	Dagger	1
Glassric's Wares	Deep Mushroom	21
Glassric's Wares	Demonslayer*	1
Glassric's Wares	Distillation Agent	1
Glassric's Wares	Dwarven Armor	1
Glassric's Wares	Dwarven Armored Boots	1
Glassric's Wares	Dwarven Armored Gloves	1
Glassric's Wares	Dwarven Helmet	1
Glassric's Wares	Dwarven Large Round Shield	1
Glassric's Wares	Engraved Mace*	1
Glassric's Wares	Exalted Maul*	1
Glassric's Wares	Expert Cold Iron Rune Tracing	1
Glassric's Wares	Expert Hale Rune Tracing	1
Glassric's Wares	Expert Reservoir Rune Tracing	1
Glassric's Wares	Expert Silverite Rune Tracing	1
Glassric's Wares	Expert Stout Rune Tracing	1
Glassric's Wares	Explosive Bolt	30
Glassric's Wares	Fire Arrow	99
Glassric's Wares	Fire Bolt	99
Glassric's Wares	Fire Bomb	2
Glassric's Wares	Fire Bomb Recipe	1
Glassric's Wares	Freeze Bomb Recipe	1
Glassric's Wares	Frenzy*	1
Glassric's Wares	Glamour Charm	16
Glassric's Wares	Grandmaster Cold Iron Rune Tracing	1
Glassric's Wares	Grandmaster Stout Rune Tracing	1
Glassric's Wares	Gravity Trap	1
Glassric's Wares	Greater Elixir of Grounding	4
Glassric's Wares	Greater Health Poultice	3
Glassric's Wares	Greater Ice Salve	4
Glassric's Wares	Greater Nature Salve	2
Glassric's Wares	Greater Spirit Balm	1
Glassric's Wares	Greater Stamina Draught	3
Glassric's Wares	Greater Warmth Balm	3
Glassric's Wares	Greatsword	1
Glassric's Wares	Heraldry: Aeducan	1
Glassric's Wares	Heraldry: Legion of the Dead	1
Glassric's Wares	Imperial Edge*	1
Glassric's Wares	Injury Kit	7
Glassric's Wares	Journeyman Cold Iron Rune Tracing	1
Glassric's Wares	Journeyman Hale Rune Tracing	1
Glassric's Wares	Journeyman Reservoir Rune Tracing	1
Glassric's Wares	Journeyman Silverite Rune Tracing	1
Glassric's Wares	Journeyman Stout Rune Tracing	1
Glassric's Wares	Knockback Bolt	80
Glassric's Wares	Large Caltrop Trap	4
Glassric's Wares	Large Caltrop Trap Plans	1
Glassric's Wares	Large Claw Trap	6

Merchant Name	Item Name	Item Quantity
Amaranthine (continued)		
Glassric's Wares	Large Claw Trap Plans	1
Glassric's Wares	Large Shrapnel Trap	3
Glassric's Wares	Large Shrapnel Trap Plans	1
Glassric's Wares	Longshot*	1
Glassric's Wares	Longsword	1
Glassric's Wares	Mace	1
Glassric's Wares	Manual: Legionnaire Scout	1
Glassric's Wares	Master Cold Iron Rune Tracing	1
Glassric's Wares	Master Hale Rune Tracing	1
Glassric's Wares	Master Reservoir Rune Tracing	1
Glassric's Wares	Master Silverite Rune Tracing	1
Glassric's Wares	Master Stout Rune Tracing	1
Glassric's Wares	Maul	1
Glassric's Wares	Menacing Rune Tracing	1
Glassric's Wares	Metal Shard	99
Glassric's Wares	Poisoned Caltrop Trap	2
Glassric's Wares	Poisoned Caltrop Trap Plans	1
Glassric's Wares	Potent Health Poultice	2
Glassric's Wares	Pure Iron	1
Glassric's Wares	Rock Salve	43
Glassric's Wares	Seeker's Chain*	1
Glassric's Wares	Shock Bomb Recipe	1
Glassric's Wares	Shock Coating	2
Glassric's Wares	Small Caltrop Trap Plans	1
Glassric's Wares	Small Claw Trap Plans	1
Glassric's Wares	Small Shrapnel Trap	8
Glassric's Wares	Small Shrapnel Trap Plans	1
Glassric's Wares	Snow Globe*	1
Glassric's Wares	Spring Trap Plans	1
Glassric's Wares	Sureshot Bolt	80
Glassric's Wares	Talon of the Skies*	1
Glassric's Wares	Thorval's Luck*	1
Glassric's Wares	Trap Trigger	99
Glassric's Wares	Yusaris*	1
Henley's Apothecary	Concentrator Agent	1
Henley's Apothecary	Corrupter Agent	1
Henley's Apothecary	Deep Mushroom	12
Henley's Apothecary	Distillation Agent	1
Henley's Apothecary	Elfroot	98
Henley's Apothecary	Emerald	1
Henley's Apothecary	Fire Crystal	4
Henley's Apothecary	Flame Coating	7
Henley's Apothecary	Flask	1
Henley's Apothecary	Flawless Ruby	1
Henley's Apothecary	Freezing Coating	6
Henley's Apothecary	Frostrock	6
Henley's Apothecary	Frozen Lightning	8
Henley's Apothecary	Garnet	1
Henley's Apothecary	Greater Elixir of Grounding	6
Henley's Apothecary	Greater Health Poultice	16
Henley's Apothecary	Greater Health Poultice Recipe	1
Henley's Apothecary	Greater Ice Salve	7
Henley's Apothecary	Greater Lyrium Potion	5
Henley's Apothecary	Greater Nature Salve	4
Henley's Apothecary	Greater Spirit Balm	2
Henley's Apothecary	Greater Stamina Draught	8
Henley's Apothecary	Greater Warmth Balm	11

Vendor Shopping

Basics ~ Classes ~ The Party ~ Companions ~ Supporting Cast ~ **Equipment** ~ Bestiary ~ Walkthrough ~ Side Quests ~ Random Encounters ~ Achievements/Trophies

Merchant Name	Item Name	Item Quantity
Amaranthine (continued)		
Henley's Apothecary	Health Poultice	22
Henley's Apothecary	Health Poultice Recipe	1
Henley's Apothecary	Heraldry: Dragon's Peak Bannorn	1
Henley's Apothecary	Heraldry: Templars	1
Henley's Apothecary	Incense of Awareness Recipe	1
Henley's Apothecary	Injury Kit Recipe	1
Henley's Apothecary	Lesser Elixir of Grounding	11
Henley's Apothecary	Lesser Elixir of Grounding Recipe	1
Henley's Apothecary	Lesser Health Poultice	36
Henley's Apothecary	Lesser Ice Salve	13
Henley's Apothecary	Lesser Ice Salve Recipe	1
Henley's Apothecary	Lesser Lyrium Potion	12
Henley's Apothecary	Lesser Lyrium Potion Recipe	1
Henley's Apothecary	Lesser Nature Salve	7
Henley's Apothecary	Lesser Nature Salve Recipe	1
Henley's Apothecary	Lesser Spirit Balm	4
Henley's Apothecary	Lesser Stamina Draught	18
Henley's Apothecary	Lesser Stamina Draught Recipe	1
Henley's Apothecary	Lesser Warmth Balm	9
Henley's Apothecary	Lesser Warmth Balm Recipe	1
Henley's Apothecary	Lyrium Dust	1
Henley's Apothecary	Lyrium Potion	8
Henley's Apothecary	Lyrium Potion Recipe	1
Henley's Apothecary	Magebane	3
Henley's Apothecary	Manual: Keeper*	1
Henley's Apothecary	Potent Health Poultice	9
Henley's Apothecary	Potent Lyrium Potion	3
Henley's Apothecary	Potent Stamina Draught	5
Henley's Apothecary	Rock Salve Recipe	1
Henley's Apothecary	Shock Coating	5
Henley's Apothecary	Spirit Shard	7
Henley's Apothecary	Stamina Draught	12
Henley's Apothecary	Swift Salve Recipe	1
Octham's Goods	Amplification Rune Tracing	1
Octham's Goods	Archon Robes*	1
Octham's Goods	Ashen Gloves*	1
Octham's Goods	Black Hand Gauntlets*	1
Octham's Goods	Cinderfel Gauntlets*	1
Octham's Goods	Collective Arming Cowl*	1
Octham's Goods	Elementalist's Grasp*	1
Octham's Goods	Enchanter's Arming Cap*	1
Octham's Goods	Enchanter's Footing*	1
Octham's Goods	Expert Dweomer Rune Tracing	1
Octham's Goods	Expert Immunity Rune Tracing	1
Octham's Goods	Expert Paralyze Rune Tracing	1
Octham's Goods	Expert Slow Rune Tracing	1
Octham's Goods	Fire Crystal	11
Octham's Goods	First Enchanter Robes*	1
Octham's Goods	First Enchanter's Cowl*	1
Octham's Goods	Frostrock	8
Octham's Goods	Frozen Lightning	13
Octham's Goods	Golden Vase*	1
Octham's Goods	Grandmaster Immunity Rune Tracing	1
Octham's Goods	Grandmaster Paralyze Rune Tracing	1
Octham's Goods	Grandmaster Slow Rune Tracing	1
Octham's Goods	Heaven's Wrath*	1
Octham's Goods	Heraldry: City of Amaranthine	1

Merchant Name	Item Name	Item Quantity
Amaranthine (continued)		
Octham's Goods	Journeyman Dweomer Rune Tracing	1
Octham's Goods	Journeyman Immunity Rune Tracing	1
Octham's Goods	Journeyman Paralyze Rune Tracing	1
Octham's Goods	Journeyman Slow Rune Tracing	1
Octham's Goods	Lucky Cap*	1
Octham's Goods	Magister's Staff*	1
Octham's Goods	Magus Ward*	1
Octham's Goods	Manual: Spirit Warrior*	1
Octham's Goods	Master Dweomer Rune Tracing	1
Octham's Goods	Master Immunity Rune Tracing	1
Octham's Goods	Master Paralyze Rune Tracing	1
Octham's Goods	Master Slow Rune Tracing	1
Octham's Goods	Oven Mitts*	1
Octham's Goods	Reinforced Magus Cowl*	1
Octham's Goods	Robes of the Gifted*	1
Octham's Goods	Shaperate's Blessing*	1
Octham's Goods	Silk Weave Gloves*	1
Octham's Goods	Spellfury*	1
Octham's Goods	Spirit of the Woods*	1
Octham's Goods	Spirit Shard	7
Octham's Goods	Staff of the Ephemeral Order*	1
Octham's Goods	Storm Talons*	1
Octham's Goods	Tevinter Mage Robes*	1
Octham's Goods	The Libertarian's Cowl*	1
Octham's Goods	Winter Boots*	1
Octham's Goods	Wintersbreath*	1
Crown and Lion Inn		
Dwarven Bartender	Acid Flask Recipe	1
Dwarven Bartender	Acidic Coating Recipe	1
Dwarven Bartender	Acidic Grease Trap Plans	1
Dwarven Bartender	Antivan Leather Boots	1
Dwarven Bartender	Armsman's Tensioner*	1
Dwarven Bartender	Bow of the Golden Sun*	1
Dwarven Bartender	Choking Powder Cloud Trap Plans	1
Dwarven Bartender	Concentrated Crow Poison Recipe	1
Dwarven Bartender	Concentrated Deathroot Extract Recipe	1
Dwarven Bartender	Concentrated Venom Recipe	1
Dwarven Bartender	Concentrator Agent	99
Dwarven Bartender	Corrupter Agent	99
Dwarven Bartender	Crossbow	1
Dwarven Bartender	Crow Dagger	1
Dwarven Bartender	Crow Poison Recipe	1
Dwarven Bartender	Deathroot	22
Dwarven Bartender	Deathroot Extract Recipe	1
Dwarven Bartender	Demonic Ichor	8
Dwarven Bartender	Distillation Agent	99
Dwarven Bartender	Fingers of the Nimble*	1
Dwarven Bartender	Flaming Coating Recipe	1
Dwarven Bartender	Flask	99
Dwarven Bartender	Fleet Feet*	1
Dwarven Bartender	Heraldry: Antivan Crows	1
Dwarven Bartender	Intensifying Rune Tracing	1
Dwarven Bartender	Interesting Lure Trap Plans	1
Dwarven Bartender	Lifestone	1
Dwarven Bartender	Longbow	1
Dwarven Bartender	Magebane Poison Recipe	1
Dwarven Bartender	Mage's Eye*	1
Dwarven Bartender	Manual: Blood Mage*	1

PRIMA Official Game Guide

Merchant Name	Item Name	Item Quantity
Crown and Lion Inn (continued)		
Dwarven Bartender	Manual: Reaver*	1
Dwarven Bartender	Misery*	1
Dwarven Bartender	Poisoned Caltrop Trap Plans	1
Dwarven Bartender	Potent Health Poultice	5
Dwarven Bartender	Potent Stamina Draught	3
Dwarven Bartender	Shadow of the Empire*	1
Dwarven Bartender	Shock Coating Recipe	1
Dwarven Bartender	Shortbow	1
Dwarven Bartender	Sleeping Gas Trap Plans	1
Dwarven Bartender	Soldier's Bane Recipe	1
Dwarven Bartender	Studded Leather Armor	1
Dwarven Bartender	Studded Leather Boots	1
Dwarven Bartender	Studded Leather Gloves	1
Dwarven Bartender	Studded Leather Helm	1
Dwarven Bartender	Thorn of the Dead Gods*	1
Dwarven Bartender	Toxin Extract	1
Dwarven Bartender	Venom Recipe	1
Dwarven Bartender	Voice of Velvet*	1
Silverite Mine		
Armaas's Goods	Adder's Kiss	5
Armaas's Goods	Arrow of Filth	40
Armaas's Goods	Concentrated Deathroot Extract	6
Armaas's Goods	Darkspawn Greatsword	1
Armaas's Goods	Darkspawn Longsword	1
Armaas's Goods	Demonic Poison	3
Armaas's Goods	Fire Arrow	40
Armaas's Goods	Fire Bolt	40
Armaas's Goods	Fire Bomb	13
Armaas's Goods	Flame Coating	6
Armaas's Goods	Fleshrot	4
Armaas's Goods	Freeze Bomb	8
Armaas's Goods	Freezing Coating	5
Armaas's Goods	Shock Bomb	4
Armaas's Goods	Shock Coating	4
Armaas's Goods	Soulrot Bomb	3
Vigil's Keep		
Herren's Merchandise	Axe	1
Herren's Merchandise	Backpack	1
Herren's Merchandise	Battleaxe	1
Herren's Merchandise	Clamshell Plate Armor*	1
Herren's Merchandise	Commander's Helm	1
Herren's Merchandise	Dagger	1
Herren's Merchandise	Denerim Guard Shield	1
Herren's Merchandise	Executioner's Helm*	1
Herren's Merchandise	Fire Arrow	99
Herren's Merchandise	Greatsword	1
Herren's Merchandise	Heavy Chainmail	1
Herren's Merchandise	Heavy Chainmail Boots	1
Herren's Merchandise	Heavy Chainmail Gloves	1
Herren's Merchandise	Heavy Infantry Helmet	1
Herren's Merchandise	Heavy Maul	1
Herren's Merchandise	Heavy Metal Shield	1
Herren's Merchandise	Heavy Plate Armor	1
Herren's Merchandise	Heavy Plate Boots	1
Herren's Merchandise	Heavy Plate Gloves	1
Herren's Merchandise	Helmet	1
Herren's Merchandise	Heraldry: Bear's Paw	1

Merchant Name	Item Name	Item Quantity
Vigil's Keep (continued)		
Herren's Merchandise	Heraldry: Grey Wardens	1
Herren's Merchandise	Knight-Commander's Helm*	1
Herren's Merchandise	Large Wooden Round Shield	1
Herren's Merchandise	Longsword	1
Herren's Merchandise	Mace	1
Herren's Merchandise	Mage-Hunter*	1
Herren's Merchandise	Manual of Focus	1
Herren's Merchandise	Manual: Guardian*	1
Herren's Merchandise	Metal Kite Shield	1
Herren's Merchandise	Metal Shard	1
Herren's Merchandise	Panacea*	1
Herren's Merchandise	Rainswept*	1
Herren's Merchandise	Small Metal Round Shield	1
Herren's Merchandise	Soldier's Heavy Helm	1
Herren's Merchandise	Soldier's Helm	1
Herren's Merchandise	Splintmail	1
Herren's Merchandise	Splintmail Boots	1
Herren's Merchandise	Splintmail Gloves	1
Herren's Merchandise	Stormchaser Gauntlets*	1
Herren's Merchandise	Templar Shield	1
Herren's Merchandise	Tevinter Shield	1
Herren's Merchandise	Wade's Dragonbone Plate Armor*	1
Herren's Merchandise	Wade's Dragonbone Plate Boots*	1
Herren's Merchandise	Wade's Dragonbone Plate Gloves*	1
Herren's Merchandise	Wade's Dragonskin Armor*	1
Herren's Merchandise	Wade's Dragonskin Boots*	1
Herren's Merchandise	Wade's Dragonskin Gloves*	1
Herren's Merchandise	Wade's Drakeskin Boots*	1
Herren's Merchandise	Wade's Drakeskin Gloves*	1
Herren's Merchandise	Wade's Drakeskin Leather Armor*	1
Herren's Merchandise	Wade's Heavy Dragonscale Armor*	1
Herren's Merchandise	Wade's Heavy Dragonscale Boots*	1
Herren's Merchandise	Wade's Heavy Dragonscale Gloves*	1
Vigil's Keep Throne Room		
Yuriah's Wares	Acidic Grease Trap	7
Yuriah's Wares	Acidic Trap Plans	1
Yuriah's Wares	Backpack	1
Yuriah's Wares	Blood of the Warrior*	1
Yuriah's Wares	Choking Powder Trap	5
Yuriah's Wares	Concentrator Agent	1
Yuriah's Wares	Corrupter Agent	1
Yuriah's Wares	Crossbow	1
Yuriah's Wares	Deathroot	14
Yuriah's Wares	Distillation Agent	1
Yuriah's Wares	Fire Arrow	60
Yuriah's Wares	Fire Bolt	60
Yuriah's Wares	Fire Trap Plans	1
Yuriah's Wares	Freeze Trap	6
Yuriah's Wares	Freeze Trap Plans	1
Yuriah's Wares	Frostrock	3
Yuriah's Wares	Glamour Charm	15
Yuriah's Wares	Golden Cog*	1
Yuriah's Wares	Greater Elixir of Grounding	5
Yuriah's Wares	Greater Health Poultice	3
Yuriah's Wares	Greater Ice Salve	9
Yuriah's Wares	Greater Injury Kit	13
Yuriah's Wares	Greater Warmth Balm	8

Vendor Shopping

Basics ~ Classes ~ The Party ~ Companions ~ Supporting Cast ~ **Equipment** ~ Bestiary ~ Walkthrough ~ Side Quests ~ Random Encounters ~ Achievements/Trophies

Merchant Name	Item Name	Item Quantity
Vigil's Keep Throne Room (continued)		
Yuriah's Wares	Health Poultice	9
Yuriah's Wares	Heraldry: Cousland	1
Yuriah's Wares	Heraldry: Cross	1
Yuriah's Wares	Injury Kit	22
Yuriah's Wares	Large Grease Trap Plans	1
Yuriah's Wares	Large Shrapnel Trap	6
Yuriah's Wares	Lesser Elixir of Grounding	11
Yuriah's Wares	Lesser Health Poultice	12
Yuriah's Wares	Lesser Ice Salve	15
Yuriah's Wares	Lesser Ice Salve Recipe	1
Yuriah's Wares	Lesser Injury Kit	35
Yuriah's Wares	Lesser Nature Salve	7
Yuriah's Wares	Lesser Nature Salve Recipe	1
Yuriah's Wares	Lesser Spirit Balm	5
Yuriah's Wares	Lesser Warmth Balm	14
Yuriah's Wares	Lesser Warmth Balm Recipe	1
Yuriah's Wares	Lifestone	1
Yuriah's Wares	Longbow	1
Yuriah's Wares	Manual: Shadow*	1
Yuriah's Wares	Mild Choking Powder Trap Plans	1
Yuriah's Wares	Mild Lure Plans	1
Yuriah's Wares	Mild Sleeping Gas Trap	9
Yuriah's Wares	Mild Sleeping Gas Trap Plans	1
Yuriah's Wares	Scout's Bow	1
Yuriah's Wares	Scout's Medal*	1
Yuriah's Wares	Shock Trap Plans	1
Yuriah's Wares	Small Grease Trap Plans	1
Yuriah's Wares	Trap Trigger	1
Yuriah's Wares upgrade 1	Backpack	1
Yuriah's Wares upgrade 1	Charlatan's Walking Stick*	1
Yuriah's Wares upgrade 1	Deep Mushroom	20
Yuriah's Wares upgrade 1	Elf-Flight Arrow	40
Yuriah's Wares upgrade 1	Endurance Rune Tracing	1
Yuriah's Wares upgrade 1	Flaming Coating Recipe	1
Yuriah's Wares upgrade 1	Freezing Coating Recipe	1
Yuriah's Wares upgrade 1	Grandmaster Dweomer Rune Tracing	1
Yuriah's Wares upgrade 1	Grandmaster Lightning Rune Tracing	1
Yuriah's Wares upgrade 1	Grandmaster Reservoir Rune Tracing	1
Yuriah's Wares upgrade 1	Grandmaster Silverite Rune Tracing	1
Yuriah's Wares upgrade 1	Ice Arrow	40
Yuriah's Wares upgrade 1	Ice Bolt	40
Yuriah's Wares upgrade 1	Masterpiece Lightning Rune Tracing	1
Yuriah's Wares upgrade 1	Shock Bomb Recipe	1
Yuriah's Wares upgrade 1	Shock Coating Recipe	1
Yuriah's Wares upgrade 1	Stormchaser Mail*	1
Yuriah's Wares upgrade 2	Backpack	1
Yuriah's Wares upgrade 2	Cap of the Nimble*	1
Yuriah's Wares upgrade 2	Choking Powder Cloud Trap Plans	1
Yuriah's Wares upgrade 2	Concentrated Magebane Recipe	1
Yuriah's Wares upgrade 2	Concentrated Soldier's Bane Recipe	1
Yuriah's Wares upgrade 2	Deathroot	13
Yuriah's Wares upgrade 2	Deep Mushroom	70
Yuriah's Wares upgrade 2	Explosive Bolt	40
Yuriah's Wares upgrade 2	Fire Bolt	99
Yuriah's Wares upgrade 2	Grandmaster Frost Rune Tracing	1
Yuriah's Wares upgrade 2	Greater Health Poultice Recipe	1
Yuriah's Wares upgrade 2	Ice Bolt	99
Yuriah's Wares upgrade 2	Icicle*	1

Merchant Name	Item Name	Item Quantity
Vigil's Keep Throne Room (continued)		
Yuriah's Wares upgrade 2	Injury Kit Recipe	1
Yuriah's Wares upgrade 2	Knockback Bolt	40
Yuriah's Wares upgrade 2	Lesser Injury Kit Recipe	1
Yuriah's Wares upgrade 2	Mage's Running Boots*	1
Yuriah's Wares upgrade 2	Masterpiece Dweomer Rune Tracing	1
Yuriah's Wares upgrade 2	Masterpiece Reservoir Rune Tracing	1
Yuriah's Wares upgrade 2	Masterpiece Silverite Rune Tracing	1
Yuriah's Wares upgrade 2	Novice Immunity Rune	1
Yuriah's Wares upgrade 2	Novice Tempest Rune	1
Yuriah's Wares upgrade 2	Overpowering Lure Trap Plans	1
Yuriah's Wares upgrade 2	Paragon Lightning Rune Tracing	1
Yuriah's Wares upgrade 2	Paragon Reservoir Rune Tracing	1
Yuriah's Wares upgrade 2	Sash of Power*	1
Yuriah's Wares upgrade 2	Sleeping Gas Cloud Trap Plans	1
Yuriah's Wares upgrade 2	Soulrot Bomb Recipe	1
Yuriah's Wares upgrade 2	Soulrot Coating Recipe	1
Yuriah's Wares upgrade 2	Soulrot Trap Plans	1
Yuriah's Wares upgrade 2	Stamina Draught Recipe	1
Yuriah's Wares upgrade 2	Superb Health Poultice Recipe	1
Yuriah's Wares upgrade 2	Sureshot Bolt	40
Yuriah's Wares upgrade 3	Backpack	1
Yuriah's Wares upgrade 3	Concentrated Demonic Poison Recipe	1
Yuriah's Wares upgrade 3	Deathroot	50
Yuriah's Wares upgrade 3	Dispel Grenade	3
Yuriah's Wares upgrade 3	Elemental Grenade	4
Yuriah's Wares upgrade 3	Fire Bomb	7
Yuriah's Wares upgrade 3	Fire Crystal	50
Yuriah's Wares upgrade 3	Freeze Bomb	5
Yuriah's Wares upgrade 3	Frostrock	50
Yuriah's Wares upgrade 3	Frozen Lightning	50
Yuriah's Wares upgrade 3	Greater Ice Salve Recipe	1
Yuriah's Wares upgrade 3	Greater Injury Kit Recipe	1
Yuriah's Wares upgrade 3	Greater Lyrium Potion Recipe	1
Yuriah's Wares upgrade 3	Greater Stamina Draught Recipe	1
Yuriah's Wares upgrade 3	Greater Warmth Balm Recipe	1
Yuriah's Wares upgrade 3	Master Health Poultice Recipe	1
Yuriah's Wares upgrade 3	Novice Reservoir Rune	1
Yuriah's Wares upgrade 3	Overpowering Lure Trap Plans	1
Yuriah's Wares upgrade 3	Paragon Dweomer Rune Tracing	1
Yuriah's Wares upgrade 3	Paragon Silverite Rune Tracing	1
Yuriah's Wares upgrade 3	Potent Stamina Draught Recipe	1
Yuriah's Wares upgrade 3	Quiet Death Recipe	1
Yuriah's Wares upgrade 3	Sleeping Gas Cloud Trap Plans	1
Yuriah's Wares upgrade 3	Spirit Shard	50
Yuriah's Wares upgrade 3	Superb Lyrium Potion Recipe	1
Cera's Rune Stock	Blank Runestone	7
Cera's Rune Stock	Etching Agent	25
Cera's Rune Stock	Evasion Rune Tracing	1
Cera's Rune Stock	Expert Flame Rune Tracing	1
Cera's Rune Stock	Expert Frost Rune Tracing	1
Cera's Rune Stock	Expert Lightning Rune Tracing	1
Cera's Rune Stock	Expert Paralyze Rune Tracing	1
Cera's Rune Stock	Expert Slow Rune Tracing	1
Cera's Rune Stock	Expert Tempest Rune Tracing	1
Cera's Rune Stock	Grandmaster Flame Rune Tracing	1
Cera's Rune Stock	Grandmaster Tempest Rune Tracing	1
Cera's Rune Stock	Greater Lyrium Potion	2

Merchant Name	Item Name	Item Quantity
Vigil's Keep Throne Room (continued)		
Cera's Rune Stock	Journeyman Cold Iron Rune Tracing	1
Cera's Rune Stock	Journeyman Dweomer Rune Tracing	1
Cera's Rune Stock	Journeyman Flame Rune Tracing	1
Cera's Rune Stock	Journeyman Frost Rune Tracing	1
Cera's Rune Stock	Journeyman Hale Rune Tracing	1
Cera's Rune Stock	Journeyman Immunity Rune Tracing	1
Cera's Rune Stock	Journeyman Lightning Rune Tracing	1
Cera's Rune Stock	Journeyman Paralyze Rune Tracing	1
Cera's Rune Stock	Journeyman Reservoir Rune Tracing	1
Cera's Rune Stock	Journeyman Silverite Rune Tracing	1
Cera's Rune Stock	Journeyman Slow Rune Tracing	1
Cera's Rune Stock	Journeyman Stout Rune Tracing	1
Cera's Rune Stock	Journeyman Tempest Rune Tracing	1
Cera's Rune Stock	Lesser Lyrium Potion	5
Cera's Rune Stock	Lyrium Potion	3
Cera's Rune Stock	Manual: Battlemage*	1
Cera's Rune Stock	Master Flame Rune Tracing	1
Cera's Rune Stock	Master Frost Rune Tracing	1
Cera's Rune Stock	Master Lightning Rune Tracing	1
Cera's Rune Stock	Master Reservoir Rune Tracing	1
Cera's Rune Stock	Master Tempest Rune Tracing	1
Cera's Rune Stock	Novice Cold Iron Rune	1
Cera's Rune Stock	Novice Dweomer Rune	1
Cera's Rune Stock	Novice Flame Rune	1
Cera's Rune Stock	Novice Frost Rune	1
Cera's Rune Stock	Novice Hale Rune	1
Cera's Rune Stock	Novice Immunity Rune	1
Cera's Rune Stock	Novice Lightning Rune	1

Merchant Name	Item Name	Item Quantity
Vigil's Keep Throne Room (continued)		
Cera's Rune Stock	Novice Paralyze Rune	1
Cera's Rune Stock	Novice Reservoir Rune	1
Cera's Rune Stock	Novice Silverite Rune	1
Cera's Rune Stock	Novice Slow Rune	1
Cera's Rune Stock	Novice Stout Rune	1
Cera's Rune Stock	Novice Tempest Rune	1
Vigil's Keep (Siege only)		
Medic's Supply	Elfroot	48
Medic's Supply	Greater Health Poultice	9
Medic's Supply	Greater Health Poultice Recipe	1
Medic's Supply	Greater Injury Kit	3
Medic's Supply	Greater Injury Kit Recipe	1
Medic's Supply	Greater Spirit Balm Recipe	1
Medic's Supply	Health Poultice	23
Medic's Supply	Health Poultice Recipe	1
Medic's Supply	Injury Kit	4
Medic's Supply	Injury Kit Recipe	1
Medic's Supply	Lesser Health Poultice	32
Medic's Supply	Lesser Health Poultice Recipe	1
Medic's Supply	Master Health Poultice Recipe	1
Medic's Supply	Master Stamina Draught Recipe	1
Medic's Supply	Potent Health Poultice	6
Medic's Supply	Potent Health Poultice Recipe	1
Medic's Supply	Potent Stamina Draught Recipe	1
Medic's Supply	Superb Health Poultice	4
Medic's Supply	Superb Health Poultice Recipe	1
Medic's Supply	Superb Lyrium Potion Recipe	1

Weapons

If your character loves to hack-and-slash, you'll be happy to scrutinize every weapon. Even if you don't jump into the thick of things often, a weapon can still provide valuable bonuses to attributes and special abilities.

What weapon is the right fit for you? First, identify what sort of weapon you want to carry around: a one-handed melee weapon, a two-hander, or a ranged bow or crossbow for distance damage. Next, check out the weapon's tier level. Tiers range from tier 1 to tier 9. Generally the higher tier equals more damage and will prove more useful. Compare the weapon's damage score to other weapons you have in your inventory (or at local vendors) and choose the highest damage score if other bonuses don't matter. For stats on the general Tier 8 and Tier 9 weapons in *Awakening*, see the following table.

General Weapon Stats

NOTE - Complete coverage of tier 1–7 weapons can be found in the *Dragon Age: Origins* strategy guide.

Type	Tier	Requirement	Damage	Armor Penetration	Critical Chance	Range	Spellpower	Rune Slots
Staff	Tier 8 - White Steel	40 Magic	6.8	45	NA	60	8	3
	Tier 9 - Volcanic Aurum	46 Magic	7.2	50	NA	62.5	10	3
Axe	Tier 8 - White Steel	35 Strength	10.2	4.5	1.7	NA	NA	3
	Tier 9 - Volcanic Aurum	41 Strength	10.8	5	1.8	NA	NA	3
Battleaxe	Tier 8 - White Steel	42 Strength	17	6.75	5.1	NA	NA	3
	Tier 9 - Volcanic Aurum	48 Strength	18	7.5	5.4	NA	NA	3
Dagger	Tier 8 - White Steel	34 Dexterity	6.8	9	5.1	NA	NA	3
	Tier 9 - Volcanic Aurum	40 Dexterity	7.2	10	5.4	NA	NA	3
Greatsword	Tier 8 - White Steel	42 Strength	18.7	6.75	2.55	NA	NA	3
	Tier 9 - Volcanic Aurum	48 Strength	19.8	7.5	2.7	NA	NA	3
Longsword	Tier 8 - White Steel	35 Strength	11.9	4.5	3.4	NA	NA	3
	Tier 9 - Volcanic Aurum	41 Strength	12.6	5	3.6	NA	NA	3

Vendor Shopping - Weapons

Basics ~ Classes ~ The Party ~ Companions ~ Supporting Cast ~ Equipment ~ Bestiary ~ Walkthrough ~ Side Quests ~ Random Encounters ~ Achievements/Trophies

Type	Tier	Requirement	Damage	Armor Penetration	Critical Chance	Range	Spellpower	Rune Slot
Mace	Tier 8 - White Steel	36 Strength	8.5	9	0.85	NA	NA	3
	Tier 9 - Volcanic Aurum	42 Strength	9	10	0.9	NA	NA	3
Maul	Tier 8 - White Steel	42 Strength	15.3	15.75	0.85	NA	NA	3
	Tier 9 - Volcanic Aurum	48 Strength	16.2	17.5	0.9	NA	NA	3
Longbow	Tier 8 - Vhenadahl	38 Dexterity	10.2	10	1.7	49	NA	3
	Tier 9 - Ancestral Heartwood	44 Dexterity	10.8	11	1.8	52.5	NA	3
Short bow	Tier 8 - Vhenadahl	34 Dexterity	8.5	7.5	1.7	28	NA	3
	Tier 9 - Ancestral Heartwood	40 Dexterity	9	8.25	1.8	30	NA	3
Crossbow	Tier 8 - Vhenadahl	34 Strength	13.6	12.5	3.4	56	NA	3
	Tier 9 - Ancestral Heartwood	40 Strength	14.4	13.75	3.6	60	NA	3

Certain weapons have restrictions, such as staves can only be used by mages. Sell those items you receive if nobody in your party can use them. Below your damage score, critical chance shows you the likelihood of dealing critical strikes, and armor penetration calculates how much more damage you can punch through armor. Higher values in critical chance and armor penetration can lean you toward one weapon over another that may have a similar damage score.

As you level up, more and more weapons (as well as armor and accessories) will come with attribute bonuses and special abilities. Now you must decide: Do you take the weapon with the greater damage score, or do you choose the weapon with the better bonuses? If you're playing pure DPS, damage may be the most important factor. If your play style is more versatile, bonuses tend to be the way to go. Ideally, you will find a weapon that has the maximum damage score for your level range and great bonuses to power your character up.

TIP

Higher-tier weapons may come with rune slots (generally three), which you can use to customize your weapon with powers that you choose (damage bonuses, paralysis, spell resistance, etc.). Don't underestimate weapons with rune slots! It may be better to hold a rune-slot weapon with fewer natural bonuses because it becomes more powerful as you equip better runes.

Unique Weapons

Axes							
Item Name	Material	Quality #1	Quality #2	Quality #3	Quality #4	Quality #5	Item Location
Ancient Dwarven Axe	Dragonbone	Damage +1	Armor Penetration +2	—	—	—	Sigrun
Aodh	Silverite	+3% Melee Critical Chance	+20 Fire Resistance	-5 Cold Resistance	+1 Fire Damage	—	Glassric's Wares in Amaranthine
Biteback Axe	Silverite	Armor Penetration +1.5	+15% Critical Damage	Required: Rogue	No Attribute Requirements	—	Glassric's Wares in Amaranthine
Daisycutter	Volcanic Aurum	Telekinetic	Melee Crit Chance +3	—	—	—	Avvar Sarcophagus in Vigil's Keep Basement
Darkspawn Waraxe	All Metal	Cunning +2	Armor Penetration +2	—	—	—	Kal'Hirol
Heirsplitter	Dragonbone	Damage +2	Attack +4	Crit Damage +10%	—	—	Kal'Hirol

Battleaxes							
Item Name	Material	Quality #1	Quality #2	Quality #3	Quality #4	Quality #5	Item Location
Darkspawn Battleaxe	All Metal	Cunning +2	Armor Penetration +2	—	—	—	Kal'Hirol
Darkspawn Ravager	Silverite	Melee Crit Chance +2	Attack +4	—	—	—	Oghren
Frenzy	White Steel	Combat Health Regen +0.5	Damage +5	Chance to Ignore Hostile Magic +10%	Attack +10	—	Shrine of Korth or Glassric's Wares

Crossbows							
Item Name	Material	Quality #1	Quality #2	Quality #3	Quality #4	Quality #5	Item Location
Beastmaster	Dragonthorn	Damage +2	Faster Aim +0.3	—	—	—	Chest on Vigil's Keep Battlements
Darkspawn Crossbow	Ash Wood	Cunning +2	Damage +2	Ranged Crit Chance +3	—	—	Kah'Hirol
Longshot	Ancestral Heartwood	Faster Aim +0.4	Attack +10	Damage +10	Ranged Crit Chance +15	—	Glassric's Wares in Amaranthine

Daggers							
Item Name	Material	Quality #1	Quality #2	Quality #3	Quality #4	Quality #5	Item Location
Crow Dagger	Silverite	Critical/Backstab Damage +15%	—	—	—	—	Dwarven Bartender in Crown and Lion
Darkspawn Dagger	All Metal	Cunning +2	Damage +2	—	—	—	Kal'Hirol

primagames.com

Item Name	Material	Quality #1	Quality #2	Quality #3	Quality #4	Quality #5	Item Location
Daggers (continued)							
Dumat's Claw	Dragonbone	Attack +2	Damage +2	Defense +9	When equipped with the sword Dumat's Spine, the character is immune to flanking.	—	Pirate Leader in Random Encounter
Fang	Veridium	+6 Attack					Crow Assassin
The Rose's Thorn	Dragonbone	+2 Dexterity	+1.0 Combat Health Regeneration	+3 Damage	+5% Melee Critical Chance	+30% Critical Damage	Smuggler Leader
Scout's Dirk	Dragonbone	—	—			—	Sigrun
Talon of the Skies	Dragonbone	Attack +4	Melee Crit Chance +10	Fire Damage +2	When equipped with the dagger Tooth of the Mountain-Father, the character gains a bonus to stamina regeneration.	—	Glassric's Wares in Amaranthine
Thorn of the Dead Gods	Silverite	+3 Damage	Armor Penetration +3	—	—	—	Dwarven Bartender in Crown and Lion
Tooth of the Mountain-Father	Volcanic Aurum	Damage +1	Armor Penetration +5	When equipped with the dagger Talon of the Skies, the character gains a bonus to stamina regeneration.	—		Mosley the Snake in Forlorn Cove
Twinblade	Dragonbone	Restrict: Rogue	Melee Crit Chance +1	Armor Penetration +1	Attack +2	—	Character Creation
Voice of Velvet	Volcanic Aurum	Damage +3, Cold Damage +5	Combat Health Regen +1	Melee Crit Chance +5	Chance to Dodge Attacks +25%	Crit Damage +100%	Dwarven Bartender in Crown and Lion
Greatswords							
Balanced Greatsword	Iron	No Attribute Requirements	—	—	—	—	Garevel
Darkspawn Greatsword	Grey Iron	Cunning +2	Damage +2				Kal'Hirol
Dragonbrand	Volcanic Aurum	Armor Penetration +3	Combat Stamina Regen +1	Attack +10	Constitution +5	—	Dragonhunter Corpse in Random Encounter
The Mother's Chosen	White Steel	Cunning +2	Armor Penetration +2	Attack +4			The First
Ornamental Sword	Iron	Lucky	-5 Attack	-1 Damage	—	—	Garevel or Varel
Ser Alvard's Sword	Dragonbone	Fire Resistance +20	Attack +10	Chance to ignite target +10%	—	—	Decomposing Crate in Blackmarsh or Avvar Lord
Warden's Reach	Dragonbone	Restrict: Warrior or Rogue	Crit Damage +15%	—	—	—	Character Creation
Yusaris	Silverite	+20 Fire Resistance	Damage vs. Dragons +10	—	—	—	Glassric's Wares in Amaranthine
Longbows							
Bow of the Golden Sun	Sylvanwood	+4 Attack	—	—	—	—	Dwarven Bartender in Crown and Lion
Chasind Arm	Dragonbone	Damage +3	Attack +8	—	—	—	Goodwife Turnoble
Commission	Dragonthorn	Restrict: Warrior or Rogue	Faster Aim +0.1	Attack +4	Ranged Crit Chance +3		Character Creation
Darkspawn Longbow	Ash Wood	Attack +2	Cunning +2	Armor Penetration +2	—	—	Kal'Hirol
Howe Bow	Ancestral Heartwood	Restriction: Nathaniel	Faster Aim +.2	Attack +4	Damage +3	Ranged Crit Chance +5%	Bag in Avvar Crypt
Mage's Eye	Dragonthorn	+3% Ranged Critical Chance	+4 Attack	—	—	—	Dwarven Bartender in Crown and Lion
Misery	Ancestral Heartwood	Faster Aim +0.5	Armor Penetration +2.5	Attack +10	Ranged Crit Chance +10	—	Dwarven Bartender in Crown and Lion
Spear-Thrower	Sylvanwood	0.3s Faster Aim	+5 Armor Penetration	—	—	—	Smuggler Leader

Weapons

Basics ~ Classes ~ The Party ~ Companions ~ Supporting Cast ~ **Equipment** ~ Bestiary ~ Walkthrough ~ Side Quests ~ Random Encounters ~ Achievements/Trophies

Longswords

Item Name	Material	Quality #1	Quality #2	Quality #3	Quality #4	Quality #5	Item Location
Darkspawn Longsword	Grey Iron	Cunning +2	Damage +2	—	—	—	Kal'Hirol
Dumat's Spine	White Steel	Combat Stamina Regen +0.75	Attack +6	Crit Damage +25%	When equipped with the dagger Dumat's Claw, the character is immune to flanking.	—	Weapon Stand in Throne Room
Gorim's Sword	Red Steel	—	—	—	—	—	Constable Aidan
Imperial Edge	Silverite	Damage +2	Melee Critical Chance +3%	Attack +6	—	—	Glassric's Wares in Amaranthine
Kallak	White Steel	Crit Damage +10%	When equipped with the shield Partha, the character gains a bonus to stamina regeneration.		—	—	Avvar Lord in Vigil's Keep Basement
Keening Blade	Dragonbone	+4 Armor Penetration	+6 Attack	Required: Warrior	+3 Cold Damage	—	Avvar Lord in Vigil's Keep Basement
Warden's Companion	Dragonbone	Restrict: Warrior or Rogue	Armor Penetration +1	Attack +4	Dexterity +2	—	Character Creation
The Winter Blade	Dragonbone	Armor Penetration +1	Attack +4	—	—	—	Utha in Drake's Fall

Maces

Item Name	Material	Quality #1	Quality #2	Quality #3	Quality #4	Quality #5	Item Location
Chevalier's Mace	Steel	+5 Cold Resistance	Spirit Resistance -5	+2 Cold Damage	—	—	Weapon Stand in Throne Room
Darkspawn Mace	Grey Iron	Attack +2	Cunning +2	—	—	—	Kal'Hirol
Engraved Mace	Veridium	+1 Dexterity	+1 Damage	+5 Mental Resistance	—	—	Glassric's Wares in Amaranthine
The Lamented	Dragonbone	Strength +3	Constitution +3	—	—	—	Justice
Liberator's Mace	Red Steel	+1 Dexterity	+3% Melee Critical Chance	—	—	—	Ser Rylock
Skullcrusher	White Steel	Armor Penetration +2	Attack +6	—	—	—	Chest in Blackmarsh
Vanguard	Silverite	+3 Strength	+3 Constitution	+1.0 Combat Stamina Regeneration	—	—	Kristoff's Corpse in Blackmarsh

Mauls

Item Name	Material	Quality #1	Quality #2	Quality #3	Quality #4	Quality #5	Item Location
Darkspawn Maul	Grey Iron	Attack +2	Cunning +2	—	—	—	Kal'Hirol
Demonslayer	Dragonbone	Armor Penetration +2	Damage +5	Damage vs. Possessed Creatures +20	—	—	Glassric's Wares in Amaranthine
Exalted Maul	Silverite	+2 Willpower	+10 Mental Resistance	Damage vs. Possessed Creatures +4	—	—	Glassric's Wares in Amaranthine
Leg-Crusher	White Steel	Melee Crit Chance +5	—	—	—	—	Hurlock Dragno-Tamer in Silverite Mine
Thorval's Luck	Silverite	+10% to Healing Spells	+4 Attack	+10 Physical Resistance	—	—	Glassric's Wares in Amaranthine
Valos Atredum	White Steel	Combat Health Regen +4	Crit Damage +25%	—	—	—	Kal'Hirol

Shortbows

Item Name	Material	Quality #1	Quality #2	Quality #3	Quality #4	Quality #5	Item Location
Dragonspite	Vhenadahl	Damage vs. Dragons +20	Rapid Aim	Reduces Hostility	Damage +4	Attack +10	Silverite Mine

Staves

Item Name	Material	Quality #1	Quality #2	Quality #3	Quality #4	Quality #5	Item Location
Call of the Inferno	Vhenadahl	Cold Resistance +5	Required: Mage	Faster Aim +0.2	Increases all Fire Damage +15%	Spellpower +10	Urn in Vigil's Keep Deep Roads
Charlatan's Walking Stick	Dragonbone	Required: Mage	Combat Mana Regen +1	Willpower +5	Spellpower +7	—	Yuriah's Wares (upgrade 1)
Darkspawn Staff	Iron	Cunning +1	Required: Mage	Increases all Sprit Damage +5%	Spellpower +2	—	Kal'Hirol
The Dragon's Call	Dragonbone	Restrict: Mage	Combat Mana Regen +1	Willpower +3	Spellpower +5	—	Character Creation
Flemeth's Broomstick	Dragonbone	Required: Mage	Increases all Nature Damage (+2.5% per power)	Spellpower +10	—	—	Disciple General in Amaranthine Siege

primagames.com

Staves (continued)						
Item Name	Material	Quality #1	Quality #2	Quality #3	Quality #4	Quality #5	Item Location
Heart of the Forest	Dragonbone	Required: Mage	Increases all Fire Damage +10%	Spellpower +6	Willpower +6	Combat Mana Regen +8	Velanna
Heaven's Wrath	Silverite	+1.0 Combat Mana Regeneration	+5 Spellpower	+10% to Electricity Damage	Required: Mage	—	Octham's Goods in Amaranthine
Lamppost in Winter	Ancestral Heartwood	Fire Resistance +5	Required: Mage	Faster Aim +0.2	Increases all Cold Damage +20%	Spellpower +12	Disciple General in Amaranthine Siege
Lightning Rod	Dragonbone	Required: Mage	Increases all Lightning Damage +10%	Spellpower +8	—	—	Crate in Abandoned Warehouse
Magister's Staff	Silverite	+1.0 to Combat Mana Regeneration	+5 Spellpower	+10% to Spirit Damage	Required: Mage	—	Anders
Shaperate's Blessing	Silverite	+2 Willpower	+0.5 Combat Mana Regeneration	+10% to Cold Damage	Required: Mage	—	Octham's Goods in Amaranthine
Spellfury	Ancestral Heartwood	Required: Mage	All Attributes +4	Faster Aim +0.4	Combat Mana Regen +1	Spellpower +20	Octham's Goods in Amaranthine
Staff of Shadows	Dragonbone	Restrict: Mage	Increases all Fire Damage +5%	Magic +2	Spellpower +3	—	Character Creation
Staff of the Ephemeral Order	Silverite	+3 Willpower	+5% to Spirit Damage	Required: Mage	—	—	Octham's Goods in Amaranthine
Staff of the Lost	Ancestral Heartwood	Required: Mage	Stamina +75	Spirit Resistance +15	Magic +10	Spellpower +15, Increases all Sprit Damage +50%	The Lost
Staff of Vigor	Ancestral Heartwood	Required: Mage	Faster Aim +0.3	Combat Health Regen +4	Constitution +5	Spellpower +10	Hurlock Emissary in Kal'Hirol
Wintersbreath	Dragonbone	+25 Cold Resistance	+3 Spellpower	+10% to Cold Damage	Required: Mage		Octham's Goods in Amaranthine

Vigilance—Once in a dozen generations, a truly legendary weapon is forged. This blade, created in a time of war from the bones of an ancient dragon, sings with power.

This legendary weapon is crafted for your character when you complete the "Worked to the Bone" side quest from Master Wade in Vigil's Keep. During your conversation with him, he will ask you a series of questions which will ultimately determine what type of weapon he crafts. Below you can find each dialog selection, along with the stats for each weapon variation.

Greatsword Dialog Options	
Flexible, Sharp	Greatsword 1
Flexible, Defense	Greatsword 2
Flexible, Effortless	Greatsword 3
Flexible, Wade's Recommendation	Greatsword 4
Power, Sharp	Greatsword 5
Power, Defense	Greatsword 6
Power, Effortless	Greatsword 7
Power, Wade's Recommendation	Greatsword 8

Longsword Dialog Options	
Flexible, Sharp	Longsword 1
Flexible, Defense	Longsword 2
Flexible, Effortless	Longsword 3
Flexible, Wade's Recommendation	Longsword 4
Power, Sharp	Longsword 5
Power, Defense	Longsword 6
Power, Effortless	Longsword 7
Power, Wade's Recommendation	Longsword 8

Crafted						
Item Name	Material	Quality #1	Quality #2	Quality #3	Quality #4	Quality #5	Item Location
Heartwood Bow	Ancestral Heartwood	Attack +6	Faster Aim +0.3	Ranged Crit Chance +5	Dexterity +5	Cunning +5	Crafted by Master Wade
Vigilance Greatsword 1	Volcanic Aurum	Armor Penetration +1	All Attributes +1	Melee Crit Chance +3	Crit Damage +15%	Attack +8	Crafted by Master Wade
Vigilance Greatsword 2	Volcanic Aurum	All Attributes +1	Armor Penetration +1	Chance to Dodge Attacks +10%	Defense +6	Attack +8	Crafted by Master Wade
Vigilance Greatsword 3	Volcanic Aurum	All Attributes +1	Armor Penetration +1	Combat Stamina Regen +0.5	Stamina +50	Attack +8	Crafted by Master Wade
Vigilance Greatsword 4	Volcanic Aurum	Armor Penetration +1	Attack +8	All Attributes +4	—	—	Crafted by Master Wade
Vigilance Greatsword 5	Volcanic Aurum	All Attributes +1	Attack +2	Crit Damage +15%	Melee Crit Chance +3	Armor Penetration +4	Crafted by Master Wade

Weapons - Armor

Basics ~ Classes ~ The Party ~ Companions ~ Supporting Cast ~ **Equipment** ~ Bestiary ~ Walkthrough ~ Side Quests ~ Random Encounters ~ Achievements/Trophies

Item Name	Material	Quality #1	Quality #2	Quality #3	Quality #4	Quality #5	Item Location
				Crafted (continued)			
Vigilance Greatsword 6	Volcanic Aurum	All Attributes +1	Attack +2	Chance to Dodge Attacks +10%	Defense +6	Armor Penetration +4	Crafted by Master Wade
Vigilance Greatsword 7	Volcanic Aurum	Attack +2	All Attributes +1	Stamina +50	Combat Stamina Regen +0.5	Armor Penetration +4	Crafted by Master Wade
Vigilance Greatsword 8	Volcanic Aurum	Attack +2	All Attributes +4	Armor Penetration +4	—	—	Crafted by Master Wade
Vigilance Longsword 1	Volcanic Aurum	All Attributes +1	Armor Penetration +1	Melee Crit Chance +3	Crit Damage +15%	Attack +8	Crafted by Master Wade
Vigilance Longsword 2	Volcanic Aurum	All Attributes +1	Armor Penetration +1	Chance to Dodge Attacks +10%	Defense +6	Attack +4	Crafted by Master Wade
Vigilance Longsword 3	Volcanic Aurum	All Attributes +1	Armor Penetration +1	Combat Stamina Regen +0.5	Stamina +50	Attack +8	Crafted by Master Wade
Vigilance Longsword 4	Volcanic Aurum	Armor Penetration +1	Attack +8	All Attributes +4	—	—	Crafted by Master Wade
Vigilance Longsword 5	Volcanic Aurum	All Attributes +1	Attack +2	Crit Damage +15%	Melee Crit Chance +3	Armor Penetration +4	Crafted by Master Wade
Vigilance Longsword 6	Volcanic Aurum	All Attributes +1	Attack +2	Defense +6	Chance to Dodge Attacks +10%	Armor Penetration +4	Crafted by Master Wade
Vigilance Longsword 7	Volcanic Aurum	All Attributes +1	Attack +2	Stamina +50	Combat Stamina Regen +0.5	Armor Penetration +4	Crafted by Master Wade
Vigilance Longsword 8	Volcanic Aurum	Attack +2	All Attributes +4	Armor Penetration +4	—	—	Crafted by Master Wade

Armor

There are four armor slots on a character's equipment panel: helmet, gloves, chest, and boots. Warriors can also take advantage of a fifth slot for a shield, especially if they train in the Sword and Shield school. Combined, the armor slots add up to your total armor rating, which protects you from all forms of physical damage.

What armor fits you best? First, consider any restrictions your class may have. A mage, for example, cannot wear the more durable armors (with the exception of the Arcane Warrior mage). Armor may also have a strength or dexterity requirement. Next, check out the armor's tier level; tiers range from Tier 1 to Tier 9, and generally the higher tiers equal more protection. Compare the armor's armor score to other armor you have in your inventory (or at local vendors) and choose the highest armor score if other bonuses don't matter. For stats on the general Tiers 8 and Tier 9 armor and shields in *Awakening*, see the following table.

General Armor Stats

NOTE - Complete coverage of tier 1–7 armor can be found in the *Dragon Age: Origins* strategy guide.

Type	Tier	Requirement	Armor	Missile Defense	Fatigue	Rune Slots
		Armor				
Massive Boots	Tier 8 - White Steel	46 Strength	4.05	NA	4.5	3
	Tier 9 - Volcanic Aurum	52 Strength	4.5	NA	5.25	3
Heavy Boots	Tier 8 - White Steel	42 Strength	3.375	NA	3.375	3
	Tier 9 - Volcanic Aurum	48 Strength	3.75	NA	3.938	3
Medium Boots	Tier 8 - White Steel	38 Strength	2.7	NA	2.25	3
	Tier 9 - Volcanic Aurum	44 Strength	3	NA	2.625	3
Light Boots	Tier 8 - Dragonwing	22 Strength	2.498	NA	0.625	3
	Tier 9 - High Dragon Hide	24 Strength	2.745	NA	0.65	3
Massive Chest	Tier 8 - White Steel	46 Strength	23.625	NA	31.5	3
	Tier 9 - Volcanic Aurum	52 Strength	26.25	NA	36.75	3
Heavy Chest	Tier 8 - White Steel	42 Strength	16.875	NA	21	3
	Tier 9 - Volcanic Aurum	48 Strength	18.75	NA	24.5	3
Medium Chest	Tier 8 - White Steel	38 Strength	11.475	NA	10.5	3
	Tier 9 - Volcanic Aurum	44 Strength	12.75	NA	12.25	3
Light Chest	Tier 8 - Dragonwing	22 Strength	9.99	NA	2.5	3
	Tier 9 - High Dragon Hide	24 Strength	10.98	NA	2.6	3
Mage Robes / Head Gear	Stats for these are still only measured in the bonuses of the item	—	—	—	—	NA
Massive Gloves	Tier 8 - White Steel	46 Strength	3.375	NA	4.5	3
	Tier 9 - Volcanic Aurum	52 Strength	3.75	NA	5.25	3

Type	Tier	Requirement	Armor	Missile Defense	Fatigue	Rune Slots
Armor (continued)						
Heavy Gloves	Tier 8 - White Steel	42 Strength	2.7	NA	2.625	3
	Tier 9 - Volcanic Aurum	48 Strength	3	NA	3.063	3
Medium Gloves	Tier 8 - White Steel	38 Strength	2.025	NA	1.875	3
	Tier 9 - Volcanic Aurum	44 Strength	2.25	NA	2.188	3
Light Gloves	Tier 8 - Dragonwing	22 Strength	1.665	NA	1.25	3
	Tier 9 - High Dragon Hide	24 Strength	1.83	NA	1.3	3
Massive Helmet	Tier 8 - White Steel	46 Strength	4.05	NA	4.5	3
	Tier 9 - Volcanic Aurum	52 Strength	4.5	NA	5.25	3
Heavy Helmet	Tier 8 - White Steel	42 Strength	3.375	NA	3.375	3
	Tier 9 - Volcanic Aurum	48 Strength	3.75	NA	3.938	3
Medium Helmet	Tier 8 - White Steel	38 Strength	2.7	NA	2.25	3
	Tier 9 - Volcanic Aurum	44 Strength	3	NA	2.625	3
Light Helmet	Tier 8 - Dragonwing	22 Strength	2.498	NA	0	3
	Tier 9 - High Dragon Hide	24 Strength	2.745	NA	0	3
Shields						
Kite, Metal	Tier 8 - White Steel	42 Strength	NA	9	4.8	3
	Tier 9 - Volcanic Aurum	48 Strength	NA	10.5	5.6	3
Kite, Wood	Tier 8 - Vhenadahl	30 Strength	NA	9	4	3
	Tier 9 - Ancestral Heartwood	32 Strength	NA	10.5	4.16	3
Large Round Metal	Tier 8 - White Steel	38 Strength	NA	6.75	3.75	3
	Tier 9 - Volcanic Aurum	44 Strength	NA	7.875	4.375	3
Large Round Wood	Tier 8 - Vhenadahl	26 Strength	NA	6.75	3.125	3
	Tier 9 - Ancestral Heartwood	28 Strength	NA	7.875	3.25	3
Small Round Metal	Tier 8 - White Steel	34 Strength	NA	4.5	0	3
	Tier 9 - Volcanic Aurum	40 Strength	NA	5.25	0	3
Small Round Wood	Tier 8 - Vhenadahl	22 Strength	NA	4.5	0	3
	Tier 9 - Ancestral Heartwood	24 Strength	NA	5.25	0	3
Heavy, Metal	Tier 8 - White Steel	46 Strength	NA	12	7.2	3
	Tier 9 - Volcanic Aurum	52 Strength	NA	14	8.4	3
Heavy, Wood	Tier 8 - Vhenadahl	34 Strength	NA	12	6	3
	Tier 9 - Ancestral Heartwood	36 Strength	NA	14	6.24	3

NOTE

Tier 8 and 9 for the wooden shields have a lower strength requirement than Tiers 6 and 7 because Vhenadahl and Ancestral Heartwood are extremely light and strong materials, enabling players with lower strength to wield top-notch shields.

Something else to keep in mind: if you collect pieces of armor from the same set, you may gain item set bonuses. These can range from fatigue reduction to fire resistance with any of Master Wade's drake and dragon armor items. In general, it's worth collecting an armor set that's in your level range if you can find all the pieces.

As you level up, most armor will come with attribute bonuses and special abilities. Now you have decisions to make: Do you take the armor with the greater defensive value, or do you choose the armor with the better bonuses? If you're playing the tank role, defense may be the most important factor. If your play style is more versatile, bonuses tend to be the way to go. Ideally, you will find four pieces of armor that have great defense scores for your level range and excellent bonuses.

CAUTION

You can't just look at the highest armor score for your equipment. Armor also comes with a fatigue score. The fatigue percentage equals how much extra a talent will cost in stamina or a spell will cost in mana. A character with a 50 percent fatigue rating from armor will have all of his abilities cost 50 percent more. Balance your need for physical defense with the impact fatigue has on your stamina or mana.

Armor

Basics ~ Classes ~ The Party ~ Companions ~ Supporting Cast ~ **Equipment** ~ Bestiary ~ Walkthrough ~ Side Quests ~ Random Encounters ~ Achievements/Trophies

							Boots

Item Name	Material	Quality #1	Quality #2	Quality #3	Quality #4	Quality #5	Item Location
				Light			
Antivan Leather Boots	Inscribed Leather	+4% Chance to Ignore Hostile Magic	—	—	—	—	Crow Assassin, Dwarven Bartender, Smuggler Leader, Shady Character (Amaranthine)
Blackblade Boots	High Dragon Hide	Required: Rogue	Dexterity +4	Willpower +4	Cunning +4, Chance to Ignore Hostile Magic +8%	When equipped with the Blackblade tunic, gloves, and helm, the character gains a bonus to armor and the character's spells or talents cost less to activate.	High Dragon in Dragonbone Wastes
Enchanter's Footing	All Leather	Defense +6	Required: Mage	No Attribute Requirements	—	—	Octham's Goods in Amaranthine
Fadewalker	High Dragon Hide	Required: Mage	Spirit Resistance +15	Willpower +5	Defense +15		Pile of Bones in Dragonbone Wastes
Feet of the Nimble	Dragonwing	Required: Rogue	Stamina +50	When equipped with the vest, fingers, and cap of the Nimble, the character gains bonuses to cold resistance and fire resistance.	—	—	Smuggler's Cache in Smuggler's Cache
Firestompers	Dragonwing	Required: Mage	Dexterity +4	Fire Resistance +20	Physical Resistance +10	—	Baroness in Blackmarsh
Grey Warden Leather Boots	Drakescale Leather	Restrict: Rogue	Chance to Dodge Attacks +5%	Armor +2	When equipped with Grey Warden light armor, gloves, and helm, the character gains bonuses to dexterity and constitution.	—	Character Creation
Imperial Weavers	All Leather	+10% Chance to Dodge Attacks	Required: Mage	No Attribute Requirements	—	—	Octham's Goods or Velanna
Lorekeeper's Boots	Dragonwing	Required: Mage	Dexterity +2	Defense +6	Electricity Resistance +15	When equipped with the Lorekeeper's robe, mittens, and cowl, the character gains bonuses to armor and physical resistance.	Armoire in Abandoned Warehouse in Amaranthine
Mage's Running Boots	Dragonwing	Required: Mage	Chance to Dodge Attacks +10%	Defense against Missiles +20	—	—	Yuriah's Wares (upgrade 2)
Magus War Boots	Drakescale Leather	+12 Defense	Required: Mage	No Attribute Requirements	—	—	Anders
Trickster's Boots	Dragonwing	Required: Rogue	Fatigue Reduction +2	Electricity Resistance +20	When equipped with the Trickster's tunic, gloves, and cap, the character's spells or talents cost less to activate.	—	Skeleton in Vigil's Keep Deep Roads
Wade's Drakeskin Boots	Drakescale	+5 Fire Resistance	When equipped with the other Dragonskin items, fatigue -10%	—	—	—	Herren's Merchandise or Crow
Winter Boots	High Dragon Hide	Required: Mage	Armor +2	Defense +15	Cold Resistance +40	Constitution +8	Octham's Goods in Amaranthine
Wolf Treads	High Dragon Hide	Required: Rogue	Defense +6	Dexterity +3	Cunning +3	Defense against Missiles +10	Crow Assassin or Avvar Sarcophagus in Vigil's Keep Basement
Item Name	Material	Quality #1	Quality #2	Quality #3	Quality #4	Quality #5	Item Location
				Medium			
Legionnaire Scout Boots	Dragonbone	Decrease Fire resistance +15	—	—	—	—	Sigrun
Wade's Dragonskin Boots	Dragonbone	+5 Fire Resistance	When equipped with the other Dragonskin items, fatigue -25%	—	—	—	Herren's Merchandise in Vigil's Keep

primagames.com

				Boots (continued)			
Item Name	Material	Quality #1	Quality #2	Quality #3	Quality #4	Quality #5	Item Location
				Heavy			
Boots of Diligence	Silverite	+6 Defense	+2 Armor	When equipped with other Diligence items, willpower +5	—	—	Garevel or Varel
Ceremonial Armored Boots	Red Steel	When equipped with the other Ceremonial items, +6 Defense vs. Missiles	—	—	—	—	Constable Aidan or Lieutenant
Fleet Feet	Volcanic Aurum	Defense +6	Chance to Dodge Attacks +10%	Dexterity +4	Chance to Ignore Hostile Magic +10%	Defense against Missiles +10	Dwarven Bartender in Crown and Lion
Stormchaser Boots	White Steel	Defense +3	Electricity Resistance +5	Dexterity +4	When equipped with the Stormchaser armor, gauntlets, and helm, the character gains a bonus to electricity resistance.	—	Templar Corpse on Turnoble Estate
Wade's Heavy Dragonscale Boots	Dragonbone	+5 Fire Resistance	When equipped with the other Dragonscale items, fatigue -20%	—	—	—	Herren's Merchandise in Vigil's Keep
Item Name	Material	Quality #1	Quality #2	Quality #3	Quality #4	Quality #5	Item Location
				Massive			
Boots of the Legion	Dragonbone	When equipped with the other Legion items, Damage +3 and Constitution +3	—	—	—	—	Oghren, Jukka, or Legionnaire
Boots of the Sentinel	Volcanic Aurum	Defense +3	Physical Resistance +5	Strength +8	When equipped with the armor, gauntlets, and helm of the Sentinel, the character gains a bonus to armor and the character's spells or talents cost less to activate.	—	Iron Chest in Blackmarsh or Avvar Lord in Vigil's Keep Basement
Greaves of Hirol's Defense	White Steel	Constitution +6	When equipped with the breastplate, gauntlets, and helm of Hirol's Defense, the character's spells or talents cost less to activate.	—	—	—	Kal'Hirol
Grey Warden Plate Boots	Silverite	Restrict: Warrior	Chance to Dodge Attacks +5%	Armor +2	When equipped with Grey Warden plate armor, gauntlets, and helm, the character gains bonuses to strength and constitution.	—	Character Creation
Wade's Dragonbone Plate Boots	Dragonbone	+5 Fire Resistance	When equipped with the other Dragonbone items, fatigue -10%	—	—	—	Herren's Merchandise in Vigil's Keep
				Chest			
Item Name	Material	Quality #1	Quality #2	Quality #3	Quality #4	Quality #5	Item Location
				Light			
The Bear's Embrace	Drakescale Leather	Armor +1	Dexterity +3	Physical Resistance +5	—	—	Nathaniel or Prisoner's Effect in Vigil's Keep Dungeon
Blackblade Tunic	High Dragon Hide	Defense +12	Fire Resistance +20	Cold Resistance +20	When equipped with the Blackblade gloves, boots, and helm, the character gains a bonus to armor and the character's spells or talents cost less to activate.	—	Crow Assassin or Chest in Silverite Mine
The Felon's Coat	Drakescale	+6 Dexterity	+9 Defense	+4 Armor	+1.0 Combat Stamina Regeneration	+15 Physical Resistance	Smuggler Leader or Shady Character (Amaranthine)

Armor

Basics ~ Classes ~ The Party ~ Companions ~ Supporting Cast ~ **Equipment** ~ Bestiary ~ Walkthrough ~ Side Quests ~ Random Encounters ~ Achievements/Trophies

Chest (continued)

Item Name	Material	Quality #1	Quality #2	Quality #3	Quality #4	Quality #5	Item Location
Light (continued)							
Grey Warden Light Armor	Drakescale Leather	Restrict: Rogue	Dexterity +2	Combat Stamina Regen +0.5	Armor +4	When equipped with Grey Warden light boots, gloves, and helm, the character gains bonuses to dexterity and constitution.	Character Creation
Orlesian Warden's Light Armor	Drakescale Leather	Restrict: Rogue	Dexterity +2	Combat Stamina Regen +0.5	Armor +4	When equipped with the Warden light gloves, boots, and helm, the character gains bonuses to dexterity and constitution.	Character Creation
Rainswept	High Dragon Hide	Armor +2	Nature Resistance +10	Spirit Resistance +10	Combat Stamina Regen +1	Defense against Missiles +20	Herren's Merchandise in Vigil's Keep
Shadow of the Empire	Drakescale	+2 Strength	+2 Dexterity	+1.0 Combat Stamina Regeneration	—	—	Dwarven Bartender in Crown and Lion
Trickster's Tunic	Dragonwing	Armor +1	Defense +9	Physical Resistance +10	When equipped with the Trickster's gloves, boots, and cap, the character's spells or talents cost less to activate.	—	Armor Stand in Throne Room
Vest of the Nimble	Dragonwing	Armor +1	Dexterity +5	Cunning +5	When equipped with the fingers, feet, and cap of the Nimble, the character gains bonuses to cold resistance and fire resistance.	—	Crow Assassin
Wade's Drakeskin Leather Armor	Drakescale	+25 Fire Resistance	When equipped with the other Dragonskin items, fatigue -10%	—	—	—	Herren's Merchandise or Crow
Item Name	**Material**	**Quality #1**	**Quality #2**	**Quality #3**	**Quality #4**	**Quality #5**	**Item Location**
Medium							
Legionnaire Scout Armor	Dragonbone	Stamina +25	Dexterity +3	—	—	—	Sigrun
Wade's Dragonskin Armor	Dragonbone	+25 Fire Resistance	When equipped with the other Dragonskin items, fatigue -25%	—	—	—	Herren's Merchandise in Vigil's Keep
Item Name	**Material**	**Quality #1**	**Quality #2**	**Quality #3**	**Quality #4**	**Quality #5**	**Item Location**
Heavy							
Armor of Diligence	Silverite	+0.5 Combat Health Regeneration	+2 Armor	When equipped with the other Diligence items, willpower +5	—	—	Garevel or Varel
Ceremonial Armor	Red Steel	-3 Armor	+10 Mental Resistance	When equipped with the other Ceremonial items, +6 Defense vs. Missiles	—	—	Constable Aidan or Lieutenant
Stormchaser Mail	White Steel	Defense +3	Armor +1	Electricity Resistance +10	When equipped with the Stormchaser gauntlets, boots, and helm, the character gains a bonus to electricity resistance.	—	Yuriah's Wares (upgrade 1)
Sturdy Heavy Chainmail	Dragonbone	Armor +2	Strength +3	When equipped with heavy chainmail gloves and boots, the character's spells or talents cost less to activate.	—	—	Justice
Venture	Volcanic Aurum	Defense +12	Constitution +12	—	—	—	Avvar Sarcophagus in Vigil's Keep Basement
Wade's Heavy Dragonscale Armor	Dragonbone	+25 Fire Resistance	When equipped with the other Dragonscale items, fatigue -20%	—	—	—	Herren's Merchandise in Vigil's Keep

primagames.com

Item Name	Material	Quality #1	Quality #2	Quality #3	Quality #4	Quality #5	Item Location
Chest (continued)							
Massive							
Armor of the Legion	Dragonbone	+3 Willpower	When equipped with the other Legion items, Damage +3 and Constitution +3	—	—	—	Oghren, Jukka, or Legionnaire
Armor of the Sentinel	Volcanic Aurum	Combat Health Regen +4	Strength +6	Defense against Missiles +20	Physical Resistance +20	When equipped with the gauntlets, boots, and helm of the Sentinel, the character gains a bonus to armor and the character's spells or talents cost less to activate.	The First
Breastplate of Hirol's Defense	White Steel	Fatigue Reduction +2	Fire Resistance +30	When equipped with the gauntlets, greaves, and helm of Hirol's Defense, the character's spells or talents cost less to activate.	—	—	Kal'Hirol
Clamshell Plate Armor	Volcanic Aurum	Defense +6	Strength +8	Defense against Missiles +30	Physical Resistance +25	—	Herren's Merchandise in Vigil's Keep
Grey Warden Plate Armor	Silverite	Restrict: Warrior	Stamina +25	Constitution +2	Armor +4	When equipped with Grey Warden plate gauntlets, boots, and helm, the character gains bonuses to strength and constitution.	Character Creation
Juggernaut Plate Armor	Silverite	+10 Fire Resistance	+10 Cold Resistance	+10 Electricity Resistance	+10 Nature Resistance	+10 Spirit Resistance	Ser Derren
Knight Commander's Plate	Silverite	+5 Willpower	+40% Chance to Ignore Hostile Magic	+10 Mental Resistance	Required: Templar	—	Ser Rylock
Orlesian Warden's Plate Armor	Silverite	Restrict: Warrior	Stamina +25	Constitution +2	Armor +4	When equipped with the Warden plate gauntlets, boots, and helm, the character gains bonuses to strength and constitution.	Character Creation
Templar Armor	Steel	+3 Willpower	+20% Chance to Ignore Hostile Magic	+5 Mental Resistance	Required: Templar	—	Ser Rylien, Ser Rylock, Templar (Abandoned Warehouse in Amaranthine)
Wade's Dragonbone Plate Armor	Dragonbone	+25 Fire Resistance	When equipped with the other Dragonbone items, fatigue -10%	—	—	—	Herren's Merchandise in Vigil's Keep
Item Name	Material	Quality #1	Quality #2	Quality #3	Quality #4	Quality #5	Item Location
Mage							
Apprentice Robes	Robes	+1 Willpower	—	—	—	—	Experimental Subject in Silverite Mine
Archon Robes	Robes	+0.75 Combat Health Regeneration	+3 Armor	+2 Spellpower	—	—	Octham's Goods in Amaranthine
Blood Promise	Volcanic Aurum	Required: Mage	Improves Blood Magic	Combat Mana Regen +1	Willpower +3	Magic +3, Natural Armor +6	Armoire in Abandoned Warehouse
First Enchanter Robes	Robes	+3 Willpower	+3 Magic	+9 Defense	—	—	Octham's Goods in Amaranthine
Grey Warden Robes	Robes	Required: Mage	Cold Resistance +10	Combat Mana Regen +2	Magic +4, Natural Armor +3	—	Character Creation
Lorekeeper's Robe	Volcanic Aurum	Required: Mage	Magic +3	Fire Resistance +15	Natural armor +5	When equipped with the Lorekeeper's mittens, boots, and cowl, the character gains bonuses to armor and physical resistance.	Hired Goon Leader in Amaranthine

Armor

Basics ~ Classes ~ The Party ~ Companions ~ Supporting Cast ~ **Equipment** ~ Bestiary ~ Walkthrough ~ Side Quests ~ Random Encounters ~ Achievements/Trophies

Chest (continued)

Item Name	Material	Quality #1	Quality #2	Quality #3	Quality #4	Quality #5	Item Location
				Mage (continued)			
Robe of the Witch	Robes	+10 Cold Resistance	+5% Chance to Dodge Attacks	+3 Armor	—	—	Fen Witches
Robes of the Architect		Required: Mage	Stamina +50	Combat Mana Regen +3	Chance to Ignore Hostile Magic +10%	Natural Armor +9	The Architect in Drake's Fall
Robes of the Gifted	Robes	+6% Chance to Ignore Hostile Magic	Reduces Hostility	—	—	—	Octham's Goods in Amaranthine
Robes of the Magister Lords	Robes	+5 Willpower	+10 Fire Resistance	+10 Cold Resistance	—	—	Blood Mages
Robes of the Orlesian Magister	Robes	Required: Mage	Cold Resistance +10 per power)	Combat Mana Regen +2	Magic +4, Natural Armor +3	—	Character Creation
Skins of the Keeper	Robes	All Attributes +1	Defense +6	Spellpower +6	—	—	Velanna
Spellminder	Volcanic Aurum	Required: Mage	Combat Mana Regen +4	Natural Armor +8	Magic +8	—	Queen of the Blackmarsh
Tevinter Mage Robes	Robes	+1.0 Combat Mana Regeneration	+4% Chance to Ignore Hostile Magic	+5 Spellpower	—	—	Anders or Octham's Goods
Vestments of Urthemiel	Robes	Required: Mage	Combat Mana Regen +2	Magic +6	Natural Armor +7	—	Apostate Mage in Amaranthine or Flesh Pod in Drake's Fall

Item Name	Material	Quality #1	Quality #2	Quality #3	Quality #4	Quality #5	Item Location
				Crafted			
Golem Shell Armor	Volcanic Aurum	Armor +2	Fire Resistance +25	Strength +8	Constitution +8	Physical Resistance +20	Crafted by Master Wade

Gloves

Item Name	Material	Quality #1	Quality #2	Quality #3	Quality #4	Quality #5	Item Location
				Light			
Ashen Gloves	Inscribed Leather	+20% to Cold Damage	Required: Mage	No Attribute Requirements	—	—	Octham's Goods in Amaranthine
Backhands	Hardened Leather	+10% Critical Damage	Required: Rogue	—	—	—	Crow Assassin
Black Hand Gauntlets	Inscribed Leather	+20% to Spirit Damage	Required: Mage	No Attribute Requirements	—	—	Octham's Goods in Amaranthine
Blackblade Gloves	High Dragon Hide	Required: Rogue	Fire Resistance +20	Constitution +8	When equipped with the Blackblade tunic, boots, and helm, the character gains a bonus to armor and the character's spells or talents cost less to activate.	—	High Dragon in Dragonbone Wastes
Cinderfel Gauntlets	Inscribed Leather	+20% to Fire Damage	Required: Mage	No Attribute Requirements	—	—	Octham's Goods in Amaranthine
Elementalist's Grasp	Dragonwing	Required: Mage	Increases all Fire Damage +5%	Increases all Sprit Damage +5%	Increases all Cold Damage +5%	Increases all Nature Damage +5%, Increases all Lightning Damage +5%	Disciple General in Amaranthine Siege or Octham's Goods
Fingers of the Nimble	Dragonwing	Required: Rogue	Crit Damage +15%	Faster Aim +0.5	Dexterity +6, Ranged Crit Chance +10	When equipped with the vest, feet, and cap of the Nimble, the character gains bonuses to cold resistance and fire resistance.	Dwarven Bartender in Crown and Lion
Gloves of Guile	Drakescale	+5 Armor Penetration					Smuggler Leader in Smuggler's Cove
Grey Warden Light Gloves	Drakescale Leather	Restrict: Rogue	Attack +4	When equipped with Grey Warden light armor, boots, and helm, the character gains bonuses to dexterity and constitution.	—	—	Character Creation

Item Name	Material	Quality #1	Quality #2	Quality #3	Quality #4	Quality #5	Item Location
Gloves (continued)							
Light (continued)							
Lorekeeper's Mittens	Dragonwing	Required: Mage	Constitution +3	Cold Resistance +15	When equipped with the Lorekeeper's robe, boots, and cowl, the character gains bonuses to armor and physical resistance.	—	Armoire in Abandoned Warehouse
Ornate Leather Gloves	Drakescale Leather	Armor +1	Dexterity +2	—	—	—	Nathaniel or Prisoner's Effects in Vigil's Keep Dungeon
Oven Mitts	High Dragon Hide	Required: Mage	Fire Resistance +30	Cold Resistance +30	Increases all Fire Damage +30%	Increases all Cold Damage +30%	Octham's Goods in Amaranthine
Pocketed Searing Gloves	Hardened Leather	+10% to Fire Damage	Required: Mage	No Attribute Requirements	—	—	Velanna
Polar Gauntlets	Hardened Leather	+10% to Cold Damage	Required: Mage	No Attribute Requirements	—	—	Anders
Pushback Strikers	Drakescale	+5% Melee Critical Chance	Required: Rogue	—	—	—	Shady Character (Amaranthine)
Shock Treatment	Dragonwing	Required: Mage	Electricity Resistance +10	Increases all Lightning Damage +20%	—	—	Dragon Thrall in Silverite Mine
Silk Weave Gloves	Inscribed Leather	+20% to Nature Damage	Required: Mage	No Attribute Requirements	—	—	Octham's Goods in Amaranthine
The Slippery Ferret's Gloves	High Dragon Hide	Required: Rogue	Armor +1	Dexterity +4	Cunning +8	Ranged Crit Chance +10, Melee Crit Chance +10	Dragon Thrall in Silverite Mine
Spirit of the Woods	Dragonwing	Required: Mage	Nature Resistance +30	Spirit Resistance +30	Increases all Sprit Damage +30%	Increases all Nature Damage +30%	Octham's Goods in Amaranthine
Storm Talons	Inscribed Leather	+20% to Electricity Damage	Required: Mage	No Attribute Requirements	—	—	Octham's Goods in Amaranthine
Trickster's Gloves	Dragonwing	Required: Rogue	Attack +4	Dexterity +3	When equipped with the Trickster's tunic, boots, and cap, the character's spells or talents cost less to activate.	—	Smuggler's Cache in Smuggler's Cove
Wade's Drakeskin Gloves	Drakescale	+5 Fire Resistance	When equipped with the other Drakeskin items, fatigue -10%	—	—	—	Herren's Merchandise, Crow Assassin, Crow
Item Name	Material	Quality #1	Quality #2	Quality #3	Quality #4	Quality #5	Item Location
Medium							
Legionnaire Scout Gloves	Dragonbone	Attack +6	—	—	—	—	Sigrun
Wade's Dragonskin Gloves	Dragonbone	+5 Fire Resistance	When equipped with the other Dragonskin items, fatigue -25%	—	—	—	Herren's Merchandise in Vigil's Keep
Item Name	Material	Quality #1	Quality #2	Quality #3	Quality #4	Quality #5	Item Location
Heavy							
Barbed Fists	White Steel	Armor +1	Armor Penetration +2	Attack +6	—	—	Armored Ogre Alpha in Vigil's Keep Siege
Ceremonial Armored Gloves	Red Steel	When equipped with the other Ceremonial items, +6 Defense vs. Missiles	—	—	—	—	Constable Aidan or Lieutenant
Gloves of Diligence	Silverite	+4 Armor	When equipped with the other Diligence items, willpower +5	—	—	—	Garevel or Varel
Stormchaser Gauntlets	Volcanic Aurum	Defense +6	Armor +3	Dexterity +4	Electricity Resistance +30, Combat Stamina Regen +2	When equipped with the Stormchaser armor, boots, and helm, the character gains a bonus to electricity resistance.	Herren's Merchandise in Vigil's Keep

Armor

Item Name	Material	Quality #1	Quality #2	Quality #3	Quality #4	Quality #5	Item Location
Gloves (continued)							
Heavy (continued)							
Sturdy Chainmail Gloves	Dragonbone	Armor +1	Attack +2	When equipped with heavy chainmail armor and boots, the character's spells or talents cost less to activate.	—	—	Justice
Wade's Heavy Dragonscale Gloves	Dragonbone	+5 Fire Resistance	When equipped with the other Dragonscale items, fatigue -20%	—	—	—	Herren's Merchandise in Vigil's Keep

Item Name	Material	Quality #1	Quality #2	Quality #3	Quality #4	Quality #5	Item Location
Massive							
Gauntlets of Hirol's Defense	White Steel	Armor Penetration +2	Melee Crit Chance +3	Strength +4	When equipped with the breastplate, greaves, and helm of Hirol's Defense, the character's spells or talents cost less to activate.	—	Sarcophagus in Kal'Hirol
Gauntlets of the Sentinel	Volcanic Aurum	Melee Crit Chance +3	Attack +6	When equipped with the armor, boots, and helm of the Sentinel, the character gains a bonus to armor and the character's spells or talents cost less to activate.	—	—	Iron Chest in Blackmarsh
Gloves of the Legion	Dragonbone	+4 Attack	When equipped with the other Legion items, Damage +3 and Constitution +3	—	—	—	Oghren, Jukka, Legionnaire
Grey Warden Plate Gauntlets	Silverite	Restrict: Warrior	Attack +4	When equipped with Grey Warden plate armor, boots, and helm, the character gains bonuses to strength and constitution.	—	—	Character Creation
Wade's Dragonbone Plate Gloves	Dragonbone	+5 Fire Resistance	When equipped with the other Dragonbone items, fatigue -10%	—	—	—	Herren's Merchandise in Vigil's Keep

Item Name	Material	Quality #1	Quality #2	Quality #3	Quality #4	Quality #5	Item Location
Helmets							
Light							
Armsman's Tensioner	Inscribed Leather	0.3s Faster Aim	+6 Attack	—	—	—	Dwarven Bartender in Crown and Lion
Blackblade Helm	High Dragon Hide	Required: Rogue	Crit Damage +5%	Combat Stamina Regen +0.5	Willpower +4	When equipped with the Blackblade tunic, gloves, and boots, the character gains a bonus to armor and the character's spells or talents cost less to activate.	Chest in Silverite Mine
Cap of the Nimble	High Dragon Hide	Armor +2	Cunning +6	Chance to Ignore Hostile Magic +20%	Mental Resistance +10	When equipped with the vest, fingers, and feet of the Nimble, the character gains bonuses to cold resistance and fire resistance.	Yuriah's Wares (upgrade 2)
Free Scout Arming Cap	Hardened Leather	+2 Dexterity	—	—	—	—	Crow
Grey Warden Light Helm	Drakescale Leather	Restrict: Warrior	Defense +3	Cunning +2	When equipped with Grey Warden light armor, gloves, and boots, the character gains bonuses to dexterity and constitution.	—	Character Creation

primagames.com

Helmets (continued)

Item Name	Material	Quality #1	Quality #2	Quality #3	Quality #4	Quality #5	Item Location
Light (continued)							
Quicksilver	High Dragon Hide	Chance to Dodge Attacks +5%	Defense +9	Cunning +6	—	—	Pile of Bones in Dragonbone Wastes
Studded Leather Helm	Drakeskin	Physical Resistance +2	—	—	—	—	Dwarven Bartender in Crown and Lion
Trickster's Cap	Dragonwing	Willpower +2	Mental Resistance +15	Physical Resistance +15	When equipped with the Trickster's tunic, gloves, and boots, the character's spells or talents cost less to activate.	—	Avvar Sarcophagus in Vigil's Keep Basement

Item Name	Material	Quality #1	Quality #2	Quality #3	Quality #4	Quality #5	Item Location
Medium							
Dwarven Helmet	Dragonbone	Physical Resistance +2	—	—	—	—	Glassric's Wares in Amaranthine
Legionnaire Scout Helm	Dragonbone	Cold Resistance +15	—	—	—	—	Sigrun

Item Name	Material	Quality #1	Quality #2	Quality #3	Quality #4	Quality #5	Item Location
Heavy							
Executioner's Helm	Silverite	Stamina +25	—	—	—	—	Herren's Merchandise in Vigil's Keep
Helm of Dragon's Peak	Volcanic Aurum	Combat Stamina Regen +.5	Defense +9	Strength +6	—	—	Armored Ogre Alpha in Vigil's Keep Siege
Helm of the Legion	Dragonbone	—	—	—	—	—	Oghren or Legionnaire
Helm of the Red	Steel	+1 Dexterity	+10 Fire Resistance	—	—	—	Lieutenant in Amaranthine
Knight Commander's Helm	Dragonbone	Physical Resistance +5	—	—	—	—	Herren's Merchandise in Vigil's Keep
Stormchaser Helm	White Steel	Defense +6	Electricity Resistance +10	Mental Resistance +15	When equipped with the Stormchaser armor, gauntlets, and boots, the character gains a bonus to electricity resistance.	—	Chest in Vigil's Keep

Item Name	Material	Quality #1	Quality #2	Quality #3	Quality #4	Quality #5	Item Location
Massive							
Duty	Silverite	+2 Constitution	When equipped with the other Duty items, fatigue -10%	—	—	—	Avvar Lord
Grey Warden Plate Helm	Silverite	Restrict: Warrior	Defense +3	Mental Resistance +5	Physical Resistance +5	When equipped with Grey Warden plate armor, gauntlets, and boots, the character gains bonuses to strength and constitution.	Character Creation
Helm of Hirol's Defense	White Steel	Defense +6	Constitution +4	Chance to Ignore Hostile Magic +10%	Mental Resistance +15	When equipped with the breastplate, gauntlets, and greaves of Hirol's Defense, the character's spells or talents cost less to activate.	Stone Chest in Kal'Hirol
Helm of the Sentinel	Volcanic Aurum	Combat Health Regen +2	Defense +9	Constitution +8	When equipped with the armor, gauntlets, and boots of the Sentinel, the character gains a bonus to armor and the character's spells or talents cost less to activate.	—	Iron Chest in Blackmarsh

Item Name	Material	Quality #1	Quality #2	Quality #3	Quality #4	Quality #5	Item Location
Mage							
Collective Arming Cowl	Cowl	+2 Constitution	Required: Mage	—	—	—	Octham's Goods in Amaranthine

Armor

Helmets (continued)

Mage (continued)

Item Name	Material	Quality #1	Quality #2	Quality #3	Quality #4	Quality #5	Item Location
Enchanter's Arming Cap	Cowl	+1 Willpower	+10 Mental Resistance	Required: Mage	—	—	Octham's Goods in Amaranthine
First Enchanter's Cowl	Cowl	Chance to Ignore Hostile Magic +2%	Chance to Dodge Attacks +10%	Required: Mage	—	—	Apostate Mage, Octham's Goods, Architect's Chest
Grey Warden Cowl	Cowl	Restrict: Mage	Required: Mage	Willpower +2	Mental Resistance +15	—	Character Creation
The Liber-tarian's Cowl	Cowl	+12 Defense	+0.25 Combat Mana Regeneration	Required: Mage	—	—	Octham's Goods in Amaranthine
Lorekeeper's Cowl	Cowl	Required: Mage	Willpower +2	Spirit Resistance +15	When equipped with the Lorekeeper's robe, mittens, and boots, the character gains bonuses to armor and physical resistance.	—	Armoire in Abandoned Warehouse
Lucky Cap	Cowl	Required: Mage	Armor +2	Mental Resistance +7	Physical Resistance +7	—	Octham's Goods in Amaranthine
Reinforced Magus Cowl	Cowl	+2 Willpower	+20 Mental Resistance	-1 Dexterity	Required: Mage	—	Octham's Goods or Fen Witch
Sage's Fuzzy Head-Sweater	Cowl	Required: Mage	Dexterity +4	Willpower +4	Magic +4	Cunning +4	Disciple General in Amaranthine Siege
Toque of the Oblivious	Cowl	Required: Mage	Armor +5	Chance to Ignore Hostile Magic +10%	Mental Resistance +10	Physical Resistance +10, Magic +10	Queen of the Blackmarsh

Shields

Small Round

Item Name	Material	Quality #1	Quality #2	Quality #3	Quality #4	Quality #5	Item Location
Small Darkspawn Shield	All Metal	Defense +3	Defense against Missiles +6	—	—	—	Kal'Hirol

Large Round

Item Name	Material	Quality #1	Quality #2	Quality #3	Quality #4	Quality #5	Item Location
Large Darkspawn Shield	All Metal	Defense +3	Defense against Missiles +8	—	—	—	Kal'Hirol
Large Grey Warden Shield	Dragonthorn	Restrict: Warrior	Defense +3	Defense against Missiles +10	Decrease Damage Scale +5	—	Character Creation
Mage-Hunter	White Steel	Defense +6	Chance to Ignore Hostile Magic +8%	Willpower +4	Decrease Damage Scale +10	—	Herren's Merchandise in Vigil's Keep
Shield of the Legion	Dragonbone	+10 Mental Resistance	—	—	—	—	Legionnaire in Kal'Hirol

Kite

Item Name	Material	Quality #1	Quality #2	Quality #3	Quality #4	Quality #5	Item Location
Griffon's Crest	Dragonbone	Armor +1	Defense against Missiles +6	—	—	—	Justice
Landsmeet Shield	Volcanic Aurum	Stamina +50	Defense +12	Electricity Resistance +30	+12% damage reduction for all damage types	Physical Resistance +15	Ser Rylock, Dragon Thrall, Avvar Lord

Tower

Item Name	Material	Quality #1	Quality #2	Quality #3	Quality #4	Quality #5	Item Location
Howe's Shield	Silverite	+12 Defense	+10 Fire Resistance	+10 Cold Resistance	-2 Willpower	—	Sergeant Maverlies or Private
Partha	White Steel	Chance to Dodge Attacks +5%	Cunning +2	Defense +15	Defense against Missiles +20, Decrease Damage Scale +10	When equipped with the sword Kallak, the character gains a bonus to stamina regeneration.	Dailan's Remains in Kal'Hirol

Crafted

Item Name	Material	Quality #1	Quality #2	Quality #3	Quality #4	Quality #5	Item Location
Heartwood Shield	Ancestral Heartwood	Nature Resistance +10	Defense against Missiles +10	Defense +15	Decrease Damage Scale +15	Physical Resistance +20	Crafted by Master Wade

Accessories

Belts, amulets, and rings fall into the accessories category, and each provides more magical bonuses to augment your characters' attributes and skills. The Girdle of Kal'Hirol in the belt slot, for example, increases defense, fire resistance, cold resistance, and physical resistance. Depending on how you want to build up your character, you may opt for the Will of the Unyielding amulet to provide more willpower, or a Ring of Mastery for more spellpower. When you receive a new accessory, you may not want to drop it on your main PC each time. Think about which party member it benefits the most and give it to them. Giving an item granting extra defense to the tank benefits the party more than giving it to your PC rogue who barely needs it.

Amulets					
Item Name	Quality #1	Quality #2	Quality #3	Quality #4	Quality #5	Item Location
Blood of the Warrior	Required: Warrior	Strength +2	Defense against Missiles +10	Physical Resistance +10	—	Yuriah's Wares (original store)
Fox's Pendant	Restriction: Anders	Healing Spells +10%	Willpower +3	—	—	Anders
Halla Horn	+10 Mental Resistance	—	—	—	—	Velanna
Illumination	All Attributes +3	Mental Resistance +3	—	—	—	Mystic Chest in Wending Wood
Kristoff's Locket	Restriction: Justice	All Attributes +1	Chance to Dodge Attacks +5%	—	—	Justice
Magus Ward	Required: Mage	Magic +1	Chance to Ignore Hostile Magic +10%	Mental Resistance +10	—	Octham's Goods in Amaranthine
Nature's Blessing	Combat Health Regen +6	Combat Mana Regen +6	Combat Stamina Regen +1.5		—	Sarcophagus in Kal'Hirol
Rough-Hewn Pendant	Required: Warrior	Crit Damage +10%	Fatigue Reduction +5	—	—	Queen of the Blackmarsh
Scout's Medal	Dexterity +2	Armor +2	Stamina +50	Constitution +10	—	Yuriah's Wares (original store)
Seeker's Chain	Defense +3	All Attributes +2	Combat Health Regen +1	—	—	Glassric's Wares in Amaranthine
Shaper's Amulet	+2 Willpower	—	—	—	—	Nathaniel
Smith's Heart	+20 Fire Resistance	-1 Dexterity	—	—	—	Oghren
Spirit Cord	Required: Rogue	Spirit Resistance +5	Dexterity +3	Cunning +3	Nature Resistance +15	Crown and Lion Inn
Spirit Ward	+10 Spirit Resistance	—	—	—	—	Sigrun
Talisman of Restoration	Reduces Hostility	Required: Mage	Healing Spells +15%	Willpower +3	Defense against Missiles +20	Urn in Vigil's Keep Deep Roads
Will of the Unyielding	Required: Mage	Willpower +3	Physical Resistance +15	—	—	Flesh Pod in Drake's Fall
Belts					
Item Name	Quality #1	Quality #2	Quality #3	Quality #4	Quality #5	Item Location
Battlemage's Cinch	Required: Mage	Willpower +5	Spellpower +5	—	—	The Lost—Lower Reaches of Kal'Hirol
Belt of the Architect	Required: Mage	Willpower +7	Spellpower +7	—	—	The Architect in Drake's Fall
Deep Roads Girdle	Restriction: Sigrun	Crit Damage +15%	—	—	—	Sigrun
Doge's Dodger	Strength +4	Dexterity +4	Defense against Missiles +10	—	—	Utha in Drake's Fall
Enduring Faith	Cold Resistance +20	Combat Stamina Regen +1	Defense +15	—	—	Disciple General in Amaranthine Siege
Girdle of Kal'Hirol	Defense +6	Fire Resistance +10	Cold Resistance +10	Physical Resistance +10	—	Hirol's Sarcophagus in Kal'Hirol
Gladiator's Belt	Strength +2	Dexterity +2	Willpower +2	Attack +4	—	Runic Pedestal in Blackmarsh
Lucrosian's Silken Cord	Required: Mage	Magic +2	Constitution +4	—	—	Chest in Vigil's Keep
Magister's Cinch	Reduces Hostility	+10% to Healing Spells	—	—	—	Anders
One for the Ditch	Restriction: Oghren	Constitution +3	Physical Resistance +15	—	—	Oghren
Panacea	Dexterity +3	Healing Spells +25%	—	—	—	Herren's Merchandise in Vigil's Keep
Sash of Power	Fire Resistance +50	Cold Resistance +50	Electricity Resistance +50	Nature Resistance +50	Physical Resistance +10	Yuriah's Wares (upgrade 2)

Accessories

Basics ~ Classes ~ The Party ~ Companions ~ Supporting Cast ~ **Equipment** ~ Bestiary ~ Walkthrough ~ Side Quests ~ Random Encounters ~ Achievements/Trophies

Belts (continued)

Item Name	Quality #1	Quality #2	Quality #3	Quality #4	Quality #5	Item Location
Swordsman's Girdle	+2% Melee Critical Chance	—	—	—	—	Justice
Wasp's Sting	Crit Damage +5%	Armor Penetration +2	Attack +6	—	—	Ogre Commander in Vigil's Keep Deep Roads

Rings

Item Name	Quality #1	Quality #2	Quality #3	Quality #4	Quality #5	Item Location
Ash	Required: Mage	Fire Resistance +10	Increases all Fire Damage +20%	When equipped with the ring Icicle, the character gains a bonus to magic.	—	Darkspawn Corpse in Wending Wood
Blessing of the Divine	Required: Warrior	Stamina +25	Chance to Ignore Hostile Magic +12%	Mental Resistance +10	When equipped with the Mark of the Divine, the character gains a bonus to health regeneration.	The Herald in Vigil's Keep Siege
Corin's Proposal	All Attributes +2	—	—	—	—	Floating Bottle in Blackmarsh
Dawn Ring	+4 Strength	-1 Cunning	If worn with Dusk Ring, armor +2	—	—	Justice
Dusk Ring	+3 Cunning	-1 Strength	If worn with Dawn Ring, armor +2	—	—	Nathaniel
Earthbound	Required: Mage	Nature Resistance +15	Increases all Nature Damage +15%	When equipped with the ring Soulbound, the character gains a bonus to willpower.	—	Queen of the Blackmarsh
Golden Cog	Required: Mage	Willpower +4	Magic +4	When equipped with the Silver Cog, the character gains a bonus to health regeneration.	—	Yuriah's Wares (original store)
Hailstone	+5% to Cold Damage	—	—	—	—	Anders
Icicle	Required: Mage	Willpower +3	Increases all Cold Damage +30%	Cold Resistance +70	When equipped with the ring Ash, the character gains a bonus to magic.	Yuriah's Wares (upgrade 2)
Keeper's Charm	Restriction: Velanna	Willpower +2	Magic +2	Increases all Fire Damage +5%	—	Velanna
Lyrium Ring	Restriction: Justice	Chance to Ignore Hostile Magic +10%	Willpower +6	—	—	Justice through personal quest
Mark of the Divine	Required: Warrior	Fire Resistance +10	Cold Resistance +10	Electricity Resistance +10, Healing Spells +10%	When equipped with the Blessing of the Divine, the character gains a bonus to health regeneration.	Blighted Shadow Wolf in Blackmarsh
Ring of Discipline	Required: Mage	Willpower +15	When equipped with the Ring of Mastery, the character gains a bonus to constitution.	—	—	Architect's Chest in Silverite Mine
Ring of Faith	+10% to Fire Damage	Required: Mage	—	—	—	Anders
Ring of Mastery	Required: Mage	Spellpower +10	When equipped with the Ring of Discipline, the character gains a bonus to constitution.	—	—	Adria in Vigil's Keep Basement
Ring of Resistance	+1 Willpower	+1 Constitution	—	—	—	Oghren & Sigrun
Ring of Severity	Required: Rogue	Constitution +6	Combat Health Regen +6	When equipped with the Ring of Subtlety, the character gains a bonus to health regeneration.	—	Chest in Blackmarsh
Ring of Study	+1 Magic	—	—	—	—	Velanna
Ring of Subtlety	Dexterity +3	Cunning +3	When equipped with the Ring of Severity, the character gains a bonus to health regeneration.	—	—	Packed Earth in Amaranthine

primagames.com

Rings (continued)					
Item Name	Quality #1	Quality #2	Quality #3	Quality #4	Quality #5	Item Location
Ring of the Warrior	+2 Strength	+2 Dexterity	—	—	—	Oghren
Silver Cog	Required: Mage	Electricity Resistance +15	Increases all Lightning Damage +15%	When equipped with the Golden Cog, the character gains a bonus to health regeneration.	—	Personal Storage in Throne Room
Sleeper	Spirit Resistance +15	Electricity Resistance +25	—	—	—	Chest in Keep Interior
Soulbound	Required: Mage	Spirit Resistance +50	Chance to Ignore Hostile Magic +20%	Increases all Sprit Damage +100%	When equipped with the ring Earthbound, the character gains a bonus to willpower.	Baroness in Blackmarsh
Tingler	Combat Health Regen +3	Healing Spells +15%	Constitution +4	—	—	Chest in Vigil's Keep Basement
Worn Golden Ring	Restriction: Nathaniel	Chance to Dodge Attacks +10%	Cunning +3	—	—	Nathaniel

Ammo					
Item Name	Quality #1	Quality #2	Quality #3	Quality #4	Quality #5	Item Location
Arrow of Filth	+3 Nature Damage	—	—	—	—	Various
Elf-Flight Arrow	+6 Attack	Chance to Stun	—	—	—	Various
Explosive Bolt	+4 Fire Damage	—	—	—	—	Various
Fire Arrow	+2 Fire Damage	—	—	—	—	Various
Fire Bolt	+3 Fire Damage	—	—	—	—	Various
Ice Arrow	+2 Cold Damage	—	—	—	—	Various
Ice Bolt	+3 Cold Damage	—	—	—	—	Various
Knockback Bolt	Chance to Knock Target Back	—	—	—	—	Various
Sureshot Bolt	Massive Damage to Darkspawn	—	—	—	—	Various

Runes

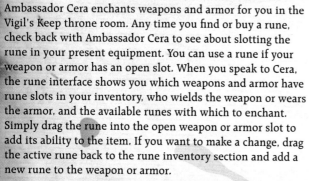

Ambassador Cera enchants weapons and armor for you in the Vigil's Keep throne room. Any time you find or buy a rune, check back with Ambassador Cera to see about slotting the rune in your present equipment. You can use a rune if your weapon or armor has an open slot. When you speak to Cera, the rune interface shows you which weapons and armor have rune slots in your inventory, who wields the weapon or wears the armor, and the available runes with which to enchant. Simply drag the rune into the open weapon or armor slot to add its ability to the item. If you want to make a change, drag the active rune back to the rune inventory section and add a new rune to the weapon or armor.

There are seven rune categories, which increase in potency with each level: novice, journeyman, expert, master, grandmaster, masterpiece, and paragon. A novice flame rune, for example, grants +1 fire damage, while a grandmaster flame rune gives +5. See the following charts for weapon, armor, and special rune powers.

Weapon Rune Powers

Rune Name	Ability
Cold Iron	Damage vs. Spirits
Dweomer	Spell Resistance
Flame	Bonus Fire Damage
Frost	Bonus Cold Damage
Hale	Bonus Physical Resistance
Lightning	Bonus Electrical Damage
Paralyze	Chance to Root Target
Silverite	Damage vs. Darkspawn
Slow	Reduce Movement Speed

Armor Rune Powers

Rune Name	Ability
Barrier	Increases Armor
Immunity	Cold, Electricity, Fire Resistance
Reservoir	Increases Willpower
Stout	Increases Constitution
Tempest	Defense Against Missiles

Accessories - Runes

Basics ~ Classes ~ The Party ~ Companions ~ Supporting Cast ~ **Equipment** ~ Bestiary ~ Walkthrough ~ Side Quests ~ Random Encounters ~ Achievements/Trophies

Special Rune Powers

Rune Name	Ability
Amplification	Increase Cold, Fire, Lightning, Nature, and Spirit Damage +5
Diligence	Flank Immunity
Elemental	Deals Chromatic Damage (+1 all damage types at once)
Endurance	Fatigue Reduction
Evasion	Increases Dodge Chance
Intensifying	Increases Crit Chance and Crit Damage
Menacing	Increases Hostility
Momentum	Grants Haste

As you collect runes and add them to your weapons and armor, parcel them out based on party needs and class specialties. The damage-based runes generally go to DPS characters or the tank. Hale and barrier, of course, go to a tank, while dweomer and reservoir tend to go on mages (they tend to draw the return fire from enemy spellcasters in the rear and need the extra mana). Paralyze and slow runes are excellent on a tank or DPSer weapon to keep the enemy in place while they wallop on them. Special runes can go anywhere, based on your characters' tactics and your play style. As with everything, play to your party members' strengths and mind their weaknesses. If your tank keeps getting hurt by ranged fire, naturally give him the tempest rune.

Weapon Runes

Name	Bonuses
Novice Cold Iron Rune	Damage +1 vs. Spirits
Novice Dweomer Rune	+2% Chance to Ignore Hostile Magic
Novice Flame Rune	+1 Fire Damage
Novice Frost Rune	+1 Cold Damage
Novice Hale Rune	+5 Physical Resistance
Novice Lightning Rune	+1 Electricity Damage
Novice Paralyze Rune	Chance of Paralysis
Novice Silverite Rune	Damage +1 vs. Darkspawn
Novice Slow Rune	Chance to Reduce Movement Speed
Journeyman Cold Iron Rune	Damage +2 vs. Spirits
Journeyman Dweomer Rune	+4% Chance to Ignore Hostile Magic
Journeyman Flame Rune	+2 Fire Damage
Journeyman Frost Rune	+2 Cold Damage
Journeyman Hale Rune	+10 Physical Resistance
Journeyman Lightning Rune	+2 Electricity Damage
Journeyman Paralyze Rune	Chance of Paralysis
Journeyman Silverite Rune	Damage +2 vs. Darkspawn
Journeyman Slow Rune	Chance to Reduce Movement Speed
Expert Cold Iron Rune	Damage +3 vs. Spirits
Expert Dweomer Rune	+6% Chance to Ignore Hostile Magic
Expert Flame Rune	+3 Fire Damage
Expert Frost Rune	+3 Cold Damage
Expert Hale Rune	+15 Physical Resistance
Expert Lightning Rune	+3 Electricity Damage
Expert Paralyze Rune	Chance of Paralysis
Expert Silverite Rune	Damage +3 vs. Darkspawn
Expert Slow Rune	Chance to Reduce Movement Speed
Master Cold Iron Rune	Damage +4 vs. Spirits
Master Dweomer Rune	+8% Chance to Ignore Hostile Magic
Master Flame Rune	+4 Fire Damage
Master Frost Rune	+4 Cold Damage
Master Hale Rune	+20 Physical Resistance
Master Lightning Rune	+4 Electricity Damage
Master Paralyze Rune	Chance of Paralysis
Master Silverite Rune	Damage +4 vs. Darkspawn
Master Slow Rune	Chance to Reduce Movement Speed
Grandmaster Cold Iron Rune	Damage +5 vs. Spirits
Grandmaster Dweomer Rune	+10% Chance to Ignore Hostile Magic
Grandmaster Flame Rune	+5 Fire Damage
Grandmaster Frost Rune	+5 Cold Damage

Weapon Runes (continued)

Name	Bonuses
Grandmaster Hale Rune	+25 Physical Resistance
Grandmaster Lightning Rune	+5 Electricity Damage
Grandmaster Paralyze Rune	Chance of Paralysis
Grandmaster Silverite Rune	Damage +5 vs. Darkspawn
Grandmaster Slow Rune	Chance to Reduce Movement Speed
Masterpiece Cold Iron Rune	Damage +6 vs. Spirits
Masterpiece Dweomer Rune	+12% Chance to Ignore Hostile Magic
Masterpiece Flame Rune	+6 Fire Damage
Masterpiece Frost Rune	+6 Cold Damage
Masterpiece Hale Rune	+30 Physical Resistance
Masterpiece Lightning Rune	+6 Electricity Damage
Masterpiece Paralyze Rune	Chance of Paralysis
Masterpiece Silverite Rune	Damage +6 vs. Darkspawn
Masterpiece Slow Rune	Chance to Reduce Movement Speed
Paragon Cold Iron Rune	Damage +7 vs. Spirits
Paragon Dweomer Rune	+14% Chance to Ignore Hostile Magic
Paragon Flame Rune	+7 Fire Damage
Paragon Frost Rune	+7 Cold Damage
Paragon Hale Rune	+35 Physical Resistance
Paragon Lightning Rune	+7 Electricity Damage
Paragon Paralyze Rune	Chance of Paralysis
Paragon Silverite Rune	Damage +7 vs. Darkspawn
Paragon Slow Rune	Chance to Reduce Movement Speed

Armor Runes

Name	Bonuses
Novice Barrier Rune	Armor +1
Novice Immunity Rune	Cold, Electricity and Fire Resistances +3
Novice Reservoir Rune	Willpower +1
Novice Stout Rune	Constitution +2
Novice Tempest Rune	Defense against Missiles +2
Journeyman Barrier Rune	Armor +2
Journeyman Immunity Rune	Cold, Electricity, and Fire Resistances +6
Journeyman Reservoir Rune	Willpower +2
Journeyman Stout Rune	Constitution +4
Journeyman Tempest Rune	Defense against Missiles +4
Expert Barrier Rune	Armor +3
Expert Immunity Rune	Cold, Electricity, and Fire Resistances +9
Expert Reservoir Rune	Willpower +3
Expert Stout Rune	Constitution +6
Expert Tempest Rune	Defense against Missiles +6

primagames.com

Armor Runes (continued)	
Name	**Bonuses**
Master Barrier Rune	Armor +4
Master Immunity Rune	Cold, Electricity, and Fire Resistances +12
Master Reservoir Rune	Willpower +4
Master Stout Rune	Constitution +8
Master Tempest Rune	Defense against Missiles +8
Grandmaster Barrier Rune	Armor +5
Grandmaster Immunity Rune	Cold, Electricity, and Fire Resistances +15
Grandmaster Reservoir Rune	Willpower +5
Grandmaster Stout Rune	Constitution +10
Grandmaster Tempest Rune	Defense against Missiles +10
Masterpiece Barrier Rune	Armor +6
Masterpiece Immunity Rune	Cold, Electricity, and Fire Resistances +20
Masterpiece Reservoir Rune	Willpower +6
Masterpiece Stout Rune	Constitution +12
Masterpiece Tempest Rune	Defense against Missiles +12

Armor Runes (continued)	
Name	**Bonuses**
Paragon Barrier Rune	Armor +7
Paragon Immunity Rune	Cold, Electricity, and Fire Resistances +25
Paragon Reservoir Rune	Willpower +7
Paragon Stout Rune	Constitution +14
Paragon Tempest Rune	Defense against Missiles +14

Special Runes	
Name	**Bonuses**
Amplification Rune	Increases all damage types +5%
Diligence Rune	Flank Immunity
Elemental Rune	Enhances chromatic damage, which is +1 for damage types
Endurance Rune	Fatigue Reduction +1
Evasion Rune	Chance to Dodge Attacks +5%
Intensifying Rune	Crit Damage +20%
Menacing Rune	Increase hostility
Momentum Rune	Haste

Crafting

Runecrafting, Herbalism, Trap-Making, and Poison-Making contribute to craft items. The new Runecrafting skill allows you to craft your own runes for weapons and armor. When you gain the Herbalism skill, you can craft medicinal items, such as health poultices, lyrium potions, and injury kits. Trap-Making creates simple but effective mechanisms for snaring and injuring enemies, such as claw traps and caltrop traps. Poison-Making extracts potent poisons from deadly plants and venom from reptiles to coat weapons with various effects detrimental to your enemies. Herbalism is absolutely essential in any group, and usually a mage will take up the craft due to their high magic score. Trap-Making is a nice luxury if you have the extra skill points to spend on it. Any warrior or rogue who wants a little extra AoE and root/snaring effects can dabble here. Poison-Making will improve DPS, which fits with a rogue or damage-dealing warrior. Runecrafting can seriously increase the effectiveness of your items, and as long as you have the extra money to spend on it (it's expensive!). One of your characters should invest in it all the way to the fourth Runecrafting level. Your main PC should probably spend skill points on the critical talents, such as Coercion and Combat Training (for warriors and rogues), while each companion can take a crafting skill to maximize your item output in the various crafting areas.

Now that you've decided you want to study up on Runecrafting, Herbalism, Poison-Making, or Trap-Making, what reagents do you need? At what rank can you make each crafting item? Read through the following table for the essentials you need to craft every item in the game.

Herbalism									
Item Name	**Craft**	**Ingredient 1**	**Count 1**	**Ingredient 2**	**Count 2**	**Ingredient 3**	**Count 3**	**Ingredient 4**	**Coun**
Lesser Health Poultice	Herbalism	Elfroot	1	Flask	1	****	0	****	0
Lesser Lyrium Potion	Herbalism	Lyrium Dust	1	Flask	1	****	0	****	0
Health Poultice	Herbalism (Improved)	Elfroot	3	Flask	1	Distillation Agent	1	****	0
Incense of Awareness	Herbalism (Improved)	Lyrium Dust	1	Deep Mushroom	1	Flask	1	Distillation Agent	1
Lyrium Potion	Herbalism (Improved)	Lyrium Dust	2	Flask	1	Distillation Agent	1	****	0
Minor Injury Repair Kit	Herbalism (Improved)	Elfroot	2	Deep Mushroom	2	Distillation Agent	1	****	0
Rock Salve	Herbalism (Improved)	Deep Mushroom	2	Flask	1	Distillation Agent	1	****	0
Greater Health Poultice	Herbalism (Expert)	Elfroot	4	Flask	1	Distillation Agent	2	Concentrator Agent	
Greater Lyrium Potion	Herbalism (Expert)	Lyrium Dust	3	Flask	1	Distillation Agent	2	Concentrator Agent	
Injury Repair Kit	Herbalism (Expert)	Elfroot	3	Deep Mushroom	3	Distillation Agent	2	Concentrator Agent	1

Runes - Crafting

Basics ~ Classes ~ The Party ~ Companions ~ Supporting Cast ~ **Equipment** ~ Bestiary ~ Walkthrough ~ Side Quests ~ Random Encounters ~ Achievements/Trophies

Herbalism (continued)

Item Name	Craft	Ingredient 1	Count 1	Ingredient 2	Count 2	Ingredient 3	Count 3	Ingredient 4	Count 4
Lesser Elixir of Grounding	Herbalism (Expert)	Frozen Lightning	1	Flask	1	Concentrator Agent	1	****	0
Lesser Ice Salve	Herbalism (Expert)	Frostrock	1	Flask	1	Concentrator Agent	1	****	0
Lesser Nature Salve	Herbalism (Expert)	Lifestone	1	Flask	1	Concentrator Agent	1	****	0
Lesser Spirit Balm	Herbalism (Expert)	Spirit Shard	1	Flask	1	Concentrator Agent	1	****	0
Lesser Warmth Balm	Herbalism (Expert)	Fire Crystal	1	Flask	1	Concentrator Agent	1	****	0
Swift Salve	Herbalism (Expert)	Lyrium Dust	2	Deep Mushroom	2	Flask	1	Concentrator Agent	1
Greater Elixir of Grounding	Herbalism (Master)	Frozen Lightning	2	Flask	1	Distillation Agent	1	Concentrator Agent	2
Greater Ice Salve	Herbalism (Master)	Frostrock	2	Flask	1	Distillation Agent	1	Concentrator Agent	2
Greater Nature Salve	Herbalism (Master)	Lifestone	2	Flask	1	Distillation Agent	1	Concentrator Agent	2
Greater Spirit Balm	Herbalism (Master)	Spirit Shard	2	Flask	1	Distillation Agent	1	Concentrator Agent	2
Greater Stamina Draught	Herbalism (Master)	Deep Mushroom	3	Flask	1	Distillation Agent	2	Concentrator Agent	1
Greater Warmth Balm	Herbalism (Master)	Fire Crystal	2	Flask	1	Distillation Agent	1	Concentrator Agent	2
Lesser Stamina Draught	Herbalism (Master)	Deep Mushroom	1	Flask	1	****	0	****	0
Major Injury Repair Kit	Herbalism (Master)	Elfroot	4	Deep Mushroom	4	Distillation Agent	2	Concentrator Agent	2
Master Health Poultice	Herbalism (Master)	Elfroot	8	Flask	1	Distillation Agent	8	Concentrator Agent	8
Master Lyrium Potion	Herbalism (Master)	Lyrium Dust	8	Flask	1	Distillation Agent	8	Concentrator Agent	8
Master Stamina Draught	Herbalism (Master)	Deep Mushroom	8	Flask	1	Distillation Agent	8	Concentrator Agent	8
Potent Health Poultice	Herbalism (Master)	Elfroot	5	Flask	1	Distillation Agent	2	Concentrator Agent	2
Potent Lyrium Potion	Herbalism (Master)	Lyrium Dust	4	Flask	1	Distillation Agent	2	Concentrator Agent	2
Potent Stamina Draught	Herbalism (Master)	Deep Mushroom	4	Flask	1	Distillation Agent	2	Concentrator Agent	2
Stamina Draught	Herbalism (Master)	Deep Mushroom	2	Flask	1	Distillation Agent	1	****	0
Superb Health Poultice	Herbalism (Master)	Elfroot	6	Flask	1	Distillation Agent	4	Concentrator Agent	4
Superb Lyrium Potion	Herbalism (Master)	Lyrium Dust	6	Flask	1	Distillation Agent	4	Concentrator Agent	4
Superb Stamina Draught	Herbalism (Master)	Deep Mushroom	6	Flask	1	Distillation Agent	4	Concentrator Agent	4

Poison-Making

Item Name	Craft	Ingredient 1	Count 1	Ingredient 2	Count 2	Ingredient 3	Count 3	Ingredient 4	Count 4
Deathroot Extract	Poison-Making	Deathroot	1	Flask	1	****	0	****	0
Venom	Poison-Making	Toxin Extract	1	Flask	1	****	0	****	0
Acid Flask	Poison-Making (Improved)	Lifestone	1	Flask	1	Corrupter Agent	1	****	0
Concentrated Deathroot Extract	Poison-Making (Improved)	Deathroot	2	Flask	1	Distillation Agent	1	****	0
Concentrated Venom	Poison-Making (Improved)	Toxin Extract	2	Flask	1	Distillation Agent	1	****	0
Crow Poison	Poison-Making (Improved)	Toxin Extract	2	Deathroot	2	Flask	1	Distillation Agent	1
Fire Bomb	Poison-Making (Improved)	Fire Crystal	1	Flask	1	Corrupter Agent	1	****	0

primagames.com

Item Name	Craft	Ingredient 1	Count 1	Ingredient 2	Count 2	Ingredient 3	Count 3	Ingredient 4	Count 4
Poison-Making (continued)										
Freeze Bomb	Poison-Making (Improved)	Frostrock	1	Flask	1	Corrupter Agent	1	****	0
Shock Bomb	Poison-Making (Improved)	Frozen Lightning	1	Flask	1	Corrupter Agent	1	****	0
Soulrot Bomb	Poison-Making (Improved)	Spirit Shard	1	Flask	1	Corrupter Agent	1	****	0
Acidic Coating	Poison-Making (Expert)	Lifestone	2	Flask	1	Corrupter Agent	2	Concentrator Agent	1
Adder's Kiss	Poison-Making (Expert)	Toxin Extract	3	Flask	1	Distillation Agent	2	Concentrator Agent	1
Concentrated Crow Poison	Poison-Making (Expert)	Toxin Extract	3	Deathroot	3	Flask	1	Concentrator Agent	1
Demonic Poison	Poison-Making (Expert)	Demonic Ichor	1	Flask	1	Concentrator Agent	1	****	0
Flaming Coating	Poison-Making (Expert)	Fire Crystal	2	Flask	1	Corrupter Agent	2	Concentrator Agent	1
Fleshrot	Poison-Making (Expert)	Deathroot	3	Flask	1	Distillation Agent	2	Concentrator Agent	1
Freezing Coating	Poison-Making (Expert)	Frostrock	2	Flask	1	Corrupter Agent	2	Concentrator Agent	1
Magebane	Poison-Making (Expert)	Lyrium Dust	3	Flask	1	Corrupter Agent	2	Concentrator Agent	1
Shock Coating	Poison-Making (Expert)	Frozen Lightning	2	Flask	1	Corrupter Agent	2	Concentrator Agent	1
Soldier's Bane	Poison-Making (Expert)	Deep Mushroom	3	Flask	1	Corrupter Agent	2	Concentrator Agent	1
Soulrot Coating	Poison-Making (Expert)	Spirit Shard	2	Flask	1	Corrupter Agent	2	Concentrator Agent	1
Concentrated Demonic Poison	Poison-Making (Master)	Demonic Ichor	2	Flask	1	Concentrator Agent	2	****	0
Concentrated Magebane	Poison-Making (Master)	Lyrium Dust	4	Flask	1	Corrupter Agent	2	Concentrator Agent	2
Concentrated Soldier's Bane	Poison-Making (Master)	Deep Mushroom	4	Flask	1	Corrupter Agent	2	Concentrator Agent	2
Dispel Coating	Poison-Making (Master)	Rashvine Nettle	2	Flask	1	Corrupter Agent	4	Concentrator Agent	2
Dispel Grenade	Poison-Making (Master)	Rashvine Nettle	1	Flask	1	Corrupter Agent	2	Concentrator Agent	1
Elemental Coating	Poison-Making (Master)	Blood Lotus	2	Flask	1	Corrupter Agent	4	Concentrator Agent	2
Elemental Grenade	Poison-Making (Master)	Blood Lotus	1	Flask	1	Corrupter Agent	2	Concentrator Agent	1
Quiet Death	Poison-Making (Master)	Toxin Extract	4	Deathroot	4	Flask	1	Concentrator Agent	2
Runecrafting										
Diligence Rune	Runecrafting	Novice Tempest Rune	1	Menacing Rune	1	Blank Runestone	1	Etching Agent	1
Expert Barrier Rune	Runecrafting	Journeyman Barrier Rune	2	Blank Runestone	1	Etching Agent	0	****	0
Expert Cold Iron Rune	Runecrafting	Journeyman Cold Iron Rune	2	Blank Runestone	1	Etching Agent	0	****	0
Expert Dweomer Rune	Runecrafting	Journeyman Dweomer Rune	2	Blank Runestone	1	Etching Agent	0	****	0
Expert Flame Rune	Runecrafting	Journeyman Flame Rune	2	Blank Runestone	1	Etching Agent	0	****	0
Expert Frost Rune	Runecrafting	Journeyman Frost Rune	2	Blank Runestone	1	Etching Agent	0	****	0
Expert Hale Rune	Runecrafting	Journeyman Hale Rune	2	Blank Runestone	1	Etching Agent	0	****	0
Expert Immunity Rune	Runecrafting	Journeyman Immunity Rune	2	Blank Runestone	1	Etching Agent	0	****	0

Crafting

Basics ~ Classes ~ The Party ~ Companions ~ Supporting Cast ~ **Equipment** ~ Bestiary ~ Walkthrough ~ Side Quests ~ Random Encounters ~ Achievements/Trophies

Item Name	Craft	Ingredient 1	Count 1	Ingredient 2	Count 2	Ingredient 3	Count 3	Ingredient 4	Count 4
				Runecrafting (continued)					
Expert Lightning Rune	Runecrafting	Journeyman Lightning Rune	2	Blank Runestone	1	Etching Agent	0	****	0
Expert Paralyze Rune	Runecrafting	Journeyman Paralyze Rune	2	Blank Runestone	1	Etching Agent	0	****	0
Expert Resevoir Rune	Runecrafting	Journeyman Resevoir Rune	2	Blank Runestone	1	Etching Agent	0	****	0
Expert Silverite Rune	Runecrafting	Journeyman Silverite Rune	2	Blank Runestone	1	Etching Agent	0	****	0
Expert Slow Rune	Runecrafting	Journeyman Slow Rune	2	Blank Runestone	1	Etching Agent	0	****	0
Expert Stout Rune	Runecrafting	Journeyman Stout Rune	2	Blank Runestone	1	Etching Agent	0	****	0
Expert Tempest Rune	Runecrafting	Journeyman Tempest Rune	2	Blank Runestone	1	Etching Agent	0	****	0
Journeyman Barrier Rune	Runecrafting	Novice Barrier Rune	1	Blank Runestone	1	Etching Agent	0	****	0
Journeyman Cold Iron Rune	Runecrafting	Novice Cold Iron Rune	1	Blank Runestone	1	Etching Agent	0	****	0
Journeyman Dweomer Rune	Runecrafting	Novice Dweomer Rune	1	Blank Runestone	1	Etching Agent	1	****	0
Journeyman Flame Rune	Runecrafting	Novice Flame Rune	1	Blank Runestone	1	Etching Agent	0	****	0
Journeyman Frost Rune	Runecrafting	Novice Frost Rune	1	Blank Runestone	1	Etching Agent	0	****	0
Journeyman Hale Rune	Runecrafting	Novice Hale Rune	1	Blank Runestone	1	Etching Agent	0	****	0
Journeyman Immunity Rune	Runecrafting	Novice Immunity Rune	1	Blank Runestone	1	Etching Agent	0	****	0
Journeyman Lightning Rune	Runecrafting	Novice Lightning Rune	1	Blank Runestone	1	Etching Agent	0	****	0
Journeyman Paralyze Rune	Runecrafting	Novice Paralyze Rune	1	Blank Runestone	1	Etching Agent	0	****	0
Journeyman Resevoir Rune	Runecrafting	Novice Resevoir Rune	1	Blank Runestone	1	Etching Agent	0	****	0
Journeyman Silverite Rune	Runecrafting	Novice Silverite Rune	1	Blank Runestone	1	Etching Agent	0	****	0
Journeyman Slow Rune	Runecrafting	Novice Slow Rune	1	Blank Runestone	1	Etching Agent	0	****	0
Journeyman Stout Rune	Runecrafting	Novice Stout Rune	1	Blank Runestone	1	Etching Agent	0	****	0
Journeyman Tempest Rune	Runecrafting	Novice Tempest Rune	1	Blank Runestone	1	Etching Agent	0	****	0
Menacing Rune	Runecrafting	Novice Immunity Rune	1	Novice Silverite Rune	1	Blank Runestone	1	Etching Agent	1
Endurance Rune	Runecrafting (Improved)	Journeyman Stout Rune	1	Journeyman Hale Rune	1	Blank Runestone	1	Etching Agent	2
Intensifying Rune	Runecrafting (Improved)	Journeyman Lightning Rune	1	Journeyman Cold Iron Rune	1	Blank Runestone	1	Etching Agent	2
Master Barrier Rune	Runecrafting (Improved)	Expert Barrier Rune	2	Blank Runestone	1	Etching Agent	3	****	0
Master Cold Iron Rune	Runecrafting (Improved)	Expert Cold Iron Rune	2	Blank Runestone	1	Etching Agent	3	****	0
Master Dweomer Rune	Runecrafting (Improved)	Expert Dweomer Rune	2	Blank Runestone	1	Etching Agent	3	****	0
Master Flame Rune	Runecrafting (Improved)	Expert Flame Rune	2	Blank Runestone	1	Etching Agent	3	****	0
Master Frost Rune	Runecrafting (Improved)	Expert Frost Rune	2	Blank Runestone	1	Etching Agent	3	****	0
Master Hale Rune	Runecrafting (Improved)	Expert Hale Rune	2	Blank Runestone	1	Etching Agent	3	****	0
Master Immunity Rune	Runecrafting (Improved)	Expert Immunity Rune	2	Blank Runestone	1	Etching Agent	3	****	0

primagames.com

Item Name	Craft	Ingredient 1	Count 1	Ingredient 2	Count 2	Ingredient 3	Count 3	Ingredient 4	Count 4
Runecrafting (continued)									
Master Lightning Rune	Runecrafting (Improved)	Expert Lightning Rune	2	Blank Runestone	1	Etching Agent	3	****	0
Master Paralyze Rune	Runecrafting (Improved)	Expert Paralyze Rune	2	Blank Runestone	1	Etching Agent	3	****	0
Master Resevoir Rune	Runecrafting (Improved)	Expert Resevoir Rune	2	Blank Runestone	1	Etching Agent	3	****	0
Master Silverite Rune	Runecrafting (Improved)	Expert Silverite Rune	2	Blank Runestone	1	Etching Agent	3	****	0
Master Slow Rune	Runecrafting (Improved)	Expert Slow Rune	2	Blank Runestone	1	Etching Agent	3	****	0
Master Stout Rune	Runecrafting (Improved)	Expert Stout Rune	2	Blank Runestone	1	Etching Agent	3	****	0
Master Tempest Rune	Runecrafting (Improved)	Expert Tempest Rune	2	Blank Runestone	1	Etching Agent	3	****	0
Amplification Rune	Runecrafting (Expert)	Expert Resevoir Rune	1	Expert Dweomer Rune	1	Blank Runestone	1	Etching Agent	3
Elemental Rune	Runecrafting (Expert)	Expert Flame Rune	1	Expert Frost Rune	1	Blank Runestone	1	Etching Agent	3
Grandmaster Barrier Rune	Runecrafting (Expert)	Master Barrier Rune	2	Blank Runestone	1	Etching Agent	4	****	0
Grandmaster Cold Iron Rune	Runecrafting (Expert)	Master Cold Iron Rune	2	Blank Runestone	1	Etching Agent	4	****	0
Grandmaster Dweomer Rune	Runecrafting (Expert)	Master Dweomer Rune	2	Blank Runestone	1	Etching Agent	4	****	0
Grandmaster Flame Rune	Runecrafting (Expert)	Master Flame Rune	2	Blank Runestone	1	Etching Agent	4	****	0
Grandmaster Frost Rune	Runecrafting (Expert)	Master Frost Rune	2	Blank Runestone	1	Etching Agent	4	****	0
Grandmaster Hale Rune	Runecrafting (Expert)	Master Hale Rune	2	Blank Runestone	1	Etching Agent	4	****	0
Grandmaster Immunity Rune	Runecrafting (Expert)	Master Immunity Rune	2	Blank Runestone	1	Etching Agent	4	****	0
Grandmaster Lightning Rune	Runecrafting (Expert)	Master Lightning Rune	2	Blank Runestone	1	Etching Agent	4	****	0
Grandmaster Paralyze Rune	Runecrafting (Expert)	Master Paralyze Rune	2	Blank Runestone	1	Etching Agent	4	****	0
Grandmaster Resevoir Rune	Runecrafting (Expert)	Master Resevoir Rune	2	Blank Runestone	1	Etching Agent	4	****	0
Grandmaster Silverite Rune	Runecrafting (Expert)	Master Silverite Rune	2	Blank Runestone	1	Etching Agent	4	****	0
Grandmaster Slow Rune	Runecrafting (Expert)	Master Slow Rune	2	Blank Runestone	1	Etching Agent	4	****	0
Grandmaster Stout Rune	Runecrafting (Expert)	Master Stout Rune	2	Blank Runestone	1	Etching Agent	4	****	0
Grandmaster Tempest Rune	Runecrafting (Expert)	Master Tempest Rune	2	Blank Runestone	1	Etching Agent	4	****	0
Evasion Rune	Runecrafting (Master)	Master Tempest Rune	1	Master Lightning Rune	1	Blank Runestone	1	Etching Agent	4
Masterpiece Barrier Rune	Runecrafting (Master)	Grandmaster Barrier Rune	2	Blank Runestone	1	Etching Agent	5	****	0
Masterpiece Cold Iron Rune	Runecrafting (Master)	Grandmaster Cold Iron Rune	2	Blank Runestone	1	Etching Agent	5	****	0
Masterpiece Dweomer Rune	Runecrafting (Master)	Grandmaster Dweomer Rune	2	Blank Runestone	1	Etching Agent	5	****	0
Masterpiece Flame Rune	Runecrafting (Master)	Grandmaster Flame Rune	2	Blank Runestone	1	Etching Agent	5	****	0
Masterpiece Frost Rune	Runecrafting (Master)	Grandmaster Frost Rune	2	Blank Runestone	1	Etching Agent	5	****	0
Masterpiece Hale Rune	Runecrafting (Master)	Grandmaster Hale Rune	2	Blank Runestone	1	Etching Agent	5	****	0
Masterpiece Immunity Rune	Runecrafting (Master)	Grandmaster Immunity Rune	2	Blank Runestone	1	Etching Agent	5	****	0

Crafting

Basics ~ Classes ~ The Party ~ Companions ~ Supporting Cast ~ **Equipment** ~ Bestiary ~ Walkthrough ~ Side Quests ~ Random Encounters ~ Achievements/Trophies

Runecrafting (continued)

Item Name	Craft	Ingredient 1	Count 1	Ingredient 2	Count 2	Ingredient 3	Count 3	Ingredient 4	Count 4
Masterpiece Lightning Rune	Runecrafting (Master)	Grandmaster Lightning Rune	2	Blank Runestone	1	Etching Agent	5	****	0
Masterpiece Paralyze Rune	Runecrafting (Master)	Grandmaster Paralyze Rune	2	Blank Runestone	1	Etching Agent	5	****	0
Masterpiece Resevoir Rune	Runecrafting (Master)	Grandmaster Resevoir Rune	2	Blank Runestone	1	Etching Agent	5	****	0
Masterpiece Silverite Rune	Runecrafting (Master)	Grandmaster Silverite Rune	2	Blank Runestone	1	Etching Agent	5	****	0
Masterpiece Slow Rune	Runecrafting (Master)	Grandmaster Slow Rune	2	Blank Runestone	1	Etching Agent	5	****	0
Masterpiece Stout Rune	Runecrafting (Master)	Grandmaster Stout Rune	2	Blank Runestone	1	Etching Agent	5	****	0
Masterpiece Tempest Rune	Runecrafting (Master)	Grandmaster Tempest Rune	2	Blank Runestone	1	Etching Agent	5	****	0
Momentum Rune	Runecrafting (Master)	Master Tempest Rune	1	Master Hale Rune	1	Blank Runestone	1	Etching Agent	4
Paragon Barrier Rune	Runecrafting (Master)	Masterpiece Barrier Rune	2	Blank Runestone	1	Etching Agent	6	****	0
Paragon Cold Iron Rune	Runecrafting (Master)	Masterpiece Cold Iron Rune	2	Blank Runestone	1	Etching Agent	6	****	0
Paragon Dweomer Rune	Runecrafting (Master)	Masterpiece Dweomer Rune	2	Blank Runestone	1	Etching Agent	6	****	0
Paragon Flame Rune	Runecrafting (Master)	Masterpiece Flame Rune	2	Blank Runestone	1	Etching Agent	6	****	0
Paragon Frost Rune	Runecrafting (Master)	Masterpiece Frost Rune	2	Blank Runestone	1	Etching Agent	6	****	0
Paragon Hale Rune	Runecrafting (Master)	Masterpiece Hale Rune	2	Blank Runestone	1	Etching Agent	6	****	0
Paragon Immunity Rune	Runecrafting (Master)	Masterpiece Immunity Rune	2	Blank Runestone	1	Etching Agent	6	****	0
Paragon Lightning Rune	Runecrafting (Master)	Masterpiece Lightning Rune	2	Blank Runestone	1	Etching Agent	6	****	0
Paragon Paralyze Rune	Runecrafting (Master)	Masterpiece Paralyze Rune	2	Blank Runestone	1	Etching Agent	6	****	0
Paragon Resevoir Rune	Runecrafting (Master)	Masterpiece Resevoir Rune	2	Blank Runestone	1	Etching Agent	6	****	0
Paragon Silverite Rune	Runecrafting (Master)	Masterpiece Silverite Rune	2	Blank Runestone	1	Etching Agent	6	****	0
Paragon Slow Rune	Runecrafting (Master)	Masterpiece Slow Rune	2	Blank Runestone	1	Etching Agent	6	****	0
Paragon Stout Rune	Runecrafting (Master)	Masterpiece Stout Rune	2	Blank Runestone	1	Etching Agent	6	****	0
Paragon Tempest Rune	Runecrafting (Master)	Masterpiece Tempest Rune	2	Blank Runestone	1	Etching Agent	6	****	0

Trap-Making

Item Name	Craft	Ingredient 1	Count 1	Ingredient 2	Count 2	Ingredient 3	Count 3	Ingredient 4	Count 4
Rope Trap	Trap-Making	Trap Trigger	1	****	0	****	0	****	0
Small Caltrop Trap	Trap-Making	Metal Shard	1	****	0	****	0	****	0
Small Claw Trap	Trap-Making	Metal Shard	1	Trap Trigger	1	****	0	****	0
Small Shrapnel Trap	Trap-Making	Metal Shard	1	Trap Trigger	1	****	0	****	0
Large Caltrop Trap	Trap-Making (Improved)	Metal Shard	2	****	0	****	0	****	0
Large Claw Trap	Trap-Making (Improved)	Metal Shard	2	Trap Trigger	1	****	0	****	0
Large Shrapnel Trap	Trap-Making (Improved)	Metal Shard	2	Trap Trigger	1	****	0	****	0
Mild Choking Powder Trap	Trap-Making (Improved)	Toxin Extract	1	Corrupter Agent	1	Trap Trigger	1	****	0

primagames.com

Trap-Making (continued)									
Item Name	Craft	Ingredient 1	Count 1	Ingredient 2	Count 2	Ingredient 3	Count 3	Ingredient 4	Count 4
Mild Sleeping Gas Trap	Trap-Making (Improved)	Deathroot	1	Corrupter Agent	1	Trap Trigger	1	****	0
Small Grease Trap	Trap-Making (Improved)	Lifestone	1	Distillation Agent	1	Trap Trigger	1	****	0
Small Lure	Trap-Making (Improved)	Glamour Charm	1	****	0	****	0	****	0
Acidic Trap	Trap-Making (Expert)	Lifestone	1	Corrupter Agent	1	Trap Trigger	1	****	0
Choking Powder Trap	Trap-Making (Expert)	Toxin Extract	2	Corrupter Agent	2	Concentrator Agent	1	Trap Trigger	1
Fire Trap	Trap-Making (Expert)	Fire Crystal	1	Corrupter Agent	1	Trap Trigger	1	****	0
Freeze Trap	Trap-Making (Expert)	Frostrock	1	Corrupter Agent	1	Trap Trigger	1	****	0
Large Grease Trap	Trap-Making (Expert)	Lifestone	2	Distillation Agent	2	Concentrator Agent	1	Trap Trigger	1
Large Lure	Trap-Making (Expert)	Glamour Charm	2	****	0	****	0	****	0
Poisoned Caltrop Trap	Trap-Making (Expert)	Metal Shard	2	Lifestone	1	Corrupter Agent	1	****	0
Shock Trap	Trap-Making (Expert)	Frozen Lightning	1	Corrupter Agent	1	Trap Trigger	1	****	0
Sleeping Gas Trap	Trap-Making (Expert)	Deathroot	2	Corrupter Agent	2	Concentrator Agent	1	Trap Trigger	1
Soulrot Trap	Trap-Making (Expert)	Spirit Shard	1	Corrupter Agent	1	Trap Trigger	1	****	0
Acidic Grease Trap	Trap-Making (Master)	Lifestone	3	Corrupter Agent	2	Concentrator Agent	2	Trap Trigger	1
Choking Powder Cloud Trap	Trap-Making (Master)	Toxin Extract	3	Corrupter Agent	2	Concentrator Agent	2	Trap Trigger	1
Dispel Trap	Trap-Making (Master)	Rashvine Nettle	1	Corrupter Agent	2	Trap Trigger	1	Concentrator Agent	1
Elemental Trap	Trap-Making (Master)	Blood Lotus	1	Corrupter Agent	2	Trap Trigger	1	Concentrator Agent	1
Gravity Trap	Trap-Making (Master)	Glamour Charm	4	Corrupter Agent	4	Trap Trigger	1	****	0
Irresistable Lure	Trap-Making (Master)	Glamour Charm	3	****	0	****	0	****	0
Misdirection Cloud Trap	Trap-Making (Master)	Madcap Bulb	2	Corrupter Agent	2	Concentrator Agent	2	Trap Trigger	1
Sleeping Gas Cloud Trap	Trap-Making (Master)	Deathroot	3	Corrupter Agent	2	Concentrator Agent	2	Trap Trigger	1

Usable Items

Anything you can craft, and many of the crafting components, can be considered usable items. The most common ones are health poultices and lyrium potions (Herbalism), poisons (Poison-Making), and trap kits (Trap-Making). Click on the item and you gain the effect, using up one of the item in the process. If you use an item often, add it to your quickbar/shortcut for easy access. Something that early adventurers may not be aware of is that crafting reagents also have effects if used directly. For example, deep mushroom restores 10 stamina, while lifestone gives +10 nature resistance for one minute. In general, though, if you plan on crafting, hold off on the small one-time reagent effects to gain the larger effects from crafted items.

Grenades			
Name	Quality #1	Quality #2	Quality #3
Acid Flask	Deals 80 Nature damage to creatures in the area of effect	—	—
Dispel Grenade	Required: Poison-Making	Dispels magic effects in area	—
Dworkin's Explosives	Dworkin the Mad's "safest" explosives	—	—
Dworkin's Explosives	A powerful variant of Dworkin the Mad's explosives	—	—

Crafting - Usable Items

Basics ~ Classes ~ The Party ~ Companions ~ Supporting Cast ~ **Equipment** ~ Bestiary ~ Walkthrough ~ Side Quests ~ Random Encounters ~ Achievements/Trophies

Grenades (continued)

Name	Quality #1	Quality #2	Quality #3
Dworkin's Explosives	Dworkin the Mad's explosives. They go "boom!"	—	—
Elemental Grenade	Required: Poison-Making	Deals elemental damage in area	—
Fire Bomb	Deals 80 Fire damage to creatures in the area of effect	—	—
Freeze Bomb	Deals 80 Cold damage to creatures in the area of effect	—	—
Shock Bomb	Deals 80 Electricity damage to creatures in the area of effect	—	—
Soulrot Bomb	Deals 80 Spirit damage to creatures in the area of effect	—	—

Health Poultices

Name	Quality #1	Quality #2	Quality #3
Lesser Health Poultice	Restores 50+ Health	—	—
Health Poultice	Restores 100+ Health	—	—
Greater Health Poultice	Restores 150+ Health	—	—
Potent Health Poultice	Restores 200+ Health	—	—
Superb Health Poultice	Restores 250+ Health	—	—
Master Health Poultice	Restores 300+ Health	—	—
Ethereal Health Poultice	Healing Potion	This exists only in the Fade	—

Heraldry

Name	Quality #1	Quality #2	Quality #3
Heraldry: Aeducan	The heraldry of House Aeducan can be applied to a suitable shield.	—	—
Heraldry: Antivan Crows	The insignia of the Antivan Crows can be applied to a suitable shield.	—	—
Heraldry: Bear's Paw	This outline of a bear's paw can be applied to a suitable shield.	—	—
Heraldry: City of Amaranthine	The crest of the City of Amaranthine can be applied to a suitable shield.	—	—
Heraldry: Cousland	The heraldry of the Couslands of Highever can be applied to a suitable shield.	—	—
Heraldry: Cross	This cross can be applied to a suitable shield.	—	—
Heraldry: Dragon's Peak Bannorn	The heraldry of the Bann of Dragon's Peak can be applied to a suitable shield.	—	—
Heraldry: Grey Wardens	The heraldry of the Grey Wardens can be applied to a suitable shield.	—	—
Heraldry: Legion of the Dead	The crest of the Legion of the Dead can be applied to a suitable shield.	—	—
Heraldry: Templars	The templars' insignia can be applied to a suitable shield.	—	—

Injury Repair Kit

Name	Quality #1	Quality #2	Quality #3
Lesser Injury Kit	Restores 10 Health	Removes 1 Injury	—
Injury Kit	Restores 20 Health	Removes 3 Injuries	—
Greater Injury Kit	Restores 40 Health	Removes All Injuries	—

Mana Potions

Name	Quality #1	Quality #2	Quality #3
Lesser Lyrium Potion	Restores 50+ Mana	Required: Mage	—
Lyrium Potion	Restores 100+ Mana	Required: Mage	—
Greater Lyrium Potion	Restores 150+ Mana	Required: Mage	—
Potent Lyrium Potion	Restores 200+ Mana	Required: Mage	—
Superb Lyrium Potion	Restores 250+ Mana	Required: Mage	—
Master Lyrium Potion	Restores 300+ Mana	Required: Mage	—
Ethereal Lyrium Potion	Mana Potion	Required: Mage	This exists only in the Fade

Manuals

Name	Quality #1	Quality #2	Quality #3
Manual of Focus	Re-spec Character	—	—
Manual: Battlemage	Unlocks Mage Specialization	—	—
Manual: Blood Mage	Unlocks Mage Specialization	—	—
Manual: Guardian	Unlocks Warrior Specialization	—	—
Manual: Keeper	Unlocks Mage Specialization	—	—

primagames.com

Manuals (continued)			
Name	Quality #1	Quality #2	Quality #3
Manual: Legionnaire Scout	Unlocks Rogue Specialization	—	—
Manual: Reaver	Unlocks Warrior Specialization	—	—
Manual: Shadow	Unlocks Rogue Specialization	—	—
Manual: Spirit Warrior	Unlocks Warrior Specialization	—	—

Poisons			
Name	Quality #1	Quality #2	Quality #3
Deathroot Extract	+1 Nature Damage for 60 seconds	Chance to stun target for 60 seconds	—
Venom	+1 Nature Damage for 60 seconds	Chance to slow target for 60 seconds	—
Concentrated Deathroot Extract	+2 Nature Damage for 60 seconds	Chance to stun target for 60 seconds	—
Concentrated Venom	+2 Nature Damage for 60 seconds	Chance to slow target for 60 seconds	—
Adder's Kiss	+3 Nature Damage for 60 seconds	Chance to slow target for 60 seconds	—
Crow Poison	+3 Nature Damage for 60 seconds	Chance to stun target for 60 seconds	—
Fleshrot	+3 Nature Damage for 60 seconds	Chance to stun target for 60 seconds	—
Demonic Poison	+5 Spirit Damage for 60 seconds	—	—
Magebane	+5 Mana Damage for 60 seconds	—	—
Soldier's Bane	+5 Stamina Damage for 60 seconds	—	—
Concentrated Crow Poison	+6 Nature Damage for 60 seconds	Chance to stun target for 60 seconds	—
Concentrated Demonic Poison	+10 Spirit Damage for 60 seconds	—	—
Concentrated Magebane	+10 Mana Damage for 60 seconds	—	—
Concentrated Soldier's Bane	+10 Stamina Damage for 60 seconds	—	—
Quiet Death	+10 Nature Damage for 60 seconds	instantly kills weak, injured creatures	—

Reagents			
Name	Quality #1	Quality #2	Quality #3
Blank Runestone	For crafting runes	—	—
Blood Lotus	Used for crafting Elemental items	—	—
Deep Mushroom	Restores 10 Stamina	—	—
Elfroot	Restores 10 Health	—	—
Etching Agent	For crafting runes	—	—
Fire Crystal	+10 Fire Resistance for 60 seconds	—	—
Frostrock	+10 Cold Resistance for 60 seconds	—	—
Frozen Lightning	+10 Electricity Resistance for 60 seconds	—	—
Lifestone	+10 Nature Resistance for 60 seconds	—	—
Lyrium Dust	Restores 10 Mana	—	—
Madcap Bulb	Use for crafting Misdirection items	—	—
Rashvine Nettle	Use for crafting Dispel items	—	—
Spirit Shard	+10 Spirit Resistance for 60 seconds	—	—

Resistance Potions			
Name	Quality #1	Quality #2	Quality #3
Lesser Elixir of Grounding	+30 Electricity Resistance for 180 seconds	—	—
Lesser Ice Salve	+30 Cold Resistance for 180 seconds	—	—
Lesser Nature Salve	+30 Nature Resistance for 180 seconds	—	—
Lesser Spirit Balm	+30 Spirit Resistance for 180 seconds	—	—
Lesser Warmth Balm	+30 Fire Resistance for 180 seconds	—	—
Greater Elixir of Grounding	+60 Electricity Resistance for 180 seconds	—	—
Greater Ice Salve	+60 Cold Resistance for 180 seconds	—	—
Greater Nature Salve	+60 Nature Resistance for 180 seconds	—	—
Greater Spirit Balm	+60 Spirit Resistance for 180 seconds	—	—
Greater Warmth Balm	+60 Fire Resistance for 180 seconds	—	—

Stamina Draughts			
Name	Quality #1	Quality #2	Quality #3
Lesser Stamina Draught	Restores 50+ Stamina	Required: Warrior or Rogue	—
Stamina Draught	Restores 100+ Stamina	Required: Warrior or Rogue	—
Greater Stamina Draught	Restores 150+ Stamina	Required: Warrior or Rogue	—
Potent Stamina Draught	Restores 200+ Stamina	Required: Warrior or Rogue	—
Superb Stamina Draught	Restores 250+ Stamina	Required: Warrior or Rogue	—
Master Stamina Draught	Restores 300+ Stamina	Required: Warrior or Rogue	—
Ethereal Stamina Draught	Stamina Potion	Required: Warrior or Rogue	This exists only in the Fade

Usable Items

Basics ~ Classes ~ The Party ~ Companions ~ Supporting Cast ~ **Equipment** ~ Bestiary ~ Walkthrough ~ Side Quests ~ Random Encounters ~ Achievements/Trophies

Trap Kits

Name	Quality #1	Quality #2	Quality #3
Acidic Grease Trap	Movement speed reduced	Chance to slip	Constant Nature Damage
Acidic Trap	100 Nature Damage	—	—
Choking Powder Cloud Trap	Cloud remains for 20 seconds	Dazed	Movement speed reduced
Choking Powder Trap	Dazed	Movement speed reduced	—
Dispel Trap	Dispels magical effects on target	—	—
Elemental Trap	Deal elemental damage to target	—	—
Fire Trap	100 Fire Damage	—	—
Freeze Trap	100 Cold Damage	—	—
Gravity Trap	Nullifies free movement on target	—	—
Interesting Lure	Middle rank creatures are drawn to the lure	Lure disappears after being touched	—
Large Caltrop Trap	Movement speed reduced	Enemies take constant Physical Damage	—
Large Claw Trap	Immobilized	150 Physical Damage	—
Large Grease Trap	Movement speed reduced	Chance to slip	—
Large Shrapnel Trap	80 Physical Damage	—	—
Mild Choking Powder Trap	Dazed	Movement speed reduced	—
Mild Lure	Lower rank creatures are drawn to the lure	Lure disappears after being touched	—
Mild Sleeping Gas Trap	Put to sleep	—	—
Misdirection Cloud Trap	Cast Misdirection on targets in area	—	—
Overpowering Lure	Most creatures are drawn to the lure	Lure disappears 30 seconds after being touched	—
Poisoned Caltrop Trap	Movement speed reduced	Enemies take constant Physical and Nature Damage	—
Shock Trap	100 Electricity Damage	—	—
Sleeping Gas Cloud Trap	Cloud remains for 20 seconds	Put to sleep	—
Sleeping Gas Trap	Put to sleep	—	—
Small Caltrop Trap	Movement speed reduced	Enemies take constant Physical Damage	—
Small Claw Trap	Immobilized	100 Physical Damage	—
Small Grease Trap	Movement speed reduced	Chance to slip	—
Small Shrapnel Trap	60 Physical Damage	—	—
Soulrot Trap	100 Spirit Damage	—	—
Spring Trap	Chance to slip	—	—

Weapon Coatings

Name	Quality #1	Quality #2	Quality #3
Acidic Coating	+2 Nature Damage for 60 seconds	Required: Poison-Making	—
Dispel Coating	Dispels magical effects	Required: Poison-Making	—
Elemental Coating	Deals elemental damage	Required: Poison-Making	—
Flame Coating	+2 Fire Damage for 60 seconds	Required: Poison-Making	—
Freezing Coating	+2 Cold Damage for 60 seconds	Required: Poison-Making	—
Shock Coating	+3 Electricity Damage for 60 seconds	Required: Poison-Making	—
Soulrot Coating	+2 Spirit Damage for 60 seconds	Required: Poison-Making	—

Misc

Name	Quality #1	Quality #2	Quality #3
Dwarven Regicide Antidote	Dispels magical effects	—	—
Flawless Diamond	Worth valuable coin	—	—
Flawless Emerald	Worth valuable coin	—	—
Flawless Ruby	Worth valuable coin	—	—
Flawless Sapphire	Worth valuable coin	—	—
Formari Tome	Character gains +1 Skill point	—	—
Greater Tome of the Mortal Vessel	Character gains +2 Attribute points	—	—
Incense of Awareness	+10 Defense for 120 seconds	-10 Mental Resistance for 120 seconds	—
Rock Salve	+5 Armor for 120 seconds	+10 Physical Resistance for 120 seconds	Movement speed slowed for 120 seconds
Swift Salve	Movement speed increase for 60 seconds	Attack speed increase for 60 seconds	Aim speed increase for 60 seconds
Tome of Arcane Technique	Character gains +1 Talent point	Required: Mage	—
Tome of Ethereal Suggestion	Character gains +1 Talent point	—	—
Tome of Physical Technique	Character gains +1 Talent point	Required: Warrior or Rogue	—
Tome of Skill and Sundry	Character gains +1 Skill point	—	—
Tome of the Mortal Vessel	Character gains +1 Attribute point	—	—

primagames.com

Gifts

Everyone loves to receive gifts, even grumpy, never-smiling companions such as Velanna. Presenting a gift to a companion raises their approval rating, and you always want your approval rating with a companion as high as possible. Approval rating affects how the companion responds to you, including inviting you on personal quests, following your lead, or even leaving the group permanently.

NOTE

See the "Gifts" section of the Companions chapter for the complete rundown on gifts, approval ratings, distribution recommendations, and more.

As you journey around the land, you will find or buy gifts. Consult the gift charts here for the companion who would best benefit from the new gift you have. If you deliver the gift to the correct companion, you will gain a big approval boost for that companion. If you give the special gift to another companion, expect only a minor approval boost (after a while it will only be +1). If you don't care too much about a companion—for example, you only use Justice instead of Oghren—feel free to give that companion's gifts away to whomever you want to improve relationships with more. There are also many gifts that provide a small approval boost but can be given to any companion. You need all the gifts you can get to raise a companion's level up to 100 if you ever want to max out a companion's affection for you.

Anders

Name	Plot Gift or Normal	Found In	Location
Bell Collar	Normal	Homer's Toys	Amaranthine
Engraved Silver Bracers	Normal	Pile of Bones	Kal'Hirol
Gold Earring	Normal	Knight's Corpse	Vigil's Keep Basement
Kitten	Plot	Plot Item	Eastern section of Vigil's Keep Courtyard
Knitted Scarf	Normal	Lost and Found box	Amaranthine Chantry
Phylacteries: A History Written in Blood	Normal	Books	Silverite Mine
Ser Pounce-a-lot	Plot	Inventory	Received after giving kitten to Anders

Justice

Name	Plot Gift or Normal	Found In	Location
Elven Prayer for the Dead	Normal	Crate	Wending Wood
Kristoff's Locket	Normal	Pile of Rocks	Blackmarsh
Kristoff's Mementos	Normal	Chest	Crown and Lion Inn
Lyrium Ring	Plot	Chest	Kal'Hirol's Main Hall
Lyrium: The Voice of the Maker	Normal	Bookshelf	Abandoned Warehouse in Amaranthine
Verses of Dreams	Normal	Pile of Books	Vigil's Keep Throne Room

Nathaniel

Name	Plot Gift or Normal	Found In	Location
Bronze Sextant	Normal	Corpse	Wending Wood
Delilah Howe's Letters	Normal	Howe Correspondence	Vigil's Keep Basement
Golden Vase	Normal	Octham's Goods	Amaranthine
Howe Bow	Plot	Bag	Vigil's Keep Basement
Locksmith's Tools	Normal	Crate	Smuggler's Cove
Whetstone	Normal	Stone Container	Kal'Hirol

Oghren

Name	Plot Gift or Normal	Found In	Location
Aqua Magus	Normal	Crate	Abandoned Warehouse in Amaranthine
Dragon Piss	Normal	Crate	Hubert's Den in Amaranthine
Hirol's Lava Burst	Normal	Chest	Knotwood Hills
Mackay's Epic Single Malt	Normal	Crate	Crown and Lion Inn
Toy Horse	Plot	On the ground	Blackmarsh
West Hill Brandy	Normal	Crate	Vigil's Keep Basement

Sigrun

Name	Plot Gift or Normal	Found In	Location
Potted Plant	Normal	Pot	Outside Amaranthine Chantry
Snow Globe	Normal	Glassric's Wares	Amaranthine
Soap on a Rope	Normal	Supplies	Vigil's Keep Dungeon
Spyglass	Plot	Soldier's Corpse	Silverite Mine
Toy Chariot	Normal	Toy Box	Smuggler's Cove
The Warrior's Heart	Normal	Pile of Books	Vigil's Keep Throne Room

Velanna

Name	Plot Gift or Normal	Found In	Location
Blank Journal	Plot	Pile of Books	Amaranthine Chantry
Carved Greenstone	Normal	Stone Container	Trade Quarter in Kal'Hirol
Discarded Journal	Normal	Crate	Amaranthine
Elven Runestone	Normal	Pile of Rocks	Vigil's Keep Deep Roads
Ornate Silver Bowl	Normal	Pile of Filth	Blackmarsh
Shiny Malachite	Normal	Pile of Rocks	Silverite Mine

Monster Ranks

Basics ~ Classes ~ The Party ~ Companions ~ Supporting Cast ~ Equipment ~ **Bestiary** ~ Walkthrough ~ Side Quests ~ Random Encounters ~ Achievements/Trophies

The Bestiary

Darkspawn talk. Broodmothers birth fiendish children. A more powerful dragon lurks in the ethereal regions of the Blackmarsh. In *Awakening*, more devastating monsters join the ranks of your original foes, and you'll be hard-pressed to stop the tide without a stalwart party.

As with *Dragon Age: Origins*, statistics for monsters are dynamic; they scale to the player's level. This makes for a challenging experience, because you won't run into an area that's way too easy or way too difficult; you can enjoy the gameplay right along with the story.

TIP

Monster levels scale to a party the first time they enter an area. Visit a particularly difficult area early, leave, and come back a few levels later, and your party will have a much easier time conquering the place.

The following Bestiary showcases the game's monsters, including each one's rank, class, primary stats, description, and play tips on how to avoid the monsters' attacks and how to defeat the diabolical denizens. Each creature falls in one of seven ranks. Normal is on par with the PC. Weak Normal, Critter, and One-Hit descend in power from a creature barely a challenge to the PC to a creature you can eliminate in a single stroke. On the other side, Lieutenant is a creature slightly above the PC's level, Boss is a creature meant to take on an entire party, and Elite Boss is the toughest of the tough and taking it down will require an expert party and all their skills.

NOTE

There are many monster variants among the creatures in the Amaranthine lands. For example, you could have a devouring skeleton or a frenzied devouring skeleton, but both are still skeletons. The basic monster type remains the same and the different monster looks do not affect your play strategy against them.

Rank Type	Monster Ranks									
Label	Health Scaling	Bonus Stat Points	Level Scaling	Damage Capability	Resistance to Various Attacks	Resistance Maximum	Loot Drops	Chance to Steal From	Stealth Detection
One-Hit Kill	Very Low	N/A	2 behind player	Very Low	Average	0	Very Low	Very High	Average
Critter	Low	N/A	3 behind player	Very Low	Average	0	Very Low	Very High	Average
Weak Normal	Fair	N/A	2 behind player	Low	Fair	25%	Low	Very High	Average
Normal	Moderate	N/A	1 behind player	Moderate	Average	50%	Fair	Moderate	Average
Player	Average	N/A	Average	Average	Average	75%	N/A	Very High	Moderate
Lieutenant	Above Average	Fair	Average	Average	Above Average	75%	Above Average	Fair	Above Average
Boss	High	Above Average	1 ahead of player	Average	High	100%	High	Low	High
Elite Boss	Very High	Very High	2 ahead of player	Very High	Very High	100%	Very High	Very Low	Very High

The higher the rating, the higher the health.

The higher the rating, the more stat points each target gets.

Level target is compared to the PC.

The higher the rating, the more damage the target does.

The higher the rating, the greater the resistance to an array of things.

The maximum amount of damage this rank could possibly resist from a certain type of attack (in percentage).

The higher the ratings here, the better chance of loot drops.

The higher the rating, the harder it is to steal from the target.

The higher the rating, the easier it is for the enemy to detect a stealthed character.

Creature classes can include either the base classes (like Warrior or Mage) or monster-specific classes, which determine attributes and general combat roles. The possible monster-specific classes are:

- Monster—Tank
- Monster—High Damage
- Monster—Agile
- Monster—Balanced Physical
- Monster—Spirit
- Monster—Balanced Mental
- Monster—Spellcaster

Creature attributes are all ranked on a ten-point scale, from Very Low to Superior. The possible attribute ranks, from best to worst, are:

- Superior
- Very High
- High
- Above Average
- Average
- Moderate
- Fair
- Meager
- Low
- Very Low

Knowing these attribute strengths can give you the advantage in combat. For example, A creature with a high strength score will deal significant melee damage and take less in return. A creature with a high magic score will lean toward spells in combat. A creature with low willpower won't have much stamina or mana and will not be able to continuously hit you with abilities.

primagames.com

DRAGON AGE ORIGINS — AWAKENING

PRIMA Official Game Guide

NOTE

While classes define general attribute patterns, they're also influenced by a creature's rank. For example, genlocks and high dragons both have a very high strength attribute, but this is compared to other creatures of the same rank. The poor genlock would be no match for a dragon one-on-one.

After each monster description, look for play tips on how to overcome the creature's abilities and how to defeat the beast. After you encounter a monster several times you'll probably know what to expect, but it's useful to study up on creatures for your first few encounters. When you want to know more about the creatures that inhabit the arling of Amaranthine, check out your codex. The first time you encounter a monster, you receive a codex entry which contains interesting and useful information for that monster. You'll learn anything from the telekinetic abilities of revenants to the factions of the darkspawn disciples.

The following chart presents monster abilities. They are grouped by type but may not be exclusive because some monsters share abilities (for example, the Dark Theurge relies on an array of electricity-based spells). In addition, the last chart contains a shared group of general abilities. Note that if a certain monster isn't on this chart, it's because it primarily uses basic attacks. Passive abilities cover general stats, resistances, and bonuses, while active abilities cover specific attacks or actions. You can generally react to active abilities either to prevent them by stunning the creature before it has a chance to follow through, or to escape the arrea of effect.

The Toughest of the Tough

You know when you see a red bar above your foe's name that it's going to be a long battle. Any boss-ranked creatures receive a bonus of 2,000 health while elite boss-ranked creatures receive a bonus of 5,000 health.

Monster Abilities

Monster	Category	Ability Name	Description
Abomination	Active	Rage	The abomination enters a rage, gaining bonuses to damage and movement speed for a short time.
	Active	Slam	The ash wraith slams its target, dealing critical damage and draining it of mana or stamina. The attack knocks the target down unless it passes a physical resistance check.
	Active	Triple Strike	The abomination strikes its target three times, dealing normal damage with each hit, and stunning on the third hit.
	Active	Whirlwind	The ash wraith creates a whirlwind around itself, dealing spirit damage to all nearby enemies and stunning them unless they pass a physical resistance check.
	Passive	Abomination Properties	The abomination has natural bonuses to strength and electricity resistance (strength +5, electricity +25).
Arcane Horror	Active	Drain	The arcane horror draws mana or stamina from all nearby enemies and deals spirit damage at the same time. It regains a fraction of the drained mana and stamina as health.
	Active	Restore	The arcane horror restores some health and mana or stamina to nearby allies, including itself.
	Active	Spirit Blast	The arcane horror shoots a blast of energy at its opponent, dealing spirit damage.
	Active	Swarm	The arcane horror forces its allies to attack the target, which is rooted in place unless it passes a physical resistance check.
	Passive	Arcane Horror Properties	The arcane horror has natural bonuses to magic, spellpower, and magic resistance (spellpower +10, magic +20, magic resistance +20).
The Architect	Active	Cataclysm	The caster summons a storm of flame and cascading rock that pelts targets with constant fire damage. Friendly fire possible.
	Active	Flare	The caster hurls a violent burst of energy at the target, inflicting fire damage.
	Active	Shivering Shot	The caster hurls an icy projectile at the target, inflicting cold damage.
	Passive	Architect Properties	Health +1,000, armor +11.
Armored Ogre	Active	Whirlwind	The ogre spins, inflicting tremendous damage to all surrounding foes.
	Passive	Armored Ogre Properties	Health +2,000, armor +35, magic resistance +15.
Ash Wraith	Active	Leap	The ash wraith leaps on its target, dealing critical damage and draining it of mana or stamina. The attack stuns the target unless it passes a physical resistance check.
Bear	Active	Overwhelm	The bear leaps upon its target, pinning it to the ground and attacking it repeatedly.
	Active	Rage	The bear becomes enraged, gaining a bonus to strength and a penalty to defense for a short time.
	Active	Slam	The bear slams the target. If the attack hits, it deals critical damage and knocks the target down unless it passes a physical resistance check.
	Passive	Bear Properties	The bear has natural bonuses to nature resistance and armor (nature resistance +50, armor +10).
Blighted Werewolf	Passive	Blighted Werewolf Properties	Health +100, armor +10, attack +5.
Charred Sylvan	Active	Rage	The sylvan enters a rage, giving itself a bonus to damage for a short time and waking up other nearby sylvans. If the sylvan is a boss-level creature, it also generates an insect swarm that inflicts damage over time and penalties to attack, defense, and movement speed.
	Active	Roots	The sylvan snares nearby targets with its roots, immobilizing them and dealing physical damage for a short time. Friendly fire possible.
	Active	Stomp	The sylvan stomps, damaging nearby targets and knocking them down. Friendly fire possible.
	Passive	Wild Sylvan Properties	The sylvan has natural bonuses to armor and health, but a large penalty to fire resistance (armor +5, health +25, fire -50).

Monster Abilities

Basics ~ Classes ~ The Party ~ Companions ~ Supporting Cast ~ Equipment ~ **Bestiary** ~ Walkthrough ~ Side Quests ~ Random Encounters ~ Achievements/Trophies

Monster	Category	Ability Name	Description
The Children	Active	Capricious Demise	If the childer dies while this mode is active, it detonates, inflicting significant nature damage to all nearby enemies.
	Active	Leap	The creature jumps to a targeted location.
	Active	Sprout	While this mode is active, the childer grub morphs into a more aggressive hatchling.
	Active	Metamorphosis	The childer hatchling morphs into a more aggressive adult.
	Active	Overwhelm	The childer leaps upon its target, pinning it to the ground and attacking it repeatedly. With each successful attack, the childer gains health.
	Active	Pincer Flurry	The childer begins a furious series of attacks that inflict increasing damage with each consecutive hit.
	Active	Spit	The childer spits acid at the target, inflicting nature damage.
	Active	Virulent Burst	The childer snaps its arms out, splashing surrounding enemies with mucus that causes nature damage over time, inflicts a penalty to movement speed, and knocks foes down unless they pass a physical resistance check.
	Passive	Childer Properties	Health +150, magic resistance +10.
Corpse	Passive	Cold Affinity	This creature has a large natural bonus to cold resistance, but a penalty to fire resistance (cold resistance +75, fire resistance -25).
The Dark Theurge	Active	Lightning Spells	The Dark Theurge relies on its many electricity-based spells to hamper a party.
Deepstalker	Active	Acid Spit	The stalker spits at its target, dealing nature damage for a short time and possibly stunning the opponent.
	Active	Overwhelm	The stalker leaps upon its target, pinning it to the ground and attacking it repeatedly.
	Active	Scare	The stalker scares its target, giving it a penalty to attack for a short time.
	Active	Slowing Spit	The stalker spits at its target, giving the target an attack penalty for a short time and slowing its movement rate unless it passes a physical resistance check.
Desire Demon	Active	Cursed Dance	The desire demon inflicts a curse on all nearby enemies. Females are knocked down and take penalties to all resistances. Males cannot heal for a time. Enemies also take spirit damage for a time and fall asleep unless they pass a mental resistance check.
	Active	Scream	The desire demon lets out a horrible scream, dealing spirit damage to all nearby enemies and stunning them for a short time unless they pass a mental resistance check.
Disciple	Active	Cimmerian Might	For as long as this mode is active, the disciple gains a bonus to damage.
	Active	Cimmerian Shield	For as long as this mode is active, the disciple gains a bonus to armor, although it becomes more vulnerable to damage from magic.
	Active	Wraithwall	For as long as this mode is active, the disciple gains bonuses to fire, cold, electricity, nature, and spirit resistance, but becomes more vulnerable to physical damage.
	Passive	Disciple Properties	Health +400, armor +10, magic resistance +10.
Dragon Thrall	Active	Buffet	The dragon flaps its wings, dealing physical damage to targets in the area and knocking them back. Friendly fire possible.
	Active	Flame Breath	The dragon breathes flame, dealing major fire damage to all targets in the area.
	Active	Overwhelm	The dragon leaps upon its target, pinning it to the ground and attacking it repeatedly.
	Active	Rake	The dragon rakes its opponent, dealing critical damage and knocking it down.
	Active	Roar	The dragon lets out a fearsome roar, stunning enemies within range and giving them a penalty to attack and defense for a short time.
	Active	Shred	The dragon shreds a target, dealing normal damage on each hit, but penetrating armor easily.
	Active	Slap	The dragon slaps with its tail, dealing normal damage to targets in the area and knocking them down. Friendly fire possible.
	Passive	Dragon Properties	The dragon has a large natural bonus to fire resistance (fire resistance +90, armor +5).
Dragon-ling	Active	Flame Breath	The dragonling breathes flame, dealing fire damage to enemies in the area and making them burn for a short time. Friendly fire possible.
Genlock	Passive	Genlock Properties	Magic resistance +5, mental resistance +3.
Ghoul	Passive	Unholy Swarm	Ghouls try to swarm around their target to increase flanking damage.
High Dragon	Active	Buffet	The high dragon flaps its wings, dealing physical damage to all targets in the area and knocking them back. Friendly fire possible.
	Active	Dragon Breath	The high dragon breathes fire, dealing major fire damage to all targets in the area. Friendly fire possible.
	Active	Fire Spit	The high dragon spits a ball of fire, which explodes violently. All targets in the area take fire damage and burn for a short time. Friendly fire possible.
	Active	Grab	The high dragon grabs a target and strikes it repeatedly, dealing normal damage with each hit.
	Active	Roar	The high dragon lets out a fearsome roar, stunning targets within range and giving them a penalty to attack and defense for a short time. Friendly fire possible.
	Active	Slap	The high dragon slaps with its tail, dealing normal damage to targets in the area and knocking them down. Friendly fire possible.
	Active	Sweep	The high dragon sweeps the area around it, hitting all targets in the area and knocking them down. Friendly fire possible.
	Passive	High Dragon Properties	Armor +10.

primagames.com

Monster	Category	Ability Name	Description
Hurlock	Passive	Hurlock Properties	Cold resistance +5, spirit resistance +5, +1% evasion.
Inferno Golem	Active	Ignite	The golem becomes engulfed in flame, dealing fire damage to all enemies in the area.
Inferno Golem	Active	Searing Quake	The golem slams the ground three times, dealing continual fire damage to all nearby creatures and stunning them unless they pass a physical resistance check. Friendly fire possible.
Inferno Golem	Active	Searing Slam	The golem slams the target. If the attack hits, it deals significant fire damage and knocks the target down.
The Mother	Active	Animus Lash	The broodmother whips her tentacle in a wide arc, damaging all nearby creatures and knocking them down unless they pass a physical resistance check. Friendly fire possible.
The Mother	Active	Grab	The broodmother grabs a target with her tentacle and crushes it repeatedly, dealing normal damage with each hit.
The Mother	Active	Rotting Gas	The broodmother unleashes her built-up intestinal gasses on nearby targets, inflicting nature damage for the duration the cloud persists. Friendly fire possible.
The Mother	Active	Scream	The broodmother lets out a horrible scream. Nearby targets are knocked off their feet, while those farther away are stunned and those farther still are merely disoriented. Friendly fire possible.
The Mother	Active	Slam	The broodmother slams out her tentacles, dealing normal damage to targets in the area and knocking them off their feet unless they pass a physical resistance check. Friendly fire possible.
The Mother	Active	Spit	The broodmother spits acid at its target, dealing nature damage.
The Mother	Active	Sweep	The broodmother lashes out, dealing normal damage and knocking down or stunning targets in the area. Friendly fire possible.
The Mother	Active	Tentacle Ward	For as long as this mode is active, the broodmother's tentacle curls into a defensive position, granting it a significant bonus to armor and a chance to resist hostile magic.
The Mother	Active	Vomit	The broodmother spews vomit and bile, dealing nature damage to all targets in the area. Friendly fire possible.
The Mother	Passive	Broodmother Properties	The broodmother has large natural bonuses to mental resistance, nature resistance, and armor (mental resistance +75, nature damage resistance +75, armor +2).
The Mother	Passive	The Mother Properties	Health +1,000, armor +10.
The Mother's Tentacles	Passive	Tentacle Properties	Health +750, armor +10, magic resistance +10.
Ogre	Active	Grab	The ogre picks up its opponent, striking it repeatedly for normal damage while holding it in the air.
Ogre	Active	Hurl	The ogre hurls a rock at the target, damaging all nearby targets and knocking them down unless they pass a physical resistance check. Friendly fire possible.
Ogre	Active	Ram	The ogre gores its opponent with its horns, knocking the target off its feet and dealing critical damage unless it passes a physical resistance check.
Ogre	Active	Stomp	The ogre slams the ground, sending out a shockwave. Targets in the area take physical damage and are knocked off their feet unless they pass a physical resistance check. Friendly fire possible.
Ogre	Active	Sweep	The ogre slams its target with both fists, knocking the enemy down and dealing critical damage unless the target passes a physical resistance check.
Ogre	Passive	Ogre Properties	Cold resistance +20, magic resistance +10. Ogres can only have one of the two possible passive ability sets.
Ogre	Passive	Ogre Properties 2	Spirit resistance +15, damage + 1. Ogres can only have one of the two possible passive ability sets.
Pride Demon	Active	Drain	The demon grabs a target, creating a sinister bond that drains the target's life energy to heal the demon.
Pride Demon	Active	Fire Blast	An explosion of flame bursts from the pride demon, doing fire damage to all nearby enemies and causing them to burn for a short time. Enemies are knocked back unless they pass physical resistance check.
Pride Demon	Active	Fire Bolt	The pride demon shoots a bolt of fire at a target, inflicting fire damage and causing it to burn for a short time.
Pride Demon	Active	Frost Bolt	The pride demon shoots a bolt of frost at an opponent, doing cold damage and freezing it solid unless it passes a physical resistance check.
Pride Demon	Active	Frost Burst	An explosion of frost bursts from the pride demon, doing cold damage to all nearby enemies, who are frozen solid for a short time unless they pass a physical resistance check.
Pride Demon	Active	Mana Wave	An explosion of mana bursts from the pride demon, dispelling all effects from opponents in the area and draining them of their mana or stamina.
Pride Demon	Active	Shockwave	The demon slams the ground, creating a linear shockwave that deals normal damage to all creatures in the area and knocks them off their feet unless they pass a physical resistance check. Friendly fire possible.
Pride Demon	Passive	Pride Demon Properties	The pride demon has natural bonuses to mana regeneration, spellpower, and armor (mana combat regen +1, spellpower +5, armor +5).
Queen of the Blackmarsh	Active	Lightning Breath	The dragon breathes lightning, dealing major electrical damage to all targets in the area. Friendly fire possible.
Queen of the Blackmarsh	Active	Lightning Spit	The dragon spits a ball of lightning that explodes violently. All creatures in the area take electrical damage for a short time. Friendly fire possible.
Queen of the Blackmarsh	Passive	Fade Dragon Properties	Health +5,000.
Queen of the Blackmarsh	Passive	Regen Properties	Displacement +10, armor +40, magic resistance +50.
Rage Demon	Active	Fire Bolt	The rage demon shoots a bolt of fire at a target, inflicting fire damage and causing it to burn for a short time.
Rage Demon	Active	Fire Burst	The rage demon creates a burst of lava at a targeted location. Targets in the area take fire damage for a short time. Friendly fire possible.
Rage Demon	Active	Slam	The rage demon slams an opponent, dealing critical damage, which ignores a portion of its armor.

Monster Abilities

Monster	Category	Ability Name	Description
Revenant	Active	Double Strike	The revenant strikes nearby targets twice. If the attacks hit, they deal less than normal damage. Friendly fire possible.
	Active	Mass Pull	The revenant draws all nearby enemies into melee range.
	Active	Pull	The revenant draws the target into melee range.
	Passive	Revenant Properties	The revenant has natural bonuses to mental resistance, stamina regeneration, and armor (mental resistance +75, stamina regeneration +1, armor +2).
Shriek	Active	Frenzy	The shriek strikes at its opponent four times in a frenzy, dealing normal damage each time.
	Active	Leap	The shriek leaps on its target, dealing normal damage and knocking the target down unless it passes a physical resistance check.
	Active	Overwhelm	The shriek leaps upon its target, pinning it to the ground and attacking it repeatedly.
	Active	Terrorize	The shriek wails, dealing spirit damage to nearby enemies and stunning them unless they pass a mental resistance check. Werewolves within the area are enraged, gaining a bonus to damage for a short time.
Skeleton	Passive	Rise from the Grave	Skeletons frequently lie on the ground as inert bones until enemies pass over them and then they rise up to ambush an unsuspecting party.
Spider	Active	Overwhelm	The spider leaps upon its target, pinning it to the ground and attacking it repeatedly.
	Active	Web	The spider fires a web at the target, immobilizing it for a short time.
	Passive	Spider Properties	The spider has a large natural bonus to nature resistance (nature resistance +75, fire resistance -10).
Steel Golem	Passive	Steel Golem Properties	The steel golem has large natural bonuses to electrical and cold resistance (electrical and cold resistance +50).
Stone Golem	Passive	Stone Golem Properties	The stone golem has large natural bonuses to fire resistance and cold resistance (fire and cold resistance +50).
Wild Sylvan	Active	Rage	The sylvan enters a rage, giving itself a bonus to damage for a short time and waking up other nearby sylvans. If the sylvan is a boss-level creature, it also generates an insect swarm that inflicts damage over time and penalties to attack, defense, and movement speed.
	Active	Roots	The sylvan snares nearby targets with its roots, immobilizing them and dealing physical damage for a short time. Friendly fire possible.
	Active	Stomp	The sylvan stomps, damaging nearby targets and knocking them down. Friendly fire possible.
	Passive	Wild Sylvan Properties	The sylvan has natural bonuses to armor and health, but a large penalty to fire resistance (armor +5, health +25, fire resistance -50).
Wisp	Active	Lightning Strike	The wisp fires a bolt of lightning at its target, dealing a small amount of electrical damage.
	Passive	Wisp Properties	The wisp has natural bonuses to armor and defense, but a penalty to health (armor +3, defense +10, health -20).
Wolf	Passive	Flank Attack	Wolves like to hunt in packs and surround their victims for easier attacks.

Shared Abilities

Monster Type	Category	Ability Name	Description
Darkspawn	Passive	Darkspawn Resistances	Darkspawn have a natural bonus to nature resistance, but a penalty to fire resistance. (fire resistance -15, nature resistance +25, attack +7 [off set all weapons giving -10 to attack])
Demon	Passive	Demon Properties	The demon has natural bonuses to spellpower, armor, and health regeneration (spellpower +5, armor +5, health regeneration in combat +1).
	Passive	Demon Resistances	The demon has a large natural bonus to fire resistance (fire resistance +50, spirit resistance +5).
Golem	Active	Hurl	The golem hurls a rock at the target, damaging all nearby targets and knocking them down unless they pass a physical resistance check. Friendly fire possible.
	Active	Lightning Burst	The golem unleashes a burst of energy at the target, dealing electrical damage to all enemies in the area.
	Active	Quake	The golem slams the ground three times, dealing damage to all nearby targets and stunning them unless they pass a physical resistance check. Friendly fire possible.
	Active	Slam	The golem slams the target. If the attack hits, it deals critical damage and knocks the target down.
	Passive	Golem Properties	The golem has natural bonuses to physical resistance and armor, but a penalty to defense (physical resistance +50, armor +10, defense -10).
Select Monsters	Active	Aura of Corruption	The creature radiates a damaging aura to opponents in a small radius.
	Active	Aura of Fire	An aura of flame surrounds the creature. Enemies within the aura take continuous fire damage until they leave the area.
	Active	Aura of Healing	The creature is surrounded by an aura that heals allies continuously until they leave the area.
	Active	Aura of Weakness	An aura of draining energy surrounds the creature. Enemies within the aura suffer penalties to attack and defense until they leave the area, as well as a penalty to movement speed unless they pass a physical resistance check.
	Active	Corruption Burst	A burst of corrupted energy emanates from the creature. All opponents within the area affected take spirit damage for a short time and suffer a penalty to attack.
	Active	Paralyze	The creature paralyzes its foe for a short time.
	Active	Poison Spit	The creature spits poison on its target, dealing nature damage for a short time.
	Active	Shred	The creature cuts through an opponent with a sharp melee attack.

primagames.com

Arcane Horror

Rank: Boss

Class: Monster—Spellcaster

Prime Location: Wending Wood

Special Abilities: Drain, Restore, Spirit Blast, Swarm

Description: An arcane horror is a skeleton possessed by a pride demon.

Play Tips: Interrupt an arcane horror's casting as much as possible. Up close, abilities such as Dirty Fighting and Mind Blast work great. At range, Paralyze, Pinning Shot, or Scattershot can break the thing's concentration.

Attributes

Strength	Dexterity	Willpower	Magic	Cunning	Constitution
Meager	Moderate	Superior	Superior	High	Meager

The Architect

Rank: Elite Boss

Class: Monster—Tank and Monster—Spellcaster

Prime Location: Drake's Fall

Special Abilities: Cataclysm, Flare, Shivering Shot, Spells (including Hand of Winter, Mind Blast, Chain Lightning, Glyph of Neutralization, Misdirection Hex, Affliction Hex, Drain Life)

Description: One of the two main villains of *Awakening*, he's the first sentient, reasoning darkspawn and he's discovered a technique to bring sentience to other darkspawn, which involves drinking Grey Warden blood. He leads one branch of the darkspawn terrorizing Amaranthine.

Play Tips: When you enter Drake's Fall as you hunt down the Mother, you meet the Architect face to face. You can choose to side with him (and gain some aid in the final battle against the Mother) or slay him for all the atrocities he's committed against humanity. See the "Lair of the Mother" walkthrough for complete details and strategy tips.

Attributes

Strength	Dexterity	Willpower	Magic	Cunning	Constitution
Very High	High	High	Very High	High	High

Ash Wraith

Rank: Lieutenant

Class: Monster—Spirit

Prime Location: Baroness's Manor in Blackmarsh Undying

Special Abilities: Leap

Description: A wraith is a powerful version of a shade, a spirit that has entered the physical world but does not possess a physical body. In the case of the ash wraith, the spirit has formed a quasi-material body for itself out of ashes (usually the ashes of burnt corpses, but not necessarily). This allows it to interact with and affect the physical world, but the wraith is not dependent on the ashes to survive. If wounded, it can disperse at will and reform later. Such wraiths occasionally use other materials to form their physical bodies such as bones, mold, and even blood.

Play Tips: Watch out for rear or flank attacks, as these creatures can materialize behind or on your side. High spirit resistance will reduce the damage taken from the wraith's main attacks.

Attributes

Strength	Dexterity	Willpower	Magic	Cunning	Constitution
Very High	Very High	Above Avg.	Very Low	Meager	Very High

Bear

Rank: Normal (black bear) or Lieutenant (great bear)

Class: Monster—Tank

Prime Location: Knotwood Hills

Special Abilities: Overwhelm, Rage, Slam

Description: Bears live in forests, often near settlements. They are known for breaking into cabins and stealing food. A particularly territorial bereskarn guards the area near the entrance to the Knotwood Hills.

Play Tips: Any bear form is vulnerable to magic, so mages deliver serious damage. The mage's Shapeshifter specialization transforms the caster into a bear, so you can experience its abilities firsthand.

Attributes

Strength	Dexterity	Willpower	Magic	Cunning	Constitution
Very High	High	Above Avg.	Very Low	Meager	Very High

Arcane Horror – Corpse

Basics ~ Classes ~ The Party ~ Companions ~ Supporting Cast ~ Equipment ~ **Bestiary** ~ Walkthrough ~ Side Quests ~ Random Encounters ~ Achievements/Trophies

Spoiler Alert

Bereskarn

The bereskarn variant is a lieutenant with twice as much health as the average PC.

Black Bear

Most bears you meet will be the more common black bear variety.

Great Bear

The great bear variant is a more formidable adversary, with lots more health, deadlier claws, and an Overwhelm ability.

Blighted Werewolf

Rank: Normal

Class: Warrior (Monster—Tank)

Prime Location: Blackmarsh

Special Abilities: Leap, Frenzy, Overwhelm, Terrorize

Description: Fereldan lore is full of stories of wolves possessed by rage demons with incredible speed and strength. The ability of dogs to detect werewolves even in their human guise is what first led Fereldans to adopt dogs as indispensable companions in every farmhold. Blighted werewolves have become infected with the darkspawn taint.

Play Tips: Werewolves are very fast and some use stealth. At least one point in Survival will help drastically in detecting werewolves on your mini-map before they are on you.

Attributes

Strength	Dexterity	Willpower	Magic	Cunning	Constitution
High	High	High	Low	Low	High

Blighted Shadow Wolf

These wolves use stealth to go invisible and sneak up on the unsuspecting. They inflict higher damage than the normal blighted werewolf.

The Children

Rank: Critter (grub), Normal (hatchling) or Lieutenant (adult)

Class: Warrior (Monster—Tank)

Prime Locations: Blackmarsh, Blackmarsh Undying, Dragonbone Wastes, Drake's Fall, Kal'Hirol, Vigil's Keep

Special Abilities: Capricious Demise, Leap, Metamorphosis, Overwhelm, Pincer Flurry, Spit, Sprout, Virulent Burst

Description: Larval darkspawn born to a broodmother awakened from the "hive mind" of other darkspawn, they are darkspawn children gone wrong.

Play Tips: Identify your childer target and plan accordingly. If you see grubs, expect a swarm attack against the party. Hatchlings will enter melee to use their special abilities effectively. Adults need a tank on them and the full efforts of a party to spill their guts.

Attributes

Strength	Dexterity	Willpower	Magic	Cunning	Constitution
High	High	High	Low	Low	High

Alpha Childer

The highest ranked childer of a particular type.

Childer Grub

The smallest of the childers, and only really dangerous in swarms.

Childer Hatchling

An average childer that appears frequently.

Adult Childer

Powerful boss versions of childers.

Corpse

Rank: Normal

Class: Monster—Tank

Prime Location: Shadowy Crypt

Special Abilities: Cold Affinity

Description: Weaker demons crossing over from the Fade may be able to possess a living target. Unable to distinguish that which was once living from that which still is, they sometimes end up in a corpse instead.

Play Tips: Beware of dead bodies strewn upon the ground. Frequently, what appears as the grisly remnants of a massacre is actually an ambush by the various corpse forms.

Attributes

Strength	Dexterity	Willpower	Magic	Cunning	Constitution
Very High	High	Above Avg.	Very Low	Meager	Very High

Desiccated Shambling Corpse

More powerful version of the normal shambling corpse.

Devouring Corpse

Devouring corpses are corpses possessed by a hunger demon. These attempt to feed on living victims as quickly as possible.

Enraged Corpse

Enraged corpses are corpses possessed by a rage demon. These go berserk and simply wade into opponents mindlessly.

Shambling Corpse

Shambling corpses are corpses possessed by a sloth demon. These cause enemies to become weak and fatigued.

The Dark Theurge

Rank: Boss

Class: Monster—Tank

Prime Locations: Vigil's Keep

Special Abilities: Aura of Weakness, Mana Clash, Leap, Slam, Spells (including Chain Lightning, Shock, Lightning, Arcane Bolt, Stone Fist, Misdirection Hex, Drain Life, Disorient, Horror)

Description: This spirit still haunts a series of caves beneath Vigil's Keep. It was once a villain of an Avvar tribe that previously inhabited the area. When you stumble upon it in the basement, you release the spirit, which persistently attacks you in many ways before it can finally be dispersed.

Play Tips: To complete the quest beneath Vigil's Keep, you have no choice but to release the Dark Theurge. For complete details and combat strategies see the "It Comes from Beneath" and "Sealing the Great Barrier Doors" side quests.

Attributes

Strength	Dexterity	Willpower	Magic	Cunning	Constitution
Very High	High	Above Avg.	High	Low	Very High

Deepstalker

Rank: Critter or Normal

Class: Monster—Agile

Prime Location: Kal'Hirol

Special Abilities: Acid Spit, Overwhelm, Scare, Slowing Spit

Description: This bizarre creature evolved in the deep caverns beneath the dwarven cities. When rolled up, the creature resembles a large rock; stalkers often look like boulders strewn through the dwarven tunnels. Once prey approaches, they unroll and leap at their victims.

Play Tips: Deepstalkers hunt in packs. If you see one, others are nearby ready to pounce. Try to spot the large group and raze them with AoE damage.

Attributes

Strength	Dexterity	Willpower	Magic	Cunning	Constitution
Very High	Very High	Above Avg.	Very Low	Meager	High

Deepstalker Leader

The leader ranks as normal with slightly higher attack and defense values.

Deepstalker Spitter

The spitter has a ranged poison attack. Where other deepstalkers charge into melee, this one will hang back and spit, then engage.

Desire Demon

Rank: Lieutenant

Class: Monster—Balanced Mental

Prime Location: Blackmarsh Undying

Special Abilities: Cursed Dance, Scream

Description: Of all the threats from beyond the Veil, few are more insidious and deceptively deadly than the desire demon. In popular folklore, such demons are characterized most commonly as peddlers of lust, luring their prey into a sexual encounter where they are slain at the culmination. While a desire demon can indeed deal in pleasure, in truth they deal with any manner of desire that humans can possess: wealth, power, and beauty to name a few. Far more intelligent than the bestial hunger and rage demons, and more ambitious than the demons of sloth, these dark spirits are among the greatest at tempting mages into possession. Many who serve the whims of a desire demon never realize it. They are manipulated by illusions and deceit if not through mind control, though these demons are reluctant to resort to such crude measures. Instead, they seem to take great pleasure in corruption. The greater the deceit, the greater their victory.

Play Tips: Desire demons in the Blackmarsh Undying work together as a cabal of three. Because they are intent on their unholy ceremony, drop a strong, continuous AoE attack on them and wait for the wounded desire demons to come to you for the rest of their punishment.

Attributes

Strength	Dexterity	Willpower	Magic	Cunning	Constitution
Meager	Moderate	Very High	Very High	Very High	Meager

Corpse - Dragon

The Disciples

Rank: Boss (Alpha or Emissary) or Lieutenant (Heretic)

Class: Warrior (Monster—Tank) or Mage (Monster—Spellcaster)

Prime Locations: Various

Special Abilities: See "Disciples' Special Abilities" chart

Description: The Architect awakened other darkspawn from their former "hive minds." These are known as the disciples. They're stronger, powerful warriors and mages. Some, however, were infuriated with the Architect for freeing them, so they joined sides with the Mother.

Play Tips: You face off against many of the disciples, such as the Withered and the Lost, as bosses at the end of major quests. See the individual walkthrough chapters for more details and strategy tips.

Attributes

Strength	Dexterity	Willpower	Magic	Cunning	Constitution
High	High	High	High	Low	High

Alpha
These disciples rely on melee weapons to deal high damage.

Emissary
Battlemages make up this segment of the disciples.

Heretic
Though only lieutenants, these disciples generally travel in groups and can be warriors or archers.

Disciples' Special Abilities

Alpha	Emissary	Normal
Cimmerian Might	Cimmerian Might	Berserk
Cimmerian Shield	Cimmerian Shield	Powerful Swings
Wraithwall	Wraithwall	Sunder Armor
Carapace	Arcane Field	Mighty Blow
Rally	Arcane Bolt	Sweep
War Cry	Hand of Winter	Cripple
Assault	Misdirection Hex	Shield Cover
Overpower	Mind Blast	Assault
Shield Bash	Mass Paralysis	Shield Pummel
Low Blow	Heroic Aura	Shield Bash
Unending Flurry	Heroic Defense	Rapid Shot
Punisher	Glyph of Warding	Critical Shot
Cripple	Glyph of Paralysis	Shattering Shot
—	Repulsion Field	—
—	Horror	—
—	Death Cloud	—
—	Death Magic	—
—	Curse of Mortality	—
—	Drain Life	—
—	Lightning	—
—	Chain Lightning	—
—	Crushing Prison	—
—	Heal	—
—	Fireball	—
—	Arcane Field	—
—	Stinging Swarm	—

Dragon

Rank: Lieutenant

Class: Monster—Balanced Physical

Prime Locations: Dragonbone Wastes, Silverite Mine

Special Abilities: Buffet, Fire Spit, Flame Breath, Grab, Overwhelm, Rake, Roar, Shred, Slap, Sweep

Description: At about 100 years of age, female dragonlings undergo a metamorphosis, darkening in color and growing wings. After their wings grow, these dragon females become very adventurous, traveling long distances from their original hatching grounds and feeding widely on wild beasts and livestock as they range out to find their own burrows. Human encounters happen most often with these nomadic adult females. Adult dragons are the most aggressive and commonly seen; however, while deadly, they are not regarded with the awe usually reserved for high dragons.

Play Tips: Everyone stand back except the tank. Send your tank in to pull as much threat as possible. When the dragon gets angry enough to unload its fire breath on the tank, have a mage cast Force Field to shield the tank for the duration of the attack. Everyone else unloads high-powered damage on the dragon while it concentrates on the invulnerable tank.

Attributes

Strength	Dexterity	Willpower	Magic	Cunning	Constitution
Very High	Very High	Above Avg.	Very Low	Meager	Very High

Dragon Thrall
In the depths of the Silverite Mine, the Architect nurtures two dragon thralls in his arena to test the mettle of adventurers such as yourself. The new red dragons are more fearsome than dragonlings, but not as powerful as a high dragon.

Dragonling
Baby dragons of both genders hatch from eggs into dragonlings, which are roughly the size of a deer. These dragonlings are wingless and slender and are born in vast numbers because they are still very vulnerable to predation. The dragonlings stay for a short time in their mothers' lairs, then venture out into the world where they spend several decades in their small, vulnerable state.

High Dragon

Any dragon is a formidable adversary, but a high dragon is even more: an elite boss. High dragons are adult female dragons, the mountainous classic dragons into which the dragons mature. Relatively few dragons survive to this stage of adulthood. When they do, they take possession of a burrow (either an abandoned tunnel complex that they further hollow out, or the lair of another high dragon that they challenge and displace). The high dragons then spend most of their time sleeping and mating, living off the prey that their drakes hunt and bring back. A high dragon guards the entrance to Drake's Fall in the Dragonbone Wastes.

Drake

Rank: Lieutenant

Class: Monster—Balanced Physical

Prime Location: Silverite Mine

Special Abilities: Flame Breath, Overwhelm, Rake, Roar, Shred, Slap

Description: At about 50 years of age, male dragonlings undergo a metamorphosis, as the skin of their forelimbs stretches and grows into wings, leaving them with no separate forelegs. These drakes immediately begin searching for mates, seeking out the lairs of adult female high dragons (which are many times larger). When they find high dragon mates, drakes move into the female's lair and spend the rest of their lives there, emerging only to hunt and bring food back for the female and dragonlings. For any given high dragon, usually a dozen or so drakes live in her lair and fight among themselves for the right to mate. If the high dragon or dragonlings are attacked, the drakes defend the lair. Drakes live only about 100 years, and often much less when the casualties of combat are considered.

Play Tips: Drakes guard the hurlock dragon-tamer if you try to complete the "Last Wishes" side quest. Many fine pieces of fire-resistant armor are made from the scales you find from these creatures.

Attributes

Strength	Dexterity	Willpower	Magic	Cunning	Constitution
Very High	Very High	Above Avg.	Very Low	Meager	Very High

Genlock

Rank: Normal (normal genlock) or Lieutenant (alphas and emissaries)

Class: Default or Ranged (for archers) Warrior (Monster—Tank), Monster—Spellcaster (for emissaries)

Prime Location: Anywhere

Special Abilities: Alpha (Dual Wield), Emissary (see "Genlock Special Abilities" chart)

Description: Genlocks originate from dwarven broodmothers and are the most numerous of all the darkspawn. They have stocky dwarven bodies and a robust appearance. Their skin is pale white or yellow, and their heads are large and bald, with sunken eyes and cheeks. Genlocks have both the strength and hardiness of their dwarven origins and are difficult to kill. They also commonly possess the dwarven resistance to magic, though this trait is strongest in alpha and emissary genlocks.

Play Tips: Load up on silverite runes if you know you're about to battle darkspawn. Even a novice silverite rune grants +1 damage against the fiends, and a grandmaster silverite rune gives +5!

Attributes

Strength	Dexterity	Willpower	Magic	Cunning	Constitution
Very High	High	Above Avg.	Very Low	Meager	Very High

Genlock Alpha

Alphas are more cunning versions of the base genlock and have higher magic resistance. They are ranked as lieutenants and can dual wield.

Genlock Emissary

Genlock emissaries are the most intelligent genlocks and have the highest magic resistance. They are ranked as lieutenants.

Genlock Emissary Special Abilities

Balanced	Defensive	Offensive
Arcane Bolt	Arcane Bolt	Arcane Bolt
Curse of Mortality	Crushing Prison	Chain Lightning
Death Cloud	Curse of Mortality	Curse of Mortality
Death Magic	Death Magic	Death Cloud
Drain Life	Drain Life	Death Magic
Heroic Aura	Glyph of Paralysis	Drain Life
Horror	Glyph of Warding	Fireball
Lightning	Heal	Lightning
Mass Paralysis	Heroic Aura	Stinging Swarm
Mind Blast	Heroic Defense	—
Misdirection Hex	Misdirection Hex	—
—	Regeneration	—

Ghoul

Rank: Lieutenant

Class: Monster—High Damage

Prime Location: Vigil's Keep Basement

Special Abilities: Unholy Swarm

Description: A ghoul is a man or woman twisted and corrupted by the darkspawn taint. They differ from regular darkspawn in that they are not born from broodmothers. Adria the Ghoul leads a swarm of them in the basement of Vigil's Keep.

Play Tips: Invest in cold iron runes. A novice cold iron rune grants +1 against ghouls while a grandmaster cold iron rune grants a +5 against ghouls.

Attributes

Strength	Dexterity	Willpower	Magic	Cunning	Constitution
Very High	High	Above Avg.	Very Low	Meager	Very High

Dragon - Hurlock

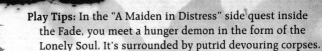

Basics ~ Classes ~ The Party ~ Companions ~ Supporting Cast ~ Equipment ~ **Bestiary** ~ Walkthrough ~ Side Quests ~ Random Encounters ~ Achievements/Trophies

Spoiler Alert

Golem

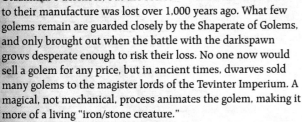

Rank: Lieutenant

Class: Monster—Tank

Prime Location: Kal'Hirol

Special Abilities: Hurl, Quake, Slam

Description: Dwarves built golems, creatures of hewn stone or sheets of metal animated with a spark of lyrium. They were once a crucial part of Orzammar's defenses, but the secret to their manufacture was lost over 1,000 years ago. What few golems remain are guarded closely by the Shaperate of Golems, and only brought out when the battle with the darkspawn grows desperate enough to risk their loss. No one now would sell a golem for any price, but in ancient times, dwarves sold many golems to the magister lords of the Tevinter Imperium. A magical, not mechanical, process animates the golem, making it more of a living "iron/stone creature."

Play Tips: The warrior's Shattering Blows talent increases damage against golems and other constructs. A warrior heading into Kal'Hirol might be wise to spend a few points in the Two-Handed school.

Attributes

Strength	Dexterity	Willpower	Magic	Cunning	Constitution
Very High	High	Above Avg.	Very Low	Meager	Very High

Inferno Golem

In addition to a large increase to armor and health, the giant inferno golem uses the abilities Ignite, Searing Quake, and Searing Slam.

Steel Golem

The steel golem has large natural bonuses to electrical resistance (+50) and cold resistance (+50).

Stone Golem

The stone golem has large natural bonuses to fire resistance (+50) and cold resistance (+50).

Hunger Demon

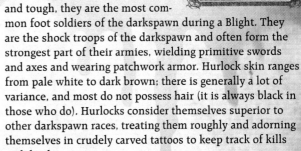

Rank: Lieutenant

Class: Monster—Spellcaster

Prime Location: Blackmarsh Undying

Special Abilities: Abomination Rage, Abomination Triple Strike

Description: When the Lonely Soul appears, she seems like an innocent and frightened young woman, and runs off into the Shadow Crypt. When you follow her, you discover that she's a hunger demon in disguise.

Play Tips: In the "A Maiden in Distress" side quest inside the Fade, you meet a hunger demon in the form of the Lonely Soul. It's surrounded by putrid devouring corpses. Lock your tank warrior on the hunger demon while the rest of the party kills off the corpses. When you have no corpses to hack, concentrate all your efforts on the hunger demon.

Attributes

Strength	Dexterity	Willpower	Magic	Cunning	Constitution
Meager	Moderate	Very High	Very High	High	Moderate

Hurlock

Rank: Normal (normal hurlock) or Lieutenant (alphas and emissaries)

Class: Warrior (Monster—Tank)

Prime Location: Anywhere

Special Abilities: See "Hurlock Special Abilities" chart

Description: Hurlocks originate from human broodmothers. Muscular and tough, they are the most common foot soldiers of the darkspawn during a Blight. They are the shock troops of the darkspawn and often form the strongest part of their armies, wielding primitive swords and axes and wearing patchwork armor. Hurlock skin ranges from pale white to dark brown; there is generally a lot of variance, and most do not possess hair (it is always black in those who do). Hurlocks consider themselves superior to other darkspawn races, treating them roughly and adorning themselves in crudely carved tattoos to keep track of kills and deeds.

Play Tips: Identify hurlocks as soon as a fight ensues. Emissaries are your immediate priority. Alphas can be trouble, but you'll probably want to eliminate the regular hurlocks first to reduce the numbers against you.

Attributes

Strength	Dexterity	Willpower	Magic	Cunning	Constitution
High	High	High	Low	Low	High

Hurlock Alpha

Darkspawn hatched by a broodmother have to fight among themselves for food during the first month of life; usually, a tenth to a quarter of the litter will survive. Occasionally one will prove stronger than the rest of its siblings and be the only one remaining at the end of the month. This is indicative of a superior version of the race and it will be known as an "alpha." Alphas are generally taller, stronger, and much more intelligent than others of their kind. They will be the commanders and generals who direct the others in combat and are intelligent enough to direct the slavery of humanoid races in lands they conquer. As lieutenants, they act as warriors with the Weapon and Shield and Two-Handed talents.

primagames.com

Hurlock Emissary

Very few alphas have proven themselves to be not only incredibly intelligent, but also naturally gifted with arcane abilities akin to blood magic in their effects. These few are known as "emissaries." Darkspawn armies are fairly disorganized, but the different races usually group together (genlocks with genlocks, hurlocks with hurlocks, etc.).

Hurlock Guardian

This tough warrior hurlock shows up in the siege of Amaranthine, and attempts to ambush you outside the Chantry.

Hurlock Sniper

These ranged DPS hurlocks show up in the siege of Amaranthine, and attempt to ambush you outside the Chantry.

Hurlock Special Abilities

Emissary Battlemage	Alpha Archer	Alpha Guardian (axe & shield)	Alpha Berserker (maul)
Arcane Field	Rally	Rally	Rally
Hand of Winter	Rain of Arrows	War Cry	War Cry
Draining Aura	Burst Shot	Assault	Sweeping Strike
Death Cloud	War Cry	Overpower	Two-Handed Sweep
Fireball	Rapid Shot	Fortifying Aura	Reaving Storm
Stinging Swarm	Scattershot	Aura of the Stalwart Defender	Indomitable
Death Magic	Arrow of Slaying	Shield Bash	Powerful Swings
Chain Lightning	Pinning Shot	—	Sunder Armor
Lightning	Critical Shot	—	Critical Strike
Curse of Mortality	Shattering Shot	—	Mighty Blow
Weakness	—	—	—
Arcane Bolt	—	—	—

The Mother

Rank: Elite Boss
Class: Monster—High Damage
Prime Locations: The Nest
Special Abilities: Animus Lash, Tentacle Ward, Scream, Rotting Gas, Vomit, Sweep, Spit, Slam, Glyph of Neutralization, Stinging Swarm, Chain Lightning

Description: The Mother was a young human woman infected with the Blight and transformed into a monstrous creature built only for birthing darkspawn. Her mind was subsumed by her dark impulses—but when the Architect freed her from those impulses, she regained a bit of her identity…only to discover that she was now a tormented, hideous creature twisted by corruption. She went insane. Now she is a creature of chaos, a gibbering mad monster determined to be queen of the darkspawn so that she can destroy herself and the world along with her.

Play Tips: Your final battle will be against the Mother. For complete details on this epic encounter see the "Lair of the Mother" walkthrough chapter.

Attributes

Strength	Dexterity	Willpower	Magic	Cunning	Constitution
Very High	Low	Very High	Very High	High	Very High

Ogre

Rank: Lieutenant or Normal
Class: Monster—High Damage
Prime Location: Anywhere
Special Abilities: Grab, Hurl, Ram, Stomp, Sweep, Whirlwind

Description: Ogres originate from qunari broodmothers; they are rare, but growing in number. They are massive: taller and broader than even hurlock alphas, with dark, rough-colored skin covered in patches of thick fur. They possess huge, curved horns and are said to charge their enemies like bulls, slamming into them with devastating effect: they can even barrel through thick stone walls.

Play Tips: Avoid the ogre's long reach: an ogre can grab and choke the life out of you. If an ogre grabs a companion, stun it with attacks like shield bash to break its hold.

Attributes

Strength	Dexterity	Willpower	Magic	Cunning	Constitution
Very High	High	Above Avg.	Very Low	Meager	Very High

Armored Ogre

A fully geared ogre is a much more dangerous foe. The armored ogre has an extra 2,000 health, +35 armor, and +15 magic resistance. An armored ogre can also spin to inflict tremendous damage to all surrounding foes.

Pride Demon

Rank: Boss (lesser is ranked Lieutenant)
Class: Monster—High Damage
Prime Location: Blackmarsh
Special Abilities: Drain, Fire Blast, Fire Bolt, Frost Bolt, Frost Burst, Mana Wave, Shockwave

Description: Demons can exist in both the real world (through possession) and in the Fade. Demons spend their time searching out new territory and pushing their boundaries. For this reason, they are the Fade dwellers most commonly seen in the mortal realm. While in the Fade, demons rail at a sleeper, forcing him into dark realms of nightmare where the demons feed off the negative energy created by his fear. The demons are, in order

Hurlock – Shade

Basics ~ Classes ~ The Party ~ Companions ~ Supporting Cast ~ Equipment ~ **Bestiary** ~ Walkthrough ~ Side Quests ~ Random Encounters ~ Achievements/Trophies

of increasing power and intelligence: rage, hunger, sloth, desire, and pride. Greater pride demons are bosses, while lesser pride demons are ranked as lieutenants.

Play Tips: Watch out for the pride demon's Drain ability. When a pride demon grabs a target, it drains health from the target to heal itself. Break the effect immediately with stuns or a spell like Force Field.

Attributes

Strength	Dexterity	Willpower	Magic	Cunning	Constitution
Very High	High	Above Avg.	Very Low	Meager	Very High

Queen of the Blackmarsh

Rank: Elite Boss

Class: Monster—Tank

Prime Locations: Blackmarsh

Special Abilities: Flurry of special melee attacks (tail, wings, arms, legs), Lightning Breath, Lightning Spit, Roar

Description: This spectral dragon now exists solely in the Fade. If you complete "The Lost Dragon Bones" side quest, you can summon forth the Queen of the Blackmarsh to the mountaintop in Blackmarsh.

Play Tips: You need a fully geared party of at least level 24 to attempt this dragon encounter. See "The Lost Dragon Bones" side quest description for strategy tips on the fight.

Attributes

Strength	Dexterity	Willpower	Magic	Cunning	Constitution
Very High	High	High	High	High	Very High

Rage Demon

Rank: Lieutenant (lesser is ranked Critter)

Class: Monster—Spirit

Prime Location: Blackmarsh Undying

Special Abilities: Fire Bolt, Fire Burst, Slam

Description: Demons can exist in both the real world (through possession) and in the Fade. Demons spend their time searching out new territory and pushing their boundaries. For this reason, they are the Fade dwellers most commonly seen in the mortal realm. While in the Fade, demons rail at a sleeper, forcing him into dark realms of nightmare where the demons feed off the negative energy created by his fear. The demons are, in order of increasing power and intelligence: rage, hunger, sloth, desire, and pride. Greater rage demons are lieutenants, while lesser rage demons are ranked as critters.

Play Tips: Stick to cold-based spells to deal extra damage. Cone of Cold or Blizzard can freeze them solid and deal significant damage; even Winter's Grasp can be effective.

Attributes

Strength	Dexterity	Willpower	Magic	Cunning	Constitution
Very High	Very High	Above Avg.	Very Low	Meager	Very High

Revenant

Rank: Lieutenant

Class: Monster—High Damage

Prime Location: Blackmarsh

Special Abilities: Double Strike, Mass Pull, Pull

Description: A revenant is a corpse possessed by a pride demon. Many possess spells, but most are armed and armored and prefer to use their martial talents.

Play Tips: A challenging foe, the revenant can pull you toward it with telekinesis; ranged DPS and healing won't be safe at the edge of the battlefield. Don't waste time on ranged positioning. If the revenant does pull, it sets aside its massive blade, which is prime time for melee combatants to get in some licks.

Attributes

Strength	Dexterity	Willpower	Magic	Cunning	Constitution
Very High	High	Above Avg.	Very Low	Meager	Very High

Shade

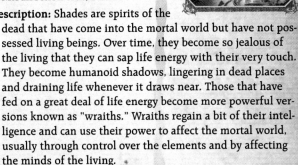

Rank: Lieutenant (lesser version is ranked Normal)

Class: Monster—Spirit

Prime Locations: Blackmarsh, Blackmarsh Undying

Special Abilities: Aura of Weakness, Disorient, Drain Life, Horror, Leap, Misdirection Hex, Slam

Description: Shades are spirits of the dead that have come into the mortal world but have not possessed living beings. Over time, they become so jealous of the living that they can sap life energy with their very touch. They become humanoid shadows, lingering in dead places and draining life whenever it draws near. Those that have fed on a great deal of life energy become more powerful versions known as "wraiths." Wraiths regain a bit of their intelligence and can use their power to affect the mortal world, usually through control over the elements and by affecting the minds of the living.

Play Tips: Mundane weapons may have a lesser effect, but spells can put a hurt on a shade. Keep your spellcasters protected and let them fire away while the tank and melee DPS hold them at bay.

Attributes

Strength	Dexterity	Willpower	Magic	Cunning	Constitution
Very High	Very High	Above Avg.	Very Low	Meager	Very High

primagames.com

Shriek

Rank: Lieutenant (Normal shriek is ranked Normal)

Class: Monster—High Damage

Prime Location: Anywhere

Special Abilities: Frenzy, Leap, Overwhelm, Terrorize

Description: Thought of as horrors of the night more than as darkspawn, shrieks are tall, lean creatures renowned for their speed, incredible agility, and stealth. Indeed, shrieks have been known to run (with their strange, loping gait; their arms are as long as their legs) as fast as a horse and disappear just as quickly into the shadows. Shrieks' talons and teeth are incredibly sharp, as their favorite tactic is to leap on their prey and tear it to ribbons within seconds. Shrieks originate from elven broodmothers, and retain both a natural elven agility and relative fragility. Only a couple of solid strikes are needed to kill the creature—getting that strike, however, tends to be the problem. Physically, shrieks stand between six and seven feet tall but weigh only perhaps 100 to 120 pounds. They are thin, with bark-like skin that ranges from light green to dark brown. Their faces are twisted, with long wild-looking hair and eyes that are sunken into their skull, appearing to be black holes with pricks of dim light shining from within.

Play Tips: Set up a defensive perimeter where each companion can watch the others' backs. Shrieks can materialize out of thin air, and you don't want them ripping and tearing at your exposed side.

Attributes

Strength	Dexterity	Willpower	Magic	Cunning	Constitution
Very High	High	Above Avg.	Very Low	Meager	Very High

Skeleton

Rank: Normal

Class: Warrior (Monster—Tank)

Prime Locations: Blackmarsh Undying, Shadowy Crypt, Silverite Mine, Vigil's Keep Deep Roads

Special Abilities: Ancient (ranked bonuses), Archer (ranged), Devouring (increased health), Fanged (Dual Weapon), Normal (Weapon and Shield), Shambling (Two-Handed)

Description: Demons that possess flesh form walking corpses; demons that possess bones form skeletons.

Play Tips: Employ standard party tactics as you would for any melee combatant or enemy archer. The shambling skeletons generally deal more damage and should be a priority, though if you spy an ancient fanged skeleton make it your number-one target.

Attributes

Strength	Dexterity	Willpower	Magic	Cunning	Constitution
Very High	High	Above Avg.	Very Low	Meager	Very High

Ancient Fanged Skeleton

These are the toughest of all the skeletons, both in terms of the punishment they can withstand and the punishment they can rake out.

Archer

Archer skeletons are bones possessed by a rage demon.

Devouring

Devouring skeletons are stronger versions of the standard skeleton. You'll encounter more than a few of them in the Shadowy Crypt.

Fanged

Fanged skeletons are bones possessed by a hunger demon. They act as warriors with the Dual Weapon talents.

Normal

Normal skeletons are bones possessed by a rage demon. They act as warriors with the Weapon and Shield talents.

Shambling

Shambling skeletons are bones possessed by a sloth demon. They act as warriors with the Two-Handed talents. In the Blackmarsh Undying, mangled shambling skeletons and desiccated shambling corpses can also plague your party.

Spider

Rank: Normal

Class: Monster—Agile

Prime Locations: Kal'Hirol, Wending Wood

Special Abilities: Poison, Overwhelm, Web

Description: These creatures (also called "deep crawlers" by the dwarves) grew in the depths of the dwarven Deep Roads, once having been encouraged to multiply to feed on the numerous species of large bats that the dwarves considered pests. Once the Deep Roads were lost to the darkspawn, these spiders began to feed on genlocks as well as bats, and their numbers were no longer controlled. Some moved up to make their lairs in the surface forests, but most have remained below ground.

Play Tips: Support each other whenever spiders arrive. If you end up apart, a spider's Web or Overwhelm attack can incapacitate a lone companion. Guard webbed allies until they're free. Against an Overwhelm attack, everyone else should immediately focus on the charging spider to kill it before it kills your companion.

Attributes

Strength	Dexterity	Willpower	Magic	Cunning	Constitution
Very High	Very High	Above Avg.	Very Low	Meager	High

Corrupted Spider

Corrupted Spiders are those that have feasted on darkspawn flesh. They are more aggressive and stronger than standard spiders.

Giant Spider

These are the most common variety of dungeon spider and will threaten you with an Overwhelm ability.

Poisonous Spider

These spiders can shoot poison at medium range and deal damage over time.

Sylvan

Rank: Lieutenant

Class: Monster—Tank

Prime Location: Wending Wood

Special Abilities: Rage, Roots, Stomp

Description: In forests where the Veil between this plane and the Fade has become one with the trees. Sylvans can retain some of the intelligence and even memories of the possessing spirit, which sometimes grow over time. More often, sylvans retain only a smattering of intelligence and are filled with an extreme jealousy of other living things. They kill any who enter their domain, animating branches to swing as fists, enveloping the living in their roots, or uprooting themselves briefly to walk (slowly). Sylvans are heavily resistant to physical damage.

Play Tips: Tread slowly when in a forest around sylvans. The tree creatures blend in with the non-hostile forest and suddenly spring to life as you near. Fire-based attacks do extra damage.

Attributes

Strength	Dexterity	Willpower	Magic	Cunning	Constitution
Very High	High	Above Avg.	Very Low	Meager	Very High

Charred Sylvan

Burnt versions of wild sylvans, charred sylvans are even angrier for what has been done to them.

The Old One

This sylvan boss can be slain in the Wending Wood for its ancient sylvanwood that is a crucial component to creating the unique Heartwood Bow or Heartwood Shield.

Wild Sylvan

The forest is "alive" with vengeful spirits who have possessed trees. These creatures are called "wild sylvans."

Wisp

Rank: Critter

Class: Monster—Spirit

Prime Location: Blackmarsh

Special Abilities: Lightning Strike

Description: Wisps are small glowing balls of electrical energy. It is not certain whether they are demon, spirit, or just a Fade disturbance of some kind.

Play Tips: Wisps won't attack you directly. They use their power to heal the Queen of the Blackmarsh, so take them out if you want to fight her effectively.

Attributes

Strength	Dexterity	Willpower	Magic	Cunning	Constitution
Very High	Very High	Above Avg.	Very Low	Meager	Very High

Wolf

Rank: Critter or Lieutenant (alpha)

Class: Monster—Agile

Prime Locations: Blackmarsh, Wending Wood

Special Abilities: Howl, Overwhelm, Shred

Description: These wolves are large and imposing. They hunt in packs and take advantage of large numbers to take down tougher targets.

Play Tips: Wolves will attempt to swarm you. Try not to get flanked and have the party concentrate firepower on one at a time as you trim down their numbers. Also watch out for their Overwhelm ability, which can take a party member down quickly if you're not prepared.

Attributes

Strength	Dexterity	Willpower	Magic	Cunning	Constitution
Very High	Very High	Above Avg.	Very Low	Meager	High

Alpha Blight and Marsh Wolf

A stronger variant of their respective wolf family, this lieutenant will lead the wolf charge as a dangerous pack closes in.

Blight Wolf

A wolf twisted by darkspawn taint.

primagames.com

Awakening Walkthrough

The Arling of Amaranthine both mystifies and terrifies its inhabitants with places of vast beauty and unflinching peril. You can journey around Amaranthine, but unless you've unlocked all major quests and the majority of side quests, it will take several plays to fully explore its majesty. For those who want a sneak peek of what's in store on your travels, study the essential locations here and the detailed world map on the pages that follow.

Essential Locations

Spoiler Alert

Vigil's Keep

Vigil's Keep occupies a strategic gateway between the coastal lowlands of Amaranthine and the rest of Ferelden. Fortifications have stood here since the time of the Avvar barbarians. This is your base of operations, and has been the home of the Grey Wardens since they acquired it from the traitor Arl Howe in *Origins.*

Amaranthine

The city of Amaranthine is the jewel of Ferelden's north and the economic heart of the arling. In more prosperous times, merchant ships filled the port to bursting. Now, the city overflows instead with refugees and despair. You will visit here many times on your various quest runs.

Sequence of Events

No matter whether you begin a new character or import an existing character, the following quest line serves as the introduction to the game and must be completed first:

- Assault on Vigil's Keep

The following three main quest lines can be completed in any order, though they are listed in most practical order:

- Shadows of the Blackmarsh
- The Righteous Path
- Last of the Legion

The primary city, Amaranthine, serves as a bustling trade center with lots of vendors and side quests. Visit this area early in your pursuit for the main quests, and return often.

- Amaranthine

Once you have completed all three main quests, you can speak with Seneschal Varel to trigger the final two quest lines to end the game:

- Siege of Vigil's Keep or Assault on Amaranthine
- Lair of the Mother

The Blackmarsh

Winds off the Amaranthine Ocean leave the Blackmarsh unpleasantly cold. A settlement was once located here, but no longer. The whole coast is reportedly haunted. You'll find out for yourself firsthand when you attempt the "Shadows of the Blackmarsh" main quest.

Wending Wood

This has long been the most perilous segment of the Pilgrim's Path, the major trade route between Amaranthine and Denerim. The trees of the Wending Wood offer refuge to bandits and worse. You'll journey to the heart of the forest in "The Righteous Path" main quest.

Silverite Mine

The hills of the Wending Wood once boasted significant mineral deposits. Only a few of the old mines still contain viable veins. The second part of "The Righteous Path" quest leads you into the mine.

Knotwood Hills

Hunters occasionally venture to the Knotwood Hills to stalk the rich wildlife, but otherwise, this remote edge of the arling is untouched by civilization. When you embark on the "Last of the Legion" main quest, you enter the hills for yourself.

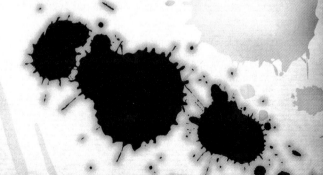

Essential Locations - How to Use the Walkthrough

Basics ~ Classes ~ The Party ~ Companions ~ Supporting Cast ~ Equipment ~ Bestiary ~ **Walkthrough** ~ Side Quests ~ Random Encounters ~ Achievements/Trophies

Kal'Hirol

The "Last of the Legion" quest sends you into this once-great dwarven thaig. It fell during the first Blight, and no civilized race has visited the site in a thousand years.

Dragonbone Wastes

Deep within the hills that border the Feravel Plains is an ancient graveyard where dragons once came to die. A younger generation of the winged beasts has turned the region dangerous yet again. To the Wastes you must go to ultimately stop the great evil plaguing the land.

⟡ NOTE ⟡

Side quests and random encounters have dedicated chapters after this walkthrough section covering all the main quests. See the Side Quests chapter and the Random Encounters chapter for all the details.

How to Use the Walkthrough

Main quests around Amaranthine can sometimes seem complex and daunting. The following walkthroughs provide in-depth, precise explanations for every main quest line in the game. If it doesn't appear in this chapter, it's not a main quest and will appear in the Side Quests or Random Encounters chapters. The walkthroughs that follow this introduction are presented in the most efficient sequence, from your introduction at Vigil's Keep to the endgame quests. Here's a quick breakdown of what's in each walkthrough:

Map

Each walkthrough contains all the necessary maps to navigate from the quest's starting point to ending point. Labels on the maps indicate NPCs, enemies, quest spots, treasure locations, general points of interest, and runthrough markings to show the best route through the area. A walkthrough will generally contain multiple maps to all the important locations.

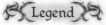

Legend

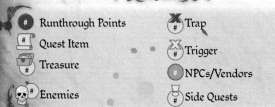

- ● Runthrough Points
- 📜 Quest Item
- 📦 Treasure
- 💀 Enemies
- ✖ Trap
- ⏃ Trigger
- ● NPCs/Vendors
- ⚗ Side Quests

Runthrough

This small sidebar boils the walkthrough down to essential steps. The steps are marked on the map in red numbered circles. To progress through an area effectively, start with "1" and continue in numerical order to the last number. If you're familiar with an area, you can use the runthrough as a guide to moving through a map very quickly.

Cheatsheet

Each main map has a cheatsheet that tracks the main quest, important NPCs, key items, monsters, and side quests. Use this cheatsheet to make sure you didn't miss anything critical on your journey, or to scout out what you need to accomplish in the area.

Walkthrough Text

We pack as much comprehensive strategy and expert guidance as we can into each section. The runthrough can give you a nice overview, but if you really want to know how to avoid the traps, tackle the monsters, and collect the important items, read the walkthrough. Whenever you encounter a really difficult enemy—whether it be a boss or other ranked, troublesome adversary—we'll give you tips on its battle tendencies and how to defeat it.

Reference the world map for your global questions, then flip to the appropriate walkthrough section for the nitty gritty of that quest line. We'll get you through the underground maze of Kal'Hirol and show you how to escape the Fade that has swallowed the Blackmarsh.

Waking Sea

North to
Free Marches

The Coastlands

West to
Highever

8

C

2

The Pilgrim's Path

Feravel Plains

D

The North Road

A

Knottwood
Hills

7

6

1

Hafter River

The Arling
of Amaranthine

The Pilgrim

Tarcaisme Ridge

The Bannorn

Hafter River

Hafter River

Amaranthine Map

Basics ~ Classes ~ The Party ~ Companions ~ Supporting Cast ~ Equipment ~ Bestiary ~ **Walkthrough** ~ Side Quests ~ Random Encounters ~ Achievements/Trophies

Spoiler Alert

Amaranthine Highlights

1 Vigil's Keep
- Intro quest ("Assault on Vigil's Keep")
- Anders (mage companion)
- Oghren (warrior companion)
- Nathaniel Howe (rogue companion)

2 Amaranthine
- Major trade center
- All main quests route here
- Many side quests

3 Blackmarsh
- First main quest ("Shadows of the Blackmarsh")
- Justice (warrior companion)
- Essence Rewards (permanent stat bonuses)

4 Wending Wood
- Second main quest ("The Righteous Path")
- Velanna (mage companion)

5 Silverite Mine
- Continuation of second main quest

6 Knotwood Hills
- Third main quest ("Last of the Legion")
- Sigrun (rogue companion)

7 Kal'Hirol
- Continuation of third main quest

8 Dragonbone Wastes
- Final quest line to slay the Mother

A Turnoble Estate

B Forlorn Cove

C Anselm's Reef

D Old Stark's Farm

Color Coding
Side Quest Locations

primagames.com

Assault on Vigil's Keep

NOTE

You begin your journey into *Awakening* at the entrance to Vigil's Keep. It doesn't matter whether you created a new character for the expansion or imported your hero from *Dragon Age: Origins*, there is only a single origin story this time around.

Vigil's Keep: Exterior

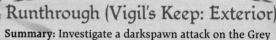

Runthrough (Vigil's Keep: Exterior)

Summary: Investigate a darkspawn attack on the Grey Warden stronghold.

1. You arrive at Vigil's Keep with the warrior Mhairi, only to discover it's under attack by darkspawn.

2. Reach the main gate and battle through marauding darkspawn.

3. To reach the upper level, approach the closed gate and survive the darkspawn push to drive you back.

4. The courtyard to the east has pockets of darkspawn all around. Be careful of ambush.

5. Reach the portcullis to the Inner Keep.

Legend

1 Genlocks	15 Shriek	
2 Genlocks	1 Blood Lotus	
3 Genlocks	2 Chest	
4 Genlocks	3 Blood Lotus	
5 Hurlock	4 Chest	
6 Shriek	5 Chest	
7 Ogre	6 Wooden Crate	
8 Hurlocks	7 Chest	
9 Genlocks & Hurlock	8 Wooden Crate	
10 Hurlocks	9 Chest & Wooden Crate	
11 Genlock Emissary & Hurlocks	10 Chest (locked)	
12 Hurlocks	Mhairi	
13 Hurlocks	1 "A Medical Necessity"	
14 Genlock & Hurlocks		

Assault on Vigil's Keep

Basics ~ Classes ~ The Party ~ Companions ~ Supporting Cast ~ Equipment ~ Bestiary ~ **Walkthrough** ~ Side Quests ~ Random Encounters ~ Achievements/Trophies

Vigil's Keep: Exterior Cheatsheet

Main Plot Quest
- The Assault on Vigil's Keep

Important NPCs
- Mhairi

Key Items
- Stormchaser Helm

Monsters
- Genlock Emissary
- Genlocks
- Hurlocks
- Ogre
- Shrieks

Side Quests
- A Medical Necessity

Spoiler Alert

1 As your story begins, you reach the outskirts of Vigil's Keep, a Grey Warden stronghold south of Amaranthine, which you are set to take over as Warden-Commander (this is your title no matter if you arrive with a new character or an existing character). You travel with a Grey Warden recruit, the warrior Mhairi, and you both soon realize that something is definitely wrong when no one comes out to greet you. Within seconds, a soldier races out of the keep with darkspawn hot on his heels. Rally behind the soldier and slay the initial trio of genlocks.

2 You can explore around the main gate and trigger a few darkspawn encounters if you like while hunting for the scattered loot. Once you pass by the main gate, prepare for three darkspawn to attack from different directions. The hurlock and shriek come from your left, and after a few seconds delay, the ogre charges from directly ahead. Let Mhairi take the brunt of the damage (unless your character is a warrior tank too), while you deal damage quickly to the ogre before it pounds you both.

TIP

Once inside the Keep's main gate, fight your way west through two groups of genlocks and a shriek. Once you have cleared the area of foes, you can rescue a scared merchant (by chest point 5 on the map). When you encounter the merchant Yuriah in the throne room later, he will have more extensive stock to sell you.

NOTE

Try to save as many of the Vigil's Keep soldiers as you can. They fight the darkspawn throughout the fortress grounds and can work with you to defeat the darkspawn in their areas.

3 After clearing out the lower level, climb up the ladder and approach the closed gate. The gate explodes outward and knocks you off your feet. Fortunately, Mhairi is light on hers and she races ahead to intercept the two hurlocks who charge out. In the back, a genlock emissary will begin casting nasty AoE spells. Don't give him a chance. Interrupt with a disruptive attack such as Paralyze, or charge straight for him and stun him with a melee talent. Keep the battle close to the shattered gate so you don't pull in any other enemies while you take these three down.

4 If you head to the right, watch out for a major ambush when you enter the open courtyard. Hurlocks, a genlock, and a shriek all lurk in the area and love to converge as you approach. Deal with the shriek first, because it will appear behind you and try to deal damage to your exposed side.

5 To the left after the shattered gate lies the portcullis entrance to the Inner Keep. Two hurlocks patrol the area, and you'll have to get through them to gain the exit point. If you can kill these two hurlocks before they kill the nearby Vigil's Keep soldier, the grateful soldier offers the "A Medical Necessity" side quest. See the "Vigil's Keep" section in the Side Quest chapter for complete details.

NOTE

Loot is generally random. In the cases where an item is fixed or codex entry occurs, we've listed the actual reward in parentheses after the treasure location.

primagames.com

Keep Interior

Runthrough (Keep Interior)

Summary: Root out the darkspawn inside the keep and confront a new talking darkspawn.

1. Enter the inside of the keep.
2. Meet up with the mage Anders.
3. Battle darkspawn to reach the outer battlements.
4. Carve through the darkspawn on the battlements to reach the barricaded area.
5. Pull the portcullis lever to access the keep's northern section.
6. More genlocks and hurlocks pour through the portcullis and engage you in the first chamber.
7. Hurlocks ambush you in the central chamber.
8. Join forces with the warrior Oghren.
9. A huge battle finishes off the darkspawn inside the keep.
10. Exit to the second battlement and confront the Withered.

Keep Interior Cheatsheet

Main Plot Quest
- The Assault on Vigil's Keep

Important NPCs
- Anders
- Oghren
- Rowland

Key Items
- Portcullis Lever

Monsters
- Genlock Alpha
- Genlock Emissary
- Genlocks
- Hurlock Alphas

- Hurlock Emissary
- Hurlocks
- Ogre
- Shriek Alpha
- Shrieks

Side Quests
- The Survivors of Vigil's Keep

Assault on Vigil's Keep

Basics ~ Classes ~ The Party ~ Companions ~ Supporting Cast ~ Equipment ~ Bestiary ~ **Walkthrough** ~ Side Quests ~ Random Encounters ~ Achievements/Trophies

Legend

💀① Shriek Alpha & Shrieks

💀② Hurlocks

💀③ Genlocks & Hurlocks

💀④ Hurlock Emissary & Hurlocks

💀⑤ Genlock, Genlock Emissary, & Hurlocks

💀⑥ Hurlock Alpha & Hurlock Emissary

💀⑦ Genlock Emissary, Genlocks, & Hurlock Alpha

💀⑧ Genlocks

💀⑨ Genlocks & Hurlocks

💀⑩ Genlocks & Hurlocks

💀⑪ Genlock Alpha

💀⑫ Hurlocks

📦① Wooden Crate

📦② Wooden Crate

📦③ Chest

📦④ Wooden Crate

📦⑤ Chest (Sleeper ring)

📦⑥ Chest

📦⑦ Pile of Books

📦⑧ Pile of Books

📦⑨ Chest

📦⑩ Wooden Crate

📦⑪ Chest

📦⑫ Chest

① Anders

② Oghren

③ Rowland

🏺① "The Survivors of Vigil's Keep"

📜① Portcullis Lever

📜② Keep Survivor ("Survivors of Vigil's Keep")

📜③ Keep Survivor ("Survivors of Vigil's Keep")

📜④ Keep Survivor ("Survivors of Vigil's Keep")

📜⑤ Keep Survivor ("Survivors of Vigil's Keep")

Spoiler Alert

① The keep's first chamber may look empty, but it's an illusion. As soon as you take a step forward, three shrieks materialize and attack.

Dispatch them with Mhairi taking the lead. If you look up to the western ledge, you'll spot a portcullis lever that raises the sealed portcullis in front of you, but you can't access the area directly because the door is barricaded. Instead, you have to climb the stairs on the eastern side and work your way around.

② Open the eastern door. The mage Anders polishes off the last of his enemies with a burst of flame. Dead templars and darkspawn litter the floor. After a brief conversation, you find out that Anders is an apostate mage who was brought to the keep by the templars. He escaped during the chaos with the darkspawn. Invite him to join your party to add a capable mage.

③ In the next room, hurlocks stalk a lone keep survivor. Rush in to his aid and intercept the hurlocks before they kill the man. Draw the hurlocks' attention with targeted attacks and spells—no AoE or you'll kill the keep survivor—and use Anders to heal the keep survivor if he starts taking damage. If you slay the hurlocks before they slay the keep survivor, you unlock "The Survivors of Vigil's Keep" side quest. See the "Vigil's Keep" section in the Side Quest chapter for complete

④ details. The door in this small side chamber leads outside to the battlements. You must cross this outer ledge to reach the door that leads to the portcullis lever back in the first chamber.

Genlocks and hurlocks swarm the confined ledge, and you have to make sure you get some ranged fire on the genlock emissary in the rear or you'll be tasting AoE damage for the whole fight. Be sure to retrieve the Beastmaster crossbow in the treasure chest by the ballista.

⑤ Enter the western side from the battlements door and pull the portcullis lever out in the first chamber. Destroy the barricade blocking the stairs that lead down to the first chamber, or stand up on the western ledge and rain destruction down on the genlocks and hurlocks that charge in.

6 You can find the invading genlocks and hurlocks in any number of places. The dwarf Dworkin detonates some of his homemade explosives in the first chamber and kills a few of the darkspawn for you. Finish off the rest before heading north through the now-opened portcullis.

7 A hurlock emissary and a handful of hurlocks set up an ambush in this central chamber. Don't rush in or you can be surrounded quickly. Instead, launch a ranged attack at the hurlock emissary and hold back near the door. Let them come to you and pick them off one by one. When the dust settles, grab the loot from the chest and wooden crate in the western stock room.

Now you have a choice: head north or east. North continues the main quest and brings you to the next major encounter. East gives you more genlocks and hurlocks, and some more loot, including the Sleeper ring in the next room's chest. If you're trying to complete "The Survivors of Vigil's Keep," you have to head east and rescue the two keep survivors being savaged by darkspawn.

8 When you finally decide to clear out the northern section of the keep, you rendezvous with a blast from the past: the sometimes drunk, but always lovable, dwarven warrior Oghren. He's convinced himself he wants to become a Grey Warden, and, because trouble seems to follow him around, Oghren has found himself mixed up with another darkspawn invasion. Oghren can hold his own against his foes, so take the group that advances on you (usually led by the hurlock alpha) and teach them what it really means to anger a Grey Warden. After the fight, Oghren joins your party and you're at full strength for the final keep battles.

9 As you near the final set of rooms, a dying soldier, Rowland, calls out to you. Despite your healing magics, there's nothing you can do for the poisoned man, but he warns you of a talking darkspawn who has seized Seneschal Varel.

Tread carefully after speaking with Rowland. Two darkspawn fire arrows down at you from the top of the stairs in the next room. As soon as you ascend those stairs, more darkspawn will crash out into the room from the side room to the north. Tons more darkspawn, led by a genlock alpha, clog up the room to the east and will join the fray as soon as you come into range. Expect lots of heavy resistance, and Anders should be ready with Heals and Group Heals throughout the long fight. Proceed methodically, slaying each band as it comes, and try not to pull extra foes or get caught in the middle of flanking enemy groups.

10 The door in the northeast corner leads out to the second battlement. The talking darkspawn Rowland mentioned, the Withered, holds Seneschal Varel hostage out on the corner tower. The Withered has a genlock and two hurlocks as bodyguards. Send in Mhairi or Oghren to pin down the Withered, while the other warrior charges at the other three darkspawn. The PC should help take down the weaker darkspawn quickly, while Anders stays back and heals.

Once the three lesser darkspawn bleed out on the stone, all four party members concentrate damage on the Withered. The talking darkspawn can hit hard, but it won't be able to out-damage four heroes laying it on. Slay the Withered and speak with Seneschal Varel. He fills you in partially on events, when a new army arrives.

King Alistair (or Queen Anora, depending on who became ruler at the end of *Dragon Age: Origins*) rides into the keep with a small army to aid

with the darkspawn incursion. He's happy to see you've taken matters into your own hands and, though he wishes he could join back in and pal around with Grey Wardens again, he gives you his blessing before leaving for other courtly matters. The templars accompanying the king insist on taking Anders back into custody. If you want to keep him in your party—and you should!—ask Alistair for the Rite of Conscription on Anders before the king leaves. He sides with you and Anders becomes a Grey Warden. You can also permanently recruit Oghren at this point—but if you choose the wrong dialog option (choice three), Oghren will no longer be a possible party member.

Assault on Vigil's Keep

Basics ~ Classes ~ The Party ~ Companions ~ Supporting Cast ~ Equipment ~ Bestiary ~ **Walkthrough** ~ Side Quests ~ Random Encounters ~ Achievements/Trophies

Throne Room

Runthrough (Throne Room)

Summary: Conduct the Joining ceremony for the new Grey Warden recruits and explore Vigil's Keep's throne room.

1. Conduct the Joining ceremony.

2. Exit the throne room after speaking with relevant NPCs, shopping at the vendors, and collecting some of your stored possessions.

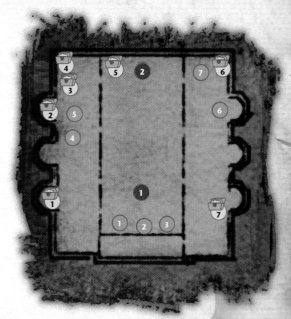

Throne Room Cheatsheet

Main Plot Quest
- The Awakening

Important NPCs
- Ambassador Cera
- Anders
- Captain Garevel
- Mhairi
- Mistress Woolsey
- Oghren

- Seneschal Varel
- Yuriah

Key Items
- Warden-Commander possessions

Monsters
- None

Side Quests
- None

Legend

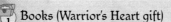
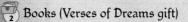
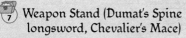

1. Books (Warrior's Heart gift)
2. Books (Verses of Dreams gift)
3. Armor Stand (Trickster's Tunic)
4. Book (Vassals and their Liege codex)
5. Personal Storage (Silver Cog ring)

6. Book (The First Warden codex)
7. Weapon Stand (Dumat's Spine longsword, Chevalier's Mace)

1. Captain Garevel
2. Seneschal Varel

3. Mistress Woolsey
4. Anders
5. Ambassador Cera (Enchanter)
6. Oghren
7. Yuriah (General Goods)

Spoiler Alert

1. You reconvene in the throne room, and Varel has made preparations to once again fill the Grey Warden ranks. You should have Anders, Mhairi, and Oghren in your party, and all three will partake in the darkspawn blood that either kills or transform one into a Grey Warden. Oghren completes the rite without even losing consciousness. Anders passes out, but survives. Poor Mhairi, however, doesn't make it. There's nothing you can do about it; Mhairi dies in the Joining trying to realize her lifelong dream of serving the land as a Warden.

2. After the Joining, you can leave at any time, but there are several things to do around the throne room first. You can speak with your NPCs, and if you click on the cask next to Oghren, you catch him drunk as a skunk guzzling from the tap. Listen to his amusing, drunken imaginations, but don't try to embarrass him with your dialogue choices or you'll end up with a disapproval rating. Ambassador Cera sells runes and crafting gear, plus she'll enchant weapons and armor for you. On the other side of the room, Yuriah sells general goods. Comb the room for all the Warden-Commander possessions in the piles of books, armor stand, weapon stand, and personal storage chest (which serves as an extension of your party inventory, accessed only in the throne room).

primagames.com

The three main NPCs—Captain Garevel, Seneschal Veral, and Mistress Woolsey—hold the three main quests to progress through the game. Captain Garevel gives you the "Last of the Legion" quest. Veral sends you on the "Shadows of the Blackmarsh" quest. Mistress Woolsey entrusts you with "The Righteous Path" quest. Feel free to pick them all up now, or come back and pick up each one as you need it.

►NOTE◄

The throne room serves as the scene for many courtly events and many Vigil's Keep side quests. Check back often to heal up and follow up on the matters of state. See the Side Quest chapter for complete details.

Vigil's Keep Courtyard

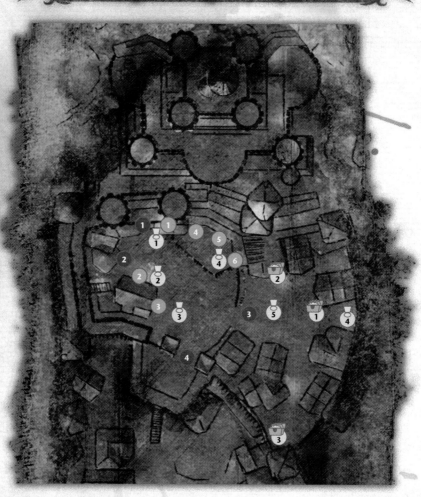

Legend

 Kitten (gift)

 Chest (locked)

 Wooden Crate

 Chest (locked)

(1) Private

(2) Sergeant Maverlies

(3) Voldrik

(4) Dworkin

(5) Herren

(6) Wade

 "A Daughter Ransomed" & "Far Afield"

(2) "It Comes from Beneath"

(3) "Cost of Doing Business"

(4) "Elemental Requirements"

(5) "The Howe Family"

Assault on Vigil's Keep

Basics ~ Classes ~ The Party ~ Companions ~ Supporting Cast ~ Equipment ~ Bestiary ~ **Walkthrough** ~ Side Quests ~ Random Encounters ~ Achievements/Trophies

Runthrough (Vigil's Keep Courtyard)

Summary: Seek out Nathaniel Howe and visit a few other Vigil's Keep inhabitants before leaving for the world map.

1 Enter the courtyard.

2 Go see Nathaniel Howe in the dungeon.

3 Visit the eastern section of the courtyard and speak with Samuel (with Nathaniel in your party).

4 After final preparations are made, leave for the lands outside Vigil's Keep.

Vigil's Keep Courtyard Cheatsheet

Main Plot Quest
- The Prisoner

Important NPCs
- Dworkin
- Herren
- Private
- Samuel
- Sergeant Maverlies
- Voldrik
- Wade

Key Items
- Kitten

Monsters
- None

Side Quests
- A Daughter Ransomed
- Cost of Doing Business
- Elemental Requirements
- Far Afield
- It Comes from Beneath
- Salvage Operation
- The Howe Family
- The Terrified Merchant

Spoiler Alert

1 Exit the throne room area and enter the courtyard. Before you leave for the lands outside the keep and embark on any of the main quests, you need to pick up one more companion. When you leave the throne room, the private at the gate hands you two letters that open up the side quests "A Daughter Ransomed" and "Far Afield." See the Side Quest chapter and follow up on them when you have a chance. Once you complete these two side quests, you can return to the private for one more, "Salvage Operation." The private also tells you that the keep guards have a prisoner in the dungeon. It's the prisoner that you want to see.

2 Descend into the dungeon and ask the dungeon guard to let you see the prisoner. The man behind the bars is Nathaniel Howe, son of Arl Howe, who plotted against the Grey Wardens with Loghain in *Dragon Age: Origins.* If you imported your character, you may even be Arl Howe's murderer! Nathaniel wants nothing to do with you at first, but you sense a good heart in this rogue's body. Call the seneschal and conscript Nathaniel Howe into the Wardens. The next time you return to the throne room and speak with Varel, Nathaniel survives the Joining and becomes a Grey Warden.

3 With Nathaniel Howe in your party, head to the eastern section of the courtyard. The groundskeeper Samuel walks by and Nathaniel recognizes him. Samuel tells Nathaniel that his sister Delilah is alive, and he gives you "The Howe Family" side quest. While you're in the area, pick up the stray cat that meows along the far buildings. The kitten is actually a gift for Anders.

4 Level up your characters. Buy and sell at the vendors. Add runes to your more powerful magic equipment. When you've completed all that and finished off any Vigil's Keep side quests that you want to tackle at the moment, head out the gates to the world at large. It's time to journey to Amaranthine and tackle your first major quest.

primagames.com

Shadows of the Blackmarsh

NOTE

There are three main quests in *Awakening*: "Shadows of the Blackmarsh," "The Righteous Path," and "Last of the Legion." You can attempt the quests in any order, but it's probably best to do "Shadows of the Blackmarsh" first. Here, you gain Justice, the best tank warrior of the companions, and you can enhance your PC's attributes through the various essences you find in the Fade.

Beginning the Quest

When you're ready to begin your first major quest out in the lands of Amaranthine, speak with Varel in Vigil's Keep's throne room. He tells you that one of the Grey Wardens, Kristoff, has been away tracking down a lead on why the darkspawn were still active after the Blight. The seneschal believes Kristoff can be found in the city of Amaranthine. At the conversation's conclusion, you gain the "Shadows of the Blackmarsh" quest.

Amaranthine

When you enter Amaranthine, look for the Crown and Lion Inn in the city's eastern section. Proceed north by Constable Aidan and turn right at the intersection. Climb the stairs and the Crown and Lion entrance is on your left (just before you turn for the steps leading up to the Chantry). Inside you'll find a clue to Kristoff's whereabouts.

NOTE

If this is your first time visiting Amaranthine, there is a lot to do in the bustling city. See the "Amaranthine" section in the Side Quests chapter for all the events and quests not directly related to the main quests.

The Crown and Lion

~ See map on next page ~

Runthrough (The Crown and Lion)

Summary: Speak with the innkeeper for the key to Kristoff's room and find the clue to his location inside.

1. In the common room, speak with the innkeeper and gain Kristoff's room key.
2. Search Kristoff's room for the Map of Ferelden, which unlocks the Blackmarsh world map location.

The Crown and Lion Cheatsheet

Main Plot Quest
- Shadows of the Blackmarsh

Important NPCs
- Innkeeper
- Bartender
- Sorcha

Key Items
- Map of Ferelden

Monsters
- None

Side Quests
- The Blight Orphans?

Shadows of the Blackmarsh

Basics ~ Classes ~ The Party ~ Companions ~ Supporting Cast ~ Equipment ~ Bestiary ~ **Walkthrough** ~ Side Quests ~ Random Encounters ~ Achievements/Trophies

Legend

 Book (The Crown and Lion codex)

 Chest (locked)

Chest

Chest (Kristoff's Mementos gift)

Book (Kristoff's Journal codex)

Chest (Spirit Cord, A Letter from Aura codex)

1 Innkeeper

2 Bartender

3 Sorcha

1 "The Blight Orphans?"

1 Map of Ferelden

2 Secret Entrance to Smuggler's Cove (Amaranthine Smugglers quests)

1 Once inside the Crown and Lion, speak with the innkeeper in the common room. Ask him if he's seen Kristoff, and then tell him that you're Kristoff's commanding officer to get the key to Kristoff's room. The dwarven bartender to the innkeeper's left sells goods and holds many secrets regarding the smugglers in town, if you choose to do some of the Amaranthine side quests. You can also question Sorcha, the barmaid up the stairs toward Kristoff's room, and she'll reveal some insight about Kristoff's general mannerisms.

2 Use the key the innkeeper gave you and open Kristoff's room. Pick up Kristoff's Mementos, a gift item, in the chest to your right, and gain Kristoff's Journal codex entry from the book on the table. The chest by the bed holds the Spirit Cord amulet (+3 dexterity, +3 cunning, +15% nature resistance, +5% spirit resistance) and A Letter from Aura codex entry. When you interact with the Map of Ferelden on the back wall, the Blackmarsh location opens up on the world map. You can now follow Kristoff to the marsh and see where his pursuit of the new darkspawn led.

Spoiler Alert

The Blackmarsh

~ See map on next page ~

Runthrough (The Blackmarsh)

Summary: Follow the trail of clues to discover Kristoff's whereabouts.

1 Enter the Blackmarsh.
2 Encounter marsh wolves as you navigate the marsh.
3 Discover a darkspawn corpse slain by Kristoff.
4 Leave the ruins and head north out into the deep swamp.
5 Discover Kristoff's camp.
6 Kristoff didn't make it. The First set a trap for any Grey Wardens seeking Kristoff.

The Blackmarsh Cheatsheet

Main Plot Quest
• Shadows of the Blackmarsh

Important NPCs
• None

Key Items
• Darkspawn Corpse
• Cot
• Kristoff's Body

Monsters
• Alpha Marsh Wolves

• Blighted Shadow Werewolves
• Blighted Werewolves
• Childer Grubs
• Marsh Wolves
• The First

Side Quests
• The Burden of Guilt
• The Lost Dragon Bones
• Tears in the Veil
• The Trail of Love

Veil Tear

Veil Tear

Veil Tear

Veil Tear

Spoiler Alert

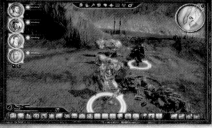

1 The Blackmarsh exudes creepiness, and there is something super-natural in the air. Nathaniel warns of this if you interact with the Blackmarsh tree a few paces up the path on the left. Beware of the nearby marsh wolves that bear down on you as you approach them feasting on some unlucky critter. As with all wolf encounters in the marsh, AoE stunning abilities such as Repulsion Field keep them at bay. Pay attention to Group Heal because everyone will likely take damage simultaneously as the creatures nip away.

As you explore the Blackmarsh, you come across tears in the Veil. These Veil tears block your passage in the physical world. If you attempt the "Tears in the Veil" side quest, you can close these tears once you reach the Fade on the Blackmarsh Undying map.

2 Fight through more wolves at the first inter-section. If you take the left (north) fork, the path leads to a dead end at one of the sealed Veil tears. Take the right (east) fork to continue on the main quest to find Kristoff.

Shadows of the Blackmarsh

Basics ~ Classes ~ The Party ~ Companions ~ Supporting Cast ~ Equipment ~ Bestiary ~ **Walkthrough** ~ Side Quests ~ Random Encounters ~ Achievements/Trophies

Legend

1. Alpha Marsh Wolf & Marsh Wolves
2. Alpha Marsh Wolves & Marsh Wolves
3. Blighted Werewolves
4. Blighted Werewolves
5. Blighted Werewolves & Marsh Wolf
6. Blighted Shadow Wolves
7. Blighted Werewolves & Blighted Shadow Wolves
8. Blighted Werewolves
9. Childer Grub

1. Rashvine
2. The Blackmarsh tree (party dialogue)
3. Blood Lotus
4. Chest
5. Rashvine
6. Chest
7. Toy Horse (gift)
8. Madcap
9. Town Records (Records of the Blackmarsh codex)
10. Chest
11. Elfroot
12. Blighted Shadow Wolf Corpse (Mark of the Divine ring)

13. Chest (Skullcrusher)
14. Rocks (Kristoff's Locket gift)
15. Ripped Page (The Baroness's Secret codex)
16. Chest

1. "The Trail of Love"
2. "The Lost Dragon Bones"
3. "The Burden of Guilt"
4. "Tears in the Veil"

1. Darkspawn Corpse (clue to Kristoff's whereabouts)
2. Cot (clue to Kristoff's whereabouts)
3. Kristoff's Body

3 Go right (east) and you'll see a darkspawn corpse in front of you after you take on a group of blighted werewolves. Slay the werewolves and interact with the darkspawn corpse. You surmise that Kristoff killed the darkspawn, so he must be close.

4 After combing through the ruins for loot, side quest items, and codex entries, head north out of the broken town and deeper into the marshes. (You can't get through the locked town gates to the east at this point.) There are many enemy ambushes in the area, so be on your toes.

5 In the middle of the northern section of the marsh, you find Kristoff's camp. You can tell from more dead darkspawn and Kristoff's cot that he must be very close now. Recover Kristoff's Locket, a gift, in the rock pile near the cot.

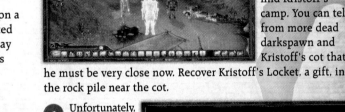

6 Unfortunately, Kristoff was slain by the very darkspawn he tracked. His body lies in the map's far northeast corner.

Kristoff's body is a darkspawn trap. Once you interact with it, your party gets transported to the Fade. Make sure you accomplish everything you wanted to in the Blackmarsh before touching Kristoff's body or it will be a long time before you return.

When you interact with Kristoff's body, darkspawn surround you. It's a trap meant to slay any Grey Wardens who followed Kristoff. The First, a loyal servant of the mysterious Mother, casts a powerful spell that rips a tear in the Veil and transports your party to the Fade. You must now battle through the Blackmarsh Undying to return to the real world.

The Blackmarsh Undying

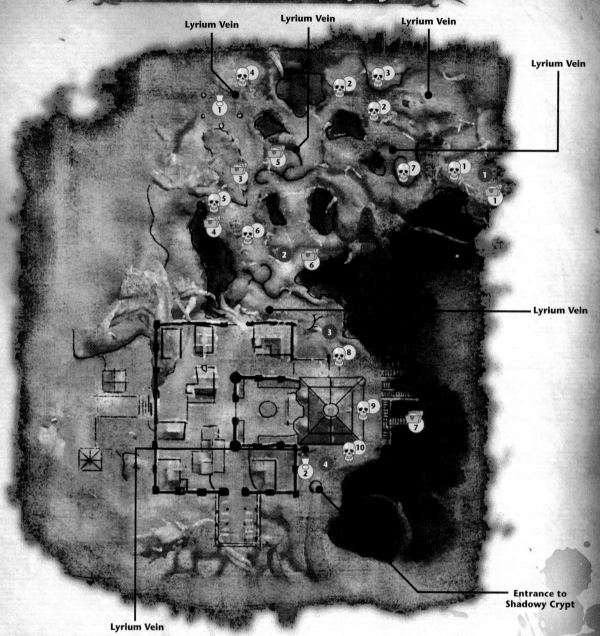

Lyrium Vein · Lyrium Vein · Lyrium Vein · Lyrium Vein · Lyrium Vein · Lyrium Vein

Entrance to Shadowy Crypt

Legend

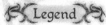
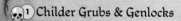

1 Childer Grubs & Genlocks
2 Greater Shades & Lesser Shades
3 Desire Demons
4 Desire Demons
5 Desire Demons
6 Greater Rage Demons & Lesser Rage Demons

7 Greater Shades & Lesser Shades
8 Greater Shades & Lesser Shades
9 Skeleton Archers
10 Devouring Skeletons & Mangled Shambling Skeletons
1 Fade (party dialogue)
2 Essence of Constitution

3 Essence of Willpower
4 Essence of Magic
5 Essence of Strength
6 Essence of Dexterity
7 Essence of Cunning
1 "The Stone Circle"
2 "A Maiden in Distress"

Shadows of the Blackmarsh

Basics ~ Classes ~ The Party ~ Companions ~ Supporting Cast ~ Equipment ~ Bestiary ~ **Walkthrough** ~ Side Quests ~ Random Encounters ~ Achievements/Trophies

Runthrough (The Blackmarsh Undying)

Summary: Escape the Fade by locating the baroness.

1. Enter the Fade and fight the First's minions.
2. Proceed toward the Baroness's Manor.
3. Head around the manor and battle the shades and skeletons that arise to thwart you.
4. Follow the Lonely Soul into the Shadowy Crypt.

The Blackmarsh Undying Cheatsheet

Main Plot Quest
- Shadows of the Blackmarsh

Important NPCs
- The Lonely Soul

Key Items
- Essence of Constitution
- Essence of Cunning
- Essence of Dexterity
- Essence of Magic
- Essence of Strength
- Essence of Willpower

Monsters
- Childer Grubs
- Desire Demons
- Devouring Skeletons
- Genlocks
- Greater Rage Demons
- Greater Shades
- Lesser Rage Demons
- Lesser Shades
- Mangled Shambling Skeletons
- Skeleton Archers

Side Quests
- A Maiden in Distress
- The Stone Circle

Spoiler Alert

1 When the First drops you into the Fade, he unexpectedly follows along with you. The First leaves you to fight off a group of childer grubs and genlocks. Dispatch them, get your bearings, and start your journey across the Fade. You can interact with a boat next to your starting point, which begins a dialogue about the Fade in your party, but be careful—it might reflect negatively on your companion approval rating.

> **NOTE**
> Lyrium veins can power you back up after a difficult battle. Touch one to recharge your health and mana/stamina.

> **TIP**
> Check the map for all essence locations. Each of the essence items grants you a permanent +1 to one of your attributes. Gather all of these attribute bonuses if you can.

2 Work your way south and battle through the various shades and demons whose paths you cross. Don't advance too quickly or you can draw two enemy groups toward you at once. Go slowly, deal with an enemy group, and move on. If you plan to finish off the side quests, slay the desire demons to shut down the Veil tears for "Tears in the Veil" and try your hand at the puzzle for "The Stone Circle" in the map's northwest corner.

3 Continue around the outside of the manor house along the docks. You encounter a group of shades at the first corner. After you slay the shades, tread carefully over the "corpses" on the waterfront. These corpses animate when you turn the next corner, and you'll have skeleton archers behind you and devouring skeletons and mangled shambling skeletons animating around you. Stuns and defensive abilities that repel enemies, such as War Cry/Superiority and Repulsion Field, come in handy.

> **TIP**
> Rather than use up your health poultices and stamina/mana potions in the Fade, drink the ethereal ones you find in the Blackmarsh Undying. These are only good while traveling the Fade, so why waste your other hard-earned stockpile?

4 Finish off any skeletons and follow the Lonely Soul into the Shadowy Crypt entrance to your left. You can't reach the rest of the Baroness's Manor without first traveling through the Shadowy Crypt.

primagames.com

Shadowy Crypt

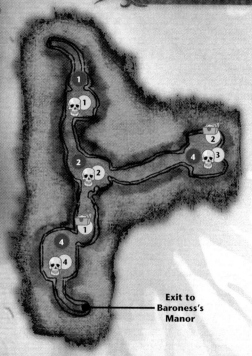

Exit to
Baroness's
Manor

Shadowy Crypt Cheatsheet

Main Plot Quest
- Shadows of the Blackmarsh

Important NPCs
- The Lonely Soul

Key Items
- Essence of Cunning
- Essence of Magic

Monsters
- Ancient Fanged Skeleton

- Desiccated Shambling Corpse
- Devouring Skeletons
- Frenzied Devouring Skeleton
- Hunger Demon
- Putrid Devouring Corpses
- Shambling Corpses
- Skeleton Archers

Side Quests
- A Maiden in Distress

Legend

1 Frenzied Devouring Skeleton, Devouring Skeletons, & Shambling Corpses

3 Hunger Demon & Putrid Devouring Corpses

2 Desiccated Shambling Corpse, Devouring Skeletons, & Skeleton Archer

4 Ancient Fanged Skeleton, Devouring Skeletons, & Skeleton Archers

1 Essence of Cunning

2 Essence of Magic

Runthrough (Shadowy Crypt)

Summary: Pass through the Shadowy Crypt to enter the Baroness's Manor.

1 Enter the crypt.

2 Deal with the corpses and skeletons in your way.

3 Choose to follow the Lonely Soul if you want to complete the "A Maiden in Distress" side quest.

4 Defeat the skeletons in the final chamber to exit the crypt.

Spoiler Alert

1 When you enter the crypt's first chamber, corpses and skeletons will attack. Corpses rise from the floor, and enemies emerge from the upright coffins throughout the crypt. The extra surprise attackers can easily flank you and disturb your battle plan if you don't act accordingly.

2 A desiccated shambling corpse and its skeletal buddies make your life difficult in the second chamber. Don't charge into the room and get surrounded; stick back near the entrance and fight from cover. After the fight, proceed south if you want to leave the crypt quickly. If you want to pursue the "A Maiden in Distress" side quest, follow the Lonely Soul to the east.

Spoiler Alert

3 The "maiden in distress" reveals herself as a hunger demon. The demon has been looking for a stronger body to inhabit, and you fit the bill. The fight is on unless you have a high Coercion score and can talk the demon out of a conflict. Putrid devouring corpses join the battle a few seconds in. Lock your tank warrior on the hunger demon while the rest of the party kills off the corpses.

When you have no corpses to hack, concentrate all your efforts on the hunger demon. After the hunger demon falls, the Lonely Soul will thank you for freeing her true soul. Don't forget to grab the essence of magic in the back corner before you leave.

4 Pick up an essence of cunning in the corridor leading to the final chamber. Clear out the skeletons in the chamber to reach the exit to the Baroness's Manor.

Baroness's Manor

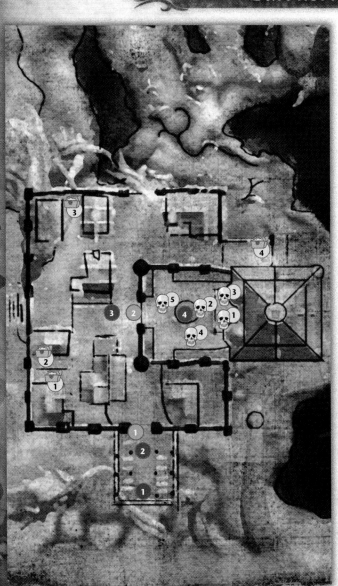

Runthrough (Baroness's Manor)

Summary: Meet up with the Spirit of Justice and confront the baroness.

1 Enter the manor grounds.

2 Speak with the Village Watch.

3 Join the Spirit of Justice at the manor gate and explain your intentions.

4 Battle the First and the baroness's pets.

Baroness's Manor Cheatsheet

Main Plot Quest
- Shadows of the Blackmarsh

Important NPCs
- Spirit of Justice

Key Items
- Essence of Dexterity
- Essence of Strength

- Essence of Willpower

Monsters
- Ash Wraiths
- The First
- Genlocks
- Hurlocks

Side Quests
- None

Legend

- **1** The Baroness
- **2** The First
- **3** Ash Wraiths
- **4** Genlocks & Hurlocks
- **5** Genlocks & Hurlocks
- **1** Essence of Strength
- **2** Book (The Blackmarsh codex)
- **3** Essence of Dexterity
- **4** Essence of Willpower
- **1** Village Watch
- **2** Spirit of Justice

1 You exit the Shadowy Crypt and return to the Fade outside the Baroness's Manor. You can hear a commotion in the distance at the manor gates.

2 Speak with the Village Watch and he'll fill you in on the events in the village. When you're finished, walk around the outskirts of the village, being careful not to approach the center where Justice and the other villagers pound at the gates. You don't want to trigger that event yet. Collect the three essences and the codex entry before approaching Justice.

3 When you enter the middle of the village, Justice and the villagers question you. Once you explain your true intentions, Justice teams up with you for the attack on the Baroness's Manor. Though probably not wise, you can choose not to align with Justice and the villagers. See the "Siding with the Baroness" sidebar.

Siding with the Baroness

If you don't want to team up with Justice, you can side with the baroness. To help the baroness, refuse to help Justice and then examine the gate of the Baroness's Manor to begin a dialogue with the doorman. He will allow you to have an audience with the baroness in which you may agree to help her defeat the villagers in exchange for returning you to the real world. It is still possible to side with Justice at the last moment, though. No matter what, you will face the First in combat and must defeat him. If you side with Justice you face the baroness's ash wraiths, while if you side with the baroness, you face the villagers instead.

4 Assuming you ally with Justice, enter the manor courtyard and confront the baroness. She dismisses your remarks and sends the First to slay you so he can earn a trip back to the real world. The baroness also sends genlocks, hurlocks, and a pair of ash wraiths into the fray. Back your healer out of the chaos and concentrate on healing the tank who should engage the First. Your second warrior or rogue should hold the ash wraiths' attention. The third party member should pick off the genlocks and hurlocks or help out with one of the other foes when they look like they're about to fall. If your healer can keep up with the enemy damage spikes and drop a few Group Heals during the fight, you'll defeat the First and confront the baroness again.

Before you can seize power from the baroness, she sacrifices the First's life essence to open a portal back to the physical world. You leave the Fade, but not without a few surprises.

Return to the Blackmarsh

~ See map on next page ~

Runthrough (Return to the Blackmarsh)

Summary: Slay the baroness.

1 Return to the real world.
2 Destroy the Fade Portal and emerging enemies.
3 Destroy the Fade Portal and emerging enemies.
4 Destroy the Fade Portal and emerging enemies.
5 Destroy the Fade Portal and emerging enemies.
6 Battle the baroness.
7 Claim extra rewards on the docks.

Return to the Blackmarsh Cheatsheet

Main Plot Quest
- Shadows of the Blackmarsh

Important NPCs
- Justice

Key Items
- Armor of the Sentinel
- Dock Storage Key
- The Mother's Chosen

Monsters
- The Baroness
- Blighted Shadow Wolf
- Fade Portal
- Revenants
- Shades

Side Quests
- The Lost Dragon Bones
- The Stone Circle
- Tears in the Veil

Shadows of the Blackmarsh

Basics ~ Classes ~ The Party ~ Companions ~ Supporting Cast ~ Equipment ~ Bestiary ~ **Walkthrough** ~ Side Quests ~ Random Encounters ~ Achievements/Trophies

Dock Gate

Legend

 1 Fade Portal

2 Revenant & Shade

 3 Fade Portal

4 Revenants & Shade

5 Fade Portal

 6 Revenant & Shade

7 Fade Portal

8 Revenant & Shade

 9 The Baroness

 10 Blighted Shadow Wolf

1 The First's corpse (Armor of the Sentinel, The Mother's Chosen greatsword)

2 Debris (Ornate Silver Bowl gift)

3 Chest (Ring of Severity)

4 Chest

Spoiler Alert

1 The trip back to the real Blackmarsh comes with two unexpected passengers: the baroness, who lurks somewhere near the manor  gates, and Justice, whose spirit has somehow crossed the divide and joined with the body of the dead Grey Warden, Kristoff. The new Justice decides to work with you against the baroness and enchants your weapons so that they can attack the Fade Portals that the baroness has ripped in the Veil. Be sure to loot the First's body for the powerful Armor of the Sentinel and the Mother's Chosen greatsword.

primagames.com

NOTE

If you want to deck out Justice, or any other party member, in the uber Sentinel armor set, you must complete the "Tears in the Veil" side quest while in the Fade. You must then recover the other three armor pieces from the iron chests that materialize in the physical world upon completion of the quest. See the Side Quests chapter for complete details.

2 The baroness's Fade Portals release more and more creatures from the Fade into the physical world. You must shut these portals down one by one. Head west from your return point and you'll see a Fade Portal almost immediately. A revenant and shade guard most portals, and the longer you wait on destroying the portal, the more creatures will pour forth. When engaging, send your tank to occupy the revenant, ignore the shade, and put all three others on the Fade Portal to destroy it as quickly as possible. Once the portal is gone, cut down any creatures that have spilled forth and finish off the revenant as a group if it's still standing.

3 Repeat your Fade Portal destruction on the second portal. Rest and recuperate before moving on to the next portal.

4 Repeat your Fade Portal destruction on the third portal. Rest and recuperate before moving on to the next portal.

5 Repeat your Fade Portal destruction on the fourth portal. Rest and recuperate before moving on to battle the baroness.

6 Open the gate to the village area after all the portals have been destroyed. The baroness waits in the middle near the manor gate.

Prepare for a battle royale. The baroness morphs into a huge pride demon, armed with several attacks meant to cripple your party. The most dangerous is her ability to open up new Fade Portals. Shut these portals down immediately, even if means leaving yourself exposed to the baroness for a few seconds. If you let these Fade Portals fester, they'll begin pouring out creatures that will soon overwhelm you.

The baroness herself can blast away with fire bolts and frost bolts. If you have high resistances to fire and cold, you should be fine. If not, the party healer will have to watch for one of these attacks and immediately throw a Regeneration or Heal after it lands.

A shockwave attack from the baroness deals normal damage and knocks you off your feet if you fail a physical resistance check. Even worse, her drain ability consumes health from the target she grabs and transfers that health to the baroness.

Keep up the constant pressure and stay patient while you chip away at the baroness's health total. The fight will be long, and the healer will probably tap into a few lyrium potions to keep up with the healing. With the right teamwork, you will survive her barrage of attacks and finally bring the baroness down.

Achievement & Trophy Tip: Pride Comes Before the Fall

When you defeat the baroness you earn the "Pride Comes Before the Fall" Achievement/Trophy.

7 Search the baroness's corpse for nice loot (Firestompers, Soulbound ring, and 14 sovereigns) and the Dock Storage Key. Use the key to open the gate that leads out to the docks at the northeast corner of the manor. You gain a lot more cool loot from the docks, and if you're completing side quests, the fifth dragon bone rests here, as does Ser Alvard's Sword in one of the decomposing crates.

You've now completed the "Shadows of the Blackmarsh" quest line and can have Justice join your party as a burly warrior tank! Now it's time to return to Vigil's Keep for your next major quest.

The Righteous Path

Basics ~ Classes ~ The Party ~ Companions ~ Supporting Cast ~ Equipment ~ Bestiary ~ **Walkthrough** ~ Side Quests ~ Random Encounters ~ Achievements/Trophies

The Righteous Path

Spoiler Alert

◆◆◇◆ NOTE ◆◇◆◆

There are three main quests in *Awakening*: "Shadows of the Blackmarsh," "The Righteous Path," and "Last of the Legion." You can attempt the quests in any order; however, it's probably best to do "The Righteous Path" second. You gain Velanna, a second mage companion, which may fill out your needs for more spellcasting, and you get introduced to the mysterious Architect.

Beginning the Quest

When you're ready to begin your second major quest out in the lands of Amaranthine, speak with Mistress Woolsey in the Vigil's Keep throne room. She tells you that the caravan route has been disrupted in the southeast, and that the kingdom can't survive without free-flowing trade (more information about the merchant attacks can be found in "Trading Troubles" in the "Side Quests" chapter). Mistress Woolsey sends you to speak with Mervis, a wealthy merchant in the city of Amaranthine. At the conversation's conclusion, you gain the "The Righteous Path" quest.

Amaranthine

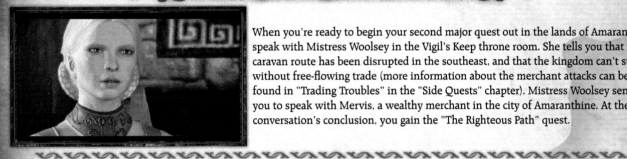

When you enter Amaranthine, look for Mervis to the north of the Market District (western side of the city). He explains that caravans have been ransacked in

◆◆◇ NOTE ◆◇◆◆

If this is your first time visiting Amaranthine, there is a lot to do in the bustling city. See the "Amaranthine" section in the Side Quests chapter for all the events and quests not directly related to the main quests.

the Wending Wood and asks you to investigate. He also promises you a reward if you can stop whoever or whatever is disrupting the trade route. When you're finished in Amaranthine, travel to the new location on the world map: the Wending Wood.

Wending Wood

~ See map on next page ~

Wending Wood Cheatsheet

Main Plot Quest
- The Righteous Path

Important NPCs
- Militia Survivor
- Velanna

Key Items
- Bronze Sextant
- Elven Prayer for the Dead
- Elven Trinket

Monsters
- Alpha Blight Wolf

- Alpha Shriek
- Bandits
- Blight Wolves
- Charred Sylvans
- Enraged Wolves
- Genlocks
- Giant Spiders
- Hurlock Alpha
- Hurlock Emissaries
- Hurlocks
- Ogre

- The Old One
- Poisonous Spiders
- Scavengers
- Shrieks
- Wild Sylvans

Side Quests
- Fire Puzzle
- Brothers of Stone
- Heart of the Forest

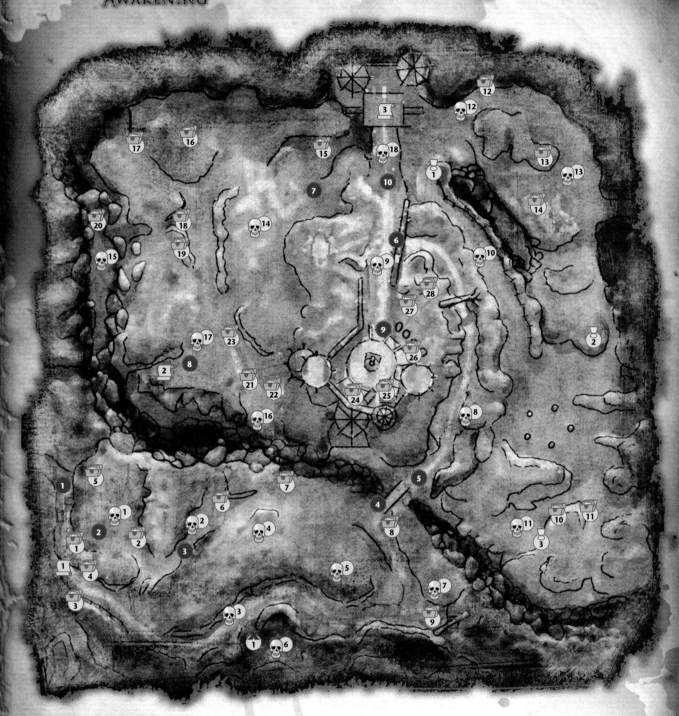

Runthrough (Wending Wood)

Summary: Investigate the Wending Wood for clues on who or what is responsible for the caravan attacks.

1 Enter the Wending Wood.

2 Dispatch the raiding bandit and scavengers.

3 Intercept a charred sylvan attack on scavengers.

4 Find the bridge to cross to the northern section.

5 Velanna warns you not to continue.

6 Battle another charred sylvan and bandits at the wood's main intersection.

7 Descend into the western section of the wood.

8 Speak with the militia survivor to piece together the truth about the caravan attacks.

9 Return to the Dalish camp and speak with Velanna.

10 Battle a host of darkspawn to enter the Silverite Mine.

The Righteous Path

Basics ~ Classes ~ The Party ~ Companions ~ Supporting Cast ~ Equipment ~ Bestiary ~ **Walkthrough** ~ Side Quests ~ Random Encounters ~ Achievements/Trophies

Legend

- 1 Bandit & Scavengers
- 2 Charred Sylvan & Scavengers
- 3 Charred Sylvan & Scavengers
- 4 Charred Sylvan & Wild Sylvan
- 5 Bandits
- 6 Scavengers
- 7 Wild Sylvans
- 8 Bandits
- 9 Charred Sylvan & Bandits
- 10 Alpha Shriek & Shrieks
- 11 The Old One & Wild Sylvan
- 12 Genlocks & Hurlocks
- 13 Genlocks, Hurlock Alpha, & Hurlocks
- 14 Charred Sylvans
- 15 Alpha Blight Wolf & Blight Wolves
- 16 Giant Spiders & Poisonous Spiders
- 17 Hurlock Alpha, Hurlock Emissary, Genlock, & Hurlocks

- 18 Genlocks, Hurlock Emissary, Hurlock, & Ogre
- 1 Broken Crate
- 2 Wooden Crate & Scroll (Orders to the Militia codex)
- 3 Blood Lotus
- 4 Chest (Fine Silks)
- 5 Rashvine
- 6 Chest
- 7 Rashvine
- 8 Elfroot
- 9 Chest (Fine Silks)
- 10 Deathroot
- 11 Corpse (Bronze Sextant gift)
- 12 Blood Lotus
- 13 Chest
- 14 Chests
- 15 Deathroot & Rashvine
- 16 Rashvine
- 17 Charred Corpse
- 18 Blood Lotus

- 19 Chest
- 20 Darkspawn Corpse
- 21 Madcap
- 22 Darkspawn Corpse (Ash ring) & Cocoon (Apprentice Cowl)
- 23 Hurlock Emissary corpse (Elven Trinket gift)
- 24 Chest
- 25 Wooden Crate
- 26 Blood Lotus
- 27 Elf Corpse (party dialogue)
- 28 Crate (Elven Prayer for the Dead gift, Dalish Gloves)
- 1 Velanna
- 1 Fire Puzzle
- 2 "Brothers of Stone"
- 3 "Heart of the Forest"
- 1 Destroyed Caravan
- 2 Militia Survivor
- 3 Silverite Mine
- 1 Leghold Traps

Spoiler Alert

1 As you enter the Wending Wood, you immediately spot bandits trying to ransack a caravan. They bolt at your appearance, and if you interact with the caravan, you notice that something else must have caused the caravan destruction. No human hand did that. As you approach the broken caravan, the "Trading Troubles" quest pops up. You'll finish it as part of "The Righteous Path" major quest.

2 It's time to punish the bandit and scavengers that tried to loot the broken caravan. Turn left and you'll see the hoodlums up on the hill. Hit them at range and charge at the bandit leader with your melee fighters. Some of the scavengers will stay back and fire at range, but your range attacks are superior and will take them down shortly.

3 Outside the bandit camp, take the northern road. Around the corner, a charred sylvan attacks two scavengers. The natural wildlife in the wood hates humans, and the two sides slug it out. Regardless of which side you aid at first, the other side will turn on you and attack, so burn down the charred sylvan first and then pick off whatever remains of the scavengers.

4 If you stay to the north and hug the cliff, you come to the bridge that leads into the larger northern section of the wood. If you explore the area around the south road, you'll run into more sylvans and bandits. You can also pick up extra loot from a chest in the southeast corner.

Spoiler Alert

5 Once you cross the bridge, a bandit runs down the hill in a panicked frenzy. He claims someone is hunting him down, and before

he can fully explain himself, an elven mage appears and threatens you all. Her name, as you find out later, is Velanna, and she's terrorizing the humans because she believes they are responsible for an atrocity against her people. She warns you to turn back now or suffer the consequences.

6 Climb up the hillside path and take out the bandits on the cliff. At the top, you reach the main inter-section, which branches off into six main areas: the path leading back to the southern woods (which you just climbed up), a path winding down to the fire puzzle area (green 1, 2, and 3), the area adjacent to the granite quarry, the entrance to the Silverite Mine, a path leading to the western section of the wood, and a road leading south to the abandoned Dalish camp. Battle the charred sylvan and bandits that clog your way.

7 Proceed to the western section of the wood. Work down to the southwest corner as you fight more charred sylvans. If you keep to the open area in the middle of the western section you'll only have to battle the sylvans before you reach the lean-to camp.

Spoiler Alert

8 A militia survivor rests here under a lean-to. Somehow he's been affected with a darkspawn disease—he's dying and decom-posing before your eyes. He does, however, have enough wits about him to clue you in on the truth behind the caravan attacks. The elf Velanna has been misled. Darkspawn killed the Dalish people and may have kidnapped Velanna's sister, Seranni. The darkspawn planted evidence to make it look like the humans did the deed. Never having known a darkspawn capable of such wit, the elf mage assumed that humans are to blame. At the end of your conversation, darkspawn surround you. It's an ambush. Send your toughest party members at the hurlock alpha and hurlock emissary, and follow with a punishing talent/spell on the hurlock emissary, such as Crushing Prison, to keep it from casting AoE. Clear up the remaining genlocks and hurlocks after the two main darkspawn die.

Spoiler Alert

9 Return up the hill toward the Dalish camp. Velanna intercepts you with two wild sylvans and a group of enraged wolves, refusing

to believe your "lies" about the humans. Fight through the wild sylvans and confront Velanna up in the Dalish camp. Convince her of the truth about the darkspawn and invite her to join your party. She will add her mage abilities to the group and point you in the direction of the Silverite Mine to track down the darkspawn responsible for these crimes.

The Righteous Path

Basics ~ Classes ~ The Party ~ Companions ~ Supporting Cast ~ Equipment ~ Bestiary ~ **Walkthrough** ~ Side Quests ~ Random Encounters ~ Achievements/Trophies

10 The Silverite Mine lies just down the hill from the Dalish camp. Except, a large group of darkspawn now guards the entrance. Concentrate your ranged attack on the ogre and let it charge toward you. You may slay the ogre before it reaches you if your damage is high enough; if not, you'll wound it severely and take it down with a melee strokes. Then take on the rest of the darkspawn and pave a path to the Silverite Mine.

Trapped by the Architect

All is quiet when you first enter the mine. A rickety wooden staircase descends to an empty room. At the base of the staircase is a scroll with "A Miner's Letter" codex. You can walk right by it if you're not looking for it.

As you might guess, all is not as it seems. When you approach the inscribed circle stone floor, the Architect appears (there's way around this, even

if you try to avoid the circle). You're not sure what this talking darkspawn has planned for you, but you won't be happy about the first part of it. His magic knocks the whole party out, and you wake up in a strange prison cell without any of your equipment!

Silverite Mine

~ See map on next page ~

Silverite Mine Cheatsheet

Main Plot Quest
- The Righteous Path

Important NPCs
- Armaas
- Seranni

Key Items
- Dragonspite Bow
- Blackblade Helm
- Blackblade Tunic
- Phylacteries: A History

Written in Blood
- Spyglass

Monsters
- Darkspawn Necromancer
- Drake
- Dragon Thralls
- Dragonlings
- Genlock Emissaries
- Genlocks
- Hurlock Alpha

- Hurlock Dragon-Tamer
- Hurlock Emissaries
- Hurlocks

Side Quests
- Elemental Requirements
- Last Wishes
- Trade Must Flow
- Worked to the Bone
- Bombs Away!

primagames.com

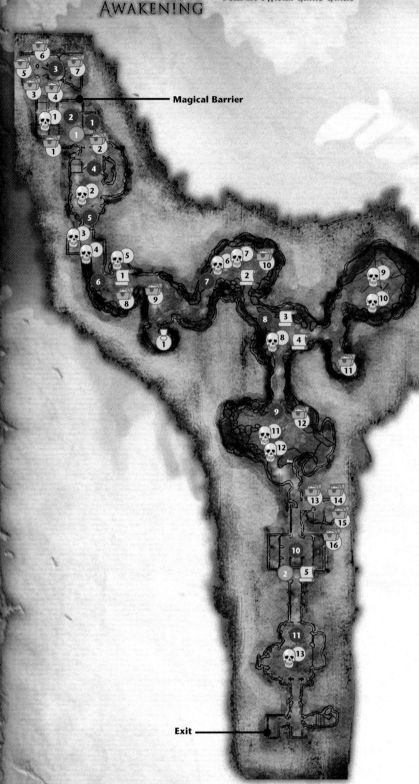

Magical Barrier

Exit

Runthrough (Silverite Mine)

Summary: Captured in the mine, you must recover all your gear and escape.

1 You wake in a prison cell after being captured by the mysterious Architect.

2 Seranni provides for your escape from the cell just before hurlocks arrive.

3 Complete the Architect's puzzle to receive an extra reward.

4 Use the ballista batter of the enemy group in the chamber below.

5 Fight back-to-back enemy groups after opening the next door.

6 Slay the first experimental subject to regain equipment for your party.

7 Slay the second experimental subject to regain equipment for your party.

8 Slay the third and fourth experimental subjects to regain equipment for your party.

9 Deal with a darkspawn necromancer and its animated dead.

10 Speak with Armaas the trader and recover the rest of your party equipment.

11 In the arena under the watchful eyes of the Architect, defeat two dragon thralls and finally escape the Silverite Mine.

TIP

You lack your equipment when you begin the Silverite Mine. Until you can find and slay experimental subjects (the enemies in the mine who are equipped with your gear), you must use whatever is on hand. As you defeat genlocks and hurlocks, loot the corpses. Common items that may have only fetched you a few coins are now worth their weight in sovereigns as you gear up one weapon or chunk of armor at a time.

The Righteous Path

Basics ~ Classes ~ The Party ~ Companions ~ Supporting Cast ~ Equipment ~ Bestiary ~ **Walkthrough** ~ Side Quests ~ Random Encounters ~ Achievements/Trophies

Legend

1. Hurlocks
2. Genlock Emissary, Genlocks, Hurlock Alpha, & Hurlocks
3. Hurlocks
4. Genlock Emissary & Genlocks
5. Dragonlings
6. Genlocks & Hurlocks
7. Hurlock Alpha
8. Dragonlings & Genlocks
9. Dragonlings & Drake
10. Hurlock Dragon-Tamer
11. Darkspawn Necromancer & Skeletons
12. Drake & Genlocks
13. Dragon Thralls

1. Dwarf Corpse
2. Fractured Stone
3. Chest
4. Books (Phylacteries: A History Written in Blood gift)
5. Journal Page (The Architect's Journal codex)
6. Experiment Notes (The Architect's Notes)
7. Chest (Dragonspite bow, Black-blade Tunic)
8. Fractured Stone
9. Stones
10. Soldier Corpse (Spyglass gift)
11. Wooden Crate
12. Fractured Stone

13. Chest (locked)
14. Letter (A Letter from the Architect codex)
15. Pile of Books & Cabinet
16. Chest (First Enchanter's Cowl & Ring of Discipline)

1. Seranni
2. Armaas

1. "Last Wishes"

1. Experimental Subject
2. Experimental Subject
3. Experimental Subject
4. Experimental Subject
5. Chest (party inventory)

Spoiler Alert

1 You awake in a cell with your companions, all stripped of your gear. Velanna's sister, Seranni, speaks to you from the cell door. She tries to explain that the Architect isn't truly an enemy, but before she can elaborate, darkspawn are at the main cell area door. Rather than risk an unfortunate end at the hands of these darkspawn, Seranni releases you from the cell and flees. If you maxed out your Coercion skill, you can persuade Seranni to give you a key that unlocks the special treasure chest in the Architect's room later in the mine.

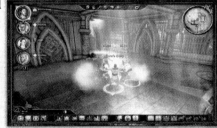

2 Leave the cell and confront the onrushing hurlocks with your bare hands! Pound them old school and pick up whatever equipment you gain off their battered corpses. Your mages rules this fight; they have few limitations on damage, while warriors and rogues without weapons can only rely on certain talents to really make a difference. Loot the corpses until you find the Holding Cell Key on one of the dead hurlocks. You can use that key to explore the other cells and gain some extra loot from the poor dwarf corpse in one and the fractured stone in another. The shimmering magical barrier to the north remains closed until you figure out the Architect's lab puzzle in the next room.

3 Enter the Architect's lab to the north and explore the tables for various notes and codex entries. On the east side of the room are two experiment control rods. If you look below, you can see the section of the lab where the Architect experiments on unfortunate victims. A deadly looking green gas swirls around. Under that gas are a lot of dead bodies and a treasure chest that you really want. To deactivate the shimmering magical barrier on the wall to your right and disperse the gas in the lower chamber, you must figure out the lever and beacon configuration. The lever on the left moves the active beacons one space clockwise. The lever on the right toggles the back two beacons active/inactive. With that in mind, the easiest method for solving the puzzle is to pull the levers in this order: left, right, left, right.

Once the gas disperses, leave the lab and go back to the magical barrier in the prison block. Enter the lower lab floor through the now-opened barrier. The chest in the middle of the lower lab floor contains two awesome rewards: Dragonspite and the Blackblade Tunic. The tunic will make any rogue's day with +12 defense, +20% fire resistance, +20% cold resistance, and three rune slots; and the Dragonspite bow with its +20 damage against dragons and +20% fire resistance will come in particularly handy in the final battle against the dragon thralls in the arena.

4 Enter the room south of the prison block carefully. If you peek over the balcony to the floor below, you spot a cluster of genlocks and hurlocks guarding the area. Rather than take them all at once, tiptoe over to the ballista and fire it at the large statue next to the enemy group. The statue crumbles on top of most of them. If any stragglers survive, meet them in the side passage to the east and finish them off there.

5 The door in the south wall of the ballista room alerts two separate darkspawn groups to your presence. Hurlocks immediately charge after you, while genlocks follow in the rear. The genlock emissary, who likes to hang back in the rear, is the most dangerous foe of the group. Send

your tank into the main fray and use your ranged party members to harass the emissary with stuns and continuous damage to take him down without a big counterattack. There is a hidden room in the east wall; inside you willfind the Blackblade Helm.

6 In the next room, you'll spot your first experimental subject. Throughout the mine, experimental subjects hold your missing

equipment. Each experimental subject wears a specific party member's gear, so if you see your tank's armor, for example, expect a bruising opponent who deals out major melee damage. Attack the experimental subject with your melee DPSers and hold back your ranged attackers. Dragonlings will pour into the area from the hole in the wall to the north. Concentrate your stuns and ranged damage on the dragonlings, while the melee fighters finish off the experimental subject. Turn the group's attention to the dragonlings after the experimental subject no longer poses a threat. Loot the experimental subject and one of your companions is back with all his or her gear.

--- ◆ TIP ◆ ---

If you need a quick advantage in any fight against the experimental subject and surrounding enemies, slay the experimental subject first, loot the corpse in the middle of combat, and equip the appropriate party member with his or her gear. Suddenly, one of you is back at full strength!

--- ◆ NOTE ◆ ---

If you go south instead of east after leaving the first experimental subject room, you'll find Keenan for the "Last Wishes" side quest. See the "Wending Wood" section in the Side Quest chapter for full details.

7 Repeat your battle tactics in the next room, only this time on the second experimental subject surrounded by genlocks and hurlocks. Half

your party is back to normal when you recover your second set of equipment.

The Righteous Path

Basics ~ Classes ~ The Party ~ Companions ~ Supporting Cast ~ Equipment ~ Bestiary ~ **Walkthrough** ~ Side Quests ~ Random Encounters ~ Achievements/Trophies

8 Two experimental subjects, including your PC's doppelganger, wait in this chamber with a mix of dragonlings and genlocks. This fight can get a bit chaotic with all the enemies in a relatively small space. It's important for the healer to focus exclusively on keeping the party alive, especially the party members who haven't recovered their gear yet. After the battle, all your party members will be back at full strength. Now all you have to do is find the rest of your miscellaneous inventory items.

NOTE

In this room you'll find silverite ore for the "Elemental Requirements" side quest. If you go east instead of south after leaving the last experimental subject room, you'll find the hurlock dragon-tamer for the "Last Wishes" side quest. You'll also find lyrium sand for "Bombs Away!" and a fresh dragon egg for "Worked to the Bone." See the "Wending Wood" section in the Side Quest chapter for full details on all these side quests.

9 A new foe, the darkspawn necromancer, sets a trap for you in the next room. When he spots you, the necromancer animates several skeletons to engage the party while he retreats to the upper platform on the chamber's south side. Meanwhile, a drake and genlocks enter from the south passage. As you try to reach the necromancer to stop his death magic, you must battle this large mix of foes. Stick the tank on the drake to eliminate its massive attacks from striking the whole team. Ranged attackers should stay at the north entrance and pick off the closest foes. Melee attackers can aid with the tank against or help the ranged attackers remove lesser foes. Once the drake dies, go after the darkspawn necromancer.

The corridor on the left after the necromancer chamber holds the Architect's room. Enter it and loot all its goodies. If Seranni gave you the key in your first dialogue, you can open the Architect's chest and gain the Ring of Discipline and the First Enchanter's Cowl.

10 At the top of the stairs in the next room, you meet up with a lone qunari, Armaas. He's a trader who doesn't take sides and is more than happy to trade with the darkspawn for a nice profit. You can trade with him yourself, and with a high enough Coercion skill, you can get him to give you a discount. Armaas can also be convinced to trade with Vigil's Keep, which helps fulfill the "Trade Must Flow" side quest. The chest to the left of the arena door holds the rest of your party's inventory items.

TIP

If you figured out the puzzle in the Architect's lab and gained the treasure, equip Dragonspite now. With its +20 damage versus dragons, it's the best weapon you can ask for in the arena battle.

11 The final room is a giant arena overseen by the Architect and his allies. You enter at full strength, ready to take on any challenge, even two dragon thralls at once! The Architect apparently wants to test your battle prowess, so he sends the two dragons on you. Spread out immediately so the dragons' fire breath doesn't hit multiple party members at once. After landing and engaging briefly, the dragon thralls launch back into the air and reposition. When they land, glance at both dragons and see which one's health is lower. Send all your attacks at that dragon. It's important to kill one first, rather than deal with two wounded yet dangerous dragons, and it's very easy to mix them up when they take to the air. If you can slay one without heavy losses, the damage will pile up on the remaining one quickly and you'll win the day.

Achievement & Trophy Tip: Blind Vengeance

When you defeat the two dragon thralls and finally escape the Silverite Mine you earn the "Blind Vengeance" Achievement/Trophy. Follow the walkthrough strategies for slaying the twin dragons. You earn this achievement/trophy after you physically leave the arena and mine.

The Architect makes a strategic retreat and you can finally escape the Silverite Mine through the exit to the south. Be sure to loot the dragon corpses for the Slippery Ferret's Gloves, Landsmeet Shield, and Shock Treatment light gloves. Return to Vigil's Keep to report on your progress and resupply for the next undertaking.

Last of the Legion

NOTE

There are three main quests in *Awakening*: "Shadows of the Blackmarsh," "The Righteous Path," and "Last of the Legion." You can attempt the quests in any order; however, it's probably best to do "Last of the Legion" third. You gain Sigrun, a second rogue companion, but because you begin with your first rogue, Nathaniel Howe, at Vigil's Keep, it's not essential to find Sigrun early in the game.

Beginning the Quest

When you're ready to begin your third major quest out in the lands of Amaranthine, speak with Captain Garevel in the Vigil's Keep throne room. He tells you a hunter stumbled upon a mysterious darkspawn chasm in the Knotwood Hills. At the conversation's conclusion, you gain the "Last of the Legion" quest.

Amaranthine

When you enter Amaranthine, look for Colbert near the main entrance. Colbert explains that he and his partner Micah saw darkspawn emerge from a chasm in

NOTE

If this is your first time visiting Amaranthine, there is a lot to do in the bustling city. See the "Amaranthine" section in the Side Quests chapter for all the events and quests not directly related to the main quests.

the Knotwood Hills, and he marked the spot on his hunting map. He has no interest in pursuing that sort of danger, but guesses that you do. When you're finished in Amaranthine, travel to the new location on the world map: Knotwood Hills.

Knotwood Hills

~ See map on next page ~

Runthrough (Knotwood Hills)

Summary: Search the Knotwood Hills for the chasm that Colbert mentioned.

1. Enter the Knotwood Hills.
2. Cross the bridge over the chasm.
3. Beware of deepstalkers near the entrance to the Deep Roads.
4. Save Sigrun from hurlock clutches.

Knotwood Hills Cheatsheet

Main Plot Quest
- Last of the Legion

Important NPCs
- Sigrun

Key Items
- Hirol's Lava Burst

Monsters
- Bereskarn

- Deepstalker Leader
- Deepstalkers
- Hangmen
- Hurlock Alpha
- Hurlocks

Side Quests
- The Long-Buried Past
- Lucky Charms

Last of the Legion

Basics ~ Classes ~ The Party ~ Companions ~ Supporting Cast ~ Equipment ~ Bestiary ~ **Walkthrough** ~ Side Quests ~ Random Encounters ~ Achievements/Trophies

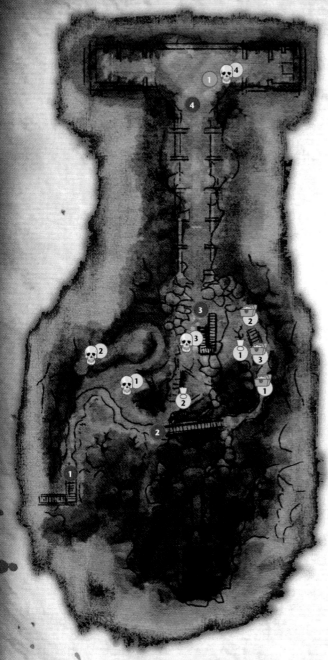

Spoiler Alert

1 A short distance down the path after entering Knotwood Hills, a lone bereskarn attacks. It tries to ambush you after the short rise as the path first crests; if you send your tank to intercept first, you party will have no trouble. Up on the hill to your left, two hangmen conduct dark business. You can bypass them completely, unless you want the extra experience from these human thugs.

2 Wind down to the bridge that crosses the chasm. On the far side, look for the beginning of criss-crossing stairs that continue down. At the foot of the first set lies a chest with "The Long-Buried Past" side quest and a Hirol's Lava Burst gift (ideally for Oghren).

3 At the base of the next set of stairs, deepstalkers attack if you head to the south away from the northern Deep Roads entrance. If you brave the deepstalkers, you can gain the "Lucky Charms" side quest when you find Micah's lucky deer foot in a bag.

4 Continue north to the T-intersection. Hurlocks are overwhelming a female rogue in golden armor. She fights valiantly, but it's up to you to step in and save her from the swarm. Send your tank at the hurlock alpha and the rest will fall easily once you take the alpha down. Sigrun lends her rogue melee expertise to the fight too. After the battle, she explains that she's the last of a failed Legion foray against the darkspawn at Kal'Hirol, an ancient dwarven fortress. She intends to avenge her fallen comrades, and you can invite her to join your party as you descend into the Deep Roads to continue unraveling the mystery of sentient darkspawn.

◄◄◄ TIP ►►►

Take Sigrun in your party. You can leave her behind, but her trap-detecting skills will help you throughout Kal'Hirol, and if Sigrun is present when you reach Kal'Hirol's main gate, Sigrun points out a secret side entrance that will save you a lot of aggravation.

⊰⊱ Legend ⊰⊱

💀¹ Bereskarn

💀² Hangmen

💀³ Deepstalker Leader & Deepstalkers

💀⁴ Hurlock Alpha & Hurlocks

🗃¹ Madcap

🗃² Madcap

🗃³ Chest (Hirol's Lava Burst gift & Darran Lyle's Missive codex)

① Sigrun

⚱¹ "The Long-Buried Past"

⚱² "Lucky Charms"

primagames.com

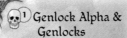

DRAGON AGE
ORIGINS
AWAKENING
PRIMA Official Game Guide

Kal'Hirol

Main Entrance
to Kal'Hirol

Hidden
Entrance to
Kal'Hirol

Legend

💀1 Genlock Alpha &
      Genlocks

💀2 Genlocks

💀3 Shriek Alpha &
      Shrieks

💀4 Hurlock Alpha &
      Hurlocks

💀5 Hurlocks

💀6 Deepstalkers

💀7 Hurlock Alpha &
      Hurlocks

💀8 Childer Grubs

📦1 Vase

📦2 Ancient Dwarven
      Crate (Ancient Boots)

📦3 Crate (Whetstone gift)

📦4 Darkspawn Corpse

📦5 Vase

📦6 Darkspawn Corpse

📦7 Vase

📦8 Vase

⬤1 Jukka

✕1 Hidden Switch

Runthrough (Kal'Hirol)

Summary: Travel through the Deep Roads to reach
Kal'Hirol.

1. Follow the Deep Roads to the outskirts of Kal'Hirol.

2. Speak with the dying legionnaire, Jukka.

3. Darkspawn try to ambush you after you speak with
   Jukka.

4. More darkspawn challenge you.

5. Cross the bridge and engage more deepstalkers.

6. Combat the darkspawn at the far gate.

7. Survey the front courtyard after dealing with childer
   grubs.

8. Enter Kal'Hirol.

Kal'Hirol Cheatsheet

Main Plot Quest
- Last of the Legion

Important NPCs
- Jukka

Key Items
- Ancient Boots
- Whetstone

Monsters
- Childer Grubs

- Deepstalkers
- Genlock Alpha
- Genlocks
- Hurlock Alpha
- Hurlocks
- Shriek Alpha
- Shrieks

Side Quests
- None

Last of the Legion

Basics ~ Classes ~ The Party ~ Companions ~ Supporting Cast ~ Equipment ~ Bestiary ~ **Walkthrough** ~ Side Quests ~ Random Encounters ~ Achievements/Trophies

Spoiler Alert

1 Take in the dramatic view as you enter Kal'Hirol. Soon you'll be on ground level eye to eye with angry darkspawn.

2 You meet a dying legionnaire, Jukka. He tells you that the darkspawn are breeding an army in the depths of Kal'Hirol. To stop the army, you must destroy the broodmothers responsible.

3 Several paces after leaving Jukka, the darkspawn ambush you. Genlocks flank you on either side after you cross into the open area. Send your tank against one side and your next strongest melee DPSer against the opposite side. The healer and fourth party member support whichever side looks like they need it more. After the genlocks go down, shrieks will sneak attack when you think the battle is over.

4 Hurlocks ambush you before the bridge. Look for two groups to swarm out from behind the rocky outcropping to the southwest. As with the genlock ambush, split the tank and second melee DPSer to separate enemy groups.

5 On the far side of the bridge, deepstalkers harass you on the climb up the hill. Finish them off and pick up your first signs of treasure in the area with the nearby vase and ancient dwarven crate.

➤ **NOTE** ➤

You will find broken items around Kal'Hirol, such as the ancient boots in the ancient dwarven crate near the deepstalkers. Don't toss this gear. It can prove very valuable later in the Trade Quarter when you find the special smith to repair each piece.

6 You reach the outer walls of Kal'Hirol at the top of the hill. A host of darkspawn guard the outer gate. Expect a swarm of skirmishing hurlocks to pin you down while the hurlock archers take shots at you from range. Send your melee characters into the charge and hold the line. Ranged attackers should bring down the darkspawn ranged attackers (if they're in range) first, then turn the fireworks on the melee darkspawn. Heal often to avoid losing anyone in this fight.

7 Inside the courtyard, deal with the childer grubs that spring forth from the pods in the area. Stay near each other as the grubs attack. If someone gets overwhelmed, turn the party's attention to that character's aid. The grubs aren't difficult on their own, but they can swarm you quickly if you aren't careful. Loot the area and then make your way up the steps to Kal'Hirol's main entrance (if you don't have Sigrun in your party).

➤ **TIP** ➤

To avoid the trap room inside Kal'Hirol's Main Hall, use the side entrance that Sigrun shows you. The side entrance bypasses the first room in the Main Hall and deposits you next to the golem master.

8 If you have Sigrun in your party, search the western courtyard wall for a hidden switch near the carved visage. Open the secret door and enter the side courtyard. The side entrance into Kal'Hirol routes you to the upper level where you can sneak attack the golem master that coordinates the darkspawn's main gate defenses.

Main Hall

Hidden Entrance

Runthrough (Main Hall)

Summary: Navigate the Main Hall as you descend deeper into Kal'Hirol.

1 Enter the Main Hall and hold your party.

2 Send your rogue through the traps gingerly.

3 Bring down the golem master and surrounding darkspawn.

4 Avoid more traps as you crush genlocks.

5 Continue through the southern section of the hall.

6 Fend off a disciple scout and hurlocks in the narrow corridor.

7 Genlocks try to lock down the next room.

8 Corrupted spiders ambush you as you near the end of the hall.

9 Exit the Main Hall.

Main Hall Cheatsheet

Main Plot Quest
- Last of the Legion

Important NPCs
- None

Key Items
- Cracked Breastplate
- Lyrium Ring

Monsters
- Corrupted Spiders
- Disciple Scout

- Genlock Alpha
- Genlock Emissary
- Genlocks
- Golem Master
- Hurlock Alpha
- Hurlock Emissary
- Hurlocks
- Stone Golems

Side Quests
- Bombs Away!

Spoiler Alert

NOTE

It's best to bypass this first room with Sigrun's help. If you don't have Sigrun in your group, switch to another rogue and have them lead through the traps, disarming as many as possible before the rest of the group comes through. If you don't have a rogue, go very slowly and watch your step.

1 Assuming you haven't used the secret side entrance, hold your party at the entrance to this first room. It's full of fire traps that trigger with pressure plates in the floor. Hurlock archers stand at the ready shortly inside, so you'll have to take them out as well, and the golem master on the upper level periodically sends magic bolts down to animate stone golems along the walls, making for more enemies to combat amid deadly traps.

Last of the Legion

Basics ~ Classes ~ The Party ~ Companions ~ Supporting Cast ~ Equipment ~ Bestiary ~ **Walkthrough** ~ Side Quests ~ Random Encounters ~ Achievements/Trophies

Legend

1 Hurlocks	12 Hurlock Emissary & Genlocks
2 Hurlocks	13 Corrupted Spiders
3 Hurlocks	14 Disciple Scout & Hurlocks
4 Hurlocks	15 Genlock Alpha, Genlock Emissary, & Genlocks
5 Stone Golem	16 Corrupted Spiders
6 Stone Golem	17 Hurlock Alpha, Hurlock Emissary, & Hurlocks
7 Stone Golem	1 Chest
8 Stone Golem	2 Scrolls
9 Stone Golem	3 Pile of Bones (Cracked Breastplate)
10 Hurlocks	4 Scrolls
11 Golem Master	

5 Pile of Bones	
6 Note (A Scout's Report codex)	
7 Chest	
8 Scrolls	
9 Moldy Journal (Dailan's Journal codex)	
10 Crate	
11 Chest (Lyrium Ring)	
12 Wall Carving (The Fortress of Kal'Hirol codex)	
14 Crate	
1 Fire Trap	

2 The trick to surviving the trap room is patience. Send your rogue and any ranged party member a few paces into the room. The rogue should point out the pressure point triggers in front of you. Stop your party before these and use ranged attacks only to kill all the hurlock archers in sight. Before the first golem activates, your rogue should drop down and deactivate as many of the nearby pressure plates as possible. Now, when the stone golems activate, you have a trap-free area to fight in.

3 Repeat the process until you reach the stairs up to the next level. If you have no active stone golems, race your party up the stairs and attack the golem master and his surrounding darkspawn. The golem master drops a golem control rod when ou defeat him. If you pick up the golem control rod, you can click on a golem in the next hallway; it will come to life and fight on our side for a while. Note that if you enter via the secret side entrance, you arrive in the Main Hall at this point.

4 After the golem master, take the stairs down and watch the various dwarven spirits reenacting the fall of Kal'Hirol. These harmless spirits deliver interesting information about Kal'Hirol's story. Pause as you enter the next room. Again, you have pressure plates on the floor in front of you, ready to spit fire on any party member foolish enough to charge in. Fire at range on any darkspawn you spot on the stairs flanking the room while your rogue disables the pressure plates. Then charge in and deal with the darkspawn up the stairs.

5 Enter the grand concourse and head south (the north section is blocked). In the room to the south, corrupted spiders drop from the ceiling. After you crush the vile bugs, search the surrounding area for loot. You'll find a cracked breastplate among the plunder.

6 There are two exits to the south. Take the one on the left and blast a strong ranged AoE down the corridor at the waiting disciple scout and hurlocks. As they charge, switch to melee and fight them at the doorway. Your whole group can attack while only one or two enemies will fit through at the choke point.

7 As you round the corner after the disciple scout's group, genlocks swarm out and try to overrun you. Throw your tank into the fray and try to clog up the doorway. The healer should concentrate on the tank as the rest of the group chips away at the flanking genlocks. If the tank stays up, the genlocks should slowly fall.

NOTE

If you're collecting lyrium sand for the "Bombs Away!" side quest, search the eastern room between the genlocks and corrupted spiders for another pile.

8 Continue north as you wind between the irregularly shaped underground chambers. Corrupted spiders will once again drop down on you as you near the main hall exit. Squash them into pulp unless you want to taste the inside of a cocoon.

TIP

Find the Lyrium Ring in the small side passage next to the corrupted spiders. Pick it up for Justice and earn a hefty approval bump.

9 The exit to the Trade Quarter lies to the east in the last large chamber. Nothing prevents you from leaving at this point. However, if you want some more experience and loot, head north and battle the hurlock alpha and his hurlock buddies. A somewhat hidden crate rests atop the platform at the center of the room, and you can grab the Staff of Vigor and a shattered maul off the dead hurlock emissary.

Trade Quarter

~ See map on next page ~

Runthrough (Trade Quarter)

Summary: Navigate the Trade Quarter as you try to find the Lower Reaches.

1 Enter the Trade Quarter.
2 Investigate an interesting burial chamber.
3 Jump into a battle of darkspawn versus darkspawn.
4 Advance to the forge.
5 Use the forge to repair your broken equipment.
6 Rescue a trapped explorer from cruel darkspawn.
7 Survive an ambush by childer hatchlings.
8 Solve the mystery of the runes to earn greater treasure.
9 Enter into a passage full of the various childer monstrosities.
10 Battle childer hatchlings and invading hurlocks.
11 Descend to the Lower Reaches.

Trade Quarter Cheatsheet

Main Plot Quest
• Last of the Legion

Important NPCs
• Steafan

Key Items
• Carved Greenstone
• Engraved Silver Bracers
• Gauntlets of Hirol's Defense
• Girdle of Kal'Hirol
• Helm of Hirol's Defense
• Nature's Blessing

Monsters
• Childer Alphas
• Childer Grubs

• Childer Hatchlings
• Genlocks
• Hurlock Alpha
• Hurlock Emissary
• Hurlocks
• Invading Genlocks
• Invading Hurlocks
• Steel Golems

Side Quests
• Bombs Away!
• Elemental Requirements
• Wrong Place, Wrong Time
• Memories of the Stone

Last of the Legion

Basics ~ Classes ~ The Party ~ Companions ~ Supporting Cast ~ Equipment ~ Bestiary ~ **Walkthrough** ~ Side Quests ~ Random Encounters ~ Achievements/Trophies

Lever for Secret Door

⊱Legend⊰

1 Hurlocks

2 Steel Golems

3 Invading Genlock & Invading Hurlocks

4 Invading Hurlocks

5 Invading Genlocks, Invading Hurlocks, & Hurlocks

6 Invading Hurlocks, & Hurlocks

7 Hurlock Alpha, Hurlock Emissary, & Hurlocks

8 Childer Hatchlings

9 Childer Grubs

10 Childer Grub Alphas, Childer Grubs, & Genlocks

11 Childer Grubs & Childer Hatchlings

12 Childer Alphas & Childer Hatchlings

13 Childer Hatchlings & Invading Hurlocks

1 Hirol's Sarcophagus (Girdle of Kal'Hirol)

2 Wall Carving (The Paragon Hirol codex)

3 Scrolls

4 Crate

5 Pile of Bones (Engraved Silver Bracers gift)

6 Crate

7 Crate

8 Crate

9 Damaged Axe

10 Scrolls

11 Lyrium Bucket (party dialogue)

12 Pile of Bones

13 Sarcophagus (Gauntlets of Hirol's Defense & Nature's Blessing amulet)

14 Vase

15 Crate

16 Treasury (Helm of Hirol's Defense & Carved Greenstone gift)

17 Pile of Bones

18 Scrolls

19 Dailan's Bones (Partha shield)

1 "Wrong Place, Wrong Time"

2 "Memories of the Stone"

primagames.com

Spoiler Alert

1 When you enter the Trade Quarter, you witness a rather strange sight: darkspawn battle darkspawn in front of you. Throughout the level, invading genlocks and hurlocks attack normal genlocks and hurlocks. Eventually, all darkspawn will attack you, but if you sit back and let them slug it out, you can take advantage of wounded darkspawn.

CAUTION

Avoid the steel golem room with the Girdle of Kal'Hirol if you fear fighting three steel golems at once. The loot makes it worth it, but only if you don't wipe.

2 Turn left and go up to the burial chamber up north. Dispatch the two hurlocks and then search the sarcophagus. You'll receive the powerful Girdle of Kal'Hirol. However, the three steel golems around the room will activate. The healer has to be in top form to keep up with the pounding. Concentrate party attacks on one golem and take it down quickly. If you run into trouble, back out of the room in a slow retreat and hit the remaining golems with ranged attacks to weaken them. Repeat all attacks on the second golem, and finish off the third before your healing runs out.

3 In the central square room, invading darkspawn battle regular darkspawn. Circle the room and pick off any survivors of the small skirmishes. Try not to pull multiple enemy groups at your party at once.

NOTE

In the side chamber northeast of the central square chamber, you can find more lyrium sand for the "Bombs Away!" side quest. If you head south into the small side room, you can also discover the "Memories of the Stone" side quest.

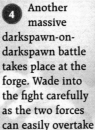

4 Another massive darkspawn-on-darkspawn battle takes place at the forge. Wade into the fight carefully as the two forces can easily overtake you if you plunge in between the two main groups. Rather, stand back on the stairs and rain AoE on each group. When darkspawn splinter off and charge, your tank and melee DPSers can meet them at the base of the stairs. Eventually, there will be piles of darkspawn bodies everywhere.

NOTE

On the western side of the forge, search the iron deposit for iron ore if you want to advance the "Elemental Requirements" side quest.

5 On the eastern side of the forge, pick up the damaged axe on the floor and search the area for more loot. The lyrium bucket near the forge will trigger a party dialogue (if you have Anders in your party and agree with his thoughts on lyrium, you gain +10 approval boost). Use the nearby anvil to repair the damaged equipment you've been picking up throughout Kal'Hirol. If you have them all, the repairs will fetch you the following magic items: Heirsplitter (axe), Valos Atredum (maul), Greaves of Hirol's Defense (massive boots), and Breastplate of Hirol's Defense (armor).

NOTE

All the damaged equipment you picked up throughout Kal'Hirol can be repaired on the anvil at the forge.

6 Leave the forge and travel south. A few hurlocks block your path as you enter the next chamber. After you slay the hurlocks, speak with Steafan imprisoned in the cage hanging over the lava. See the "Wrong Place, Wrong Time" quest in the Side Quest chapter for the various possibilities regarding Steafan's release.

Last of the Legion

Basics ~ Classes ~ The Party ~ Companions ~ Supporting Cast ~ Equipment ~ Bestiary ~ **Walkthrough** ~ Side Quests ~ Random Encounters ~ Achievements/Trophies

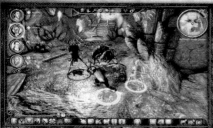

7 You witness a gruesome sight in the next passage: childer hatchlings feast on what appears to be decaying darkspawn bodies. Slay these despicable creatures one by one before they have any chance of surrounding you.

8 In the southeast chamber, a series of runes lines the walls around a sealed sarcophagus. Activate the runes so that each rune matches the symbol on the stone wall behind it. Once all runes are properly aligned, the sarcophagus opens and reveals the Gauntlets of Hirol's Defense and the Nature's Blessing amulet.

9 The next set of passages holds many childer creatures. Proceed slowly and engage only a single group at a time before moving on. West

is the exit to the Lower Reaches; however, you don't want to miss the treasury to the south and its five treasure chests.

10 In the final chamber, invading hurlocks hack away at childer hatchlings. It's a large brawl, so keep your party back to avoid flanking. Use your stronger ranged attacks to whittle down either side and let the stragglers come to you. A few well-placed AoE attacks will reduce the numbers to manageable levels quickly.

NOTE

A lever to the north of the Lower Reaches entrance opens a secret passage back up to the earlier Trade Quarter rooms. It's a quick way back in case you missed something.

11 You've found the entrance to the Lower Reaches! Heal up and descend once you're ready for two epic battles.

Lower Reaches

~ See map on next page ~

Runthrough (Lower Reaches)

Summary: Slay the Lost and the broodmothers to avenge the fallen legionnaires.

1. Enter the Lower Reaches.
2. Battle the Lost and the inferno golem.
3. Prepare for the first tentacle barrage from the brood-mothers.
4. Enter the broodmother chamber.
5. Destroy the first chain.
6. Destroy the second chain and crush the broodmothers.

Lower Reaches Cheatsheet

Main Plot Quest
• Last of the Legion

Important NPCs
• Sigrun

Key Items
• None

Monsters
• Inferno Golem
• The Lost
• Tentacles

Side Quests
• Golem's Might

Legend

- 1 Inferno Golem
- 2 The Lost
- 3 Tentacles
- 4 Tentacles
- 5 Tentacles
- 6 Tentacles
- 7 Tentacles
- 8 Tentacles
- 1 Chain
- 2 Chain
- 3 Chain
- 4 Chain

Spoiler Alert

1 Enter the Lower Reaches and turn left at the first platform. It's a long run down to the next chamber, but don't rush in unless you're prepared for a big battle.

2 When you enter the second chamber, you witness the Lost's pet, an inferno golem, tear apart the commander of the invading darkspawn sent by the Architect to destroy the Lost. After a moment, the Lost turns his attention on your party. He sends

Last of the Legion

Basics ~ Classes ~ The Party ~ Companions ~ Supporting Cast ~ Equipment ~ Bestiary ~ **Walkthrough** ~ Side Quests ~ Random Encounters ~ Achievements/Trophies

the inferno golem to smash you to pieces as he summons forth an Inferno. You can't retreat back down the corridor (it magically seals behind you), so your only choice is a fight to the death.

Match your tank on the inferno golem and keep it off the rest of the party. The golem hits really, really hard, so keep your healer on the tank. Send Sigrun (or any other rogue) directly at the Lost and stun him immediately to prevent the Inferno from finishing. If you have ranged attacks, use those to impede the Lost's spellcasting. Stay close to the Lost so that he can't catch you in a nasty AoE. The tank should circle the battle against the Lost in the chamber's center, holding the golem's full attention until the other two party members kill the Lost. At that point the full party strength can finish off the golem. You'll be rewarded with the Staff of the Lost, the Battlemage's Cinch, the Inferno Golem Shell, a flawless ruby, and a flawless diamond. The shell is one of the ingredients in the "Golem's Might" side quest.

3 Exit the Lost's chamber and follow the passage down to the broodmother chamber. After you turn the corner, expect your first attack from broodmother tentacles. They burst out of the stone floor around the corner and ambush you. As with all tentacle attacks, send the melee DPSers to engage the tentacles and back everyone else out to ranged attack range to minimize damage.

4 Enter the broodmother chamber and fight through more tentacles. You'll spot four chains at the corners of the broodmother pit. You need to destroy two of these chains to crash the ceiling down on the broodmothers.

5 Turn right and go for the first chain. You can also go around to the left, but there's a little more resistance that way. Cut the chain and move to the next corner.

6 Battle more tentacles and then cut the second chain. The ceiling caves in, and it's the end of this broodmother birthing chamber. Sigrun thanks you for the help, and you can ask her to join the Grey Wardens before she departs for more Deep Roads adventures. Return to Vigil's Keep when you're ready for the next challenge: saving Amaranthine.

Achievement & Trophy Tip: Savior of Kal'Hirol

When you crush the broodmothers at the end of Kal'Hirol, you earn the "Savior of Kal'Hirol" Achievement/Trophy.

primagames.com

Siege of Vigil's Keep

◆ NOTE ◆

After you complete the three main quests and speak with Varel, you will go to war against the invading darkspawn armies. Your party will head to Amaranthine where the battle is already underway. After combat at Amaranthine's main gate ends, you will be given a choice: save Amaranthine or save Vigil's Keep. You can only choose one; the other will be destroyed.

Spoiler Alert

Going to War

When you return to Vigil's Keep's throne room after completing the three major quests—"Shadows of the Blackmarsh," "The Righteous Path," and "Last of the Legion"—Seneschal Varel will have one final quest for you. Speak to him when you are fully geared and have spent most of your money upgrading runes, bulking up your store of potions, and swapping inventory equipment until your four main characters have the best of the best.

News reaches you that a darkspawn army advances on the city of Amaranthine. It will take too long to mobilize the keep's forces to stop an attack, so you volunteer your party to intercept. Choose your party wisely. Depending on your forthcoming actions, these may be the final party members for the rest of the game.

Go straight to Amaranthine, where the battle has already begun. Darkspawn swarm the city, and you enter combat as soon as you arrive at the front gate. Fight through the genlocks, hurlocks, and childers to save the citizens at the gate. If your party starts to get flanked, retreat to your starting location where you can only be attacked head on.

Once the first combat ends, Constable Aidan approaches and explains that the city may be lost. Darkspawn somehow poured into the city during the night and ravaged the population. The city guard is in disarray and under constant attack. Before you can make a decision, a messenger from the Architect arrives and informs you that the Mother's darkspawn army moves on Vigil's Keep. While you're occupied here, the Mother wants Vigil's Keep destroyed.

You now have a choice: save Amaranthine or save Vigil's Keep. You cannot save both. Despite the current state of affairs in Amaranthine, it can be saved with some hard work, or you can give the command to burn the city to the ground and race back to Vigil's Keep to support your fellow Grey Wardens. If you choose to save Vigil's Keep, read the next section; if you choose to save Amaranthine, skip the next section and read the following section.

Siege of Vigil's Keep

Basics ~ Classes ~ The Party ~ Companions ~ Supporting Cast ~ Equipment ~ Bestiary ~ **Walkthrough** ~ Side Quests ~ Random Encounters ~ Achievements/Trophies

Siege of Vigil's Keep

Runthrough (Siege of Vigil's Keep)

Summary: Survive the siege on Vigil's Keep.

① Enter the courtyard.

② Battle the first wave at the front gate.

③ Rally to the east gate defenses.

④ Battle the second wave at the front gate.

⑤ Battle the third wave at the front gate.

⑥ Return to the courtyard to slay the heretic disciples.

⑦ Survive the mighty armored ogre.

⑧ Finish off the Herald.

Siege of Vigil's Keep Cheatsheet

Main Plot Quest
- The Awakening

Important NPCs
- Captain Garevel
- Seneschal Varel

Key Items
- Barbed Fists
- Blessing of the Divine
- Helm of Dragon's Peak

Monsters
- Armored Ogre
- Childer Hatchling Alphas
- The Herald
- Heretic Disciples
- Ogres
- Shriek Alphas

Side Quests
- None

Achievement & Trophy Tip: The Enduring Vigil

You earn "The Enduring Vigil" Achievement/ Trophy if you fully upgrade Vigil's Keep for the siege. You must have the city walls constructed by the dwarf Voldrik, your men completely outfitted by Master Wade, and Vigil Keep's basement cleared of all darkspawn and the Deep Roads sealed off. To do all this and earn the achievement/trophy, you need to complete the following side quests: pay 80 sovereigns and find granite for Voldrik in the quests "Cost of Doing Business" and "What Is Built Endures," find iron ore, silverite ore, and veridium ore for "Elemental Requirements," and seal off the Deep Roads beneath the keep by completing "It Comes from Beneath" and "Sealing the Great Barrier Doors." See the Side Quest chapter for complete details.

Legend

💀① Heretic Disciples

💀② Childer Hatchling Alphas

💀③ Ogres

💀④ Shriek Alphas

💀⑤ Heretic Disciples

💀⑥ Armored Ogre

💀⑦ The Herald

① Captain Garevel

② Seneschal Varel

primagames.com

Spoiler Alert

1 The darkspawn have already launched the first attack on the keep walls as you leave the throne room. How long the keep lasts depends on the Vigil's Keep side quests you performed throughout the game. If you upgraded the walls through Voldrik ("Cost of Doing Business" and "What Is Built Endures"), ogres will not be able to break through the walls. If you upgraded your soldiers' armor through Herren and Wade ("Elemental Requirements"), the soldiers will be tougher. If you sealed off the underground entrance in the Vigil's Keep Basement ("It Comes from Beneath" and "Sealing the Great Barrier Doors"), darkspawn will not sneak through the basement and attack women and children during the siege.

Captain Garevel meets you in the courtyard and tells you that darkspawn attack different sections of the keep. You'll need to bounce around to the different sections to ensure that no darkspawn breach the inner defenses. Your first battle is to the south at the front gates.

The Army Picker

You have allies in the battle to save Vigil's Keep. Depending on your actions and accomplishments throughout the game, various factions join to fight the darkspawn. The Army Picker allows you to select armies to be deployed in specific areas. Each army is represented by an icon and number that shows how many combatants comprise the army. Each army can be deployed only once, and only a single army can be active in one area. Once an army has been defeated in an area, you can deploy another army. Your allies are composed of:

Archer: A skilled archer in a high perch awaits the Warden-Commander's choice of target. Note that if you acquired Jacen, the archer ability will cause 50 percent more damage.

Dworkin: The dwarf will bombard any area the Warden-Commander orders. Friendly fire possible. Note that if you upgraded Dworkin's bomb-making ability by completing the "Bombs Away!" side quest, his damage will be 50 percent higher.

Infantry (18): The Vigil's infantry are competent, professional soldiers sworn to defend the arling of Amaranthine.

Knights (12): The knights of Amaranthine are elite warriors, each the product of a lifetime of individual training.

Militia: The arling's commoners are comfortable with bows, but cannot stand as long as professional soldiers in melee combat.

NOTE

During the siege, darkspawn swarm different sections of the keep. Expect heavy resistance from all forms of childers, genlocks, hurlocks, and shrieks. The enemies marked on the map are the primary foes for each encounter, not the hundreds of darkspawn grunts. Defeating the primary foes in each keep section prevents more darkspawn from spawning in the area.

2 As you descend the steps to the front gate, genlocks and childer grubs assail you left and right. Wade through the creatures as best you can to reach the front gate. Stay together as a party for maximum support and try to pick your fights in areas where you can't get flanked easily. While fighting the normal darkspawn, look for heretic disciples to emerge through the gate.

TIP

Deploy the Militia from the Army Picker during the first wave at the front gate or the childer attack on the east gate. If you can hold off while fighting the heretic disciples' forces, save the Militia for the later battles.

Once you spot a heretic disciple, cut free from whatever foes you're currently battling and go after the disciple. You must defeat the disciples to stop the other darkspawn from spawning in the area. After you slay the heretic disciples, finish off whatever darkspawn remain in the area and wait for Captain Garevel to signal that the area is secure.

3 Swing back up to the courtyard and go east to the side gate. All forms of childers rush into the small courtyard and attack the soldiers between the buildings. Seek out the childer hatchling alphas and make them your priority. Deal with all the childer hatchling alphas to prevent more spawning and you can get a handle on the remaining childers in the area. Eventually, Captain Garevel will signal that the area is secure.

Spoiler Alert

TIP

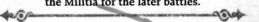

Deploy the Infantry from the Army Picker during the ogre attack on the front gate for much-needed defensive support.

4 After the childers are slain, return to the front gates. Seneschal Varel is under attack by ogres and even greater numbers of darkspawn. Target the ogres to shut down the spawn in the area. Rush to Varel's aid, but you will be too late. Varel dies in his attempt to defend the keep, though you can finish what he could not.

Siege of Vigil's Keep

Basics ~ Classes ~ The Party ~ Companions ~ Supporting Cast ~ Equipment ~ Bestiary ~ **Walkthrough** ~ Side Quests ~ Random Encounters ~ Achievements/Trophies

NOTE

After defeating the ogres at the front gate, you gain access to the keep medic. She sells you health poultices and lyrium potions at a very large discount.

5 Stand tall for the next enemy wave at the front gate. After you have a moment's rest where you can stock back up at the keep medic, alpha shrieks and more darkspawn charge through the front gates. If you haven't used the Militia or Infantry yet from the Army Picker, you can deploy them here to help out. Stay together as a party, move from alpha shriek to alpha shriek slaying each, then clean up the rest of the miscellaneous darkspawn in the area. Captain Garevel will signal when the area is secure.

TIP

Deploy the Knights from the Army Picker during the heretic disciples' attack on the courtyard for much-needed defensive support.

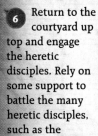 

6 Return to the courtyard up top and engage the heretic disciples. Rely on some support to battle the many heretic disciples, such as the Knights from the Army Picker. This fight will likely take longer due to your foes' toughness, so take it slowly and don't engage multiple disciples if you can help it.

TIP

Deploy Dworkin's bombardment attack from the Army Picker during the battle against the armored ogre. It takes serious damage to take it down. Just be sure you back up when Dworkin unleashes his explosions.

7 After the heretic disciples are down, a massive armored ogre assaults the keep. It will take all your efforts to bring the beast down. Send the tank directly at the ogre and keep the party healing on the tank so that he stays above 50 percent health at all times. Try to sneak a rogue behind the ogre for backstabbing, or another melee DPSer for maximum damage while staying relatively protected in the ogre's blindside. Unless you have

superior gear, the ogre's grab maneuver will take a character down quickly; the healer must Heal, Group Heal, Lifeward, or throw up a Force Field immediately when this occurs or you'll have one dead party member. Also, watch out for its whirlwind attack, which deals tremendous damage to all adjacent melee attackers. When the ogre begins to spin, jump out of the way or activate a defensive maneuver, such as a rogue's Ghost talent. Hit the armored ogre with everything you've got to slay it before it slays you.

After the battle, you can loot the armored ogre for two superb magic items: the Helm of Dragon's Peak and Barbed Fists.

TIP

Deploy the Archer from the Army Picker when you confront the Herald. The Archer's single-target damage supplements your party's attacks well.

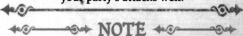

NOTE

If you have completed all the necessary side quests and earned the Enduring Vigil achievement, you will face the Herald as described in the next section. If you do not have Enduring Vigil, the armored ogre is the last foe you must defeat in the siege.

8 With all its minions fallen in battle, the Herald enters the keep as the last foe to carry out the Mother's plan to destroy Vigil's Keep.

After dispatching the armored ogre, heal up and descend the stairs to the front gate. You'll see the Herald in the distance. Similar to the armored ogre battle, send the tank and melee DPSers directly at the Herald with ranged attackers and healers hanging back. Maintain steady healing on the tank, and as long as the tank can hold the Herald's attention, you should bring him down in a long fight. If the general of the darkspawn army gets loose and starts one-shotting your weaker companions, you're in trouble. If damage mounts on a party member, immediately activate your best defensive talent or spell to survive the Herald's barrage. It's better to keep your characters alive than to worry about sneaking in extra damage. You're in the fight for the long haul.

After the battle, you can loot the Herald for the excellent Blessing of the Divine ring.

Achievement & Trophy Tip: Keeper of the Vigil

Once you save Vigil's Keep from the darkspawn siege, you earn the "Keeper of the Vigil" Achievement/Trophy. Note that you can only receive this reward or "Amaranthine's Last Hope" during a single playthrough.

When the armored ogre and the Herald finally fall, Vigil's Keep is saved. Now all that remains is to journey to the Mother's nest and slay the abomination that has caused all this death and misery.

primagames.com

Siege of Amaranthine

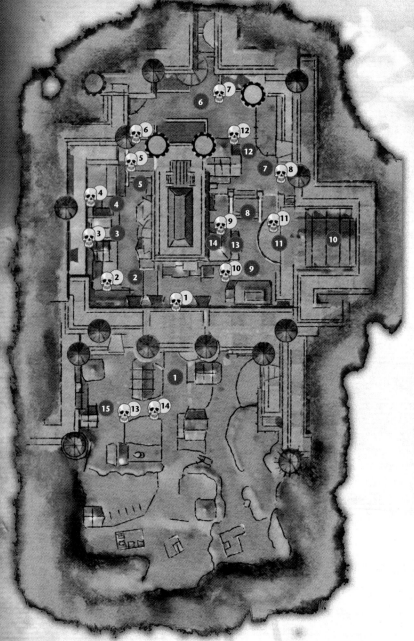

Runthrough (Siege of Amaranthine)

Summary: Survive the siege on Amaranthine.

1. Approach the fighting within the city.

2. Save the first group of city guards.

3. Save the second group of city guards.

4. Save the third group of city guards.

5. Withstand the darkspawn reinforcements on the stairs.

6. Save the fourth group of city guards.

7. Save the fifth group of city guards.

8. Save the sixth group of city guards.

9. Save the seventh group of city guards.

10. Regroup in the Chantry.

11. Exit the Chantry and rejoin the fray.

12. Slay the childers pouring out of the Crown and Lion.

13. Track the disciple general into the Crown and Lion.

14. Enter Smuggler's Cove and destroy the second disciple general and adult childer.

15. Save Amaranthine by defeating the armored ogre and final disciple general.

Legend

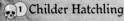

1. Childer Hatchling

2. Genlocks & Hurlocks

3. Adult Childer & Hurlocks

4. Childer Grubs & Genlocks

5. Genlocks Shadows & Shrieks

6. Hurlock Emissary & Grunts

7. Hurlock & Ogre

8. Childer Hatchling, Genlock, & Hurlock

9. Hurlock Emissary & Hurlocks

10. Genlock Alpha & Genlocks

11. Genlocks, Hurlock Guardian, & Hurlock Snipers

12. Adult Childers & Childer Hatchlings

13. Armored Ogre

14. Disciple General

Siege of Vigil's Keep

Basics ~ Classes ~ The Party ~ Companions ~ Supporting Cast ~ Equipment ~ Bestiary ~ **Walkthrough** ~ Side Quests ~ Random Encounters ~ Achievements/Trophies

Siege of Amaranthine Cheatsheet

Main Plot Quest
- The Awakening

Important NPCs
- Captain Garevel
- Constable Aidan

Key Items
- None

Monsters
- Adult Childers
- Armored Ogre
- Childer Grubs
- Childer Hatchlings
- Disciple Generals

- Genlock Alpha
- Genlock Shadows
- Genlock Grunts
- Genlocks
- Hurlock Emissary
- Hurlock Grunts
- Hurlock Guardian
- Hurlock Snipers
- Hurlocks
- Ogre
- Shrieks

Side Quests
- None

NOTE

If you ask the Messenger to fight with you, the Architect's minion will accompany you as a roving NPC to battle the darkspawn.

Spoiler Alert

1 Once you choose to abandon Vigil's Keep and save Amaranthine, prepare for a nonstop run through the city to thwart the darkspawn siege. From the battle at the main gates, run north to the first intersection and pick off a straggler childer hatchling as you turn left toward the Market District.

2 Genlocks and hurlocks attack the first city guard group in the Market District. Rally to the guards' defense and charge right in. The longer you wait, the better chance the darkspawn have to defeat the guards, so don't waste any time with elaborate battle plans. It's time for brute force.

3 An adult childer and hurlocks pin the second guard group in the side alley north of the first market encounter. Get to them as quickly as you can and let your high DPSers do their thing. The more guards that you save early on, the easier it will get as you proceed. Guards that you save join you to fight darkspawn in the immediate area.

4 Genlocks and childer grubs surround the third guard group near the northern stairs out of the market to the back of the city. This third group isn't as tough as the second enemy group; however, darkspawn reinforcements will pour down the nearby stairs and try to overwhelm you as you approach.

5 When you near the stairs, watch for the genlock shadows and shrieks who will suddenly appear behind you for backstab attempts. Keep your party together and advance on the stairs slowly after you've saved the third city guard group. A second wave of reinforcements, including a hurlock emissary, will slow you down on the steps. Proceed only after dispatching these enemies or else you'll be harassed later from the back and front.

6 An ogre and its smaller hurlock companion terrorize the fourth city guard group. Run your tank toward the ogre and taunt it away from the guards or they'll be dead in seconds flat. Let your tank absorb damage with healing backup as the rest of the team mounts damage on both the ogre and hurlock. Once the two enemies fall, continue southeast to the next enemy targets with more guards in tow.

primagames.com

7 Your momentum should start building by this point, and the battles should go smoother with more city guards aiding each other. Wipe out the childer hatchling, genlock, and hurlock surrounding the fifth city group and save them.

8 Head south to the stairs and attack the hurlock emissary and hurlocks at the corner of the Crown and Lion Inn. If the guards are near death,

switch to range at the top of the stairs and kill the enemies with single-target damage (not AoE damage!).

9 The last city guard group defends against a genlock alpha and genlocks. Hit the darkspawn from behind as they focus on the guards. They won't stand a chance if you hit them hard and get even a little bit of support from the remaining guards.

10 With all seven city guard groups saved, the militia captain warns you that a greater wave of enemies is about to roll into the city. He suggests that you retreat to the Chantry where a stronger defense can be mounted. You retreat to the Chantry, where you can heal up and collect your thoughts before part two of the battle.

11 While in the Chantry you learn that the darkspawn continue to enter the city through the Crown and Lion Inn. You must shut down

their entry point to save the city guard (it's the trapdoor in the back of the inn that leads to Smuggler's Cove). Exit the Chantry and battle the darkspawn immediately outside the

Chantry doors. The tank should match up against the hurlock guardian, and ranged attackers should take down the hurlock snipers. If you have a rogue capable of deadly backstabs, flank the rogue around to the guardian or a sniper, whichever is giving you more trouble.

12 Childers begin to emerge from the Crown and Lion. If you give these darkspawn time, they will build up to unholy numbers. You must slay the adult childers to shut down the enemy spawn in the area (otherwise the childers will continue to arrive from the Crown and Lion doorway). Once all the adults are dead, clean up the remaining childers and then enter the Crown and Lion.

13 Inside the Crown and Lion, genlocks and childers protect a disciple general. Cut through the weaker darkspawn and try to get at the disciple

general near the stairs. Once he takes a few blades to the chin, the disciple general will retreat to the back rooms (in front of Kristoff's room from the "Shadows of the Blackmarsh" quest). Finish off him and any remaining darkspawn. The trapdoor to Smuggler's Cove is in the back corner of the storage room. You must enter it to chase down the remaining generals.

14 Down in Smuggler's Cove, exit the basement area to the secret beach. The disciple general will send genlocks, hurlocks, and more childers at you. Stay together and fend off these foes as you advance on the general. When you can reach him with melee, stun the general with several party attacks in a row to pin him down and deliver the killing blow quickly. You can loot Flemeth's Broomstick and the Elementalist's Grasp light gloves from the general's corpse.

The fight down in the cove, however, isn't over yet. Darkspawn continue to attack. Press into the constricted southwest corridor and go after the adult childer in the rear. You must defeat the adult childer to stop the enemy spawn in the area. After you slay all remaining foes, you can return to the city streets.

Siege of Vigil's Keep

Basics ~ Classes ~ The Party ~ Companions ~ Supporting Cast ~ Equipment ~ Bestiary ~ **Walkthrough** ~ Side Quests ~ Random Encounters ~ Achievements/Trophies

15 Track down the final disciple general back up in the city streets (in almost a full circle from where you started the whole run). Unfortunately, the general is not alone; a massive armored ogre joins him for the final assault. Take out the ogre first because its damage output is much more dangerous.

Send the tank directly at the ogre and keep the party healing on the tank so that he stays above 50 percent health at all times. Try to sneak a rogue behind the ogre for backstabbing, or another melee DPSer for maximum damage while staying relatively protected in the ogre's blindside. Unless you have superior gear, the ogre's grab maneuver will take a character down quickly; the healer must Heal, Group Heal, Lifeward, or throw up a Force Field immediately when this occurs or you'll have one dead party member. Also, watch out for its whirlwind attack that deals tremendous damage to all adjacent melee attackers. When the ogre begins to spin, jump back out of the way or activate a defensive maneuver, such as a rogue's Ghost talent. Hit the armored ogre with everything you've got to slay it before it slays you.

Achievement & Trophy Tip: Amaranthine's Last Hope

Once you save Amaranthine from the darkspawn siege, you earn the "Amaranthine's Last Hope" Achievement/Trophy. Note that you can only receive this reward or "Keeper of the Vigil" during a single playthrough.

After the armored ogre falls, turn toward the disciple general. With no other minions left to defend him, the general will eventually go down to your synchronized party attacks. The surviving citizens will gather and applaud your heroic efforts. Among the cheering citizens are a merchant and an enchanter. Visit them as you complete your preparations for the final battle. You have saved the city, but at a terrible price to your own home. It's time for the Mother to pay for her crimes.

Achievement & Trophy Tip: Commander of the Grey

You earn the "Commander of the Grey" Achievement/ Trophy if you reach level 30. You have to be a dedicated adventurer to reach the milestone, as it will take all the main quests completed plus 50 percent or more of the side quests. If you're level 29, you may be able to reach level 30 with the experience gained from Dragonbone Wastes, Drake's Fall, and the Nest. If you're level 28 or lower, and want to earn the Commander of the Grey reward, complete some more side quests before venturing into Dragonbone Wastes at level 29.

prima games.com

Lair of the Mother

NOTE

Journey to the Dragonbone Wastes when you are ready for your final quest to destroy the Mother. The game ends after defeating the Mother, so make sure you have finished off any side quests and equipped your end-game gear before leaving for the Wastes.

Spoiler Alert

Dragonbone Wastes

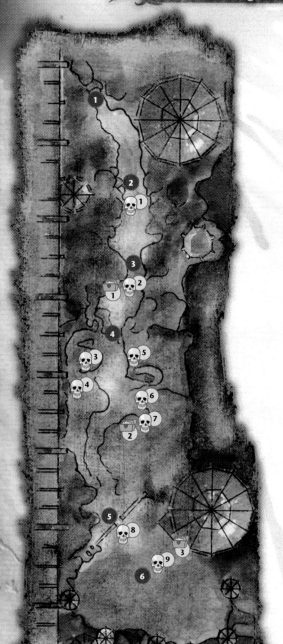

Runthrough (Dragonbone Wastes)

Summary: Discover the entrance to Drake's Fall.

1. Enter the Dragonbone Wastes.
2. Encounter childer hatchlings versus a disciple and genlocks.
3. Fight more childer hatchlings.
4. Prepare for an ambush in the canyons.
5. Slay the childer hatchlings before entering the Drake's Fall courtyard.
6. Beat the high dragon to enter Drake's Fall.

Dragonbone Wastes Cheatsheet

Main Plot Quest
- Depths of Depravity

Important NPCs
- None

Key Items
- Fadewalker
- Quicksilver

Monsters
- Armored Ogre

- Childer Hatchlings
- Disciple
- Genlock Emissary
- Genlocks
- The High Dragon
- Hurlocks

Side Quests
- None

You arrive in the

Legend

1. Childer Hatchlings, Disciple, & Genlocks
2. Childer Hatchlings
3. Genlocks & Hurlocks
4. Genlock Emissary
5. Genlocks
6. Genlock Emissary
7. Armored Ogre
8. Childer Hatchlings & Hurlocks
9. The High Dragon

1. Pile of Bones (Fade-walker)
2. Note (Drake's Fall codex
3. Pile of Bones (Quicksilver helm)

Lair of the Mother

Basics ~ Classes ~ The Party ~ Companions ~ Supporting Cast ~ Equipment ~ Bestiary ~ **Walkthrough** ~ Side Quests ~ Random Encounters ~ Achievements/Trophies

1 Dragonbone Wastes to a full moon and an empty landscape. Nothing is around at the entrance. That will soon change.

2 Up the path, a disciple battles a group of childer hatchlings. Let the two sides damage each other for a few seconds before you approach too close. Hit the largest group with a powerful AoE to thin the numbers before engaging in melee to crush the rest.

3 Slice through a second group of childer hatchlings to reach the pile of bones along the right side of the slight hill. Slip into the new Fadewalker boots found in the bones, which are likely an upgrade for one of your party members.

4 A stretch of short canyons wrinkles the land over the slight hill. Genlocks lie in ambush on either side, including two genlock emissaries and an armored ogre. Inch up and pick off the normal genlocks with single-target ranged attacks. When you spot a genlock emissary or the armored ogre, cast a powerful AoE on the unsuspecting darkspawn (Inferno or Blizzard work great). Hold your ground and let the AoE damage hurt or kill your target. Anything that charges out of the AoE at you will be weakened and an easier foe for your melee DPSers.

✦✦ CAUTION ✦✦

Do not enter the Drake's Fall courtyard until all the childer hatchlings are dead. Once you set foot in the courtyard, a high dragon arrives, and you don't want to fight a dragon and childers at the same time.

5 Head south to the gate leading into the Drake's Fall courtyard. Childer hatchlings attack hurlocks in a chaotic sea of limbs and froth.

Wait for the childer hatchlings to defeat the hurlocks and then face off against them at the gate. Only after the childer hatchlings are dead, and you've healed back up to full, should you enter the courtyard.

6 Setting foot in the courtyard summons a high dragon. You can't enter Drake's Fall until you beat the dragon. Fan your party out so the

dragon's AoE breath attack can't hit more than a single party member. Send in the tank to hold the dragon's attention. The healer concentrates all healing on the tank, unless the dragon catches another party member unaware. Use whatever tricks you have at your disposal: Force Field to protect a wounded ally, Time Spiral to double-cast spells such as Inferno or Group Heal, poison on your weapons, etc. You'll go through quite a few stamina draughts, lyrium potions, and health poultices before you're through. When you're ready to enter Drake's Fall, search the pile of bones near the door for the Quicksilver helmet.

Drake's Fall

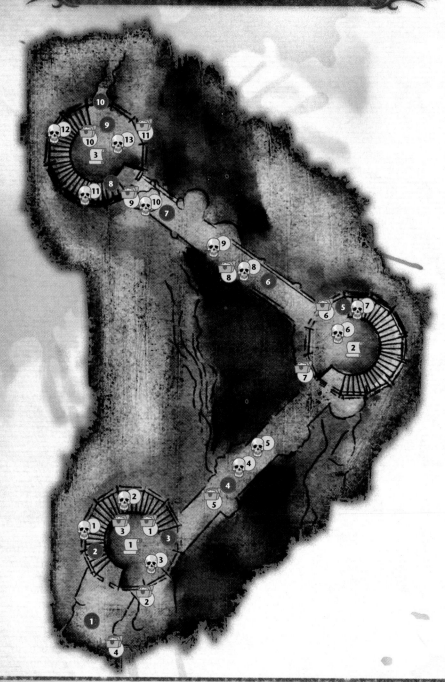

Runthrough (Drake's Fall)

Summary: Reach the bottom of Drake's Fall to discover the Mother's lair.

1 Enter Drake's Fall.

2 Battle down the first spiral staircase.

3 Combat the heretic disciple and armored ogre. Activate the Tower of Flame.

4 Out on the walkway, battle more disciples and grubs.

5 Choose to side with the Architect or slay him. Activate the Tower of Trauma.

6 Fight through more childers.

7 Survive the charge from the adult childers and armored ogre.

8 Battle down the third spiral staircase.

9 Kill the final heretic disciple. Activate the Tower of Healing.

10 Enter the Mother's nest.

Lair of the Mother

Basics ~ Classes ~ The Party ~ Companions ~ Supporting Cast ~ Equipment ~ Bestiary ~ **Walkthrough** ~ Side Quests ~ Random Encounters ~ Achievements/Trophies

Legend

- (1) Genlocks & Hurlock Alpha
- (2) Genlocks & Hurlock Alpha
- (3) Armored Ogre & Heretic Disciple
- (4) Childer Grubs, Disciple, & Disciple Alpha
- (5) Childer Grubs
- (6) The Architect
- (7) Utha
- (8) Adult Childers & Childer Grubs
- (9) Childer Grubs & Childer Hatching Alpha

- (10) Adult Childers & Armored Ogre
- (11) Childer Grubs
- (12) Adult Childers
- (13) Heretic Disciple & Childer Grubs
- (1) Flesh Pod (Crystal)
- (2) Flesh Pod (Crystal)
- (3) Flesh Pod (Will of the Undying amulet)
- (4) Chest (Crystal)
- (5) Flesh Pod (Crystal)

- (6) Flesh Pod (Crystal)
- (7) Flesh Pod (Crystal)
- (8) Flesh Pod (Vestments of Urthemiel)
- (9) Flesh Pod (Crystal)
- (10) Flesh Pod
- (11) Chest (Crystal)
- (1) Tower of Flame
- (2) Tower of Trauma
- (3) Tower of Healing

Crystals of the Imperium

Throughout Drake's Fall, you can activate three ancient Tevinter towers that grant you unique powers in the final battle against the Mother. You must find 12 crystals (four per tower). They can be in flesh pods, locked chests, and on creatures in the area, so search everything. Once you have four crystals, interact with the sockets of one of the towers to activate the ancient magic. The three available powers are:

Tower of Flame: Blasts a single target with high-damage flames.

Tower of Healing: Heals all allies in a battle.

Tower of Trauma: Stuns all creatures in an area.

Spoiler Alert

(1) You arrive inside Drake's Fall on a platform adjacent to a large spiral staircase. Out on the platform, look to your right and you'll spot a locked chest. If you have a skilled lockpicking rogue in your party, you can gain one of the valuable Tevinter crystals scattered throughout the area. For more details on the crystals, see the "Crystals of the Imperium" sidebar on this page.

Drake's Fall Cheatsheet

Main Plot Quest
- Depths of Depravity

Important NPCs
- None

Key Items
- Crystals
- Vestments of Urthemiel
- Will of the Undying

Monsters
- The Architect
- Adult Childers
- Armored Ogre

- Childer Grubs
- Childer Hatchlings
- Childer Hatchling Alpha
- Disciple
- Disciple Alpha
- Genlocks
- Heretic Disciples
- Hurlock Alpha
- Utha

Side Quests
- Crystals of the Imperium

(2) As soon as you enter the first spiral staircase, two groups of genlocks, each led by a hurlock alpha, charge up the stairs at you. Cut them down at the top of the stairs, or the middle of the stairs. Don't descend to the bottom yet or you'll pull the armored ogre and heretic disciple into the mix. You don't want to fight everything in the room at once.

3 After the genlocks and hurlocks are down, descend and take on the heretic disciple and armored ogre. Whichever character has the best stunning attacks should challenge the heretic disciple and disrupt his spellcasting. The rest should go after the ogre, with the healer staying on the stairs to heal whoever needs it. If you play it carefully, it's possible to pull the heretic disciple to the stairs by himself, without also pulling the ogre. Search the flesh pods and chest in the immediate area, and you should have at least four crystals to power up the first tower. Plug the crystals into the four empty sockets and activate the Tower of Flame.

4 Exit the first chamber and walk out on the high balcony leading to the second tower. About halfway across, a disciple, disciple alpha, and tons of childer grubs will attack. Walk slowly down the balcony so you only pull one group at a time. If you run across, the grubs will spawn out of their cocoons and rush at you from all sides. Search for crystals in the flesh pods and dead creatures as you proceed.

5 The Architect greets you in the second tower. He appears once you walk down to the tower base. The Architect explains how he's been trying to

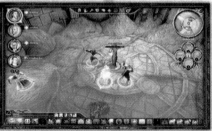

save the darkspawn by freeing them from the call of the Blight, but to do so he needs Grey Warden blood. Much like the Wardens use darkspawn blood for their Joining, the Architect needs Grey Warden blood to give the darkspawn awareness and resistance to the Blight.

CAUTION

If you choose to ally with the Architect, Justice and Sigrun refuse and will fight to the death to avoid such an alliance.

You can choose to join forces with the Architect or slay him. If you ally with the Architect, he will grant you the powerful Cataclysm AoE flame attack in the battle against the Mother. If you decide that the Architect's crimes are too much, you fight the Architect to the death.

The Architect stands in the middle of the tower and immediately attempts to launch a massive Cataclysm attack. The Architect's companion, Utha, runs down the stairs and flanks you from behind. Interrupt the Architect's spellcasting or everyone in your party is in for a world of hurt. Send the tank versus Utha to keep her at bay, while the other three concentrate on the Architect. Stay in close on the Architect and keep pounding away. You can't escape his Cataclysm when it goes off, so positioning isn't as important as the healer immediately counteracting with a timely Group Heal. When both fall, you can score some sweet loot: Robes of the Architect and Belt of the Architect, plus Doge's Dodger belt on Utha. If you have four more crystals, activate the Tower of Trauma by interacting with the sockets encircling the spot where you battled the Architect.

6 On the next balcony, advance slowly until you pull a group of childers. Deal with these childers as a tightly positioned party and raid the flesh pod a few paces to your left. This causes a second childer group to attack. If you run into flanking problems, continue to retreat and pick them off with ranged attacks to thin the numbers against you.

7 Heal back up and then cross the remainder of the balcony. Near the end, you have a difficult fight on your hands: several adult childers and an armored ogre. Try to stun or paralyze the armored ogre to give you enough time to deal with the adult childers separately. If you must deal with them all simultaneously, retreat slowly and continue to whittle enemy health down with ranged attacks. If you can retreat far enough and throw up a continuous AoE, such as Inferno, you'll force the creatures to pass through and take significant damage to enter melee with you.

8 When you reach the final tower, childers will assault you on the stairs. As with the other towers, draw the creatures up to you at the top or mid section of the stairs and slay the first two waves here.

Lair of the Mother

Basics ~ Classes ~ The Party ~ Companions ~ Supporting Cast ~ Equipment ~ Bestiary ~ **Walkthrough** ~ Side Quests ~ Random Encounters ~ Achievements/Trophies

9 Now move down to the bottom and engage the heretic disciple and childer grubs that defend the Nest entrance. Search the flesh pod and locked chest after the enemy resistance has been silenced. Take your final four crystals and activate the Tower of Healing.

10 You should now have all three Tevinter powers: flames, stuns, and heals. These will aid you greatly inside the Nest against the Mother. Take one last chance to heal, level up, and make one final equipment check for your whole party. When you're ready for the ultimate boss fight, enter the Nest and hunt down the Mother.

The Nest

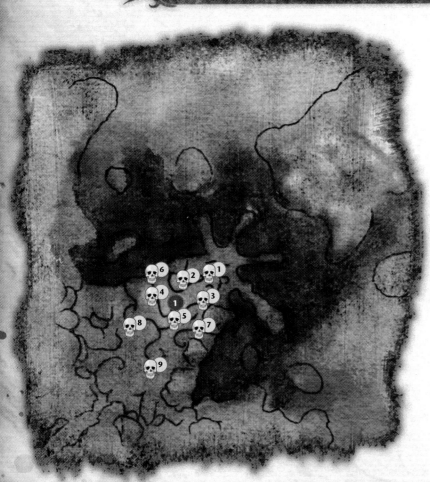

Legend

1 The Mother
2 Giant Tentacle
3 Giant Tentacle
4 Giant Tentacle
5 Giant Tentacle
6 Childer Grubs
7 Childer Grubs
8 Childer Grubs
9 Childer Grubs

Runthrough (The Nest)

Summary: Defeat the Mother once and for all.

1 Combat the Mother in a battle to the death.

The Nest Cheatsheet

Main Plot Quest
• Depths of Depravity

Important NPCs
• None

Key Items
• None

Monsters
• Childer Grubs
• Giant Tentacles
• The Mother

Side Quests
• None

primagames.com

Spoiler Alert

1 When you enter the Mother's Nest, she speaks with you. No matter what you say, expect to end this adventure with an epic battle. It will test your combat skills and party tactics to the fullest. Seasoned Wardens can slay the Mother; others won't last 40 seconds.

The Mother's Special Abilities

Animus Lash: The Mother whips her tentacle in a wide arc, damaging all nearby creatures and knocking them down unless they pass a physical resistance check. Friendly fire possible.

Grab: The Mother grabs a target with her tentacle and crushes it repeatedly, dealing normal damage with each hit.

Slam: The Mother strikes a target with her tentacle, inflicting significant damage and knocking the target down unless it passes a physical resistance check.

Tentacle Ward: For as long as this mode is active, the Mother's tentacle curls into a defensive position, granting it a significant bonus to armor and a chance to resist hostile magic.

At the start of the battle, expect to get hit hard. The Mother's giant tentacles erupt all around you: one on either side of the party and two in front of the Mother. The tentacles will begin slamming party members, or grab one and start crushing the unfortunate victim. The healer should be on alert to heal any party member in need, not just the tank, as the attacks can come from any side. If the healer gets grabbed, it's a big plus if you have a second healer, or at least a mage who can Force Field the healer. Failing that, you'll have to rely on health poultices.

TIP

Use the Tower of Flame ability to destroy one of the Mother's giant tentacles early in the battle. This cuts down on the number of attacks on the party in the long run, though you will have to deal with the first wave of childer grubs when the tentacle dies.

Spread your party out to avoid AoE attacks. You don't want to get slammed by a concentration of giant tentacles, or even get hit by your own AoE damage. Also, keep in mind that it's easier to kill the Mother's tentacles than the Mother herself; however, each time a giant tentacle is slain, the Mother calls in a wave of childer grubs to swarm you. Wiping out tentacles is a good thing; wiping out multiple tentacles in a row is maybe not so good, as you'll spawn a lot of grubs to control at once.

TIP

Use the Tower of Trauma ability to stun a childer grub swarm. During the precious stun time, reposition to avoid any potential overwhelm situation, team up on grubs, and hack away on their exposed backs.

Concentrate all your fire on a single giant tentacle and bring the second tentacle down. Don't worry about the Mother at all; you'll deal with her later, after you have the tentacles and grubs under control. The Mother doesn't move, so you know where her attacks are coming from at all times.

TIP

Use the Architect's Cataclysm spell on a grub swarm or to eliminate several injured tentacles. You can only access this powerful AoE if you allied with him earlier.

You'll hew down the third and fourth tentacles much quicker; they've already taken massive damage by the mid-point of the fight. You may even knock both of them out at once, which means you'll have twice as many grubs to control. Save some AoE to crush the grubs before they flank and overwhelm.

Once the fourth giant tentacle flops to the ground, engage the Mother. Melee DPSers need to get in tight to deal max damage, and the Mother will punish them with tentacle slaps or grabs. The healer may not be able to keep up, so melee party members should pop a health poultice whenever they drop near 50 percent.

TIP

Use the Tower of Healing ability to heal if your healer's spells are on cooldown and you need a quick boost. Of course, if anyone is in danger of dying, trigger the tower's ability, which may be early against the four giant tentacles or late against the Mother's formidable attacks.

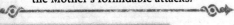

Pour on all the damage you can to kill the Mother before she kills you. At this point, it doesn't matter if an ally drops in combat; you need to out-race the Mother in damage. If you have any Tevinter powers left, trigger them in these final seconds.

With the final blow, the creature that caused so much tragedy across the land of Amaranthine comes to an end. You slay the Mother so that she can no longer breed nightmarish children to plague the land. You walk away to repair an arling that needs more devotion to its people than to the art of warfare.

Achievement & Trophy Tip: Awakening

Once you kill the Mother and finish the game, you earn the "Awakening" Achievement/Trophy. Congratulations! You've quested hard and deserve the accolades. More challenges await in a land plagued by darkspawn and other evils, but for now you can rest secure in the knowledge that you have left the world a better place than it was before you took up sword and shield.

Side Quests

Spoiler Alert

The Blackmarsh

The Blackmarsh

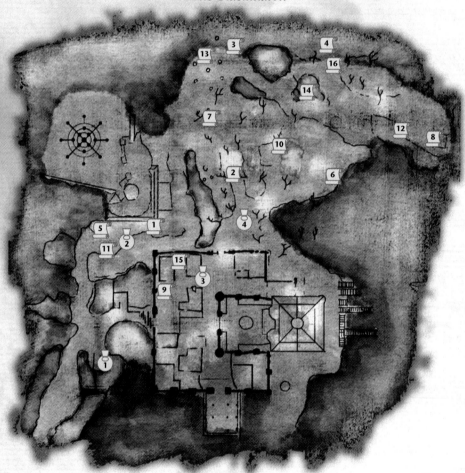

Legend

1 "The Trail of Love" & First Clue

2 "The Lost Dragon Bones"

3 "The Burden of Guilt"

4 "Tears in the Veil"

1 Veil Tear ("Tears in the Veil")

2 Veil Tear ("Tears in the Veil")

3 Veil Tear ("Tears in the Veil")

4 Veil Tear ("Tears in the Veil")

5 Dragon Bone ("The Lost Dragon Bones")

6 Dragon Bone ("The Lost Dragon Bones")

7 Dragon Bone ("The Lost Dragon Bones")

8 Dragon Bone ("The Lost Dragon Bones")

9 Second Clue ("The Trail of Love")

10 Third Clue ("The Trail of Love")

11 Fourth Clue ("The Trail of Love")

12 Fifth Clue ("The Trail of Love")

13 Final Clue ("The Trail of Love")

14 Floating Bottle ("The Trail of Love")

15 Mabari Corpse (Catgut for "Heart of the Forest")

16 Karsten's Hidden Cache ("The Burden of Guilt")

The Blackmarsh

Basics ~ Classes ~ The Party ~ Companions ~ Supporting Cast ~ Equipment ~ Bestiary ~ Walkthrough ~ **Side Quests** ~ Random Encounters ~ Achievements/Trophies

The Blackmarsh Undying

Legend

1. "The Stone Circle"
2. "A Maiden in Distress"
1. Veil Tear Apparatus ("Tears in the Veil")
2. Veil Tear Apparatus ("Tears in the Veil")
3. Runic Pedestal ("The Stone Circle")
4. Veil Tear Apparatus ("Tears in the Veil")

Return to the Blackmarsh

Legend

1. Iron Chest for "Tears in the Veil" (Boots of the Sentinel)
2. Runic Pedestal for "The Stone Circle" (Gladiator's Belt)
3. Iron Chest for "Tears in the Veil" (Gauntlets of the Sentinel)
4. Iron Chest for "Tears in the Veil" (Helm of the Sentinel)
5. Ser Alvard's Sword
6. Dragon Bone
7. Eldest Dragonbone ("Worked to the Bone")
1. Queen of the Blackmarsh
1. Queen of the Blackmarsh's corpse (Spellminder robe, Toque of the Oblivious helmet, Rough-Hewn Pendant, Earthbound ring)

Dock Gate

primagames.com

The Burden of Guilt

Type: Exploration

Start: The Blackmarsh

Destination: The Blackmarsh

Task: Find a hidden cache

Quest Tips: A merchant betrayed several people to the baroness in exchange for treasure, and his guilt drove him to suicide. The suicide note contains a map to his hidden cache. Pick up the Ancient Letter under a stack of crates (see map) and locate the hidden cache in an overturned barrel in the northern section of the Blackmarsh (see map).

XP Reward: 1,000 XP

Money Reward: Diamond, Ruby, Sapphire, 1 sovereign

Item Reward: None

The Lost Dragon Bones

Type: Exploration

Start: The Blackmarsh

Destination: The Blackmarsh

Task: Locate five missing dragon bones and reattach them to the dragon skeleton

Quest Tips: See the Blackmarsh map for the location of all five dragon bones. Return each bone to the dragon skeleton (where you first gain the quest). Four of the bones are in the main Blackmarsh area, and you find the fifth only after defeating the baroness and searching the docks. When you return the fifth bone, you summon the Queen of the Blackmarsh, a powerful spectral dragon from the Fade. Lightning strikes down and destroys the mysterious barrier previously obstructing the path up to the mountaintop. Climb the mountain and defeat the Queen of the Blackmarsh, but be forewarned—it's a very difficult fight. You must be at least level 24, and should have heavy lightning resistance gear to stand a chance.

When the Queen of the Blackmarsh arrives, spread out your party equidistantly around the dragon. The tank will most likely have to get in tight to deliver higher damage, and a rogue might sneak in for a backstab, but if you can stay back and deal moderate to high damage, stay away from the dragon's melee attacks. When you drop the dragon to approximately 75 percent health, she hides in a protective energy field in the center of the mountain. Eight charged wisps encircle her and slowly pull in toward her. Destroy these wisps as quickly as possible; the more that touch the protected dragon, the more she heals back up. These wisps appear again once or twice

more. If your party can deal continuous damage, heal through the Queen's damage spikes (which can one-shot kill a party member if you aren't careful), and prevent the wisps from healing the dragon, you can beat this epic encounter.

XP Reward: 4,000 XP

Money Reward: Flawless Diamond, 14 sovereigns, 9 silvers, 62 bits

Item Reward: Eldest Dragonbone for the "Worked to the Bone" side quest (see the Vigil's Keep section), Spellminder robe, Toque of the Oblivious, Rough-Hewn Pendant, Earthbound ring.

A Maiden in Distress

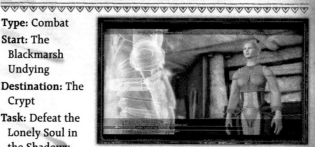

Type: Combat

Start: The Blackmarsh Undying

Destination: The Crypt

Task: Defeat the Lonely Soul in the Shadowy Crypt

Quest Tips: Follow the Lonely Soul into the Shadowy Crypt when you meet her in the Blackmarsh Undying. She will continue to run away from you as you battle corpses and skeletons in the crypt. Take the eastern passage to finally track her down in the side room. She reveals herself as a hunger demon, and unless you have a high enough Coercion score to convince her to surrender, the hunger demon attacks. Defeat the demon to free the Lonely Soul and earn your reward.

XP Reward: 500 XP (if you persuade her not to fight) or 1,000 XP (if you defeat her in combat)

Money Reward: None

Item Reward: None

Ser Alvard's Missing Sword

Type: Exploration

Start: Merchants' Guild Board in Amaranthine

Destination: The Blackmarsh Docks

Task: Locate the merchant's missing sword

Quest Tips: Accept the quest from the Merchants' Guild Board in Amaranthine. Retrieve the Dock Storage Key from the dead baroness's body and use the key to unlock the docks. Search the crates near the docks for the missing sword (see the Return to Blackmarsh map).

XP Reward: 1,000 XP

Money Reward: None

Item Reward: Ser Alvard's Sword

The Blackmarsh

Basics ~ Classes ~ The Party ~ Companions ~ Supporting Cast ~ Equipment ~ Bestiary ~ Walkthrough ~ **Side Quests** ~ Random Encounters ~ Achievements/Trophies

The Stone Circle

Type: Combat

Start: The Blackmarsh Undying

Destination: The Blackmarsh Undying

Task: Figure out the fire puzzle to unlock a reward

Quest Tips: Complete the Stone Circle puzzle by interacting with the stones in the following order: stone near the open hillside passage (west), stone opposite of the first stone (east), stone south of first stone, stone opposite the third stone, stone opposite the hillside passage, stone opposite the fifth stone. Touching the stones in this order will create a fire hexagon around the runic pedestal in the middle. Greater and lesser rage demons will spawn and attack. Defeat these demons and interact with the active runic pedestal. The quest completes, and back in the real world you gain the Gladiator's Belt if you interact with the runic pedestal there.

XP Reward: 1,000 XP

Money Reward: None

Item Reward: Gladiator's Belt

Tears in the Veil

Type: Exploration

Start: The Blackmarsh

Destination: The Blackmarsh Undying

Task: Shut down the Veil tears by slaying the desire demon cabals

Quest Tips: You gain this quest in the physical world (the Blackmarsh), but cannot complete it until you reach the Fade (the Blackmarsh Undying). In the Fade, defeat the three desire demon groups and interact with the Veil Tear Apparatus at each of the three locations (see the Blackmarsh Undying map). This completes the quest, and you can return to the physical world to claim your rewards from iron chests where each apparatus used to be.

XP Reward: 500 XP

Money Reward: None

Item Reward: Boots of the Sentinel, Gauntlets of the Sentinel, Helm of the Sentinel

The Trail of Love

Type: Exploration

Start: The Blackmarsh

Destination: The Blackmarsh

Task: Follow a trail of clues to the long-lost treasure

Quest Tips: See the Blackmarsh map for the quest starting location (exclamation point 1) and trail of clues (scrolls 9–14). Retrieve the floating bottle for the end of this heart-breaking tale and a rather nice ring (+2 to all attributes) as a consolation prize for your efforts.

XP Reward: 1,000 XP

Money Reward: None

Item Reward: Corin's Proposal ring

City of Amaranthine

~ Additional maps in two pages ~

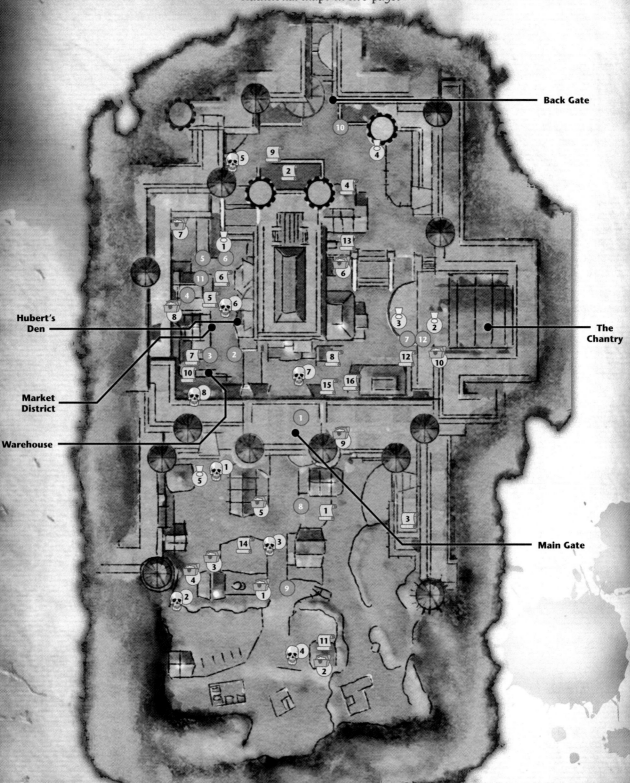

Back Gate

The Chantry

Hubert's Den

Market District

Warehouse

Main Gate

City of Amaranthine

Basics ~ Classes ~ The Party ~ Companions ~ Supporting Cast ~ Equipment ~ Bestiary ~ Walkthrough ~ **Side Quests** ~ Random Encounters ~ Achievements/Trophies

Legend

- ⚲1 Merchants' Guild Board (Includes the following quests: "Keep Out of Reach of Children," "Maferath's Monuments," "The Merchant's Goods," "Ser Alvard's Missing Sword," "Rumblings from Beneath")
- ⚲2 Chanter's Board (Includes the following quests: "A Donation of Injury Kits," "From the Living Wood," "Out of Control," "Preying on the Weak," "A Donation of Poultices")
- ⚲3 "Ines the Botanist"
- ⚲4 "Freedom for Anders"
- ⚲5 "Smuggler's Run"
- 📜1 Packed Earth ("The Long-Buried Past")
- 📜2 Wool Padding ("Golem's Might")
- 📜3 Note Fragment ("Till Death Do Us Part")
- 📜4 Pitchfork ("The Scavenger Hunt")
- 📜5 Pie ("The Scavenger Hunt")
- 📜6 Poison ("Keep Out of Reach of Children")
- 📜7 Poison ("Keep Out of Reach of Children")

- 📜8 Poison ("Keep Out of Reach of Children")
- 📜9 Poison ("Keep Out of Reach of Children")
- 📜10 Sole Shoes ("The Scavenger Hunt")
- 📜11 Karrem ("Till Death Do Us Part")
- 📜12 Doll ("The Scavenger Hunt")
- 📜13 Hammer ("The Scavenger Hunt")
- 📜14 Scarecrow ("A Present for Melisse")
- 📜15 Soft Ground ("A Present for Melisse")
- 📜16 Doorstep ("Making Amends")
- ① Constable Aidan
- ② Octham the Grocer
- ③ Glassric the Weaponsmith
- ④ Master Henley
- ⑤ Mervis
- ⑥ Kendrick
- ⑦ Wynne
- ⑧ Colbert & Micah
- ⑨ Steafan
- ⑩ Dark Wolf

- ⑪ Delilah
- ⑫ Chanter
- 📦1 Homer's Toys (Bell Collar gift)
- 📦2 Crate (Discarded Journal gift)
- 📦3 Chest (locked)
- 📦4 Chest
- 📦5 Tree (party dialogue)
- 📦6 Chest (locked)
- 📦7 Wooden Crate
- 📦8 Chest (locked)
- 📦9 Chest
- 📦10 Potted Plant gift
- 💀1 Thugs ("Preying on the Weak")
- 💀2 Thugs ("Preying on the Weak")
- 💀3 Thugs ("Preying on the Weak")
- 💀4 Thugs ("Preying on the Weak")
- 💀5 Mumbling Man ("Out of Control")
- 💀6 Rambling Elf ("Out of Control")
- 💀7 Muttering Elf ("Out of Control")
- 💀8 Apostate Mage ("Out of Control")

The Blight Orphans?

Type: Donation

Start: Blight Orphans' Notice Board

Destination: Crown and Lion Inn

Task: Donate 50 silvers to the Blight Orphans

Quest Tips: A small sign inside the door to the Crown and Lion asks for help for the destitute orphans left in the streets from the last Blight. Donate 50 silvers to the collection box to complete the quest.

XP Reward: 100 XP

Money Reward: None

Item Reward: None

The Blight Orphans (Again)

Type: Donation

Start: Blight Orphans' Notice Board

Destination: Crown and Lion Inn

Task: Donate once again to the Blight Orphans

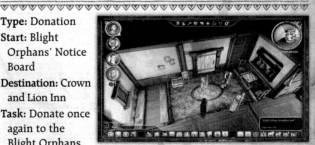

Quest Tips: You can't gain this quest until you complete "The Blight Orphans?" quest. Accept the quest from the Blight Orphans' Notice Board. Go to the bartender in the inn and buy the bottle of Antivan brandy. Interact with the orphan's donation box to donate the brandy and two sovereigns. You claim a small XP reward and work toward completing more orphan quests.

XP Reward: 200 XP

Money Reward: None

Item Reward: None

primagames.com

THE CROWN AND LION

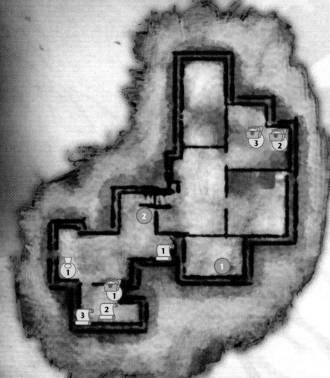

Legend

1. Blight Orphans Notice Board (Includes the following quests: "The Blight Orphans?," "The Blight Orphans (Again)," "Moonshine for the Children," "The Sermons of Justinia II," "Those Sweet Orphans," "A Present for Melisse," "The Scavenger Hunt," and "Making Amends")
1. Nida
2. Dwarven Bartender
1. Note Fragment ("Till Death Do Us Part")
2. Oil ("Heart of the Forest")
3. Kitchen Knife ("A Present for Melisse")
1. Crate (Mackay's Epic Single Malt gift)
2. Pile of Books
3. Chest (Engraved Silver Bowl gift)

Legend

1. Chest (locked)
2. Books (Blank Journal gift)
3. Chest
4. Armoire
5. Bookcase (Pilgrims and Amaranthine codex)
6. Lost and Found (Knitted Scarf gift)
1. Ser Rylien
2. Revered Mother
3. Aura
1. "Till Death Do Us Part"
1. Records ("The Long-Buried Past")
2. The Sermons of Justinia II
3. Mother Leanna's Bed ("Those Sweet Orphans")
4. Flowers ("Making Amends")

CHANTRY OF OUR LADY REDEEMER

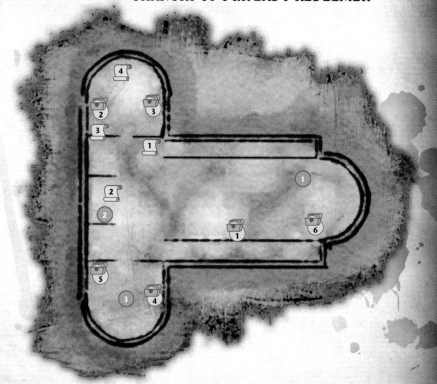

City of Amaranthine

Basics ~ Classes ~ The Party ~ Companions ~ Supporting Cast ~ Equipment ~ Bestiary ~ Walkthrough ~ **Side Quests** ~ Random Encounters ~ Achievements/Trophies

The Dark Wolf

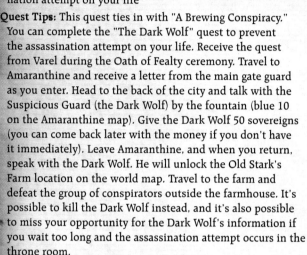

Type: Exploration

Start: Varel in Vigil's Keep Throne Room

Destination: Amaranthine

Task: Ask the Dark Wolf's help to stop an assassination attempt on your life

Quest Tips: This quest ties in with "A Brewing Conspiracy." You can complete the "The Dark Wolf" quest to prevent the assassination attempt on your life. Receive the quest from Varel during the Oath of Fealty ceremony. Travel to Amaranthine and receive a letter from the main gate guard as you enter. Head to the back of the city and talk with the Suspicious Guard (the Dark Wolf) by the fountain (blue 10 on the Amaranthine map). Give the Dark Wolf 50 sovereigns (you can come back later with the money if you don't have it immediately). Leave Amaranthine, and when you return, speak with the Dark Wolf. He will unlock the Old Stark's Farm location on the world map. Travel to the farm and defeat the group of conspirators outside the farmhouse. It's possible to kill the Dark Wolf instead, and it's also possible to miss your opportunity for the Dark Wolf's information if you wait too long and the assassination attempt occurs in the throne room.

XP Reward: 1,000 XP

Money Reward: None

Item Reward: None

A Donation of Injury Kits

Type: Donation

Start: Chanter's Board

Destination: Amaranthine Chantry

Task: Donate five injury kits to the Chantry

Quest Tips: Pick up the quest from the board in front of the Chantry. Donate five injury kits from your inventory to help out the Chantry's relief efforts. If you don't have them on you, head to the Market District and pick up additional ones. Report to the chanter outside the Chantry for your XP reward.

XP Reward: 1,000 XP

Money Reward: None

Item Reward: None

A Donation of Poultices

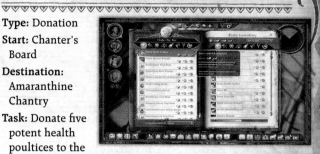

Type: Donation

Start: Chanter's Board

Destination: Amaranthine Chantry

Task: Donate five potent health poultices to the Chantry

Quest Tips: This quest becomes available after you complete "A Donation of Injury Kits." Pick up the quest from the board in front of the Chantry. Donate five potent health poultices from your inventory to help out the Chantry's relief efforts. If you don't have them on you, head to the dwarven bartender in the Crown and Lion Inn to pick up additional ones. Report to the chanter outside the Chantry for your XP reward.

XP Reward: 2,000 XP

Money Reward: None

Item Reward: None

Keep Out of Reach of Children

Type: Collection

Start: Merchants' Guild Board

Destination: Amaranthine

Task: Collect the poison bottles around the city and get them off the street

Quest Tips: The merchants want Antivan poison out of Amaranthine so no one gets hurts (and their profits don't suffer, of course). After you receive the quest from the Merchants' Guild Board, search around the city for the poison bottles in the Market District and on wayward tables (scrolls 6–9 on the Amaranthine map). Once you have them all, return to Kendrick for your XP reward.

XP Reward: 1,000 XP

Money Reward: None

Item Reward: None

primagames.com

Law and Order

◆ NOTE ◆

When you first enter the city of Amaranthine, you have to make a choice: aid the smugglers against the city guards for greater monetary reward or help the city guard against the smugglers to keep the peace. Choosing one side over the other affects certain side quests that you can gain, and companions' approval ratings will rise or fall based on your choice. "Law and Order" is the quest if you side with the guards.

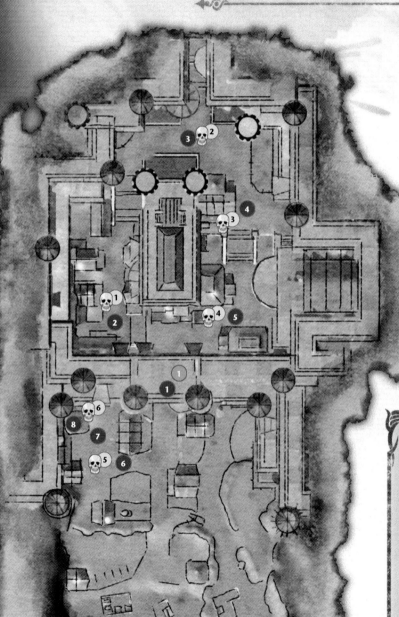

"Law and Order"
❦ Legend ❧

💀 **1** Hired Goon Leader & Hired Goons

💀 **2** Hired Goon Leader & Hired Goons

💀 **3** Hired Goon Leader & Hired Goons

💀 **4** Hired Goon Leader & Hired Goons

💀 **5** Hired Goon Leader & Hired Goons

💀 **6** Shady Character & Smugglers

1 Constable Aidan

Runthrough (Law and Order)

Summary: Side with the city guard and slay the smugglers.

1 Speak with Constable Aidan.

2 Interrogate the Suspicious Character in the market.

3 Follow the Suspicious Character and defeat his hired goons.

4 Follow the Suspicious Character and defeat his hired goons.

5 Follow the Suspicious Character and defeat his hired goons.

6 Follow the Suspicious Character and defeat his hired goons.

7 Defeat the Shady Character and gain the Smuggler's Key.

8 Enter Smuggler's Cove and slay the Smuggler Leader.

City of Amaranthine

Basics ~ Classes ~ The Party ~ Companions ~ Supporting Cast ~ Equipment ~ Bestiary ~ Walkthrough ~ **Side Quests** ~ Random Encounters ~ Achievements/Trophies

Law and Order Cheatsheet

Side Quest
- Law and Order

Important NPCs
- Constable Aidan

Key Items
- Locksmith's Tools
- Smuggler's Key
- Toy Chariot

Monsters
- Hired Goon Leaders
- Hired Goons
- Shady Character
- Smuggler Leader
- Smugglers
- Suspicious Character

Side Quests
- None

1 Upon entering the city, walk straight to the main gate and speak with Constable Aidan. He explains that the local smugglers have begun to plunder the already poor city, and the city guard wants to put a stop to their greed. If you offer to help the city guard, you gain the "Law and Order" quest.

2 Check the market area for a Suspicious Character. Travel to the northwest and interrogate the Suspicious Character in the market. He won't crack, but instead calls in some hired goons. While he flees, you must deal with the incoming enemy group. As with all the hired goon fights, concentrate your initial barrage on the hired goon leader. The leaders have more firepower, because they're mages, and you don't want a Group Heal going off. Once you finish off the goons, continue on the trail of the Suspicious Character.

3 Run to the north part of the city, near the back gate, and you'll see the next group of hired goons defending the Suspicious Character. Wipe out the hired goons and continue.

4 Round the guardhouse and attack the next group before the stairs. You may plow through the hired goons and their leader, but the Suspicious Character escapes yet again.

5 Repeat your attack pattern on the next group. After the Suspicious Character leaves, follow him to the final confrontation.

6 Battle the hired goons to get at the Suspicious Character. After you drop the last goon, the Suspicious Character flees one last time into the nearby house. You've now located the smuggler's secret entrance. Report back to Constable Aidan. He gives you the go-ahead to return to the secret entrance and look for a key.

7 Approach the Shady Character outside the smugglers' secret entrance. He immediately attacks, and two smugglers join him. Pound them in melee and grab the key from the Shady Character's corpse. Use the key on the trapdoor in the house behind him, and you're in the Smuggler's Cove.

primagames.com

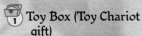

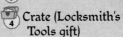
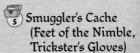
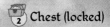

Smuggler's Cove

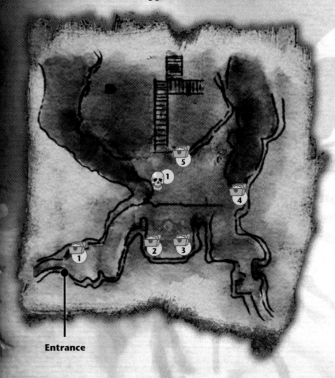

Entrance

Legend

- 1 Smuggler Leader & Smugglers
- 1 Toy Box (Toy Chariot gift)
- 2 Chest (locked)
- 3 Pile of Books
- 4 Crate (Locksmith's Tools gift)
- 5 Smuggler's Cache (Feet of the Nimble, Trickster's Gloves)

8 Approach the Smuggler Leader and his two smuggler bodyguards near the docks in Smuggler's Cove. They draw weapons and melee begins. Send the tank on the Smuggler Leader, who hits hard and has lots of health. The healer should keep single-target heals on the tank and launch a Group Heal if the other party members need help. The two other party members need to take down the smugglers as quickly as possible to help out with the Smuggler Leader.

When the Smuggler Leader finally drops to the sand, you've ended the smuggler threat. Loot the area for the many items, including the Gloves of Guile on the Smuggler Leader, and return to Constable Aidan. He thanks you for your efforts and gives you 10 sovereigns.

Making Amends

Type: Exploration
Start: Blight Orphans' Notice Board
Destination: Amaranthine
Task: Try to make up to Melisse by placing flowers on her doorstep

Quest Tips: You must accomplish all the other Blight Orphan quests before you can attempt "Making Amends." Accept the quest from the Blight Orphans' Notice Board inside the Crown and Lion. Hoping that Melisse will forgive them for their previous prank, the orphans ask you to place flowers on her doorstep. Steal the flowers out of the revered mother's room in the Chantry (see map for exact location) then place them at Melisse's house (scroll 16 on the Amaranthine map). Your quests with the Blight Orphans come to an end with a little XP reward.

XP Reward: 500 XP
Money Reward: None
Item Reward: None

Moonshine for the Children

Type: Exploration
Start: Blight Orphans' Notice Board
Destination: Hubert's Den
Task: Retrieve moonshine for the Blight Orphans from Hubert's Den

Quest Tips: You must complete "The Blight Orphans?" to gain access to this quest. Accept the quest from the Blight Orphans' Notice Board in the Crown and Lion Inn. Go to the Market District and find the new Hubert's Den location (see Amaranthine map). Enter and defeat the moonshiners inside; it won't be difficult with your fully armed party. Retrieve the moonshine and other loot from the den. Return to the orphans' donation box and drop in the moonshine to earn your small XP reward.

XP Reward: 500 XP
Money Reward: None
Item Reward: None

City of Amaranthine

Basics ~ Classes ~ The Party ~ Companions ~ Supporting Cast ~ Equipment ~ Bestiary ~ Walkthrough ~ **Side Quests** ~ Random Encounters ~ Achievements/Trophies

Out of Control

Type: Combat

Start: Chanter's Board

Destination: Amaranthine

Task: Slay the three apostate mages and their leader

Quest Tips: Once you pick up the quest from the Chanter's Board, go into the Chantry and speak with Ser Rylien. She will ask you to hunt down three apostate mages in the city. Find them wandering around the city (skulls 5–7 on the Amaranthine map). After you defeat each of the lesser mages, their leader will spawn in the back alley behind the market (skull 8 on the Amaranthine map). Slay the final mage and return to the chanter outside the Chantry for your reward.

XP Reward: 1,000 XP

Money Reward: 20 sovereigns

Item Reward: None

A Present for Melisse

Type: Exploration

Start: Blight Orphans' Notice Board

Destination: Amaranthine

Task: Plant a scarecrow in front of Melisse's house to scare her

Quest Tips: You can't access this quest unless you have completed the "Those Sweet Orphans" quest. Accept the quest from the notice board in the Crown and Lion and pick up the knife in the inn's kitchen (see Crown and Lion map for exact location). Exit the Crown and Lion and leave the city via the main gate. Look for the scarecrow in the garden to your right. With knife and scarecrow in your inventory, return to the city and plant both in the soft ground (scroll 15 on the Amaranthine map) in front of Melisse's house. The Blight Orphans will be happy with their prank and give you a small XP reward.

XP Reward: 500 XP

Money Reward: None

Item Reward: None

Preying on the Weak

Type: Combat

Start: Chanter's Board

Destination: Amaranthine

Task: Kill four groups of thugs that terrorize the villagers

Quest Tips: Accept the quest from the Chanter's Board and leave the city via the main gate. Four groups of thugs will spawn (skulls 1–4 on the Amaranthine map). Hunt each of these groups down and prevent them from harassing the local villagers any longer. Return to the chanter for your XP and monetary rewards.

XP Reward: 1,000 XP

Money Reward: 12 sovereigns

Item Reward: None

Rumblings from Beneath

Type: Combat

Start: Merchants' Guild Board

Destination: Smuggler's Cove

Task: Slay darkspawn in Smuggler's Cove

Quest Tips:
This quest is available only if you aided the smugglers and completed "Smuggler's Run" when you first entered Amaranthine. Accept the quest from the Merchants' Guild Board and enter the Crown and Lion Inn. Find the trapdoor in the back storage room and use the hatch to enter Smuggler's Cove. Kill the darkspawn that are making all the noise, and return to Kendrick for your XP and monetary rewards.

XP Reward: 1,000 XP

Money Reward: 6 sovereigns

Item Reward: None

primagames.com

The Scavenger Hunt

Type: Collection

Start: Blight Orphans' Notice Board

Destination: Amaranthine

Task: Retrieve five items scattered about the city

Quest Tips: You must complete "Those Sweet Orphans" before you can accept this quest. Once you have the quest, exit the Crown and Lion and search around the city for the hidden objects (scrolls 4, 5, 10, 12, and 13 on the Amaranthine map). With pitchfork, pie, sole shoes, doll, and hammer in your inventory, deposit them all in the orphans' donation box for your XP reward.

XP Reward: 500 XP

Money Reward: None

Item Reward: None

The Sermons of Justinia II

Type: Collection

Start: Blight Orphans' Notice Board

Destination: The Chantry

Task: Retrieve the revered mother's book for the Blight Orphans

Quest Tips: You must complete "The Blight Orphans?" to access this quest. Accept the quest from the notice board and head to the Chantry. You'll spot the revered mother's book on the altar directly in front of you down the long aisle. Take the book and place it in the orphans' donation box back at the Crown and Lion.

XP Reward: 500 XP

Money Reward: None

Item Reward: None

Smuggler's Run

~ See map on next page ~

NOTE

When you first enter the city of Amaranthine, you have to make a choice: aid the smugglers against the city guards for greater monetary reward or help the city guard against the smugglers to keep the peace. Choosing one side over the other affects certain side quests that you can gain, and companions' approval ratings will rise or fall based on your choice. "Smuggler's Run" is the quest if you side with the smugglers.

Runthrough (Smuggler's Cove)

Summary: Side with the smugglers and slay the city lieutenant.

1. Speak with the Shady Character.
2. Enter the Crown and Lion and convince the bartender to open the trapdoor to Smuggler's Cove.
3. Kill the thieves in Smuggler's Cove.
4. Climb up to the battlements.
5. Cut down the first city guard group.
6. Cut down the second city guard group and gain the Guardhouse Key.
7. Go to the guardhouse.
8. Slay the lieutenant and his men.
9. Rescue the archer Jacen.

Smuggler's Run Cheatsheet

Side Quest
- Smuggler's Cove

Important NPCs
- Jacen
- Shady Character
- Smuggler Leader

Key Items
- Cell Key
- Guardhouse Key

- Locksmith's Tools
- Toy Chariot

Monsters
- City Guards
- Lieutenant
- Sergeants
- Thieves

Side Quests
- None

City of Amaranthine

Basics ~ Classes ~ The Party ~ Companions ~ Supporting Cast ~ Equipment ~ Bestiary ~ Walkthrough ~ **Side Quests** ~ Random Encounters ~ Achievements/Trophies

"Smuggler's Run"

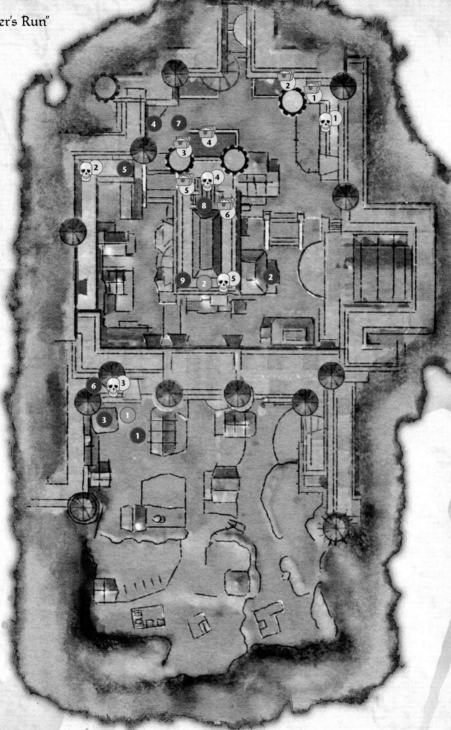

Legend

- 1 Sergeant & City Guards
- 2 Sergeant & City Guards
- 3 Sergeant & City Guards
- 4 Lieutenant & City Guards
- 5 City Guard
- 1 Wooden Crate
- 2 Wooden Crate
- 3 Chest (locked)
- 4 Chest
- 5 Chest
- 6 Chest (locked)
- 1 Shady Character
- 2 Jacen

1. When you first enter the city, you spot the Shady Character near the entrance. He mentions that he has a proposal for you and then bolts for the western section of town (before you enter the main gates). Speak with him outside the house by the refugee. So long as you are willing to get your hands dirty and work against the city guard, he offers you the "Smuggler's Run" side quest.

2. The Shady Character sends you to the Crown and Lion to speak with the dwarven bartender. He needs persuasion to open the trapdoor to Smuggler's Cove, whether it be a 1 sovereign bribe, a high Coercion check, or a high Intimidate check. Once he opens the way to the Smuggler's Cove, report back to the Shady Character.

3. After paying you 10 sovereigns, the Shady Character asks you to clear out the thieves who are stealing from the smugglers in Smuggler's Cove. Rather than go back to the Crown and Lion, use the new trapdoor entrance to Smuggler's Cove in the house behind the Shady Character.

Prepare for battle as soon as you enter Smuggler's Cove. A few feet in, you spot two groups of thieves milling about the beach. A third set of thieves appears in the midst of your party as soon as you approach (see map for the thieves' locations). Don't let them backstab you. Deal with the thieves in your midst before engaging the others fully. Send the tank to keep the beach enemies off you as you slay the backstabbing thieves. As soon as you've killed the last thief, the smugglers pour in to claim the spot. Speak with the Smuggler Leader for a 15 sovereign reward and your next task.

Smuggler's Cove

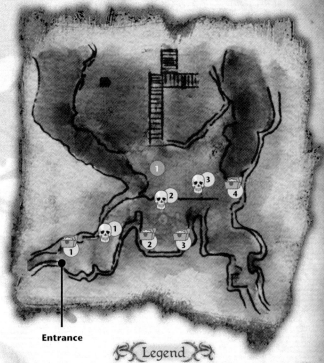

Entrance

Legend

💀¹ Thieves	📦² Chest (locked)
💀² Thieves	📚³ Pile of Books
💀³ Thieves	📦⁴ Crate (Locksmith's Tools gift)
📦¹ Toy Box (Toy Chariot gift)	⓵ Smuggler Leader

4. The Smuggler Leader asks you to kill the city lieutenant, who has been sniffing around the smugglers' business too much

for his own good. Cross to the northwest battlement entrance and ascend to the top walls.

5. Battle (or evade) the first sergeant and his surrounding city guards. You need the Guardhouse Key to go after the lieutenant, but

you won't find it on this bunch.

6 Continue to the second sergeant surrounded by his men. Slay the sergeant and take the Guardhouse Key.

8 On the battlement above, the lieutenant and half a dozen city guards survey the city. He'll ask what you're doing up on the battlement. The time for dialogue is over; attack while you have the surprise opportunity. Once you kill the lieutenant, the quest is complete. Head back to the Smuggler Leader for your 20 sovereign reward.

7 Return to the north section and open the guardhouse door with your new key. You can pick up extra loot from the two chests outside the guardhouse door.

9 Loot the Cell Key from the lieutenant's body and free the elf archer Jacen from his cage. A single city guard watches over the cage; take him down quickly so you can speak to Jacen in peace. The elf will be grateful, and if you invite him to serve at Vigil's Keep, Jacen will add his excellent bow skills to the battle during the "Siege of Vigil's Keep" later in the game.

Those Sweet Orphans

Type: Exploration
Start: Blight Orphans' Notice Board
Destination: The Chantry
Task: Plant herbs in the revered mother's bed

Quest Tips: You can't access this quest until you complete the four quests before it: "The Blight Orphans?," "The Blight Orphans (Again)," "Moonshine for the Children," and "The Sermons of Justinia II." Accept the quest from the Blight Orphans' Notice Board and pick up the pouch of herbs next to the donation box. Head to the Chantry and use the herbs in the revered mother's bed (see Chantry map for the bed's exact location).

XP Reward: 500 XP

Money Reward: None

Item Reward: None

Till Death Do Us Part

Type: Exploration
Start: Alma in the Chantry
Destination: Amaranthine
Task: Look for clue's to Alma's husband's disappearance

Quest Tips: Enter the Chantry and speak with Alma. She sends you to find her missing husband, with the first stop the Crown and Lion Inn. Search the inn for the tattered note (see the Crown and Lion map), which leads you to the city battlements (scroll 3 on the Amaranthine map). The note fragment on the battlements leads you to a house on the outskirts of the city (scroll 11 on Amaranthine map). Alma's husband, Karrem, has hung himself, unable to cope with the burdens of family life. Search the corpse for a final note, and return to Alma to give her the sad news.

XP Reward: 1,000 XP

Money Reward: None

Item Reward: None

primagames.com

Spoiler Alert

Companions

NOTE

Most companions have an associated Joining quest. These quests complete automatically the next time you talk to Varel in the Vigil's Keep throne room after the companion has agreed to join you.

Vigil's Keep Throne Room

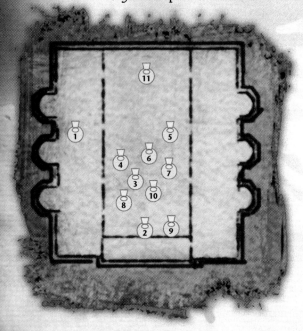

Legend

1. "A Brewing Conspiracy"
2. "A Day in Court"
3. "Defending the Land"
4. "Desertion in the Ranks"
5. "Drunk and Disorderly"
6. "Sheepherder's Lament"
7. "Solomon's Bridge"
8. "The Fate of the Ox"
9. "Trade Must Flow"
10. "Oaths of Fealty"
11. "And You, Esmerelle?"

XP Reward: 500 XP + approval bump
Money Reward: None
Item Reward: None

Freedom for Anders

Type: Combat
Start: Namaya in Amaranthine
Destination: Warehouse in Amaranthine
Task: Help Anders find his phylactery

Quest Tips: Enter Amaranthine with Anders in your party. In the back of the city, near the Dark Wolf, locate a past cohort of Anders, Namaya (see exclamation point 4 on the Amaranthine map). She tells Anders that he can find his phylactery in the Amaranthine warehouse across the city. Accompany Anders to the warehouse and search for lots of loot inside. You'll also find a group of templars, led by Ser Rylock, who will fight you for Anders. It's a trap; the phylactery was never in play. You can either give Anders over to the templars, where you will lose him from the party forever, or you can battle the templars by Anders's side. Anders will appreciate this gesture and his approval rating will bump up sizably.

The Howe Family

Type: Exploration
Start: Samuel in Vigil's Keep Courtyard
Destination: Delilah in Amaranthine
Task: Seek out Nathaniel's sister in Amaranthine

Quest Tips: After conscripting Nathaniel to your party after "The Prisoner" quest in the "Assault on Vigil's Keep" introduction, visit the eastern section of the Vigil's Keep courtyard and you'll run into Samuel. The groundskeeper informs Nathaniel that his sister is alive and married to a shopkeeper in Amaranthine. With Nathaniel in your party, head to the Amaranthine Market District where you'll find Delilah (see the Amaranthine map). Brother and sister have a good conversation, and after their talk, Nathaniel will begin to open up and become friendly with you. If your relationship with Nathaniel is warm, a final conversation with him in the throne room will complete this side quest.

XP Reward: 500 XP + approval bump
Money Reward: None
Item Reward: None

Companions

Basics ~ Classes ~ The Party ~ Companions ~ Supporting Cast ~ Equipment ~ Bestiary ~ Walkthrough ~ **Side Quests** ~ Random Encounters ~ Achievements/Trophies

Justice for Kristoff

Type: Exploration

Start: Vigil's Keep Courtyard

Destination: Aura in the Amaranthine Chantry

Task: Make amends with Kristoff's wife, Aura

Quest Tips: After you return with Justice from the "Shadows of the Blackmarsh" quest, Kristoff's wife, Aura, meets you in the Vigil's Keep courtyard. Needless to say she's shocked at seeing a spirit in her dead husband's body. She flees to the chantry in Amaranthine. With Justice in your party, enter the Amaranthine chantry later and let Justice speak to Aura. They come to an agreement that lessens the pain for both.

XP Reward: 500 XP + approval bump

Money Reward: None

Item Reward: None

Sigrun's Roguish Past

Type: Exploration

Start: Amaranthine

Destination: The Crown and Lion

Task: Let Sigrun make amends with a merchant

Quest Tips: With Sigrun in your party, the party will bump into the merchant Mischa in Amaranthine who recognizes Sigrun and accuses her of betraying their friendship. Later, if you get your approval high enough, Sigrun will ask if you can go back to find Mischa at the Crown and Lion Inn. Sigrun offers Mischa her ring, or money, and satisfies the merchant. She feels better about her past mistake and will now be eligible for friendly status.

XP Reward: 500 XP + approval bump

Money Reward: None

Item Reward: None

Oghren the Family Man

Type: Exploration

Start: Vigil's Keep Throne Room

Destination: Vigil's Keep Throne Room

Task: Listen to Oghren and Felsi's conversation

Quest Tips: In the Vigil's Keep throne room, Oghren's wife, Felsi, will eventually arrive to confront Oghren about his duties as a husband and father. She's upset that he's not taking care of her and their child, but Oghren explains he's a Grey Warden now and never wanted to settle down in the first place. No matter what you do or say, Felsi will leave unhappy and Oghren will be eligible for friendly status. If your relationship with Oghren is warm, a final conversation with him in the throne room will complete this side quest.

XP Reward: 500 XP + approval bump

Money Reward: None

Item Reward: None

Velanna's Exile

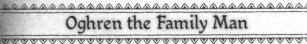

Type: Exploration

Start: Random Encounter

Destination: Random Encounter

Task: Listen to a conversation between Velanna and her past tribemates

Quest Tips: With Velanna in your party, you may come across this random encounter with Velanna's past tribe. You learn that Velanna was cast out of her clan because of her fanatical hatred of humans. Later she may confide in you about what happened and become eligible for friendly status. If your relationship with Velanna is warm, a final conversation with her in the throne room will complete this side quest.

XP Reward: 500 XP + approval bump

Money Reward: None

Item Reward: None

Knotwood Hills/Kal'Hirol

Knotwood Hills

Trade Quarter (Kal'Hirol)

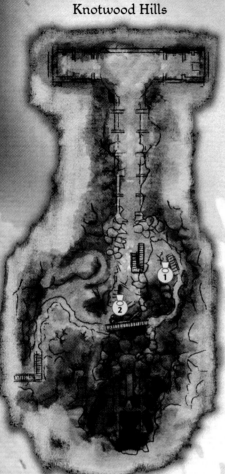

Legend

1️⃣ "Wrong Place, Wrong Time"

2️⃣ "Memories of the Stone"

1️⃣ Lyrium Sand ("Bombs Away!")

2️⃣ Iron Ore ("Elemental Requirements")

Legend

1️⃣ Inferno Golem Shell ("Golem's Might")

Main Hall

Legend

1️⃣ "The Long-Buried Past"

2️⃣ "Lucky Charms"

Legend

1️⃣ Lyrium Sand ("Bombs Away!")

Lower Reaches (Kal'Hirol)

Knotwood Hills/Kal'Hirol

Basics ~ Classes ~ The Party ~ Companions ~ Supporting Cast ~ Equipment ~ Bestiary ~ Walkthrough ~ **Side Quests** ~ Random Encounters ~ Achievements/Trophies

The Long-Buried Past

Type: Exploration

Start: Knotwood Hills

Destination: Amaranthine

Task: Go on a short treasure hunt after discovering a mysterious journal

Quest Tips: Find the treasure hunter's journal in the chest in the Knotwood Hills (see Knotwood Hills map). Return to the Amaranthine Chantry and examine the bookshelf on the right side of the main room. Exit the Chantry and find the packed earth next to a house outside Amaranthine (scroll 1 on the Amaranthine map) and retrieve the magic ring reward.

XP Reward: 1,500 XP

Money Reward: None

Item Reward: Ring of Subtlety

Lucky Charms

Type: Exploration

Start: Knotwood Hills

Destination: Colbert in Amaranthine

Task: Return the lucky deer's foot to Colbert and Micah

Quest Tips: Pick up the lucky deer's foot from a bag in the side area opposite the Deep Road entrance in the Knotwood Hills (see map for exact location). Return to Amaranthine and seek out Colbert and Micah for your XP reward.

XP Reward: 500 XP

Money Reward: None

Item Reward: None

Memories of the Stone

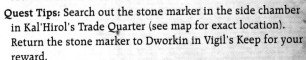

Type: Exploration

Start: Trade Quarter in Kal'Hirol

Destination: Dworkin in Vigil's Keep

Task: Return a stone marker found in Kal'Hirol to Dworkin

Quest Tips: Search out the stone marker in the side chamber in Kal'Hirol's Trade Quarter (see map for exact location). Return the stone marker to Dworkin in Vigil's Keep for your reward.

XP Reward: 1,000 XP

Money Reward: None

Item Reward: None

Wrong Place, Wrong Time

Type: Exploration

Start: Trade Quarter in Kal'Hirol

Destination: Steafan in Amaranthine

Task: Free or kill Steafan

Quest Tips: During your travels through Kal'Hirol's Trade Quarter you come across a caged man, Steafan, who may or may not have been infected with the darkspawn disease (see the Trade Quarter map for Steafan's exact location). Steafan is not infected, but you still have three choices on what to do with him. If you free Steafan and allow him to leave, you can find him again in Amaranthine outside the main gate and he'll give you a monetary reward. You can delay releasing Steafan and grill him some more until he agrees to give you a powerful flame rune in exchange for freedom. Finally, you can kick his cage into the lava if you're feeling particularly evil.

XP Reward: 1,000 XP

Money Reward: 1 sovereign (if you didn't ask for a reward up front)

Item Reward: Masterpiece Flame Rune (if you asked for a reward up front)

primagames.com

Spoiler Alert

Vigil's Keep

Vigil's Keep Throne Room

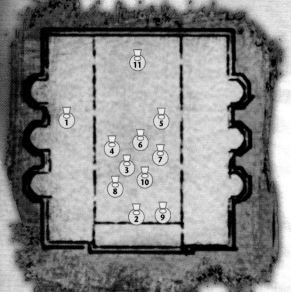

Legend

1. "A Brewing Conspiracy"
2. "A Day in Court"
3. "Defending the Land"
4. "Desertion in the Ranks"
5. "Drunk and Disorderly"
6. "Sheepherder's Lament"
7. "Solomon's Bridge"
8. "The Fate of the Ox"
9. "Trade Must Flow"
10. "Oaths of Fealty"
11. "And You, Esmerelle?"

Vigil's Keep Courtyard

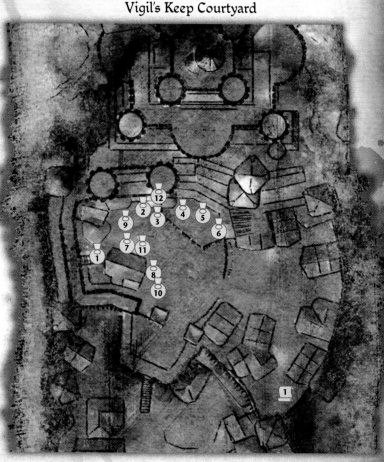

Legend

1. "A Medical Necessity"
2. "A Daughter Ransomed"
3. "Far Afield"
4. "Bombs Away!"
5. "Elemental Requirements"
6. "A Master's Work"
7. "It Comes from Beneath"
8. "Cost of Doing Business"
9. "Peasant Revolution"
10. "What Is Built Endures"
11. "Sealing the Great Barrier Doors"
12. "Salvage Operation"

1. Medical Supplies ("A Medical Necessity")

Vigil's Keep

Basics ~ Classes ~ The Party ~ Companions ~ Supporting Cast ~ Equipment ~ Bestiary ~ Walkthrough ~ **Side Quests** ~ Random Encounters ~ Achievements/Trophies

Adria's Plight

Type: Combat

Start: Mabari in Vigil's Keep Basement

Destination: Vigil's Keep Basement

Task: Find the lost soul Adria, then put her out of her misery

Quest Tips: Shortly into the first level of the Vigil's Keep basement ("It Comes from Beneath" side quest), you'll find a dying Mabari war hound surrounded by slain darkspawn. The valiant dog won't make it, but has a scroll from its mistress, Adria, tied around its neck. If you succeed at a Survival check, you can find out the dog's name and earn some extra XP. The dog's scroll gives you the "Adria's Plight" quest, and you can find Adria at the very end of the first basement level, just before the collapsed tunnel. Sadly, by the time you reach Adria, it's too late; she's turned into a ghoul, and you have no choice but to finish off her and the other ghouls.

XP Reward: 1,000 XP

Money Reward: None

Item Reward: None

And You, Esmerelle?

Type: Combat

Start: Vigil's Keep Throne Room

Destination: Vigil's Keep Throne Room

Task: Survive the conspiracy's assassination attempt

Quest Tips: You fight against any of the conspiracy members who haven't been rooted out yet, including Bann Esmerelle, Ser Temmerly the Ox, Ser Timothy, and a deadly Crow Assassin. For the first half of the battle, keep the healing flowing. You'll need to withstand the initial barrage from being surrounded by a handful of powerful enemies, at least until you can start reducing the numbers against you. Watch out for the Crow Assassin, who can score nasty critical damage from behind you. Keep on the move and stun the assassin when he materializes. Stick your tank on Ser Temmerly (if he wasn't executed earlier in "The Fate of the Ox" quest) to keep the big foe occupied. Pick off Ser Timothy and the other lesser foes first until you turn the tide in the damage department.

XP Reward: 4,000 XP

Money Reward: None

Item Reward: None

Bombs Away!

Type: Exploration

Start: Dworkin in Vigil's Keep Courtyard

Destinations: Kal'Hirol, Silverite Mine, Vigil's Keep Basement

Task: Retrieve lyrium sand for Dworkin's explosive concoctions

Quest Tips: You witness Dworkin's explosives at work early on in the fight against the darkspawn in the Inner Keep. Now you get to pocket some of those explosives yourself if you can bring back lyrium sand to the dwarf. You can find the lyrium sand in three separate locations: Kal'Hirol, Silverite Mine, and Vigil's Keep basement (see corresponding walkthrough maps in previous chapter for exact placements of lyrium sand). If you collect some lyrium sand without speaking to Dworkin first, the quest still activates, and he will accept it from you. When you give him sand, Dworkin asks you to choose what type of explosive you want: safe, pretty cool, and pure awesome. Safe makes a small boom, but won't kill you in the process. Choose "pure awesome" for high risk and high reward bangs.

XP Reward: 1,500 XP

Money Reward: None

Item Reward: Dworkin's Explosives

A Brewing Conspiracy

Type: Combat

Start: Anders or Ser Tamra in the Vigil's Keep Throne Room

Destinations: Amaranthine and Old Stark's Farm

Task: Foil an assassination plot against your life and authority

Quest Tips: A number of lords and ladies of the court are still loyal to the old ways of Arl Howe and plot to eliminate you as Warden-Commander. During your initial meeting with the nobles at court, if you give a persuasive speech, Ser Tamra will approach you with knowledge about the conspiracy. If you don't choose the persuasion option, Anders will come to you with the same information. Once you hear the information, speak with Varel. You have three options: seek to stop it by taking hostages to ensure good behavior, seek to stop it by seeking out the Dark Wolf in Amaranthine, or allow it to occur. If you take hostages, the nobles won't be too happy, but the conspiracy ends. If you choose to seek out the Dark Wolf, head to Amaranthine and look for a suspicious guard in the northern section of the city (see "The Dark Wolf" quest in the City of Amaranthine section of this chapter).

primagames.com

You can thwart the conspiracy if you complete "The Dark Wolf" quest. If you choose to ignore the conspiracy, the assassination attempt will trigger when you return to the throne room following "The Peasant Revolution" quest. See the "And You, Esmerelle?" quest for details on the fight.

XP Reward: None

Money Reward: None

Item Reward: None

Cost of Doing Business

Type: Exploration

Start: Voldrik in Vigil's Keep Courtyard

Destination: Vigil's Keep Courtyard

Task: Upgrade the walls on Vigil's Keep

Quest Tips: The walls of Vigil's Keep are in serious need of repair and upgrade. The dwarf Voldrik can perform the task, but first he needs 80 sovereigns. If you can scrape that kind of coin together, return to Voldrik and pay him the sum. You'll now have a less damaged version of the keep and open up the "What Is Built Endures" quest.

TIP

If you fully upgrade the walls of Vigil's Keep through the "Cost of Doing Business" and "What Is Built Endures," you gain a nice bonus later in the game while defending the keep during "The Siege of Vigil's Keep" quest. Ogres will not be able to break through the walls and support the darkspawn horde during the siege.

XP Reward: 500 XP

Money Reward: None

Item Reward: Stronger Vigil's Keep walls

A Daughter Ransomed

Type: Combat

Start: Private in the Vigil's Keep Courtyard

Destination: Forlorn Cove

Task: Rescue a hostage from bandits in Forlorn Cove

Quest Tips: When you exit the Vigil's Keep throne room for the first time, the private at the gate hands you two letters, one of which is this quest. Ser Edgar Bensley's daughter, Eileen, has been seized by bandits demanding a handsome ransom. Once you accept the quest, the Forlorn Cove location opens up on your world map and you can go after Eileen. The bandit leader, Mosley the Snake, can't be trusted (as you might have guessed from his name). If you pay him the 30 sovereigns, they kill Eileen and then try to kill you. If you threaten them in any way, they kill the girl and come after you. You can try to intimidate the bandits, and if your skill is high enough, some of the bandits will flee in terror, and in the midst of their chaos, you can step in and fight for Eileen's life. If your Coercion skill is high enough, the safest method of retrieving Eileen is to ask to see the girl. They will send her over, and you can pay the 30 sovereigns to leave without a fight or slay them anyway.

XP Reward: 1,000 XP

Money Reward: 5 sovereigns if Eileen is dead, 10 sovereigns if you save Ser Edgar's daughter

Item Reward: None

A Day in Court

Type: Politics

Start: Varel in Vigil's Keep Throne Room

Destination: Vigil's Keep Throne Room

Task: Hold court and make a number of judicial decisions

Quest Tips: Several quests come your way during "A Day in Court." You can try each case yourself, or leave the decision in the hands of Seneschal Varel. The quests involved include "Sheepherder's Lament," "Solomon's Bridge," and "The Fate of the Ox." See the individual quest entries for the implications of your decisions.

XP Reward: 2,000 XP

Money Reward: None

Item Reward: None

Vigil's Keep

Basics ~ Classes ~ The Party ~ Companions ~ Supporting Cast ~ Equipment ~ Bestiary ~ Walkthrough ~ **Side Quests** ~ Random Encounters ~ Achievements/Trophies

Defending the Land

Type: Politics

Start: Vigil's Keep Throne Room

Destination: Vigil's Keep Throne Room

Task: Decide how best to allocate the keep's forces

Quest Tips: During the Oath of Fealty gathering by the nobles, two nobles bicker about the keep's troops. Lord Eddelbrek believes they should safeguard the farms and country folk; Bann Esmerelle insists the soldiers should protect the city. You must choose how best to allocate your forces.

Speak with Captain Garevel. If you choose the farms, the keep and surrounding lands gets better support. If you choose the city, Amaranthine will have better protection. If you choose the roads, trade will be protected as best as you can.

XP Reward: None

Money Reward: None

Item Reward: None

Desertion in the Ranks

Type: Politics

Start: Vigil's Keep Throne Room

Destination: Vigil's Keep Throne Room

Task: Rule on Danella's desertion

Quest Tips: This quest will appear only if Anders speaks to you about the conspiracy at court. The soldier Danella left her post to protect her family's farm from the darkspawn, and now she's brought up on charges. You can choose to execute Danella for desertion, which is the decision Varel would choose if you leave the case in his hands. However, this causes unrest in the ranks and there will be some soldiers in the peasant riot later. You can choose to put Danella in prison, and you'll be seen as a just and fair ruler, though there's a chance for more soldiers deserting during the siege.

XP Reward: 1,000 XP

Money Reward: None

Item Reward: None

Drunk and Disorderly

Type: Politics

Start: Vigil's Keep Throne Room

Destination: Vigil's Keep Throne Room

Task: Deal with an unruly noble

Quest Tips:

This quest appears only if you are Orlesian (started a new character for the expansion). Ser Guy loudly proclaims his dislike for Orlesians at the fealty ceremony and tries to goad you into some kind of response. You can ignore him, have him escorted out quietly, have him executed, or try to use your Coercion skill to change his mind. The Coercion approach works best if you have a high enough skill. Though it might be a bit heartless, you may want to execute him if you don't have the Coercion skills. If not executed or persuaded, Ser Guy will participate in the assassination attempt in the "A Brewing Conspiracy" quest.

XP Reward: 100 XP

Money Reward: None

Item Reward: None

Elemental Requirements

Type: Exploration

Start: Herren in Vigil's Keep Courtyard

Destinations: Kal'Hirol, Silverite Mine, Vigil's Keep Basement

Task: Retrieve exotic materials for Wade's smithing

Quest Tips: See Herren in the Vigil's Keep courtyard to start the quest. He guarantees that Master Wade will outfit the keep's soldiers with better armor if supplies of iron ore (Kal'Hirol), silverite ore (Silverite Mine), and veridium ore (Vigil's Keep basement) can be found. See individual walkthrough maps for exact ore deposit locations. Return each time you recover one of the special ores. If you can find all three, a special regiment of soldiers will be outfitted at the keep.

XP Reward: 1,000 XP per ore; 1,000 XP more for completing quest

Money Reward: None

Item Reward: Upgrade to Vigil's Keep soldiers' armor

Far Afield

Type: Combat

Start: Private in Vigil's Keep Courtyard

Destination: Turnoble Estate

Task: Revenge the fallen inhabitants of the estate

Quest Tips: When you exit the Vigil's Keep throne room for the first time, the private at the gate hands you two letters, one of which is this quest. The Turnoble Estate location opens up on the world map, and you can travel there anytime after leaving Vigil's Keep. Alas, you're too late—the darkspawn have already killed everyone on the estate. You won't have too many problems with the marauding genlocks and hurlocks, but watch for the charging ogre who wants nothing more than to mash two party members' heads together. Clear out the darkspawn as you dodge fire from the hurlock snipers and loot the dead bodies for your rewards.

XP Reward: 1,000 XP

Money Reward: 13 sovereigns (Goodwife Turnoble)

Item Reward: Chasind Arm bow, Diamond, Stormchaser Boots (templar)

The Fate of the Ox

Type: Politics

Start: Vigil's Keep Throne Room

Destination: Vigil's Keep Throne Room

Task: Choose to release, execute, or imprison Ser Temmerly

Quest Tips: If Ser Tamra is the one to come forth with allegations about "A Brewing Conspiracy" and you don't deal with it in some fashion—either taking hostages or seeking out the Dark Wolf—then this case will be brought to court. Ser Temmerly the Ox is accused of killing Ser Tamra, but the evidence is sparse. If you let Varel decide, he will release the Ox because there is not enough evidence to convict him. If released, the Ox will take part in the assassination attempt. If you imprison the Ox or execute him, he will not show up to assassinate you.

XP Reward: 1,000 XP

Money Reward: None

Item Reward: None

Golem's Might

Type: Exploration

Start: Inferno Golem in Kal'Hirol

Destination: Various Locations

Task: Find five items for Master Wade to custom build you unique armor

Quest Tips: When you defeat the inferno golem in the Lower Reaches of Kal'Hirol, you gain a golem shell. Return the shell to Master Wade in Vigil's Keep and he'll offer you this quest. He needs you to also collect wool padding (see Amaranthine map), a master lyrium potion (create with Herbalism or buy it from a vendor), pure iron (buy it from Wade's own shop), and a blood lotus (available around the world as a wild plant). Collect them all and he crafts the superb Golem Shell Armor for you.

XP Reward: 500 XP

Money Reward: None

Item Reward: Golem Shell Armor

Heart of the Forest

Type: Exploration

Start: The Old One in Wending Wood

Destination: Various Locations

Task: Find five items for Master Wade to custom build you a unique bow or shield

Quest Tips: When you defeat the Old One in the Wending Wood, you gain special heartwood. Return with the wood to Master Wade in Vigil's Keep and he offers you this quest. He needs you to collect oil (inside the kitchen in the Crown and Lion Inn), catgut (in the ruins of Blackmarsh; see map), a flawless ruby (buy it from a store or earn it as loot), and a grandmaster lightning rune (craft this yourself). Collect them all and he makes you either the Heartwood Bow or Heartwood Shield.

XP Reward: 500 XP

Money Reward: None

Item Reward: Heartwood Bow or Heartwood Shield

Vigil's Keep

Basics ~ Classes ~ The Party ~ Companions ~ Supporting Cast ~ Equipment ~ Bestiary ~ Walkthrough ~ **Side Quests** ~ Random Encounters ~ Achievements/Trophies

"It Comes from Beneath"

NOTE

After you leave the throne room following the events of "The Assault on Vigil's Keep," seek out Sergeant Maverlies in front of the Vigil's Keep basement door. She gives you this quest as the first part of the "clearing out darkspawn from beneath the keep" task. The second part is the quest "Sealing the Great Barrier Doors."

Vigil's Keep Basement

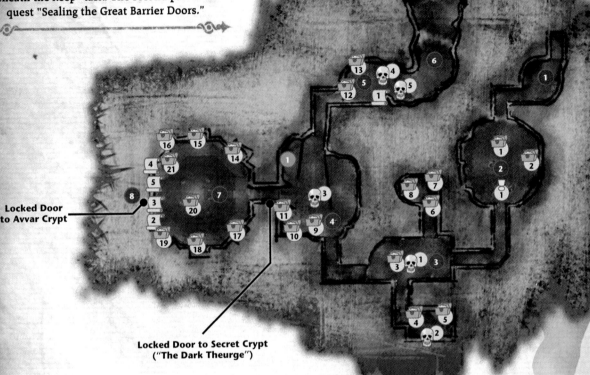

Locked Door to Avvar Crypt

Locked Door to Secret Crypt ("The Dark Theurge")

Legend

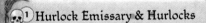

1. Hurlock Emissary & Hurlocks
2. Shriek Alpha & Shrieks
3. Prisoner Ghouls
4. Adria the Ghoul
5. Ravenous Ghouls
1. Darkspawn Corpses
2. Warrior Statue (The Great Strife codex)
3. Soldier Corpses
4. Book (The Avvars codex)
5. Book (The Howes of Amaranthine codex) & Shelves
6. Letter (Response from Rendon Howe codex)

7. Crate (West Hill Brandy gift)
8. Crates
9. Howe Correspondence (Delilah Howe's Letters gift)
10. Chest
11. Soldier Corpse
12. Letter (Letter to Rendon Howe codex)
13. Knight (Gold Earring gift)
14. Avvar Sarcophagus
15. Avvar Sarcophagus
16. Avvar Sarcophagus (Key of Kiveal)
17. Avvar Sarcophagus

18. Avvar Sarcophagus (Trickster's Cap)
19. Avvar Sarcophagus
20. Sack (Howe Bow)
21. Crypt Statue (The Great Strife codex)
1. Prisoners
1. "Adria's Plight"
1. Veridium Ore ("Elemental Requirements")
2. Keyhole–Haakon
3. Keyhole–The Lady
4. Keyhole–Korth
5. Keyhole–Kiveal

primagames.com

Runthrough (Vigil's Keep Basement)

Summary: Destroy the darkspawn in the keep's dungeon level.

1. Enter the Vigil's Keep basement.

2. Examine the Mabari war hound for the "Adria's Plight" side quest.

3. Combat the hurlock emissary and his hurlock friends.

4. Slay the prisoner ghouls before releasing the human prisoners.

5. Confront Adria and her ravenous ghouls.

6. Inform Maverlies and Voldrik that the way is currently blocked.

7. Enter the secret Avvar crypt (only available at the end of the Dark Theurge quests).

8. Defeat the Avvar war lords (only available at the end of the Dark Theurge quests).

Vigil's Keep Basement Cheatsheet

Side Quest
- It Comes from Beneath

Important NPCs
- Prisoners

Key Items
- Delilah Howe's Letters
- Gold Earring
- Howe Bow
- Key of Kiveal
- West Hill Brandy

Monsters
- Adria the Ghoul
- Hurlock Emissary
- Hurlocks
- Prisoner Ghouls
- Ravenous Ghouls
- Shriek Alpha
- Shrieks

Side Quests
- Adria's Plight
- Elemental Requirements

1 Speak with Maverlies outside Vigil's Keep's basement and she'll let you into the underground level and ask you to clean out all darkspawn. To complete the quest, you don't actually have to kill all the darkspawn. You only have to reach the end of the level, where the rocks have blocked the passage.

2 You enter the first room to the scene of a darkspawn massacre. A valiant Mabari war hound has slain many darkspawn before it was mortally wounded. Interact with the Mabari to receive the "Adria's Plight" side quest. See earlier in this section for the complete breakdown on the side quest.

3 Hurlocks infest the next room. Enter the chamber with ranged attacks firing. You can wound a few of the hurlocks before they reach you for melee, and if you have strong ranged attacks, you may even take down the deadlier hurlock emissary first. There's a lot of loot in the area; just be careful of the shrieks that pop up in the wine cellar to the south.

4 As you enter the prisoner area, ghouls rise up from the ground and defend their territory. The ghouls tend to swarm you, and with their superior numbers, it can prove difficult if you aren't careful. Don't let the ghouls flank you too much, and if they do, retreat to the entrance and battle them there for side protection. After the ghouls are sliced up, release the human prisoners to gain a small approval bump with several companions.

NOTE

A locked door in the west wall leads to the secret Avvar crypt. A rogue with lockpicking can open this door and collect the Howe Bow within, but you cannot pass the doors beyond that. You must complete the Dark Theurge quests during the "Sealing the Great Barrier Doors" side quest for the keys that allow entrance.

5 Peek around the corner to the north and you'll spy Adria on the far side of the chamber. As you approach, she reveals her ghoulish complexion. It's too late for her, and the only option for the poor woman and her ravenous ghouls is a swift death. After you defeat Adria, you can gain a ring of mastery from her corpse.

Vigil's Keep

Basics ~ Classes ~ The Party ~ Companions ~ Supporting Cast ~ Equipment ~ Bestiary ~ Walkthrough ~ **Side Quests** ~ Random Encounters ~ Achievements/Trophies

6 Continue a little farther past Adria's chamber and you'll reach a collapsed passage. Walk up to the rocks and Maverlies will show up to thank you for the job so far. While her men clear the rubble out of your way to continue, she escorts you back up to the surface.

NOTE

You can return to the underground levels beneath Vigil's Keep after you complete one main quest. See the "Sealing the Great Barrier Doors" quest for details.

7 After you've gathered all four keys from the Dark Theurge quests, return to the basement's prison block and open the locked door in the west wall with the key. The crypt contains more than a dozen lootable items, including a sack with the Howe Bow for Nathaniel. Take your time examining each one. When you descend to the bottom level, Avvar skeletons will rise up to stop you. They appear all around you, so get your party into a tight circle and watch each other's back. Keep skeletons off your healer so he or she doesn't get interrupted while casting the valuable heals. Concentrate party damage at a single target at a time to drop enemies faster and get the numbers under control.

Once all enemies are decimated and all loot claimed, use the four keys on their proper locks around the crypt. This opens another locked door into the deeper crypt room.

8 More Avvar sarcophagi greet you here. As you enter, the Dark Theurge's spirit gusts into the chamber and possesses three Avvar lords. Each lord fights as a warrior with a different style: dual wield, two-handed weapon, and sword and shield. Once you slay the Avvar lords, the Dark Theurge is finally destroyed and you can collect your hard-earned rewards.

A Master's Work

Type: Exploration

Start: Wade in Vigil's Keep Courtyard

Destination: Blackmarsh, Kal'Hirol, and the Wending Wood

Task: Receive special magic items by gathering exotic materials for Master Wade

Quest Tips: Master Wade, via Herren at the armor shop in the Vigil's Keep courtyard, promises to make special gear for you if you can retrieve various exotic materials. Three separate quests spawn from this one: "Golem's Might," "Heart of the Forest," and "Worked to the Bone." See the individual quest entries for details on how to retrieve the exotic materials. **XP Reward:** None

Money Reward: None

Item Reward: None

A Medical Necessity

Type: Exploration

Start: Soldier in Vigil's Keep Courtyard

Destination: Vigil's Keep Courtyard

Task: Save some wounded soldiers with medical supplies

Quest Tips: As you approach the portcullis entrance to the Inner Keep during "The Assault on Vigil's Keep" introduction, kill the darkspawn attacking the guard near the Inner Keep entrance. If you save the guard, you can speak to him for this quest. Cross the courtyard to the southeast corner and retrieve the medical supplies in a wooden crate. Return to the guard with the supplies to complete the quest.

XP Reward: 1,500 XP

Money Reward: None

Item Reward: None

Oaths of Fealty

Type: Politics
Start: Vigil's Keep Throne Room
Destination: Vigil's Keep Throne Room
Task: Speak with the nobles of your court

Quest Tips: When you're ready after the events of "The Assault on Vigil's Keep," speak with Varel and he'll initiate the fealty ceremony. Speak with the various nobles in the throne room and accept all quests. It's all about learning the ins and outs of court life. When you're finished talking with everyone, speak with Varel again and he ends the ceremony.

XP Reward: 2,000 XP
Money Reward: None
Item Reward: None

The Peasant Revolution

Type: Combat
Start: Vigil's Keep Courtyard
Destination: Vigil's Keep Courtyard
Task: Quell a peasant revolt in the keep

Quest Tips: After you have finished two of the three main quests, the peasant revolt will trigger when you return to Vigil's Keep. There is no avoiding it. You can try to pacify the peasants with an offer of grain if your Coercion skill is high enough, or you can Intimidate them into submission with a high enough score. Otherwise, the peasants will revolt, and it's your party and the keep soldiers against the citizens. Because you're geared and they aren't, it's a bit of a massacre. Fortunately, you've stopped future revolts with your actions.

XP Reward: 2,000 XP
Money Reward: None
Item Reward: None

> **NOTE**
> For complete details on "The Prisoner" side quest, see the "Assault on Vigil's Keep" walkthrough in the previous chapter.

Salvage Operation

Type: Combat
Start: Private in Vigil's Keep Courtyard
Destination: Anselm's Reef
Task: Retrieve trade goods from the scavengers

Quest Tips: Grab the quest from the private in Vigil's Keep courtyard and a new world location opens up: Anselm's Reef. Head to Anselm's Reef and defeat the scavengers there. Retrieve the trade goods secured by the scavengers, and when you return to civilization, you can sell the goods for profit.

XP Reward: 1,000 XP
Money Reward: None
Item Reward: None

Sealing the Great Barrier Doors

~ See map on next page ~

Runthrough (Vigil's Keep Deep Roads)

Summary: Seal the Deep Roads and protect Vigil's Keep from further darkspawn incursion.

1. Enter the Deep Roads.
2. Visit the Shrine of Korth.
3. Beware of a darkspawn ambush.
4. Collect gemstones.
5. Battle through the animated skeletons.
6. Encounter the Dark Theurge.
7. Combat the final darkspawn.
8. Slay the possessed ogre commander and seal the Deep Roads off.

> **NOTE**
> After completing one major quest, seek out Sergeant Maverlies again in front of the Vigil's Keep basement door. She will give you this quest as the second part of the "clearing out darkspawn from beneath the Keep" task. You can now finish the job in the Deep Roads.

Vigil's Keep

Basics ~ Classes ~ The Party ~ Companions ~ Supporting Cast ~ Equipment ~ Bestiary ~ Walkthrough ~ **Side Quests** ~ Random Encounters ~ Achievements/Trophies

Vigil's Keep Deep Roads

Portcullis

ᚱᚲ Legend ᚲᚱ

1 Hurlock	12 Possessed Ogre Commander
2 Hurlock	1 Darkspawn Corpse (Golden Idol of Korth)
3 Hurlocks	2 Old Book (The Great Strife codex)
4 Hurlock	3 Rocks (Elven Runestone gift)
5 Genlock Emissary & Genlocks	4 Gem Clusters
6 Hurlocks	5 Old Bones
7 Skeletons	6 Plaque (Ancient Vows codex)
8 The Dark Theurge	7 Urn
9 Skeletons	8 Urn (Talisman of Restoration, Corrupted Icon)
10 Genlocks, Hurlock Emissary, & Hurlocks	9 Urn (Call of the Inferno, Iced Band)
11 Ogre Commander	

10 Urn	
11 Scrolls	
1 "The Wraith's Vengeance"	
1 Key of Korth ("The Dark Theurge")	
2 Shrine of Korth ("The Shrine of Korth")	
3 Lyrium Sand ("Bombs Away!")	
4 Key of Haakon ("The Dark Theurge")	
5 Key of the Lady ("The Dark Theurge")	
6 Key to the Crypt ("The Dark Theurge")	

primagames.com

Vigil's Keep Deep Roads Cheatsheet

Side Quest
- Sealing the Great Barrier Doors

Important NPCs
- None

Key Items
- Call of the Inferno
- Corrupted Idol
- Elven Runestone
- Golden Idol of Korth
- Key of Haakon
- Key of Korth
- Key of the Lady
- Key to the Crypt
- Talisman of Restoration

Monsters
- Genlock Emissary
- Genlocks
- Hurlock Emissary
- Hurlocks
- Ogre Commander
- Possessed Ogre Commander
- Skeletons

Side Quests
- The Dark Theurge
- The Wraith's Vengeance

1 You can enter the Deep Roads beneath Vigil's Keep after you complete "It Comes from Beneath" and one major quest, return to Vigil's Keep, and speak with Maverlies. Clean out the darkspawn to safeguard Vigil's Keep. If you don't, during the "Siege on Vigil's Keep" the darkspawn will pour up from the basement and you won't have a chance to save the keep.

2 Take a side trip to the north to the altar of Korth area. See the "Shrine of Korth" side quest for complete details. Make sure you pick up the Key of Korth in the urn near the altar.

3 Expect a major ambush as you enter this area. Genlocks, hurlocks, and a genlock emissary surround you in the side alcoves and side passages. Inch into the main corridor and try to spot an enemy before you pull all of them on you. Pick off any targets you can see with ranged attacks, and if you see a group, throw a big AoE attack on them to weaken the full assault against you. Pick up the Key of Haakon in the south alcove's trapdoor.

NOTE
If you're working on the "Bombs Away!" side quest for Dworkin, pick up more lyrium sand in the northeast alcove.

4 After defeating the darkspawn in the ambush area, take a side trip to the gem mine. You can gain some diamonds and Elven Runestone gift in the area. If you didn't trigger them in the all-out brawl earlier with the darkspawn, watch for the genlocks to appear in the gem mine corridor as you exit.

5 Raise the portcullis in the passage that heads south and follow the corridor until you reach a chamber with statues encircling a lit center. Skeletons will animate and attack as you enter the circle, and one of the skeletons will drop the Trickster's Boots once they lie as scattered bones again.

6 The next room holds the Dark Theurge and its corresponding quest. You'll accidentally free the Dark Theurge when you enter the room (you must do this to continue). Attempt to slay the Dark Theurge, though it has a fair amount of health and will use lightning spells to keep you at distance. When it drops below 50 percent health, the Dark Theurge summons six skeletons to fight for it.

When the Dark Theurge is finally "defeated," it retreats to the side alcove in the east. There it remains motionless while it heals itself, and you can't interact with it. Instead, examine the apparatus in the center of the room. This discharges a lightning bolt that blasts through the wall behind the Dark Theurge and frees the creatures, launching "The Wraith's Vengeance" quest. It also opens the way for you to continue to the end of Vigil's Keep's Deep Roads.

7 Follow the passage to the east and then wind through some twists and turns until you reach a room containing a scroll and chest. Loot

Vigil's Keep

Basics ~ Classes ~ The Party ~ Companions ~ Supporting Cast ~ Equipment ~ Bestiary ~ Walkthrough ~ **Side Quests** ~ Random Encounters ~ Achievements/Trophies

both, and make sure you hold onto the Key of the Lady from the chest. The final mass of darkspawn defends the northern corridor. Prepare to battle genlocks, hurlocks, a hurlock emissary, and a huge ogre commander behind them. If you can engulf the corridor in AoE damage that doesn't also hit your party, that's the best course of action. Otherwise, pull the enemies toward you and seek protection in the side corridor if enemies begin to flank.

8 As if the ogre commander wasn't bad enough the first time around, the Dark Theurge possesses it after you defeat it and you must battle it a second

time. It may be a little easier to take it on this time, without all the other darkspawn to run interference; then again it may not, depending on how banged up you are after the first fight. Pop whatever potions and poultices you have and gut it out. It's the last battle before finishing the quest.

When you beat the possessed ogre, the Dark Theurge disappears, but it's not destroyed. If you want to continue with "The Wraith's Vengeance" quest, gather all four Avvar keys. You should have three of them if you looted everything in the basement and Deep Roads levels (the fourth is in the Avvar crypt itself). One of the fallen darkspawn here drops the key to the crypt. Take that key, along with the three others, and return to basement. See the "It Comes from Beneath" quest for complete details.

Finally, you reach the great doors and Voldrik arrives to seal them. You've completed your quest to clean up the keep's underground areas, and now you can rest easy that darkspawn won't spill up from the earth's bowels anymore.

Sheepherder's Lament

Type: Politics

Start: Vigil's Keep Throne Room

Destination: Vigil's Keep Throne Room

Task: Rule on the fate of Alec the sheepherder

Quest Tips: This sub-quest is part of the "A Day in Court" quest. Alec the sheepherder stole two bushels of grain to feed his family in these tough times. You can execute him, flog him, or conscript him to the keep's army. If you allow Varel to rule on the case, he will execute Alec for breaking the rules. You can do the same. You can also flog him, which will be seen as a just decision by most of the keep. If you force Alec to pay off his debt in the army, he fights valiantly in the final battle at the keep and actually goes on to form an order of knights that lasts a thousand years.

XP Reward: See "A Day in Court"

Money Reward: None

Item Reward: None

The Shrine of Korth

Type: Exploration

Start: Vigil's Keep Deep Roads

Destination: Vigil's Keep Deep Roads

Task: Visit the Shrine of Korth and pay it homage (or not)

Quest Tips: Enter the Deep Roads and visit the chamber nearest the entrance (see "Sealing the Great Barrier Doors" map). A mysterious Avvar altar to Korth waits for its next worshipper

or victim. The altar is a test and has three possible outcomes. If you take the treasure on the altar, you gain 15 sovereigns, but must fight the two golem guardians that awake to protect the altar. If you add the golden idol from the corpse near the altar, you gain experience. If you also add a diamond to the offering, you gain the magic axe Frenzy. You can also defile the altar if you bring the desecrated idol from the Dark Theurge's room back to the altar. This will cause the golems to crumble to pieces and you receive no reward.

XP Reward: 1,000 XP (if you placed the golden idol on the shrine)

Money Reward: 15 sovereigns (if you took the offering and awoke the golem guardians)

Item Reward: Frenzy axe (if you placed the golden idol on the shrine)

Solomon's Bridge

Type: Politics

Start: Vigil's Keep Throne Room

Destination: Vigil's Keep Throne Room

Task: Rule on Lady Liza's land claim

Quest Tips: This is part of the "A Day in Court" quest. Lady Liza Packton and Ser Derren are at odds over land. If you rule in Lady Liza's favor and give her the land, Ser Derren will be bitter and may join the conspiracy against you (see "A Brewing Conspiracy"). It's possible to give the land to Lady Liza and use your Coercion skill to mollify Ser Derren with a promise of future concessions. If you give the land to Ser Derren, Lady Liza will join the conspiracy. If you choose to keep the land for the Wardens, you gain 100 sovereigns, but are seen as a tyrant and both nobles will join the conspiracy against you.

XP Reward: See "A Day in Court" quest

Money Reward: 100 sovereigns (if you keep the land for yourself)

Item Reward: None

The Survivors of Vigil's Keep

Type: Combat

Start: Vigil's Keep Interior

Destination: Vigil's Keep Interior

Task: Rescue the four keep survivors trapped by the darkspawn

Quest Tips: During your initial run through the keep interior during "The Assault on Vigil's Keep" there are four survivors desperately trying to survive the darkspawn (see the walkthrough map in "The Assault on Vigil's Keep" chapter for the survivors' exact locations). As soon as you see these survivors, the nearby darkspawn will attack them. If you aren't quick to the defense, a survivor will die and the quest ends in failure. Rescue all four and you earn a large XP reward.

XP Reward: 3,000 XP

Money Reward: None

Item Reward: None

Trade Must Flow

Type: Exploration

Start: Mistress Woolsey in the Vigil's Keep Throne Room

Destination: Various Locations

Task: Convince Armaas or Lilith to trade with Vigil's Keep

Quest Tips: The keep needs trade to survive. Mistress Woolsey offers this quest to you in the hopes of resurrecting new trade routes. If you save the merchant at the start of "The Assault on Vigil's Keep" you gain an upgrade to the merchant's store and increase trade. If you convince Armaas in the Silverite Mine to trade with Vigil's Keep, you increase trade, or you can also find the traveling merchant Lilith during a random encounter and ask her to trade with Vigil's Keep. This quest completes once Armaas or Lilith agree to trade, but if you finish all the quests on the Merchants' Guild Board in Amaranthine, you increase trade. Complete a combination of these trade possibilities to gain a large monetary reward.

XP Reward: 1,000 XP

Money Reward: 60 sovereigns

Item Reward: None

What Is Built Endures

Type: Exploration

Start: Voldrik in Vigil's Keep Courtyard

Destination: Vigil's Keep Courtyard

Task: Bring back granite to increase the strength of Vigil's Keep's walls

Quest Tips: Note you must complete the "Cost of Doing Business" quest to gain access to this quest. After Voldrik gives you the quest, journey to the Wending Wood and retrieve granite from the quarry (see the Wending Wood map for the granite deposit's exact location). If you bring Voldrik back the granite and promise to send men to guard the quarry, Voldrik will finish his upgrade on the keep walls. The entire keep will look much more magnificent!

XP Reward: 1,000 XP

Money Reward: None

Item Reward: Upgrade to the Vigil's Keep walls

Worked to the Bone

Type: Exploration

Start: Queen of the Blackmarsh's Mountaintop

Destination: Various Locations

Task: Find five items for Master Wade to custom build you a unique sword

Quest Tips: When you defeat the Queen of the Blackmarsh Fade dragon on the mountaintop in the Blackmarsh, you gain a special dragon bone. Return the dragon bone to Master Wade in Vigil's Keep and he offers you this quest. He needs you to collect a diamond (buy from a vendor or gain as loot), a greater warmth potion (buy from a vendor or gain as loot), fresh dragon egg (found in the Silverite Mine; see map for exact location), and a grandmaster flame rune (you will most likely have to craft this yourself). Collect them all and he crafts the excellent Vigilance sword in the form of either a greatsword or a longsword.

XP Reward: 500 XP

Money Reward: None

Item Reward: Vigilance

NOTE

For more information on the Vigilance Longsword or Greatsword, refer to the "Crafted" weapons section in the Equipment chapter.

Vigil's Keep - The Wending Wood

Basics ~ Classes ~ The Party ~ Companions ~ Supporting Cast ~ Equipment ~ Bestiary ~ Walkthrough ~ **Side Quests** ~ Random Encounters ~ Achievements/Trophies

Spoiler Alert

The Wending Wood

~ Also see map on next page ~

Silverite Mine

Brothers of Stone

Type: Exploration

Start: Wending Wood

Destination: Wending Wood

Task: Side with the Statue of War or Statue of Peace and end their suffering

Quest Tips: Seek out the statues in the Wending Wood (see map for exact location). Speak to the Statue of War, then the Statue of Peace. You can only complete one or the other's request to end their suffering. If the brothers' longing for vengeance or peace strike a chord with you, then complete that story, or you can check the rewards and complete whichever complements your group best (a sword for the war path and recipes for the peace path). If you choose the war path, find the magister's remains a short distance down the hill (scroll 27 on the map). Defeat the Statue of War's ancient foe and collect the Winter's Blade reward next to the statue upon completion of the quest. If you choose the peace path, convince the Statue of War to be at peace instead of seeking vengeance. After doing so, return to the Statue of Peace for your recipe rewards.

XP Reward: 1,500 XP

Money Reward: None

Item Reward: The Winter's Blade (war path), or Greater Spirit Balm Recipe, Master Stamina Draught Recipe, Potent Stamina Draught Recipe (peace path)

Legend

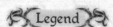

🏺 "Last Wishes"

1️⃣ Silverite Deposit ("Elemental Requirements")

2️⃣ Keenan's Wedding Ring (Hurlock Dragon-Tamer) for "Last Wishes"

3️⃣ Fresh Dragon Egg ("Worked to the Bone")

4️⃣ Lyrium Deposit ("Bombs Away!")

🔵 Armaas

primagames.com

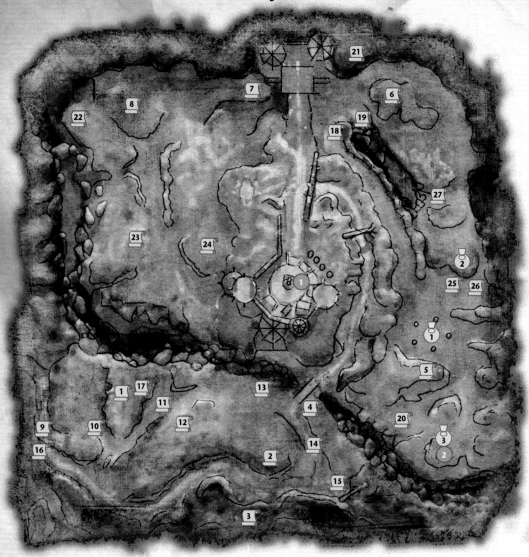

The Fire Puzzle

Type: Puzzle

Start: Wending Wood

Destination: Wending Wood

Task: Solve the fire puzzle to earn a magic amulet

Quest Tips: Examine the dead scholar near the main intersection (scroll 18 on the map) for the items necessary to start the puzzle. Descend the hill to the fire puzzle at the base. Stand on the opposite end of the puzzle (see screenshot) and interact with the missing stone. Complete the fire puzzle in the order shown (see diagram) to ignite all sides and call forth the rewards chest.

XP Reward: 1,500 XP

Money Reward: None

Item Reward: Illumination amulet

The Wending Wood

⚞ Legend ⚟

- ⚀①⚁ "The Fire Puzzle"
- ②② "Brothers of Stone"
- ③③ "Ines the Botanist"
- [1] Engraved Statue ("Maferath's Monuments")
- [2] Engraved Statue ("Maferath's Monuments")
- [3] Engraved Statue ("Maferath's Monuments")
- [4] Engraved Statue ("Maferath's Monuments")
- [5] Engraved Statue ("Maferath's Monuments")
- [6] Engraved Statue ("Maferath's Monuments")
- [7] Engraved Statue ("Maferath's Monuments")
- [8] Engraved Statue ("Maferath's Monuments")
- [9] Fine Silk (Barrel) for "The Merchant's Goods"
- [10] Fine Silk (Barrel) for "The Merchant's Goods"
- [11] Fine Silk (Bundle of Cloth) for "The Merchant's Goods"
- [12] Fine Silk (Scavenger) for "The Merchant's Goods"
- [13] Fine Silk (Crate) for "The Merchant's Goods"
- [14] Fine Silk (Crate) for "The Merchant's Goods"
- [15] Fine Silk (Chest) for "The Merchant's Goods"
- [16] Fine Silk (Chest) for "The Merchant's Goods"
- [17] Fine Silk (Scavenger) for "The Merchant's Goods"
- [18] Dead Scholar ("The Fire Puzzle")
- [19] Granite Deposit ("What Is Built Endures")
- [20] Heartwood (The Old One) for "Heart of the Forest"
- [21] Northern Prickleweed ("Ines the Botanist")
- [22] Ancient Sylvanwood ("From the Living Wood")
- [23] Ancient Sylvanwood ("From the Living Wood")
- [24] Ancient Sylvanwood ("From the Living Wood")
- [25] Ancient Sylvanwood ("From the Living Wood")
- [26] Ancient Sylvanwood ("From the Living Wood")
- [27] Magister's Remains ("Brothers of Stone")
- ① Velanna
- ② Ines the Botanist

From the Living Wood

Type: Combat
Start: Chanter's Board in Amaranthine
Destination: Wending Wood
Task: Slay ancient sylvans to collect five ancient sylvanwoods

Quest Tips: Pick up the quest at the Chanter's Board in Amaranthine and head to the Wending Wood. Throughout the northern section of the Wending Wood, five ancient sylvans slumber (scrolls 22–26 on the map). These ancient sylvans appear only if you have the quest and approach close enough for melee combat. Slay the five ancient sylvans, collect the ancient sylvanwood, and return to Kendrick in Amaranthine for your reward.

XP Reward: 1,000 XP
Money Reward: 15 sovereigns
Item Reward: None

Ines the Botanist

Type: Exploration
Start: Wynne in Amaranthine
Destination: Wending Wood
Task: Speak with Ines and find northern prickleweed

Quest Tips: Speak with Wynne outside the Chantry in Amaranthine. As long as you don't offend Wynne by being rude, she will ask you to track down Ines the Botanist in the Wending Wood. You can find Ines in the southeast corner of the Wending Wood. Agree to help her find the northern prickleweed, which is near the Silverite Mine (scroll 21 on the map), and return the seeds to Ines for your reward. This quest is unavailable if Wynne was killed in *Origins*.

XP Reward: 1,000 XP
Money Reward: None
Item Reward: Superb Health Poultice Recipe, Superb Lyrium Potion Recipe

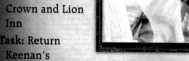

PRIMA Official Game Guide

Last Wishes

Type: Combat

Start: Keenan in Silverite Mine

Destination: Nida in Amaranthine's Crown and Lion Inn

Task: Return Keenan's wedding ring to his wife

Quest Tips: You find Keenan in a side cavern in the Silverite Mine (see map). His legs have been crushed by a hurlock dragon-tamer (scroll 2 on the map), and the vile creature stole his wedding ring. You grant Keenan's last dying wish to retrieve the ring and return it to Keenan's wife, Nida. Seek out the dragon-tamer and slay him in the side cavern. It won't be an easy fight, because he has some dragonling and drake allies. Once you slice through them all, recover Keenan's wedding ring from the dragon-tamer's corpse (you can also gain the maul that crushed Keenan's legs) and return the ring to Nida in the Crown and Lion Inn. She probably doesn't deserve the ring, as you discover after talking to her, but you gain the extra XP when you speak with her in one of the inn's side rooms.

XP Reward: 1,000 XP

Money Reward: None

Item Reward: Leg-Crusher maul

Maferath's Monuments

Type: Exploration

Start: Merchants' Guild Board in Amaranthine

Destination: Wending Wood

Task: Trace inscriptions from eight statues

Quest Tips: Pick up the quest from the Merchants' Guild Board in Amaranthine. Head to the Wending Wood and find all eight engraved statues scattered throughout the forest. Interact with each statue to update your quest. When you return to Kendrick in Amaranthine, you get some nice coin in your pocket.

XP Reward: 1,500 XP

Money Reward: 13 sovereigns

Item Reward: None

The Merchant's Goods

Type: Exploration

Start: Merchants' Guild Board in Amaranthine

Destination: Wending Wood

Task: Find the nine lost bundles of fine silk

Quest Tips: Pick up the quest from the Merchants' Guild Board in Amaranthine. Head to the Wending Wood and find all nine fine silk bundles in the southern half of the forest. Most are in the barrels and chests along the main road. A couple drop from scavengers raiding along the roads. Clear the whole southern area to find all the fine silks. Return to Kendrick in Amaranthine for a very sizable monetary reward.

XP Reward: 1,000 XP

Money Reward: 25 sovereigns

Item Reward: None

Trading Troubles

Type: Exploration

Start: Wending Wood

Destination: Wending Wood

Task: Stop the attacks on the merchant caravans

Quest Tips: This is a sub-quest to "The Righteous Path" main quest; it begins as soon as you enter the Wending Wood, and must be completed as part of "The Righteous Path." See "The Righteous Path" walkthrough for complete details. To stop the attacks on the caravans, you must either have Velanna join your party, kill her, or let her go after she realizes the error of her ways. When you return to Mervis at the completion of "The Righteous Path," he rewards you with 20 sovereigns for your efforts, unless you have a Coercion score of three or higher, in which case you can convince Mervis to pay 30 sovereigns.

XP Reward: 9,000 XP (cumulative)

Money Reward: 20 sovereigns or 30 sovereigns

Item Reward: None

The Wending Wood ~ Random Encounters

Basics ~ Classes ~ The Party ~ Companions ~ Supporting Cast ~ Equipment ~ Bestiary ~ Walkthrough ~ Side Quests ~ **Random Encounters** ~ Achievements/Trophies

Random Encounters

Darkspawn, mercenaries, blood mages, and even dragons swarm the countryside. Once you leave the safety of a secured Vigil's Keep, you always have a chance to run across wild creatures or important story moments through random encounters. There are two types of random encounters: static and repeatable. Static encounters are set story moments that trigger during certain points in your travels. In the absence of a static encounter there's a 30 percent chance of a repeatable encounter. See the next page for repeatable encounter tables, which outline the likelihood of creatures in each terrain type.

⸭⸭⸭⸭ NOTE ⸭⸭⸭⸭

In *Awakening*, you will run into fewer random encounters than your travels in *Dragon Age: Origins*. Only about 30 percent of locations on your new world map produce random encounters.

Most encounters involve enemy numbers much greater than your party's size. Don't forget your standard battle tactics: warrior tanking the toughest foes, rogues dishing out damage wisely, mage blasting out AoE damage or timely healing. Use the terrain to your advantage. Cover can shield you from ranged fire, and obstacles such as fences and rocks can minimize flanking attempts. In the encounters where it's not a pure hack-and-slash battle royale, think about consequences of your actions and what appeals most to your style of play and character's personality.

Always prepare for a fight on the road. The worst feeling is finishing off a major quest, then trying to limp back across the world, only to be smashed by a random encounter. Save before traversing the land in case of disaster, heal back to full before traveling, and don't let up even a bit when you see the small squad of darkspawn over the hill.

For each random encounter, the enemy numbers and makeup are random. For example, you may encounter four melee bandits and two archers one time, and in the next bandit random encounter, you may run into six melee bandits and one archer. Treasure is also randomly assigned.

Static Encounters

Encounter	Trigger
Meeting Nathaniel	One plot is completed, you refused to take Nathaniel with you when you encountered him in Vigil's Keep at the start of the game, but you also did not elect to have him killed (he was in a holding cell). You will only find Nathaniel in the forest either between Vigil's Keep and Amaranthine or between Vigil's keep and the Wending Wood.
Meeting Velanna's Clan	Have Velanna in party when the Righteous Path is completed. You will only find Velanna in the forest either between Vigil's Keep and Amaranthine or between Vigil's keep and the Wending Wood.
Meeting Lilith the Merchant	At least one plot is completed
Barbarian Horde	At least one plot is completed
Dragon Slayer	At least one plot is completed
Ambush by Assassins	At least one plot is completed
Pirate Encounter	At least one plot is completed

primagames.com

Forest Encounters

Chance of Encounter	Enemy
30%	Darkspawn
8%	Bandits
8%	Weak Bandits
7%	Elves
7%	Mercenaries
6%	Fen Witch
6%	Wild Sylvans
5%	Werewolves
4%	Bears
4%	Blighted Animals
4%	Wolves
3%	Barbarians
3%	Spiders
2%	Blood Mages
2%	Qunari Mercenaries
1%	Dragons

Canyon Encounters

Chance of Encounter	Enemy
30%	Darkspawn
12%	Possessed Corpses
10%	Bandits
10%	Mercenaries
9%	Dwarves
8%	Blood Mages
7%	Dragons
6%	Weak Bandits
5%	Blighted Animals
3%	Qunari Mercenaries

Beach Encounters

Chance of Encounter	Enemy
40%	Darkspawn
10%	Possessed Corpses
9%	Bandits
9%	Mercenaries
9%	Weak Bandits
8%	Blighted Animals
7%	Qunari Mercenaries
6%	Blood Mages
2%	Dragons

Farm Encounters

Chance of Encounter	Enemy
30%	Darkspawn
12%	Bandits
12%	Wolves
10%	Mercenaries
8%	Blood Mages
7%	Possessed Corpses
7%	Spiders
5%	Blight Wolves
5%	Weak Bandits
4%	Dragons

Achievements and Trophies

Basics ~ Classes ~ The Party ~ Companions ~ Supporting Cast ~ Equipment ~ Bestiary ~ Walkthrough ~ Side Quests ~ Random Encounters ~ **Achievements/Trophies**

Achievements and Trophies

Amaranthine's Last Hope

Achievement/Trophy Task: You must save the city of Amaranthine. Participate in the battle of Amaranthine and defeat the darkspawn infesting it.

After you've completed the three main quests—"Shadows of the Blackmarsh," "The Righteous Path," and "Last of the Legion"—speak with Varel to initiate the final battles leading up to game's end. Leave Vigil's Keep and journey up to Amaranthine. All will seem hopeless in the city, but you can convince the remaining city guard to let your party in to slay the sacking darkspawn and save any citizens who yet live. Follow the walkthrough advice in the "Siege of Vigil's Keep" section of the Tour of Amaranthine chapter to defeat the darkspawn infesting Amaranthine and claim your reward. Note that you must abandon Vigil's Keep to its fate to earn this achievement reward. Unless you've built up significant defenses on the keep, the Grey Warden fortress will fall along with all your friends and comrades. See The Enduring Vigil Achievement for tips on how to earn that reward and save the keep.

Awakening

Achievement/Trophy Task: You must finish the game and kill the Mother.

See the "Lair of the Mother" section of the Tour of Amaranthine chapter for tips about how best to defeat the Mother in the final battle within the Dragonbone Wastes. It's an incredibly desperate fight with little hope for survival unless you gear up a properly prepared party and play your tactics just right. Good luck.

Blind Vengeance

Achievement/Trophy Task: You must escape the Silverite Mine.

After you work out your disagreements with Velanna in the Wending Wood, she will accompany you into the Silverite Mine. Unfortunately, the Architect ambushes you almost immediately upon entering, strips your party of all your gear, and imprisons you. Velanna's sister aids you in escaping, and then it's a frantic escape attempt as you battle to retrieve your armor and weapons from the enemy. Once you've defeated all the mine foes and regained every piece of lost equipment, you leave the Silverite Mine and complete the achievement. See "The Righteous Path" section of the Tour of Amaranthine chapter for further details on how to escape the mine.

Commander of the Grey

Achievement/Trophy Task: Reach level 30.

Play long and hard to meet this goal. If you run through only the main quests and race off to slay the Mother and end the game, you'll probably top out at around level 25. Finishing all the main quests plus half the side quests will put you a couple of levels higher at level 27 or level 28. To do it right and reach level 30, you must finish all main quests and the majority of side quests. And why wouldn't you want to do that? The side quests can be just as enjoyable as the main quests, and they frequently send you off to unexplored areas of the world where you can get happily lost for hours.

primagames.com

Dragon Age: Origins
Achievements & Trophies

Here are the *Origins* achievements/trophies that can cross over into *Awakening*:

Educated: Used a tome to improve the main character's attributes, talents, spells, or skills

Heavy Hitter: Main character inflicted 250 damage with a single hit

Master of Arms: Main character achieved level 20 as a warrior

Shadow: Main character achieved level 20 as a rogue

Archmage: Main character achieved level 20 as a mage

Grey Warden: Killed 100 darkspawn

Master Warden: Killed 500 darkspawn

Blight-Queller: Killed 1,000 darkspawn

Tinkerer: Crafted an item

Persuasive: Succeeded at 5 difficult Coercion attempts

Silver Tongued: Succeeded at 25 difficult Coercion attempts

Bully: Succeeded at 5 difficult Intimidate attempts

Menacing: Succeeded at 10 difficult Intimidate attempts

Veteran: Main character learned a specialization

Elite: Main character learned 2 specializations

The Enduring Vigil

Achievement/Trophy Task: You must have all available upgrades for Vigil's Keep. This includes the following: All three of Herren's mineral requests (iron, veridium, silverite) for armoring your soldiers; find granite for Voldrik to rebuild the walls and assign troops to guard the quarry; seal off the tunnel to the Deep Roads that the darkspawn use to infiltrate the keep.

Before you set off to conquer this achievement, know that it's probably the hardest one to complete because it involves many detailed side quests and 80 disposable sovereigns. Until you have the time and money ready to go, it'll have to wait.

When you're ready to tackle it, you must speak with main NPCs around the Vigil's Keep grounds: Herren/Wade, Voldrik, and Maverlies. Herren and Wade work on beefing up your soldiers' defense, Voldrik improves the keep walls, and Maverlies secures the keep from extra darkspawn attacks from below.

Herren promises that Wade will outfit the Warden troops with better armor if you can deliver large quantities of iron, veridium, and silverite ore. Iron ore can be found in Kal'Hirol, veridium in the Vigil's Keep basement, and silverite—where else?—in the Silverite Mine. See the walkthrough maps for the deposits' exact placements. If you collect all three, Herren and Wade will arm a special regiment of soldiers to guard the keep when the "Siege of Vigil's Keep" triggers.

To upgrade your keep walls, seek out Voldrik and pay him 80 sovereigns. Leave the keep and upon your return, you will find a less damaged version of the keep. Unfortunately, the walls need more repair. Speak with Voldrik again and he asks you to find granite to strengthen the walls. Head out to the Wending Wood and find the granite deposits there (see the map in "The Righteous Path" section of the Tour of Amaranthine chapter for exact placement). Supply the men required to keep Voldrik's workers safe and he will build you walls that will withstand a siege. Your companions will survive the siege too.

Sergeant Maverlies watches over the basement and reports on any darkspawn activity below ground. After your initial clearing of darkspawn during the "Assault on Vigil's Keep," speak with Maverlies once you leave the throne room. She asks you to wipe out any darkspawn you find in the basement. Go downstairs, hack and slash through the darkspawn and click on the rocks at the farthest point. Maverlies returns and the first part of the quest completes.

Leave Vigil's Keep and complete at least one major plot quest, such as "Shadows of the Blackmarsh." When you return to the keep, Maverlies informs you of more darkspawn in the basement. Fight through all the enemies, including the Dark Theurge, who possesses once-defeated enemies that you have to fight again. See the Side Quests chapter for further details on how to beat all the Vigil's Keep basement quests. Once the final darkspawn falls, Maverlies and Voldrik will arrive to repair the ancient doors and seal them for good against the darkspawn.

If and only if you upgrade all three facets of Vigil's Keep—soldiers, walls, and basement—do you finally earn the title of "The Enduring Vigil." No one's getting into the keep now without you knowing about it.

Achievements and Trophies

Basics ~ Classes ~ The Party ~ Companions ~ Supporting Cast ~ Equipment ~ Bestiary ~ Walkthrough ~ Side Quests ~ Random Encounters ~ **Achievements/Trophies**

Keeper of the Vigil

Achievement/Trophy Task: You must save Vigil's Keep. Leave Amaranthine to its fate and return to Vigil's Keep to participate in the siege there.

After you've completed the three main quests—"Shadows of the Blackmarsh," "The Righteous Path," and "Last of the Legion"—speak with Varel to initiate the final battles leading up to game's end. Leave Vigil's Keep and journey up to Amaranthine. Listen to the guards' assessments that the city is lost and command them to burn it to the ground. Return instead to Vigil's Keep to save friends and allies. Follow the walkthrough advice in the "Siege of Vigil's Keep" section of the Tour of Amaranthine chapter to defeat the darkspawn sieging the keep and claim your reward. Note that you must abandon Amaranthine to its fate to earn this reward.

Pride Comes Before the Fall

Achievement/Trophy Task: You must defeat the baroness. Kill her in her pride demon form in the Blackmarsh after escaping the Fade.

See the "Shadows of the Blackmarsh" section of the Tour of Amaranthine chapter for tips on how best to defeat the baroness after you return from the Fade. It's nothing like the first battle you have against her in the Fade when she remains in mortal form. Here she morphs into her pride demon form, and it's a long marathon of damage and healing to survive her continuous onslaughts.

Savior of Kal'Hirol

Achievement/Trophy Task: You must destroy the brood-mothers in Kal'Hirol.

First, you have to battle through all of Kal'Hirol to reach the Lower Reaches. Next, you must defeat the Lost and an inferno golem to gain access to the broodmother chamber. The battle with the Lost will likely be more difficult even than the broodmother encounter, so make sure you haven't run out of poultices and potions by the time you reach the bottom of Kal'Hirol. Once inside the broodmother chamber, slice through the tentacle groups that reach for you through the ground. You'll spot four chains at the corners of the chamber. Make a beeline for the nearest one and cut down the chain as soon as you get a chance. Continue to bash away at the tentacles and steadily advance on a second chain. Once you cut down that second chain, the framework drops on the broodmothers and crushes them dead. Collect your reward and a well-earned deep breath. For further details on the Kal'Hirol encounters, see the "Last of the Legion" section of the Tour of Amaranthine chapter.

Achievements

Achievement	Xbox 360 Gamerscore Points Awarded	PS3 Trophy Awarded
Amaranthine's Last Hope	25	Bronze
Awakening	50	Gold
Blind Vengeance	30	Bronze
Commander of the Grey	30	Bronze
The Enduring Vigil	30	Bronze
Keeper of the Vigil	25	Bronze
Pride Comes Before the Fall	30	Bronze
Savior of Kal'Hirol	30	Bronze

primagames.com

PRIMA® OFFICIAL GAME GUIDE
• OVER 100 MAPS • EVERY SIDE QUEST DETAILED • OVER 300 PAGES

DRAGON AGE
ORIGINS

Covers PC, Xbox 360®
& PlayStation®3

BIOWARE

Prima is an authorized Electronic Arts licensee.

DRAGON AGE™ ORIGINS PRIMA OFFICIAL GAME GUIDE

OVER 100 LABELED MAPS!

PRIMA GAMES

GET 20 FREE PAGES
FROM THE OFFICIAL
DRAGON AGE™ ORIGINS STRATEGY GUIDE
www.dragonagewalkthrough.com

The Prima Games logo is a registered trademark of Random House, Inc., registered in the United States and other countries. Primagames.com is a registered trademark of Random House, Inc., registered in the United States.

PRIMA GAMES